Gardens

of the National Trust

Stephen Lacey

Gardens
of the National Trust

 National Trust

To the gardeners of the National Trust

First published in the United Kingdom in 2011
This edition published in 2016 by
National Trust Books
1 Gower Street
London WC1E 6HD

An imprint of Pavilion Books Ltd

ISBN: 9781909881792

A CIP catalogue record for this book is available from the British Library.

20 19 18 17 16
10 9 8 7 6 5 4 3 2 1

Printed in China by 1010 Printing International Ltd.
Colour Reproduction by Tag Publishing

This book can be ordered direct from the publisher at the website:
www.pavilionbooks.com, or try your local bookshop. Also available
at National Trust shops, including www.nationaltrustbooks.co.uk.

PREVIOUS PAGE Diana the Huntress in the parterre at Seaton Delaval Hall.
RIGHT The statue of Galen in front of the Temple of Piety at Fountains Abbey
and Studley Royal.

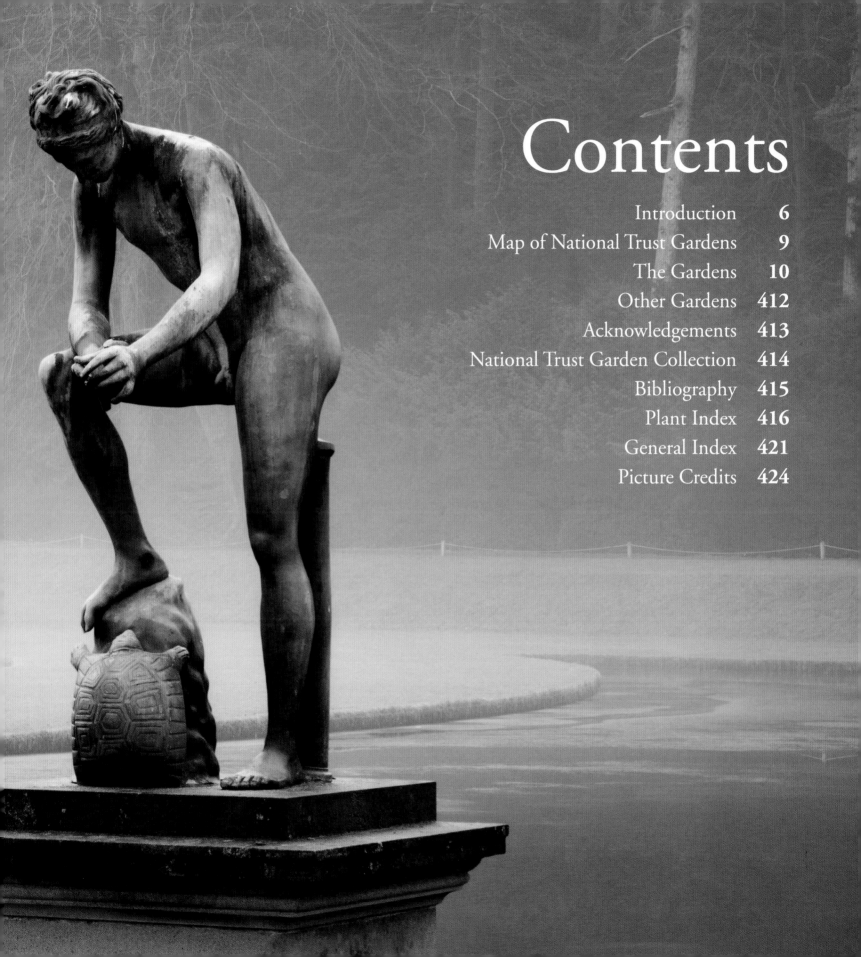

Contents

Introduction

Three recently acquired gardens appear in this revised edition of *Gardens of the National Trust* – Dyffryn Gardens and Tredegar House, both in South Wales, and Stoneywell in Leicestershire. Improvements and restoration work have been under way in many other properties, including at Attingham, Croome, Cliveden, Dunham Massey, Dunster Castle, Mount Stewart, Polesden Lacey and Quarry Bank Mill. Large new areas of woodland garden, previously private, have opened up at Bodnant, and Standen has been undergoing a major change of direction.

Otherwise, the most remarkable development of recent years is the resurgence of fruit and vegetable gardening, which, because of its high labour demands, the Trust had little opportunity to champion in the past. Today, largely thanks to the small army of volunteer and community gardeners who now work alongside the Trust's own staff, this deficiency has been comprehensively addressed, and kitchen gardens have been restored and revitalised in nearly 50 properties.

This is allowing the Trust not only to assist in the conservation of heritage fruit and vegetable varieties and traditional, even esoteric, cultivation techniques such as pineapple-growing, but also to convey a truer and more rounded picture of the life of a country house – for without their kitchen gardens, these properties, which were often far from centres of commerce, could scarcely have functioned. Some of the newly revived kitchen gardens, such as at Attingham, Clumber Park, Knightshayes Court, Llanerchaeron, Tatton Park and Wimpole Hall, are on an astonishing scale.

Wildflower and wildlife gardening has been gathering momentum, with, for instance, often just simple changes in mowing regimes producing orchid-studded tapestries. Sheffield Park, Wakehurst Place, Tyntesfield and Packwood House are prime examples of this, but in a large number of gardens the promotion of organic and more environmentally sensitive methods is also reaping rich rewards.

For me, travelling the length of Britain, meeting the head gardeners and tapping into the story of each garden's evolution and idiosyncrasies has again been an adventure and an education. The diversity of the Trust's gardens is immediately apparent from the photographs. They range from landscape park to walled town garden, box parterre to rhododendron woodland, Derbyshire hilltop to Cornish coombe. Lakes, temples, herbaceous borders, Japanese gardens, conservatories, pinetums, swathes of daffodils, roses, regional apple varieties and eighteenth-century statues, views of sea, moor and motorway, yew trees clipped as pointed Welsh hats, it is all here.

The gardens engage you on many levels. There are the straightforward pleasures of seeing, smelling, touching, listening and exploring. For home gardeners, there are ideas and plant varieties to pick up. But go deeper and invariably you tap into a story, perhaps of great individuals and family successions, designers and plant hunters, period politics and preoccupations, changing fashions, destructions and restorations.

Between them, the gardens chart some 400 years of history. To medieval times there are merely brief references, in the partnership of ancient building with flowery mead at Cotehele and Sizergh Castle, and in the presence of herb gardens at Acorn Bank and Buckland Abbey. Renaissance pleasure gardening is captured in the moated garden and banqueting house at Lyveden New Bield, the topiaries at Chastleton, the enclosures and mounts at Little Moreton Hall, the

RIGHT Foxgloves and aquilegias flower in early summer in front of fifteenth-century Great Chalfield Manor, Wiltshire.

pavilion and bowling green at Melford Hall, the covered walks and knot garden at Moseley Old Hall, and, most imposingly, by the grand Elizabethan courts, gateways and finial-capped walls at Hardwick Hall and Montacute.

The landscape movement spelled destruction for many of the great formal gardens, but those at Ham House, Westbury Court, Powis Castle, Erddig and Hanbury Hall survived in large part, or have been resurrected by the Trust, and show the European-inspired styles of the late seventeenth and early eighteenth centuries. The story of the subsequent departure from these enclosed and geometric patterns and the evolution of the landscape style through its Arcadian, Brownian and romantically Picturesque phases is recounted, in whole or in part, at Claremont, Stowe, Fountains Abbey and Studley Royal, Gibside, Wimpole Hall, Prior Park, West Wycombe Park, Croome, Stourhead, Kedleston, Petworth House and Scotney Castle.

The early nineteenth-century's renewed enthusiasm for formality and self-consciously artful gardening is marked at Calke Abbey, Ickworth and Peckover House, with grand revivals of earlier styles displayed at Oxburgh Hall, Montacute, Blickling Hall and Belton. The innovation, ingenuity and derring-do that became the order of the day is revealed in the fantasy evocations at Biddulph Grange, the engineering feats at Cragside and the multi-coloured parkland and bedding schemes at Ascott, while Waddesdon Manor, Tyntesfield, Lyme Park, Tatton Park and Polesden Lacey give a varied and luscious insight into country-house living and gardening in their Victorian and Edwardian heyday.

The influx of new trees and shrubs from the Americas, the Far East and Australasia through the nineteenth and early twentieth centuries fuelled the development of exotic woodlands, and at Killerton, Glendurgan, Nymans, Wakehurst Place, Bodnant, Rowallane, Trengwainton, Mount Stewart, Trelissick and Winkworth, we have supreme displays – equalled later at Knightshayes Court and Greenway.

Simultaneously, architectural gardening was evolving, and in time became coupled with some dreamy and painterly herbaceous planting. Gertrude Jekyll's influence pervades the gardens at Barrington Court and Lindisfarne Castle as Sir Edwin Lutyens'

does at Castle Drogo and Coleton Fishacre, while in the crisp compartments and sophisticated colour schemes of Hidcote and Sissinghurst the marriage of plantsmanship and formal design reaches a new twentieth-century zenith – with The Homewood presenting a contrasting essay in Modernism.

It is a rich legacy, but also a dynamic one. The gardens come to the Trust already many-layered – often, as in the case of Cliveden, Dunham Massey, Kingston Lacy or Shugborough, shaped by activity (destructions as well as embellishments) over many generations. Restorations by the Trust – invariably based on fragmentary evidence, and with the degree of finish and style of upkeep modified to suit the available resources – add fresh layers.

And thereafter the gardens continue to change. Plants grow and die; Mother Nature unleashes her storms, wood-boring beetles, honey fungus and, more recently, the devastating pathogen *Phytophthora ramorum*, or Sudden Oak Death, which is having a far greater impact on plants than any previous disaster. The Trust's response has been to launch the largest plant survey ever undertaken in the UK, using maps and GPS technology to record each specimen in 80 of its most important plant collections. Only now is the scale and importance of the Trust's plant collections being understood – rarities it never knew it had are being discovered.

Year by year, there is also change initiated from within the gardens which, happily, the Trust recognises as essential if a garden is to be kept alive and pulsing, and for staff to develop and demonstrate their skills. This may be a variation in bedding schemes or border planting, the continual enrichment of tree and shrub collections, or the sudden annexation of unemployed areas for new pursuits, such as winter gardening at Anglesey Abbey and Dunham Massey. Restoration always brings opportunities for innovation. And, particularly where the donor family is still in residence, the gardens may even be carried forward by bold new work from contemporary designers and artists, as at Ascott, Antony House and Plas Newydd.

Overall, the Trust's gardens seem to be in very good fettle and with ever-increasing visitor numbers. I hope there will be plenty of opportunity for you to see and enjoy for yourself.

Stephen Lacey, 2016

MAP OF NATIONAL TRUST GARDENS

Acorn Bank

TEMPLE SOWERBY, CUMBRIA

AREA 1ha (2½ acres) • SOIL slightly alkaline/clay loam • ALTITUDE 122m (400ft)
AVERAGE RAINFALL 914mm (36in) • AVERAGE WINTER CLIMATE very cold

'The ground is studded with daffodils, primroses, cranesbills and Queen Anne's lace'

Cumbria is a moody part of Britain and on a grey, wet, windswept afternoon you may find Acorn Bank rather bleak. However, on other days the sun draws out the red in the plum-coloured sandstone and reveals panoramic views across to the Lakeland fells, woodpeckers hammer the oak trees, newts rise in the well pond and the garden seems full of flowers.

The abundance of wildflowers and herbs at Acorn Bank carries you back to its medieval past, when it was home to the Knights Templar. Behind the house, where the oak-covered bank plunges steeply to the fast-flowing Crowdundle Beck – the former boundary line between Cumberland and Westmorland – the ground is studded with daffodils, primroses, cranesbills, meadowsweet and Queen Anne's lace; in the orchard grow the wild yellow tulip, *Tulipa sylvestris*, the double white wood anemone, *A. nemorosa* 'Vestal', the Lent lily, *Narcissus pseudonarcissus*, and the pheasant's eye daffodil, *N. poeticus*.

The wildflower riches of Acorn Bank were considerably boosted by Dorothy Una Ratcliffe, the Yorkshire writer and traveller who, with her husband, Capt. Noel McGrigor Phillips, bought the property in 1934. She also restored the lawns and borders, and introduced the ironwork gates and statuary. It is the balance she struck between picturesque effects and enhancing the habitats for wildlife that continues to set the tone for the garden today.

The garden is proof that a hostile climate need not preclude adventurous planting. Semi-evergreen *Rosa bracteata*, violet-flowered *Abutilon × suntense* and crimson *Schisandra grandiflora × rubriflora* all thrive unexpectedly against the sheltering walls. The shady borders around the orchard contain various Turk's cap lilies (*Lilium martagon*, *L. pyrenaicum* and *L. pardalinum*), and growing in the lawn is a fine specimen of *Aesculus × mutabilis* 'Induta', an unusual dwarf cousin of horse chestnut with pinky-yellow 'candles'. The apple trees, however, are mainly old northern or local cooking varieties which avoid frost by flowering late and fruiting early. These include 'Lemon Square', 'Scotch Bridget', 'Keswick Codlin' and 'Carlisle Codlin'. A further orchard of Cumbrian apples is also being planted beyond the walls.

Acorn Bank's most famous feature is also one of its most recent. In 1969, the long rectangular walled enclosure below the orchard was a redundant vegetable plot. Now it contains the most comprehensive collection of medicinal and culinary herbs in the north of England. The plants are backed by an early example of a flued wall, through which warm air formerly circulated; there is a record of apricots being grown here in the seventeenth century. With appropriate warnings about poisons and homespun pharmacy, the accompanying herb guide indicates unlikely remedies for nose bleeds, bruises, toothache, heart palpitations and scrofulous swellings. In inclement weather, the place to contemplate all this is the glasshouse, which, though unheated, provides enough shelter to satisfy some somewhat tender plants.

RIGHT Dovecote and orchard trees are the backdrop to a display of panther lilies, *Lilium pardalinum*, at Acorn Bank.

Alfriston Clergy House

ALFRISTON, POLEGATE, EAST SUSSEX

AREA 1.2ha (3 acres) • SOIL alkaline/well-drained light loam over chalk • ALTITUDE 0–6m (0–18ft) • AVERAGE RAINFALL 889mm (35in) • AVERAGE WINTER CLIMATE mild

In a scene of picture-postcard perfection, the half-timbered yeoman's house, dating from the mid-fourteenth century, is tucked at the edge of the village green, separated from St Andrew's church by a cluster of trees, and with its thatched roof and brick chimney silhouetted against the meadows and woods of the South Downs. Derelict by the 1890s, it was saved, at his own financial peril, by the local vicar, Rev. F.W. Benyon, and in 1896 the newly formed National Trust took it on. It was the Trust's first historic house.

The equally seductive cottage garden surrounds the house as a series of small formal terraces, intersected by walls, paths and steps of brick and flint, and framed by yew and box hedges. Immediately below, the land falls abruptly into the reed beds of the River Cuckmere, which are home to water rail, reed and sedge warblers. This means that the lower parts of the garden are subject to frequent flooding. The little orchard, with its medlar, quinces and old apple varieties (among them 'Sussex Duck Bill', 'Ribston Pippin' and 'Alfriston') is under water every winter – a cycle relished by the colonies of lady's smock, snowdrops and snakeshead fritillaries.

The Arts and Crafts design of the terraces was set out in the 1920s by the tenant, Sir Robert Witt, who was also responsible for the punctuating presence of terracotta jars, which he collected on his travels. The accompanying planting – a merry, unselfconscious jumble of colours and seasons – continues to evolve, the parameters set by the shallow chalk soil and the dangers of immersion. On the shady side of the house, Gallica roses jostle with crown imperials, Jacob's ladder, monkshood and Japanese anemones; campanulas, hollyhocks and clove-scented perennial stock bloom along the eastern path; while on the southern terraces, Alba, Damask and Bourbon roses merge with delphiniums and violets, geraniums, soapwort and Shasta daisies.

Clematis, climbing pea and summer jasmine cloak the house walls in the company of roses 'Albertine', 'New Dawn' and *R. multiflora*. From the herb garden, you pass through a pergola, where honeysuckle and a purple-leaved vine wander through a fig tree. The arch leads you into a square enclosure, swimming in the scent of wild pink, *Dianthus plumarius*, in summer, and with Corsican mint releasing odours underfoot. A sundial, commemorating the Trust's centenary, is its centrepiece, set between four impressive plants of gilt-edged box, clipped as mushroom-shaped trees. Beyond is the vegetable garden, with companion plantings of carrots and marigolds, and the contrasting architecture of rhubarb and globe artichoke leaves.

Willow, horse chestnut and other trees stand around the garden's outer edges, none more impressive than the hardy Judas tree, *Cercis siliquastrum*, which in early May is a cloud of carmine-pink against the blue sky and wheeling seagulls, and which is now recovered from the 1987 storm, when it was damaged by one of the neighbouring oaks.

ABOVE The terraces of this Arts and Crafts cottage garden are a constantly evolving mix of plants framed by yew and box hedges.

RIGHT Copper-beech hedging creates a striking foil for some of the statuary in the Anglesey Abbey garden.

Anglesey Abbey

LODE, CAMBRIDGESHIRE

AREA 49ha (120 acres) • SOIL good loam on clay base • ALTITUDE 30m (100ft)
AVERAGE RAINFALL 533mm (21in) • AVERAGE WINTER CLIMATE cold

What is one to make of this extraordinary twentieth-century garden? It is the product of one man's vision, Huttleston Broughton, 1st Lord Fairhaven, who, with grand gestures and a breathtaking sense of scale, transformed an unpromising piece of fenland into a landscape which, as Arthur Bryant has described, 'can compare with the great masterpieces of the Georgian era'. It is a garden of broad avenues, immense vistas and 12ha (30 acres) of mown lawn, decorated with extravagant flower gardens and classical statuary of the best quality, all maintained to the highest standards.

When Lord Fairhaven bought this former Augustinian priory in 1926, he inherited a small garden, laid out by Rev. John Hailstone in the 1860s, and some fine trees, including the cedars and weeping silver lime. From this nucleus he gradually expanded into 36ha (90 acres) of surrounding pastureland. The network of avenues and grass walks do not radiate from the house, but are part of a series of surprises and enticements within an independent garden design. Walking west along Coronation Avenue, you come upon a dramatic cross-vista, culminating in a marble urn, framed at one end by a triple semi-circle of fastigiate Dawyck beech (formerly Lombardy poplars) and, at the other, by silver birch. As you emerge from the beech, you are then offered a view, between island beds of coloured-leaved shrubs, towards a circle of Corinthian columns that surrounds a replica of Bernini's *David* and is guarded by a pair of eighteenth-century lead lions.

Statuary is often the reward for exploration, for Lord Fairhaven was an energetic and discerning collector. Many pieces date from the eighteenth century; some are much older. The Emperors' Walk, on the eastern edge of the garden, is especially richly endowed. It takes its name from the twelve eighteenth-century marble busts of Roman emperors displayed along its 401m (440yd) length, but there are also lead figures within a central circle of copper beech, pairs of bronze and copper urns, a bronze version of the Versailles Diana and of Silenus holding the infant Bacchus, and an open temple sheltering a Roman urn made of Egyptian porphyry.

The displays of bulbs and border plants are as extravagant as the avenues and statues are impressive. Lord Fairhaven chose plants for their impact *en masse*, and several enclosures focus on individual species. Dutch Elm Disease killed 4,000 trees here, and much of the garden has been replanted by the Trust. The new hornbeam avenue was initially underplanted with a ton of white poet's daffodils, *Narcissus poeticus var. recurvus*, and N. 'Winifred van Graven'. As this area became more shaded, an additional 10,000 bluebells, *Hyacinthoides non-scripta*, were planted in the autumn of 2002 to take over from the narcissus. Ten thousand summer snowflakes, *Leucojum aestivum*, grow in the grass of Warrior's Walk.

The rose garden beside the house was one of Lord Fairhaven's favourite areas, and contains a range of modern Bush roses. The Hyacinth Garden beyond, one of the garden's most photographed features, is a sea of 4,000 scented white 'Carnegie' and 'Blue Star' hyacinths in spring, followed in summer by 1,500 red 'Madame Simone Stappers' and gold 'Ella Britton' dahlias. The Dahlia Garden is also filled with these potent performers. Delphiniums are a feature of the vast curved border in the Herbaceous Garden, although here not in solitary splendour but accompanied by a variety of other

plants, including peonies, geraniums, campanulas and *Crambe cordifolia*, with its giant sprays of white blossom; heleniums, achillea and eupatorium help to carry the colour throughout the summer. At its peak, this is perhaps one of the most impressive herbaceous borders in the country.

In 1998, a 1ha (2½ acre) Winter Garden was opened to commemorate the centenary of the 1st Lord Fairhaven's birth. The winding route provides a succession of brilliantly coloured barks, bulbs and scented flowers, a complement to the extensive collection of snowdrops (some 240 varieties), which draws crowds of visitors in January and February. Such spectacles contrast with the dark evergreen passages of yew, ruscus, box and ivy, and the open swathes of grass and trees (including huge areas of carefully managed wildflower meadow and woodland), creating not only a stimulating pattern of light and shade, rest and drama, but also startling juxtapositions of style. In the end, Anglesey Abbey remains a triumphant anachronism; a garden to make you gasp.

LEFT The open temple with its Neo-Classical columns is one in a series of surprises throughout the garden. It shelters a Roman urn of Egyptian porphry.

ABOVE The South Park is part of the extensive former pastureland, out of which Lord Fairhaven expanded his garden.

Planting for winter interest

Richard Todd, Head Gardener
ANGLESEY ABBEY GARDEN, LODE, CAMBRIDGESHIRE

Producing colour without the benefit of plenty of flowers is a challenge in winter, but it can still be derived from other parts of a plant. Coloured stems such as are found in dogwoods (*Cornus*), willow (*Salix*) and brambles (*Rubus*) give permanent colour for at least six months of the year even on the greyest of days, while the bold yellow and green leaf colours of oleaster (*Elaeagnus*) and Mexican orange (*Choisya*) make excellent backgrounds to show off other plants. Trees with good bark interest such as birch (*Betula*), maple (*Acer*) and some cherry (*Prunus*) varieties such as *P. serrula* offer both visual and tactile qualities; berries and fruits add interest, too, although some are eaten early by birds. Species to try include holly, cotoneaster, beauty berry (*Callicarpa*), apple (*Malus*) and the unusual strawberry tree (*Arbutus unedo*).

A careful choice of ground-cover plants is important, as you will need to have colours that can complement the surrounding plants, such as Euonymus 'Emerald Gaiety' teamed with *Viburnum bodnantense* 'Dawn', or go for a strong contrast such as *Luzula sylvatica* 'Aurea' with *Mahonia aquifolium* 'Apollo'. Backgrounds of dark foliage will lift lighter-coloured plants into view, as will the use of a dark layer of leaf mould under plants such as dogwoods and brambles. Good-sized, bold groupings are important for impact, as single plants will get lost in the general mix.

Activating all the senses is what winter gardening is about and a waft of fragrance carried on the cold air is a must. There is a vast choice of shrubs that can be used, including mahonia, viburnum, honeysuckle (*Lonicera*), wintersweet (*Chimonanthus*) and Christmas box (*Sarcococca*), to name a few. These are a treat for the gardener, especially on windless, warmer days. Using the protection of nearby trees can help to prevent frost damage.

Taking note of the sun's angle in winter when planting is the key for making the most of plants with attractive thorns, flaking bark, or good branch formation, such as corkscrew hazel (*Corylus avellana* 'Contorta'). As the winter sun is low, it will provide beautiful backlighting and brightly illuminate peeling strips of bark.

Snowdrops and spring bulbs

There are varieties of snowdrops that flower from October onwards, but it is January that really heralds the arrival of this delightful flower. While snowdrops will grow in reasonably exposed sites, they tend to prefer the dappled light of woodland or the woodland edge. Growing them in thick, lush grass areas is not advised as the grass will dominate and stifle future development.

There are a host of varieties for the more serious collector to choose from, but it is usually either the common *Galanthus nivalis* or its double form 'Flore Pleno' that are seen in profusion. Clumps of bulbs can easily be divided about every five years to help increase the displays. The best time to do this is just after flowering has finished and when the leaves are still green, replanting at the same depth in groups of three or four.

Other bulbs that can give equally great displays in similar conditions include the following: winter aconite (*Eranthis*), flowering at the same time as snowdrops; *Scilla* and *Chionodoxa*, which are excellent at seeding and spreading under tree canopies; crocus species such as *C. tommasinianus*, which will readily seed and spread; *Anemone blanda*; and finally dog's tooth violet (*Erythronium*), which loves to grow in dappled sunlight in woodland.

Take advantage of planting spring bulbs under deciduous shrubs so that a good display is to be had before new foliage blocks out the light. Taller flowering bulbs can be added to ground-cover areas, for example the use of narcissus with ivy (*Hedera*) or crocus with periwinkle (*Vinca minor*).

Tips

- Regular pruning of coloured stems is essential as the best colour is always on the current year's growth; prune in late March.
- Use the low winter sun to either highlight or backlight plants for best effect.
- Strong, contrasting colours or shapes will draw immediate attention.
- Experiment with combining bulbs and other plants such as snowdrops with early miniature iris and hellebore, or using the foliage of *Cyclamen hederifolium* or bergenia as a background.

Antony

AREA 14ha (35 acres) • SOIL medium loam on shale • ALTITUDE 30m (100ft)
AVERAGE RAINFALL 1,016mm (40in) • AVERAGE WINTER CLIMATE mild

As you turn into the approach drive at Antony, a prospect of Plymouth across the estuary is a final reminder of twenty-first century bustle and congestion. The limes now lead you into parkland and woods, back into a more elegant and spacious age.

The silver-grey house was completed for Sir William Carew in 1724, though Antony had been home to his family for 250 years previously, and the garden and park radiate from it in a pattern of formal walks and enclosures and soft-edged avenues. The present design has evolved at a leisurely pace, but was much influenced by the great landscape gardener Humphry Repton, who was consulted by Reginald Pole-Carew in 1792. You can feel his hand in the uninterrupted, undulating sweeps of grass and trees, and in the gentle drama of the main views.

But other features pre-date Repton's involvement, including the terrace, the circular dovecote and the groves of holm oaks which frame the fine views from the house to the River Lynher; these were planted in the 1760s. By 1788, Reginald Pole-Carew had himself already embarked on an extensive programme of ornamental tree planting; the immense black walnut in front of the house and the cork oak at the end of the Yew Walk may date from this period.

The gravel terraces in front of the house and the formal walks and gardens to the west reveal layers of Victorian, Edwardian and more recent planting by subsequent members of the Carew family. The broad paths, high yew hedges and abundance of substantial trees continue the generous scale, but there are more intimate touches in Lady Pole-Carew's early twentieth-century Japanese garden at the east end of the terrace and in the enclosed Summer Garden and Knot Garden begun in 1983 by Lady (Mary) Carew Pole.

The planting themes at Antony tend to be focused on favourite genera. There are two magnificent rows of large, free-standing magnolias, the evergreen *M. grandiflora* 'Exmouth' and the deciduous *M. × soulangeana*; at the end of the former, overhung by an old mulberry, is the splendid Mandalay Bell brought back as booty from the Second Burmese War by General Sir Reginald Pole-Carew in 1886. Hoherias and eucryphias, which provide a mass of white blossom in summer, set new themes for the west end of the garden. Around the walls, beneath tender climbing plants such as

A

Acacia pravissima, *Senna corymbosa* (syn. *Cassia corymbosa*), *Sophora tetraptera* and various wall shrubs, is a National Collection of daylilies (*Hemerocallis*), including many American varieties, assembled and hybridised by the late Lady (Cynthia) Carew Pole between 1960 and 1977.

A romantic escape from order and elegance is offered by the 24ha (60 acres) of woodland, wilderness and wildflowers between the house and the river. This is actually outside the Trust's domain, and run by the Carew Pole Garden Trust, which allows the Trust's visitors to explore it on the days the house is open. Paths take you past an eighteenth-century bathhouse (owned by the National Trust), mature rhododendrons, long-needled pines, birches, Asiatic magnolias, and, most memorably, a long valley of pink, red and white camellias which now number over 2,000 varieties – Sir John Carew Pole's plantings being continually enhanced by those of his successors, Sir Richard and Lady (Mary) Carew Pole, with many plants grown from wild-sourced seed.

ABOVE The Summer Garden in late May.

Ardress House

PORTADOWN, CO. ARMAGH

AREA 2.4ha (6 acres) • SOIL alkaline, clay • ALTITUDE 30m (100ft)
AVERAGE RAINFALL 762mm (30in) • AVERAGE WINTER CLIMATE moderate

'A solitary whitebeam makes a focal point, a silver silhouette against the ploughed fields below'

The estate house of Ardress is washed rosy pink, the same colour as the apple-blossom buds in the surrounding orchards. For this low-lying country is the garden of Ulster, and Ardress sits on an eminence within it, commanding patchwork views of farmland, woods and acres of Bramleys. There is only a modest flower garden to accompany the farmhouse, gentrified by its architect-owner George Ensor some time after 1778. The rest of the land around the house is given over to grass, trees and apples.

As the ground drops away opposite the main, east front, the smooth lawn quickly turns into rough grass. A solitary whitebeam makes a focal point here, a silver silhouette against the ploughed fields below, and the prospect is framed by belts of taller trees. In fact, this is the beginning of a woodland walk that leads down to the Ladies' Mile, a fringe of trees to the south of the house.

The garden opposite the south front offers a contrast in mood and has been replanted by the Trust in recent years. Busts of the Four Seasons, placed in niches in the curved screen walls, together with young Irish yews on the terraced lawn, strike a classical note. As you descend the slope, past a mixed border of blue and yellow flowers, a formal rose garden is gradually revealed, centred around an oval Coade urn, which is dated 1790 and decorated with leopards' heads and bunches of grapes.

The retaining wall in this part of the garden is hung with the slightly tender, trailing rosemary *Rosmarinus officinalis* Prostratus Group, in partnership with a number of Irish-raised Climbing roses, deep pink 'Bantry Bay', coppery-orange 'Schoolgirl' and pink-tinged 'Handel'.

LEFT Apple blossom in April.

The Argory

MOY, DUNGANNON, CO. ARMAGH

AREA 2ha (5 acres) • SOIL acid/clay and peat • ALTITUDE 0–76m (0–250ft)
AVERAGE RAINFALL 838mm (33in) • AVERAGE WINTER CLIMATE very cold

The setting here is perfect. The silver-grey house sits on a rise above
the River Bracknell, amid lawns, woodland and a formal garden
designed for the barrister Walter McGeogh by the Dublin architects
John and Arthur Williamson, who also designed the house and its
outbuildings. Wrought-iron gates lead into a small rose garden,
known as the Sundial Garden, which has been replanted by the Trust
using small-flowered dwarf Polyantha and China varieties in pink
and white. It is a delicate composition that contrasts briskly with
the more solid shapes of the yew igloos and stone pavilions in the
adjacent Pleasure Ground, which slopes down to a curving rampart
wall. Over this you can see the river and, sometimes, the herd of rare
striped cattle, called moilies, grazing on the meadow.

The planting in the perimeter beds is young, but already
contains shrubs and perennials, including escallonias, brooms,
rhododendrons and heathers, together with dieramas, kniphofias
and agapanthus from the Slieve Donard nursery, as well as other
Irish-raised varieties such as *Bergenia* 'Ballawley', *Cytisus* 'Moyclare
Pink' and *Hypericum* 'Rowallane'. The sense of age is conveyed by a
few old shrubs and several good trees, including a cedar, a yew and a
knobbly buttressed tulip tree, underplanted with spotted laurel.

Recently, the 0.4ha (1 acre) walled kitchen garden has also been
revived from dereliction and is once again sporting vegetables and cut
flowers. A new timber-framed greenhouse has been built, in which
produce and flowers will be grown for sale on the estate.

RIGHT A Cedar of Lebanon beside one of the small pavilions in the Pleasure Ground.

Arlington Court

BARNSTAPLE, DEVON

AREA 12ha (30 acres) • **SOIL** acid/light, sand overlying slate • **ALTITUDE** 244m (800ft)
AVERAGE RAINFALL 1,524mm (60in) • **AVERAGE WINTER CLIMATE** moderate, occasional frost

The green combes and woods of this 971ha (2,400 acre) estate were conserved by Miss Rosalie Chichester as a wildlife sanctuary, with a lakeside nature reserve at its heart. Her domestic menagerie of dogs, canaries, budgerigars and parrots has gone, but peacocks still strut over the grass and her beloved Shetland ponies and Jacob's sheep still graze the parkland on the garden's fringe.

The house, a sober Georgian mansion, stands among trees, lawns and shrubberies, looking out over the Yeo valley. In high summer, only hydrangeas – mostly an electrifying blue, but pink-tinged where they make contact with the limestone chippings of the curving carriage drives – interrupt the greens. Earlier in the year, the grass sprouts bluebells, primroses, violets, daffodils, Siberian claytonia and, beside the main drive, colonies of cerise-pink Japanese primulas. At the same time, the rhododendrons are in bloom; like the primulas, they appreciate the high rainfall. Hidden in the south-east corner of the garden is an atmospherically Victorian wilderness pond where they grow with ferns, gunnera and pampas grass, backed by the grey stone tower of the parish church.

The moist, clean air fosters the growth of mosses and lichens and, with ferns, which also colonise the branches and trunks, they give some of the trees a jungle flavour. The backdrop is ever-changing, with the native oaks, beeches and sycamores joined by sweet chestnut, cut-leaved beech, tulip tree, redwood, hemlock, fir, cypresses, a varied collection of ash and numerous others; the walk to the lake takes in an avenue of monkey puzzles. Miss Chichester could not bear to fell trees – neither would she interfere with the advance of invasive Pontic rhododendron – with the result that the Trust inherited large tracts of derelict and senescent woodland. Much clearance and replanting has been required to rejuvenate these areas and to reopen the garden glades for wildflowers.

The chief surprise, as you stroll through the buxom plantings of these informal pleasure grounds, is suddenly to come upon the manicured terraces of the Victorian flower garden of 1865, neatly packaged in walls and grey railings. The Trust's restoration has included the rebuilding of part of the conservatory, the garden's centrepiece, which now displays plumbago, agapanthus, tibouchina, *Daphne odora* and potted azaleas and lilies, against crisp white woodwork and a slate- and tile-patterned floor. Circular beds cut into

one of the grass terraces have been enclosed in authentic, basket-weave ironwork frames to re-create a quaint, early nineteenth-century feature, the basket bed. Cobaeas are encouraged to ascend the handles in summer, and the baskets are filled with colourful ephemera. The looped pattern is echoed by the arches of common honeysuckle – alternately, the Early Dutch cultivar 'Belgica', and the redder-budded, Late Dutch cultivar 'Serotina' – which stand either side of the goldfish pool on the platform below.

The upper borders are very delicate (too delicate to pass as Victorian creations) in their fresh blue, yellow, green and deep pink colour scheme, with geraniums, alchemilla, irises, osteospermum, kniphofia, phlox and filipendula among the company. With the conservatory as their centrepiece, and the bowed, whitewashed façade of the adjoining rectory to punctuate the view, they are very photogenic indeed.

Since 1990, the Trust has also been bringing the adjacent walled Kitchen Garden back to life. The greenhouse has been rebuilt, vegetables and cut flowers have been returned to the beds, and an array of fruit trees has been trained on the walls. These include a number of local apple varieties, such as 'Devonshire Quarrenden', 'Star of Devon', 'Devonshire Buckland' and 'Lucombe's Seedling'.

FAR LEFT Sweet peas in July.

LEFT Heleniums and Shasta daisies contribute to the lively palette of summer colours.

BELOW The wilderness pond in autumn, overlooking the parish church of St. James.

Ascott

AREA 19ha (46 acres) • SOIL acid to neutral • ALTITUDE 76m (250ft)
AVERAGE RAINFALL 660mm (26in) • AVERAGE WINTER CLIMATE moderate

Ascott is a spectacular illustration of the great reversal of gardening taste that took place during the nineteenth century, when, in response to technological innovation and a new celebration of the creative mind, art and artifice became the dominant forces, with colour, bedding, exotic foliage and formality replacing the predominantly green, naturalistic landscapes of the Georgian era.

Leopold de Rothschild acquired the property from his brother, Baron Nathan Meyer, in 1876, and engaged the architect George Devey to transform the seventeenth-century farmhouse into the present, rather surprising, black-and-white residence, strung together like a row of Tudor houses and cottages and once romantically shrouded in ivy and other creepers. The task of setting out the garden was entrusted to the renowned Chelsea nurserymen James Veitch & Sons, with Rothschild, himself an enthusiastic gardener, closely involved. The principal ingredients are presented as soon as you walk down the curving entrance drive towards the house's north front: fine trees, neat lawns, pristine gravel, the splash of water from a fountain and patterns of clipped evergreens, in this case Portuguese laurels pruned into umbrella shapes.

Added to this are colourful and curious specimen plants: the autumnal flame of the large-leaved vine *Vitis coignetiae* and the seldom-seen female form of *Garrya elliptica*, producing its green and red fruits on one side of the house door while its partner drips grey catkins on the other. A quirky contoured walk, featuring serpentine hedges of beech, leads to a skating and waterlily lake, fringed in weeping willows, bold-leaved gunnera and darmera, and appointed with a thatched changing hut. Yet all this is merely a taste of what

awaits as you follow the meandering path down slopes and steps, through scented and shady shrubberies, to the main south garden. Here, the grounds open out into an extensive arboretum, the foreground to a sweeping panorama across the Vale of Aylesbury to the Chiltern Hills. Although there are acres of plain lawn and belts, groves and avenues of green trees (a number planted to commemorate royal events), it is the wealth of ornamental incident that immediately strikes you. Everywhere, there are trees of eccentric habit and hue: weeping, cut-leaved and copper beeches, blue, golden and weeping cedars, variegated sweet chestnut (a superb specimen), purple maple, cut-leaved alder, yellow catalpa – the scene further enriched in autumn by the potent tints of scarlet oak, red maple, tulip tree and liquidambar. In spring, waves of yellow and white daffodils wash over the slopes, followed by colonies of snakeshead fritillaries and native wildflowers.

Most arresting of all are the clipped and coloured evergreens. Hedges, tumps and topiaries, including yews of an electrifying yellow, are strung through the landscape, contrasting abruptly with the relaxed mood of woodland and meadow, and signalling the presence of a series of impressive formal enclosures.

The Sundial Garden is one of the first you come upon, a splendid period piece made entirely out of topiary, with the gnomon in green and golden yew (the one grafted onto the other, and aptly described in an article by Arthur Hellyer as like a giant egg in an eggcup), the Roman numerals in green box, and the quotation 'Light and shade by turn but love always' (with accompanying hearts) again in golden yew. In recent years, Sir Evelyn de Rothschild, the present tenant, has added further features including, opposite the sundial, in the former fern garden, a sunken box parterre by garden designer Arabella Lennox-Boyd patterned with circles and squares and with a central bubble fountain. These features have introduced a late twentieth-century flavour to parts of the garden, but the creativity and panache exactly echo that of Leopold de Rothschild's gardening a hundred years before.

Below the house, a long, straight run of golden yew shelters double borders of spring and summer bulbs and herbaceous plants, in a repeated pink, blue and silver colour scheme (penstemons, sedums, delphiniums, eryngiums and artemisia among the cast) that is a little soft and subtle for the garden, perhaps. The low wall behind is topped with a hedge of yellow holly and supports a range of frost-tender, winter-flowering and other shrubs and climbers, giving this garden its name of the Madeira Walk. It is when you enter the circular garden opposite that you receive your first taste of High

Victorian flower gardening in all its shocking splendour. Here, a bronze Venus rises from the sea in a great marble shell-chariot, drawn by winged horses and with cherubs in attendance; this is a work by the American sculptor Waldo Story. Enclosing it is a radiant hedge of golden yew, and in the box-edged borders there is a changing display of rich seasonal bedding.

Passages of soothing grass and trees allow the optic nerves some respite before a second, still more lavish scene is revealed. This is the Dutch Garden, a narrow strip of lawn presided over by Eros atop a slender fountain (also by Story), nestling below a high shrubbery ridge, and backed by a rock and tufa grotto, complete with mysterious dripping cavern and eruptions of hart's tongue and other ferns. The beds cut out of the grass, also filled twice yearly, are flamboyantly stocked with many of the great nineteenth-century favourites, including coloured-leaved coleus and cabbages, cannas and castor oil plants – all to provoke squeals of delight or horror, depending on your sensibilities.

ABOVE The main avenue of trees leading to the house.

Attingham Park

SHREWSBURY, SHROPSHIRE

AREA 20ha (50 acres) • **SOIL** sandy, clay • **ALTITUDE** 40–85m (131–279ft)
AVERAGE RAINFALL 711mm (28in) • **AVERAGE WINTER CLIMATE** moderate

Attingham, in an advanced stage of restoration by the Trust, has been gradually regaining the elegant finish imposed by Humphry Repton. In its overall design it has changed little since the early 1800s, and offers much insight into Georgian landscaping. There is a fine view of the grand Neo-classical mansion from Tern Bridge on the A5, which was both moved 130 yards (119m) further south to accommodate a larger park and decorated at the 1st Lord Berwick's expense in 1780. It makes an important landscape feature; reverse views take in the Wrekin and the south Shropshire hills. However, Repton was not the first landscape designer on the scene. A lesser-known practitioner, Thomas Leggett, was employed here between 1769 and 1772, before the present mansion was built, and his tree planting was extensive; a single bill of 13 February 1770 reveals that 7,000 trees were bought from Messrs Williamson of London for £42 11s 1d. Many of Repton's proposals, contained in his Red Book of 1798, consisted of alterations to this earlier work.

The tour centres principally on Leggett's mile-long pleasure walk with carefully contrived views – a popular mid-eighteenth-century garden feature. It begins above the cedar grove and leads off, between meadow and water, through a succession of stands and groves of different trees, shrubs and native daffodils. There are fine views across the river to the Repton-designed Deer Park and the Wrekin. A number of species, notably rhododendrons and azaleas, were added early in the last century, and in its replanting programme the Trust is both following Leggett's original lists and reflecting these colourful later layers. A splendid cedar of Lebanon presides over the north-east curve of the

walk, behind which a secondary path meanders beside a willow carr and across the river into the deer park. As you continue around the circumference, you pass a circle of honey locusts (*Gleditsia*), and a sombre stretch of giant fir (*Abies grandis*) before the trees suddenly part and a broad expanse of mown grass, framed by a nuttery and a high south-facing wall, carries the eye to the eighteenth-century Bee House, which now houses a display about bees and beekeeping.

The wall is clad in peaches, nectarines and apricots and belongs to the impressive 1.1 ha (2.75 acre) kitchen garden and frame yard. Built at the same time as the house and stables, in about 1780, these areas are now nearing the end of a major refurbishment. Around the centrepiece of a brick-lined well and dipping pond, the kitchen garden is once again showing a traditional quartered design planted

with many heritage varieties of fruit and vegetables, with further fan-trained fruits on the walls and espaliered and cordoned trees along the paths. Double herbaceous borders – 80m (262ft) long and filled with tulips, delphininiums, scabious, shasta daisies, and other plants with white, pink and blue flowers – run down the centre, edged in 'Hidcote' lavender. The peach house on the south wall has long gone, with only its footprint remaining, but the melon, pine and tomato houses in the adjacent frame yard have been restored and are accompanied by cut-flower beds of perennials, bulbs and roses – the varieties chosen following an inventory of 1924. The impressive range of mushroom, fruit and root storage sheds at the rear of the garden have been opened up, and there is an observation bee hive in one of the back sheds. Here also is a 0.8ha (2 acre) orchard, planted

with old and local tree varieties, including *Prunus insititia* 'Prune Damson' and the cooking apple 'Shropshire Pippin'; in the past, the apple trees would have been carefully selected to provide the family with a full year's supply of fruit.

There is further ornamental planting to the south-east of the hall, comprising rhododendrons (surrounding a brick ice-house), and a Spring Garden of trees and shrubs. The remains of formal yew and knot gardens, made in the 1920s in front of the hall, were removed by the Trust in 1976. This is now beautifully restored to grass and Reptonian tranquillity.

ABOVE The Attingham parkland is divided by the River Tern.

Baddesley

CLINTON NR KNOWLE, SOLIHULL, WARWICKSHIRE

AREA 4.5ha (11 acres) • SOIL neutral/clay and loam • ALTITUDE 113m (370ft)
AVERAGE RAINFALL 686mm (27in) • AVERAGE WINTER CLIMATE moderate

The sight of this small, moated manor house, in its pastoral setting of oaks, wildflowers, grass and sheep, cannot fail to bewitch. In spite of being a mere 26km (16 miles) from Birmingham, little appears to have ruffled the scene for centuries, its timeless air being preserved by the constant structure of moat, lake and stewponds, and the surrounding remnants of the ancient Forest of Arden. Paintings inside the house, dating from 1915, show the Walled Garden divided from the moat and south-east front by a high yew hedge and decorated elaborately with herbaceous borders, standard roses and pergolas. When it first came into the hands of the Trust, it was in a state of terrible decay, but the original arrangement is being reinstated. Rose and mixed flower borders have now returned to join the apple trees in the main lawn, with the long cross-axis border sporting nearly 500 varieties of dahlia, giving a kaleidoscope of colour in late summer. Beside the summer-house, the path leads out, past pampas grasses, to a delightful vegetable garden.

Beyond the south wall, an extensive 'flowery mead', important for its butterflies and moths, adds to this feeling of being in a rural time capsule. The grass is not mown until August to give the widest range of plants time to bloom and drop seed. Wildflowers are not confined to this area; primroses spangle the grass around the stewponds, daffodils lay trails of yellow under the oaks and limes beside the drive and along the path to the adjacent church, while bluebells colonise the ground under the oaks, sycamores and chestnuts beside the lake, which has been dredged and restored by the Trust. One of the best prospects is through a stand of Scots pine to this tranquil stretch of water, complete with its two rushy islands and rafts of waterlilies. The perimeter offers a typical nineteenth-century wilderness walk, and the native trees and shrubs have been supplemented by rhododendrons. The invasive *Rhododendron ponticum* is gradually being replaced here with other colour forms.

ABOVE Seven mascles of the Ferrers family coat of arms are laid out on the Courtyard lawn to an 1889 design.

RIGHT Lilac overhangs a lawn at Barrington Court, where the planting strongly reflects the influence of Gertrude Jekyll.

Barrington Court

ILMINSTER, SOMERSET

AREA 4.5ha (11 acres) • SOIL neutral/lime, loam over clay • ALTITUDE 20m (65ft)
AVERAGE RAINFALL 762mm (30in) • AVERAGE WINTER CLIMATE mild

Gertrude Jekyll was in her late seventies and had very poor eyesight when she was approached by architects to the Trust's tenant, Colonel Arthur Lyle, to undertake the planting at Barrington Court. The plans were submitted to her with biscuit boxes of garden soil. Although only half her schemes were put into practice, those that were rank among her finest work. Their structure and style – familiar to all students of gardening from the black-and-white photographs in her many books – remain evocatively intact, as does the warm Arts and Crafts detailing of the different outdoor rooms. In fact, the garden at Barrington Court is one of the best preserved of her gardens, especially the lily garden.

The introduction is grand. Long avenues of trees (previously of horse chestnuts, which as a result of canker have now been replaced), punctuated with 1920s farm buildings, give way to closely mown lawn, high, dark hedges (Lawson cypress as well as yew), canal ponds and scrolled stonework. Ahead is the Tudor honey-coloured mansion, and beside it an equally large stable block, built in 1674 of red brick, and known as the Strode House. The two buildings are a curious pair, particularly on the south side, where they are in alignment in the midst of open lawn and park – the house here showing its Elizabethan E-shape, and skyline of gables, finials and fin barley-twist chimneys.

Away from the house, the grandeur quickly melts into the traditional and the rustic. Cider orchards, some grazed by sheep, fringe much of the garden and are once again being harvested, producing award-winning apple juice and cider. Clipped mushrooms of Portuguese laurel sprout in front of a line of thatched cottages, and

runs of hurdle fencing provide makeshift pens. In spring, there are welcoming bursts of daffodils in the rough grass, and in summer, an assortment of wildflowers, including spotted and twayblade orchids.

This blend of the grand and formal with the homely and vernacular, the essence of the Arts and Crafts style, also characterises Gertrude Jekyll's flower gardens. The display begins to the west of the Strode House, with borders of predominantly pink and purplish shrubs and perennials – wisteria, buddleja, claret-leaved smoke bush and clove-scented *Daphne × burkwoodii* with the glossy, evergreen leaves of bergenia and *Acanthus mollis*, both much favoured by her as punctuation marks – alongside one of the most beautiful paths to be seen in this country: a straight run of mellow Tudor brick, its pattern changing every few paces, from diamond to herringbone, circle to basketweave to square.

However, it is in the adjacent Lily Garden that her influence is most keenly felt. Here, steps lead down from the Strode House's west terrace to a rectangular lawn and waterlily pool, surrounded by raised rectangular beds and, across the patterned paths, richly coloured mixed borders. In the raised beds, only the crinums, with their bold strap-like foliage and pink trumpet flowers, remain from the original scheme. Miss Jekyll's hydrangeas have been replaced with salmon-, apricot- and flame-coloured azaleas (growing in imported lime-free soil) in partnership with the early yellow daylily, *Hemerocallis dumortieri*. The inner beds echo these tones and generous stands of orange alstroemeria, helenium and lilies, scarlet crocosmia and fuchsia, and yellow hypericum and rudbeckia are blended into powerful harmonies. Miss Jekyll's supreme legacy to modern gardening is, of course, her colour teaching and this

is a wonderful demonstration of her principles. The shrubs and perennials are also interwoven, as she advocated, with splashes of spring and summer bedding, including wallflowers, marigolds, snapdragons and dahlias, to disguise gaps and prolong the display. Bergenias mark the corners again, and the foliage of tropical canna lilies helps the crinums and daylilies to provide definition and contrasting structure. It is an appealing composition.

Beyond, through another of the garden's handsome, faded oak doors, is the Rose and Iris Garden, cleaned of perennial weeds and replanted in the mid-1990s along the lines of Miss Jekyll's original scheme, with the surrounding box hedge rejuvenated from cuttings. Following rose sickness, her Rose and Peony Garden changed more dramatically; it was redesigned by Colonel Lyle's grandson Andrew in 1986 as a White Garden, such as Jekyll suggested in *Colour Schemes for the Flower Garden*. It is still strongly Edwardian in character, and the plantings of longstanding annual and perennial border favourites such as phlox, crambe, alyssum, cineraria, cosmos and silver stachys are marshalled within Jekyll's formal circular design.

The patterned brick paths run between and around these gardens, bordered by hedges of bulging boxwood and Munstead lavender, fringed by beds of catmint and pink penstemons. In one part, there is the shade of a long pergola (recently erected, but strongly Jekyllian in flavour), clad in vine, wisteria, jasmine, clematis and golden hop, and underplanted for early summer with geranium, alchemilla, aubrieta and Solomon's seal. Until 1920, this was all a cow yard, and on the north side, the calf sheds, or bustalls, are still standing, picturesquely hung with Climbing roses.

Further stretches of the canalised stream, which serves the Court as a moat, skirt the outer walls of the flower gardens, and you leave by way of an oak bridge, back into the cider orchard. A final surprise is sprung, another sudden change of scale: a long, deep, buxomly planted herbaceous border, designed by Colonel Lyle's wife Ronnie, containing massive swathes of achilleas, hollyhocks, salvias, helianthus and other flowers for cutting. Behind it is the huge walled kitchen garden, which has been in continuous production since the 1920s. Built of local stone, and with flower borders down its centre, this presents a panoply of wall fruits, from peaches and nectarines to figs, plums and gages, beds of vegetables ranging from asparagus and sea kale to aubergines and peppers, and a further scene of plump Somerset abundance. A local school has a plot within the garden.

ABOVE LEFT The circular pool in the kitchen garden.

ABOVE RIGHT The active walled kitchen garden has been in continuous production since the 1920s.

RIGHT Wisteria climbing the walls of the Walled Garden.

Basildon Park

LOWER BASILDON, READING, BERKSHIRE

AREA 2.2ha (5½ acres) • SOIL clay/sand, overlying chalk • ALTITUDE 76m (250ft)
AVERAGE RAINFALL 686mm (27in) • AVERAGE WINTER CLIMATE moderate

This fine Palladian house stands in one of those unspoilt, leafy pockets within the Thames Valley, with pastoral views of hills, beechwoods and river. It was built in the third quarter of the eighteenth century for Sir Francis Sykes, and it was set, according to the fashion of the time, in an open and elegant landscape park.

The gardens comprise a parterre (which is now lawn) and pleasure grounds east and north-east of the house. The parterre, bounded by a handsome balustraded terrace and ha-ha, was carved from the park after 1838, but its present sympathetic planting and ornament reflect the taste of Lord and Lady Iliffe, who from 1952 rescued both house and garden from an appalling state of dereliction. Roses and lavender feature prominently in the borders and do well in the free-draining soil. *Rosa* 'Sander's White Rambler' scrambles over the stone balustrade, while nearby, *Viburnum × burkwoodii, Clematis montana* and other shrubs and climbers bring light and scent to the shady courtyard between the house and its north pavilion. Out of sight of the house, the pleasure grounds, which pre-date the parterre, roll down the hillside beside the drive. A concentration of yews and holm oaks, now mature trees but once clipped tightly into tumps, gives way to glades dappled by chestnuts, limes, beeches, Japanese cherries and specimens of tulip tree and catalpa. Daffodils, primroses, anemones and vast carpets of bluebells accompany them in spring. Currently, these grounds are being reinvigorated and restored to their eighteenth-century form, with shrubberies being replanted and views opened up into the 162ha (400 acre) park.

RIGHT The grassed-over parterre and balustraded terrace.

Bateman's

BURWASH, ETCHINGHAM, EAST SUSSEX

AREA 4ha (10 acres) • SOIL acid/clay • ALTITUDE 76m (250ft) • AVERAGE RAINFALL 762mm (30in) • AVERAGE WINTER CLIMATE mild to moderate

'The Jacobean house is a solid squire's residence, set in undulating wooded countryside'

'It is a good and peaceable place, standing in terraced lawns nigh to a walled garden of old, red brick, and two fat-headed oast houses with red brick stomachs, and an aged silver grey dovecote on top … We entered and felt her spirit – her Feng Shui – to be good.' This was Rudyard Kipling's first impression of Bateman's, which was to be his home from 1902 until his death in 1936.

The Jacobean house is a solid squire's residence, set in undulating wooded countryside, 'alive with ghosts and shadows', and with rooms dark, comfortable and creaky. The garden is a spacious accompaniment to it, a blend of firm, traditional design and soft-edged planting, and, with the surrounding landscape, is rich in associations with Kipling's stories and poems, especially *Puck of Pook's Hill* and its sequel *Rewards and Fairies*, which were both set here. The mill that features in these stories is a short walk from the house, through the Wild Garden.

Visitors enter the property through the old kitchen garden, passing alongside a herb border heavy with suitable spicy and eastern odours – the curry scent comes from *Helichrysum italicum* – and then arriving at the mouth of the Pear Alley at the bottom of the slope. The pears – 'Beurré Hardy', 'Comice', 'Conference', 'Superfine', 'Williams' and 'Winter Nelis' – share their supports with clematis and are underplanted with a range of intermingling ground-cover plants, including periwinkle, bluebells, cyclamen and Corsican hellebore. Wrought-iron gates, displaying the initials RK, now lead into the Mulberry Garden opposite. The original mulberry died some time ago, and has been replaced with a young one. Since 2009, the Trust has been converting this area back to a kitchen garden, as it was in Kipling's time, the vegetables accompanied by herbs and cut flowers.

To the south of the house, the gardens are broad, open and flat, the expanse of lawn broken by some very good trees, a pleached wall lime avenue pre-dating Kipling, and other vertical and horizontal features in neat geometric shapes. Apparently, I am not the first to remark on the strange alignment of some of these – in particular the procession of stone steps, Irish yews and symmetrical pairs of *Aesculus flava* – which seem to have a life independent of the house and landscape. Other visitors have noted the absence of anticipated focal points and the quirkiness of 'paths leading nowhere'.

The main lawn is separated from the upper part, the Quarter Deck, by a low retaining wall, and as you descend, it is worth scrutinising it for its collection of lichens and rock plants. A raised platform is necessary protection from the River Dudwell, which is apt to burst its banks and submerge the lower garden.

The lily pond was constructed by Kipling so that his children could use it for swimming and boating. It had its accidental users, too; a number of names in the family visitors' book are followed by the initials F.I.P., meaning 'fell in pond'. The formal Rose Garden beyond it was also added by Kipling, and contains three varieties of Polyantha rose – pale pink 'Valentine Heart', mid-pink 'Betty Prior' and scarlet 'Frensham' – underplanted, for spring, with a yellow and blue bulb scheme comprising *Narcissus* 'Hawera' and *Muscari* 'Blue Spike'. Behind it is a sundial bearing an inscription that will have a familiar ring to all who absorb themselves in gardening: 'It is later than you think.'

LEFT Kipling's home and the surrounding kitchen garden nestles into the surrounding countryside.

ABOVE The view from the Mulberry Garden to the Pear Alley.

Belton House

GRANTHAM, LINCOLNSHIRE

AREA 14ha (35 acres) • SOIL neutral/sandy loam • ALTITUDE 52m (170ft)
AVERAGE RAINFALL 686mm (27in) • AVERAGE WINTER CLIMATE cold

This elegant composition of green and gold takes its cue from the honey-coloured mansion that presides over its level acres with the serenity of a French château. Built for Sir John Brownlow in the 1680s, its architect is thought to have been William Winde, who may also have been responsible for the elaborate geometric gardens that once accompanied it; Winde designed the grand terraces at Cliveden and, probably, Powis Castle. Most of this early formality has gone, a victim of the dramatic change in gardening taste that occurred in Britain during the eighteenth century. However, avenues continue to radiate from the house: a spectacular lime avenue to the east, punctuated with statues, sweeping up to the Bellmount Tower, constructed c.1750 to provide a prospect of the park and surrounding landscape; another of Turkey oak, leading south to the Lion Gates; and a shorter lime avenue leading west, reinstated by the Trust and framing a view of the clocktower. A mirror pond, north-east of the house, also remains, reflecting a statue of Ceres and a small Palladian temple in its water.

The linear framework therefore survived the 1740s, when the picturesque Wilderness, with its Gothic ruin, cascades, shrubberies and flower-rich meadows, was added, and the late 1770s, when the parkland planting suggested by William Emes was pursued. The resulting blend of styles is one of extreme beauty, and in the late nineteenth century when the flowing lawns were studded with specimen beech and oak, cedar and wellingtonia, the harmony merely deepened.

The Dutch Garden, a reproduction of the Georgian layout, was created by the 3rd Earl Brownlow in the 1870s. Its theme of green and gold is taken up by alternating green yew pillars and golden yew globes, the pattern complemented by honey-coloured gravel, urns and statuary. Lavenders, catmint and sea-green cedars provide scent and cool contrast. The sunken Italian Garden, designed by Jeffry Wyatville, dates from the early nineteenth century, its central axis adorned with a large fountain pool, an Orangery to the north, and an exedra with lion fountain to the south. The Orangery itself, restored and now one of the finest in the Trust's hands, contains a host of exotic plants, including palms and tree ferns; in Edwardian times, it housed a flock of free-flying budgerigars. The walled garden behind it shelters roses, sweet peas and herbaceous plants, with 'Nottingham' medlar trees set around a stone ornament, the Brownlow Basket.

Paths wind from the formal gardens and lawns to the wilder pleasure grounds, where much restoration has been taking place. You are now led through woodland gardens, full of spring colour, to a recently reopened maze, and on to the shore of the lake. The handsome architectural feature here is the chalet-style boathouse from the 1820s. Designed by Anthony Salvin, it has a fishscale slate roof and basketweave plasterwork, and was used by the family for picnics and fishing parties. The paths and terraces by the cascade have also been uncovered and planted up once again, reopening a lost world.

LEFT The early nineteenth-century Italian Garden from the north.
ABOVE Statue in the Dutch Garden, created in the 1870s by the 3rd Earl Brownlow.

Beningbrough Hall

SHIPTON-BY-BENINGBROUGH, YORK, YORKSHIRE

AREA 2.8ha (7 acres) • **SOIL** neutral/silty loam • **ALTITUDE** 15m (50ft)
AVERAGE RAINFALL 762mm (30in) • **CLIMATE** cold

'The borders feature an Edwardian theme of cool midsummer tints'

By the time restoration of this Baroque house, standing among water meadows in the Vale of York, began in 1977, the gardens too were declining. The estate records were lost and there were no clear historical guidelines for the Trust, but there had been especially active passages in the evolution, and it was decided to anchor the garden in these periods. The hall itself seems to cry out for a simple uncluttered setting that conveys a flavour of eighteenth-century elegance. Early maps show it at the centre of a formal landscape of radiating avenues, but the eighteenth-century tide of opinion against formal landscaping gathered momentum, and at Beningbrough a more natural landscape of open parkland and irregular clumps of trees replaced the avenues. Today the south front of the hall, flanked by trees, including an unusual variegated oak, surveys a pristine gravel walk and velvet lawn and, across the ha-ha, a relaxed prospect of the water meadows bordering the River Ouse.

The first Ordnance Survey map of 1852 shows the two wings of the garden, the Wilderness and the American Garden, well furnished with trees. The latter takes the form of an open glade encircled by a shady walk of trees and shrubs. Spring is its high season, when the ground is smothered with daffodils and there is blossom on cherry and amelanchier. Rhododendrons tolerant of a little lime take over in early summer – *Rhododendron* 'Cunningham's White', *R.* 'Cunningham's Blush' and *R. catawbiense*.

From 1827, Beningbrough benefited from an outstanding head gardener, Thomas Foster, and during his time the Walled Garden must have been a model kitchen garden. The walls still shelter a range of pears, apples and figs, and the original pear alley

remains as a centrepiece, with the varieties 'Black Worcester', 'Beurré Hardy' and 'Pitmaston Duchess' underplanted with herbs. Foster's home-raised grape varieties, 'Lady Downe's Seedling' (still rated one of the finest, late-keeping grapes) and 'Foster's Seedling' (one of the best early-fruiting vines) have been returned to the vinery. Among the accompanying beds of soft fruits, vegetables and cut flowers is a collection of northern rhubarb varieties and a large patch of liquorice, a plant long associated with Yorkshire. Recently, an orchard has also been planted south of the Walled Garden, featuring a collection of Yorkshire apple varieties. Now, much of this produce feeds visitors in the restaurant rather than the family.

The Victorian pleasure grounds at Beningbrough featured formal touches, and formality returned to the Park when the Lime Avenue was installed some time after 1913. Although this feature is being retained, the broad-leaved limes (*Tilia platyphyllos*) are gradually being replaced with common limes (*T. × europaea*), which are more tolerant of the high water table.

In 1916, the estate was bought by the 10th Earl and Countess of Chesterfield. Their main interest was racing and their main enterprise their stud, so they orchestrated the long South Border, below the Walled Garden, to peak during the week of the Doncaster St Leger meeting in late September. It now features buddlejas, hardy salvias and other plants attractive to bees and butterflies. To the west of the Walled Garden are further planting schemes. The double borders feature an Edwardian theme of cool midsummer tints. 'Iceberg' roses, purple berberis, philadelphus and deutzias are repeated down their length, along with standard wisteria and

varieties of clematis. In front are waves of catmint, purple sage, salvia, alchemilla and *Geranium* 'Russell Prichard', with pink and white Japanese anemones to take over later, and tulips and anemones as an appetiser for spring.

The East Formal Garden has a ground cover of cobbles and Yorkstone flags, and also a rectangular pond surrounded by clipped box and lavender, while the West Formal Garden, adjacent to the restored nineteenth-century conservatory, is filled with richly coloured bedding plants. To reflect the architecture of the hall,

a relatively recent development has been the Italianate Baroque garden, which features a small palm grove, silver-leaved plants, bulbs, annuals, and quiet sitting areas. Altogether, this now adds up to a garden of great charm.

ABOVE The parterre in the West Formal Garden which was redesigned in the style of a sixteenth-century knot garden with low-growing plants between dwarf box hedges.

NEXT PAGE The pear arch in the kitchen garden spans borders of catmint, alchemilla, red monarda and silver-leaved stachys and artemisia.

Benthall Hall

BROSELEY, SHROPSHIRE

AREA 1.2ha (3 acres) • **SOIL** alkaline/clay • **ALTITUDE** 189m (620ft)
AVERAGE RAINFALL 686mm (27in) • **AVERAGE WINTER CLIMATE** cold

Benthall Hall is tucked into well-wooded countryside close to the Severn Gorge. The approach is unassuming, along a lime-edged lane and past a whitewashed church, and suddenly the sandstone hall is revealed, flanked by topiary and softened by a sweep of flowers.

In gardening history, Benthall is most famous as the home of George Maw, the bulb and alpine specialist, who lived here for a period of 35 years from 1853. Maw, a manufacturer of ornamental tiles, travelled extensively, especially in the Alps, Pyrenees and Mediterranean, and brought a great many plants back to Shropshire, including the familiar glory of the snow, *Chionodoxa luciliae*, which bloomed for the first time in Britain at Benthall in 1877. He researched his great work *A Monograph of the Genus Crocus* here, and the garden's self-sowing carpets of spring-flowering *Crocus tommasinianus* and *C. vernus*, and autumn-flowering *C. speciosus*, *C. pulchellus* and *C. nudiflorus*, are another of his legacies.

In the June 1872 issue of *The Garden*, the thunderous Victorian gardening writer William Robinson stated that 'for the culture and introduction of valuable new and hardy plants, there is not a more noteworthy garden'. Robinson was particularly impressed by Maw's collection of saxifrages and by his method, now commonplace, of displaying alpines in broad, shallow pans instead of small pots. Until recently, the only evidence of the rockery was some large rocks beneath hollies and beech trees to the east of the lower lawn, and a strange hollow in the grass, where once was an extensive run of cold frames. The area has now been opened up and replanted with a collection of black and white hellebores; pink and white epimediums are a spring feature of the adjacent shrub border.

In the hands of his successor, Robert Bateman – son of James Bateman of Biddulph Grange – the nucleus of the garden shifted to the west side of the house. Bateman, a sculptor and painter, built the dovecote here and with his wife, Octavia Caroline, laid out the Rose Garden beneath it. It is a romantic Arts and Crafts composition with a pond and symmetrical rosebeds sheltered by walls, dissected by narrow paths and foaming with mixed beds of choice plants, many inherited from George Maw. Against the walls are the late-flowering *Clematis tibetana*, *C. viticella* subsp. *campaniflora*, *C. × jouiniana* and

ABOVE The thatched summer-house with the woodland wilderness beyond.

LEFT A view of the house across the wild flowers of the wilderness.

others. A mixture of English roses has recently been planted in the beds, accompanying magnolias and tree peonies, including the white, maroon-blotched *Paeonia rockii*. Scillas, narcissi, sisyrinchiums, hardy geraniums and dianthus are part of the varied carpet beneath them, and homage is paid to George Maw through the inclusion of a scree bed which is home to a number of alpine plants, including a collection of saxifrages.

There is a flavour of Biddulph Grange in the shady rockery behind this formal area, where you must squeeze along stone paths, mount stone steps and duck under cherry branches. Hellebores, pulmonarias, comfreys and arums make a leafy contrast to the garden below. The plantsman's theme is also carried on to the rock banks and shrubberies that frame the sweep of terraced lawn to the front of the house. Roses and brooms are here interspersed with stands of devil's walking stick, *Aralia elata*, mats of mouse plant, *Arisarum proboscideum*, and drifts of an unusual form of bear's breeches, *Acanthus balcanicus*.

The old kitchen garden, with only two of its four walls now standing, features plums, damsons and gages, together with an unusual orchard of crab apples. However, it is mostly used for flowers, with roses and sweet peas trained on decorative supports, cut flowers grown for the house, and double herbaeous borders recently replanted in shades of purple.

The relaxed and painterly style of today's garden is due in large part to members of the Benthall family, who reclaimed their ancestral home in 1934 after a gap of a hundred years. Their continuing presence and enthusiasm for Benthall and its pastoral setting ensure a homely mood. Brash blocks of plants and excessive neatness are eschewed, and a liberal view is taken over the colonising activities of ferns, campanulas, Welsh poppies and the ubiquitous *Geranium nodosum*.

LEFT *Iris sibirica* in the Rose Garden in May, with *Rosa* 'Easlea's Golden Rambler' on the dovecote.

Berrington Hall

LEOMINSTER, HEREFORDSHIRE

AREA 4.7ha (11½ acres) • SOIL clay/silty loam • ALTITUDE 76–137m (250–450ft)
AVERAGE RAINFALL 635mm (25in) • AVERAGE WINTER CLIMATE cold

The diarist Viscount Torrington, visiting in 1784, refers to Berrington as 'just finish'd and furnish'd in all the modern elegance, commanding beautiful views, a fine piece of water, and … throughout a scene of elegance and refinement'. Although they are now accompanied by the rumble of the Hereford road, the views remain pastoral. A circuit walk, opened up by the Trust in 1993, takes you across the park, fashioned by 'Capability' Brown some time after 1775, to the 5.7ha (14 acre) pool with its 1.6ha (4 acre) island. It allows the visitor the equally fine reverse views, back between the oaks, limes, beech and ash to the portico and pediments of the red sandstone hall.

The garden thus sits within an important Georgian framework, complete with ha-ha (recently reconstructed by the Trust), elegant stable block and office pavilions, and a grand triumphal archway as the entrance lodge. Around the west front of the hall, the open lawn rolls away into the park, and to the north, there is a shady shrubbery walk (the shrubbery expanded into a protective wood in 1906), offering views out over Bircher Common. Elsewhere, the Brownian scheme has been subjected to a more ornamental overlay, applied from the mid-1840s onwards.

South-east of the hall, a medley of flowering trees and shrubs now border the curving entrance drive. Bladder nut (*Staphylea colchica*), Persian lilac (*Syringa × persica*), Chinese tulip tree (*Liriodendron chinense*), *Lonicera involucrata*, *Magnolia wilsonii* and several ginkgo trees are among the company, many of which were introduced by the 3rd Lord Cawley. An avenue of clipped golden yews, planted in 1901, processes from the Triumphal Arch, and

an assortment of shrubs and climbers flank the wisteria pergola on the south-facing wall of the Walled Garden, including yellow *Rosa banksiae* 'Lutea', red *Buddleja colvilei*, white-flowered *Crinodendron patagua*, and the very unusual (and invasive) yellow-flowered climbing marrow, *Thladiantha oliveri*, found by Lord Cawley in a Surrey garden. Until recently, a further 36 flower-beds adorned the east lawns and their departure has rather stranded the remaining stone fountain.

All this jollity certainly counters the rather sombre look of the hall, but, of course, it also confuses one's initial taste of the eighteenth-century composition. The colour is much more readily appreciated in the Walled Garden, now replanted around patterns of fruit trees: medlars, mulberries, figs and, in the main grass

ABOVE The Walled Garden in May.

plots, a large collection of pre-1900 apple varieties raised in Herefordshire, such as 'Doctor Hare's', 'Warner's King' and 'Ashmead's Kernel'. These are accompanied by a lavender-edged sundial lawn, cutting beds, a herb garden, double herbaceous borders of mixed colours and the camellias and climbing plants in the adjacent laundry-drying ground. There is a further concentration of flowers behind the curtain of weeping ash to the north-east of the hall, where the woodland path meanders between handkerchief trees, maples, and a large collection of azaleas and rhododendrons,

including hybrids raised by Lord Cawley. Hydrangeas give a later wash of summer colour, together with daylilies, crocosmias, and, back along the north front of the hall, past the clipped tumps of holly, rhododendron and laurel, a pool of pink and white cyclamen in the grass. There is a fine show of snowdrops here in winter.

ABOVE As well as containing many unusual Herefordshire apple varieties, the Walled Garden at Berrington preserves medlar, fig and other fruit trees.

Biddulph Grange

BIDDULPH, STOKE-ON-TRENT, STAFFORDSHIRE

AREA 6ha (15 acres) • **SOIL** acid/loamy clay • **ALTITUDE** 145–195m (475–640ft)
AVERAGE RAINFALL 914mm (36in) • **AVERAGE WINTER CLIMATE** cold

Gardens do not come more ingenious or entertaining than Biddulph. The meandering paths have you squeezing between rock faces, crossing water by stepping stones and plunging down dark tunnels; you enter a half-timbered cottage and find yourself in an Egyptian tomb, clamber through a Scottish glen and come out in a Chinese water garden; at every turn, there are strange beasts, flamboyant flowers, eruptions of rock, or soaring exotic conifers in ambush. The genius behind it all was the Victorian plantsman James Bateman, aided by his wife Maria and their friend Edward Cooke, the marine artist. The estate, in cold hilly country below Biddulph Moor, was bought by Bateman's grandfather for its coal-mining potential, with the family living at nearby Knypersley Hall. James and Maria Bateman moved here in 1840, two years after their marriage, and soon began transforming the former farmhouse into an Italianate mansion and commissioning for the grounds some mind-boggling feats of earth-moving, contouring and stonework.

When the garden came to the Trust in 1988, a major restoration was required of the buildings and parterres. However, the garden's superstructure remained and, thanks to good documentation and on-site archaeology, a very precise reconstruction was possible. An appeal was launched and the immense and labour-intensive programme of work began.

From the south-west corner of the house, the starting point of the tour, the view is of an intimate garden, with foreground terraces, a small lake below and a heavy fringe of yews, hollies, rhododendrons and evergreen trees. There are lively splashes of colour, as you would expect, but no jarring contrasts of style. Bateman avoided falling

into the trap set by Victorian eclecticism by subdividing the garden into different compartments, each with its own theme and screened from one another by a unifying framework of hedges and walls, trees and rocky mounds. It was an innovative and influential approach. The terraces extend the width of the house. At the west end, the door opens onto an Italian garden of stone platforms, stairways and balustraded walls. To the east, within a framework of yew hedges, a range of nineteenth-century plant novelties and artful styles of cultivation is displayed. There are parterres devoted to verbenas, hybrid China roses and the quirky monkey puzzle tree (reintroduced to gardening by William Lobb in 1844). An ornamental orchard features clipped double Morello cherries, planted on raised mounds and associated with *Cotoneaster microphyllus*, pruned as bells, and various clematis, grown up posts and trained along chains. Hardy herbaceous plants, in the form of peonies, *Iris pallida*, phlox and delphiniums – favourites of Maria Bateman – also appear. Running almost the length of the terrace, is a kaleidoscopic walk of hybrid dahlias, whose tropical colours were enthusiastically embraced by many a Victorian gardener.

ABOVE The gilded water buffalo sculpture by Waterhouse Hawkins in a part of the garden named China.

Earlier in the year, it is the shrubberies around the lake that steal the show, for they are stocked with rhododendrons of every hue. At the head of the lime avenue marking the garden's western boundary, they were arranged by Bateman in rainbow bands. Beside the water, they are loosely dispersed – flashes of yellow from the scented yellow azalea *Rhododendron luteum* and mounds of pink, purple, white and cherry-red from the Hardy Hybrids. Rhododendrons also once filled the adjacent stream-fed glen. These were the new species collected by Joseph Hooker on his expeditions to Sikkim, Nepal and Bhutan in 1849–51, but their reluctance to bloom here, in spite of the provision of moist, shady pockets of peaty soil, persuaded Bateman to move them under glass. Instead, the glen was stocked with ferns, another fashionable tribe of plants to which both Bateman and Edward Cooke were devoted.

Cooke's major contribution to the garden was the architectural features, both ornamental buildings and rockwork. Here in the glen you see the results of his careful study of rock formation for his paintings: spectacular outcrops and massive boulders of locally quarried gritstone, with every crack and cascade geologically justified. Wild heather and bilberries, collected on the moor, contribute to the realism, with weeping holly added for picturesque effect and native and foreign water plants strung along the stream. From the lakeside shrubberies, you pop down a tunnel to emerge in the Pinetum, among redwoods, hemlocks, cedars and pines. The range of conifer species had been boosted by David Douglas's plant-hunting on the west coast of America in the 1820s and 1830s, and here Bateman prepared ideal conditions for them; many are planted on mounds to give improved drainage and a better display. In late spring, bluebells lap the curving walk between the grassy banks and there is carefully contrived contrast from variegated oak, golden yews and hollies – many added by Robert Heath, who bought Biddulph from the Bateman family in 1871.

The focal point of the walk is the half-timbered façade of a Cheshire cottage, sporting the date 1856 and the intertwined initials 'J & MB'. Inside, there is no cosy welcome, only a squat, subhuman creature (the Ape of Thoth, an associate of the Egyptian god of botany) bathed in bloody light by a pane of red glass in the roof. You are inside a pyramid, and you emerge from the dark into its open court to see a stone arch set into a slab of clipped yew, guarded by two pairs of sphinxes. This stands at the opposite end of the terraces

RIGHT Leading away from the Shelter House, stepped yew hedges divide the Dahlia Walk into compartments.

B

from where you began, and the main path continues east behind it, through a rough arboretum, planted with autumn-colouring North American red maples and liquidambar, gorse and other heathland shrubs, and pampas grass and osmunda fern set beside a small pool, then on to a long avenue.

To the north is the restored Woodland Terrace, one of its paths leading to Bateman's Geological Gallery, a unique entrance portal to the garden and, constructed in about 1860, one of the last major additions. Inspired by the theories of the geologist and theologian Hugh Miller, and built possibly with advice from the palaeontologist Professor Richard Owen (one of Charles Darwin's prominent adversaries), the Gallery presents its fossils contextualised within the Genesis story of creation. The principal avenue tree was intended to be the most majestic of the newly introduced conifers, the wellingtonia (brought in by William Lobb in 1853, and immediately obtained by Bateman through Messrs Veitch). He interplanted his specimens with deodar cedars for quick effect – and gave them an interesting backing formed by lines of white briar rose, red horse chestnut and Austrian pine – but unfortunately, when the time came to thin, his successor Robert Heath decided to retain the cedars instead. The Trust has returned to Bateman's original plan and in time the wellingtonias will assume their rightful dominance. From here, the sandy path leads upwards to the moor through heath and woodland, gradually narrowing as it rises to give the appearance of a natural obelisk; this land is now a country park, belonging to the local district council.

Where is the Chinese garden? So well concealed is the prize exhibit that it is possible to complete the circuit without encountering it, yet it stands at the garden's very heart. There are two points of entry: one is via a cleft in the Himalayan glen and along a dark tunnel and grotto, while the other is below Egypt. This latter route takes you through one of the most curious of Victorian garden features, the Stumpery. This involved excavating tree stumps and upturning them to create a framework for woodland perennials like ferns, ivies, hellebores and epimediums. The path descends between rocks and shrubs and then you are inside the Great Wall. There is a watchtower high on the north-east bank and a joss house to the south, above a winding flight of steps. The flora of the Far East is all about: Japanese maples, bamboos, cryptomeria, paulownia, tree peonies, hostas and a golden larch – again, many of these were collected by contemporary plant-hunters, particularly Robert Fortune, who explored China and Japan in the 1840s and 1850s. Irish yews, elegant weeping trees and coloured foliage strike contrasting notes.

Behind a stone doorway, you come upon the gilded head of a water buffalo – a Chinese idol, sculpted by Waterhouse Hawkins – and further along, an enormous stone frog. Dragons are carved out of the lawn, and more dragons and grebes perch on the corners of the temple's upturned eaves. The central water scene will look familiar, for it is based on the willow pattern featured on countless household plates, with its hump-backed footbridge joined to a zigzag railing, and waterside rocks and plants. The pagoda is the predominant structure, a glorious flight of fancy but, as always, with its surprises: one tunnel leads to the Himalayan glen and the other to an icehouse. These buildings were among the last expressions of the fashion for chinoiserie, and, painstakingly restored and freshly painted in their original livery of scarlet, buff and blue-green, are once again a sparkling contrast to the black waters and coniferous backdrop.

ABOVE The Rhododendron Ground around the lake at Biddulph Grange.

Blickling Hall

BLICKLING, NORWICH, NORFOLK

AREA 22ha (55 acres) • SOIL acid/loam • ALTITUDE 30m (100ft) • AVERAGE RAINFALL 635mm (25in) • AVERAGE WINTER CLIMATE cold

The sudden prospect of this beautiful Jacobean mansion, with its turrets and gables and salmon-red brickwork, is arresting. It sits square to the road, separated by simple railings, backed by trees and flanked by Dutch-style service ranges and ancient hedges of yew. It is a complete picture, with which horticulture does not interfere. Only as you walk up to the house do you take in the globes of *Magnolia grandiflora* either side of the stone bridge, and the shrubs and climbers in the dry moat below. These are an hors d'oeuvre to the gardens awaiting you through the arch in the east wall.

Of the early seventeenth-century design to accompany Sir Henry Hobart's house, there remains only an outline. Before you is the product of the three subsequent centuries, each layer building on the bones of its predecessor. The central axis, the vista uphill to the Doric Temple, is the work of the 1st Earl of Buckinghamshire, who swept away his great-grandfather's garden in the early part of the eighteenth century. The present grid pattern is a Victorian evolution carried out between 1861 and 1864 by the 8th Marquis of Lothian. It is a much grander and more intricate design than was here previously, with radial walks, each of a single tree species – Turkey oak, beech and lime – infilled with mixed deciduous trees with a shrubby understorey of evergreens, and leading to circular clearings. The hurricane of October 1987 wreaked havoc here but the area is now regaining a sense of maturity.

In front of the hall is the 0.8ha (2 acre), flower-filled parterre, its rich colours playing against the shadowy topiary. It, too, is Lord Lothian's creation and part of the garden's momentous return to Jacobean formality. It was excavated for him from the sloping lawn by Arthur Markham Nesfield, son of the garden designer William Andrews Nesfield, the great champion of parterres. However, the planting that colours it today is the work of Norah Lindsay, who was associated with some of the best country gardens in the 1920s and '30s, including Hidcote and Chirk Castle. Indeed, her dreamy planting style – a relaxed and billowing interpretation of Gertrude Jekyll's painterly approach, ordered by hedges and topiaries – influenced a generation of garden-makers. She was commissioned by the 11th Marquis to simplify the elaborate Victorian pattern of beds and ribbon borders, which she achieved by clearing the centre of everything but its seventeenth-century fountain and joining the corner flower-beds into four large squares. She retained the yew topiary, including the famous Blickling topiary grand pianos. To each square she gave a two-tone fringe of roses – pink and crimson Floribundas 'Else Poulsen' and 'Kirsten Poulsen', or red and orange 'Locarno' and Polyantha 'Gloria Mundi' – and underplanted them with catmint. She then filled two with herbaceous plants in tints of pink, white, violet and blue, including monkshoods, bellflowers, globe thistles and delphiniums, and the remaining two with glowing yellows, oranges and reds in the form of achilleas, heleniums, rudbeckias and the apricot Nankeen lily, *Lilium* × *testaceum* 'Apricot'. Since the gardener's palette becomes hotter as the summer advances, it is inevitable that the cooler beds should peak slightly earlier than their neighbours, soon after midsummer; nevertheless, it is a triumphant composition.

ABOVE Honeysuckle in the Secret Garden.

Over the past few years, further extensive planting in Norah Lindsay's style has taken place on the raised south side of the parterre, where a flower garden existed in Jacobean times. As they recede from the house, these new box-edged double borders warm in colouring through daylilies, crocosmias, purple berberis and striped miscanthus grass, until finally concluding in a garden of black-red dahlias, heuchera and ophiopogon. Behind them runs a border of pale and silvery plants such as artemisia, *Salvia sclarea* var. *turkestanica* and *Lilium regale*, equally handsomely composed and textured.

The subterranean world of the dry moat must certainly have appealed to Norah Lindsay's romantic temperament. It is a world of old walls and arched bridges, and she caught its spirit well in her plantings of dripping fuchsias, ferns and ghostly Japanese anemones. The shelter has since been exploited to grow a range of wall shrubs and climbers that you might not expect to see in this hostile Norfolk climate of dry summers and cold, windy winters. These include spring-flowering *Buddleja crispa* var. farreri and autumn-flowering *B. auriculata*, ceanothus, camellia and variegated *Trachelospermum jasminoides* with flowers scented of orange blossom.

Penetrate the formal woods above the parterre, or turn the corner towards the north front of the hall, and suddenly you see a further layer of the garden's history – for here is the parkland landscape moulded in the late eighteenth century by the 2nd Earl of Buckinghamshire. Living through the golden era of the English landscape garden, he set his father's classical ornaments in this more natural setting of rolling pasture, broken by groves and stands of oak, beech and sweet chestnut. There are fine elevated views of the park behind the Temple, where the remnant of an earlier fortification serves as a broad terrace and provided the 2nd Earl with a ready-made ha-ha. At one end of it he built the handsome Orangery. Probably designed by Samuel Wyatt, it was completed in 1782 and is now once again housing citrus fruit, including oranges, lemons, limes and grapefruits. Behind it, new areas of garden have recently been developed; 0.8ha (2 acres) have been planted for winter and early spring interest, with double-flowered hellebores, including yellow forms, grouped among mahonias, viburnums, *Daphne bholua* and the coloured stems of willows and dogwoods. A pedimented, rustic pavilion, topped with carved pine cones, now looks over a shady dell that includes a fine stand of tree ferns; the pavilion is a copy of that designed by John Adey Repton, who was employed extensively at Blickling after 1823, designing trellis, arbours and furniture. Hereabouts, as elsewhere along the radial

walks, vast numbers of snowdrops, crocus and white *Narcissus pseudonarcissus* flood the ground beneath the trees and shrubs.

On the south side of the woods, tucked under the oaks, hollies and sweet chestnuts, is the Secret Garden. With its 'profusion of Minionet Roses, mirtles and honeysuckles' (sic), this was the principal flower garden in the late eighteenth century and the domain of Lady Buckinghamshire, with John Adey Repton's father, Humphry Repton, offering suggestions on its improvement. The garden took on its present shape and reduced size in the 1860s,

and is now a quiet green retreat of grass and beech hedge, brick paths and sundial. The cool shrubbery, fronted with hostas and daylilies, by which it is approached, is the work of Norah Lindsay (although largely supplemented by the Trust), and is quite a contrast to her plantings near the house. The soil is more acidic here and joining the laurel, philadelphus, bamboo and dogwood are rhododendrons and blue-flowered hydrangeas.

The centrepiece for the 2nd Earl's park was the great lake, which comes into view suddenly as you walk from the parterre to the north front. It makes a dramatic moment, linked in my mind to the scent of the vast Oriental plane trees growing on this corner, whose leaves, on the right day, infuse the air with sweet resin. The ancient Turkey oak is also a major feature, and in spring both it and the plane trees are knee-deep in bulbs and wildflowers.

ABOVE The Jacobean-style parterre is a nineteenth-century re-creation, with later planting schemes around the topiaries designed by Norah Lindsay.

Bodnant Garden

TAL-Y-CAFN, COLWYN BAY, CONWY

AREA 32ha (80 acres) • **SOIL** acid/clay • **ALTITUDE** 52m (170ft) • **AVERAGE RAINFALL** 1,016mm (40in) • **AVERAGE WINTER CLIMATE** moderate

'The drama of the view greets you as you approach the front of the house'

The scale, grandeur and scenic beauty of this garden are nothing short of stupendous. Set on a west-facing slope, 52m (170ft) above the tidal River Conwy, the massive granite house (privately owned) commands panoramic views of the eastern edge of the Snowdonia range. Below, a series of five gigantic Italianate terraces anchor the house majestically in its mountainous setting. To the south, the precipitous-sided valley of the River Hiraethlyn is embraced, manipulated and coloured to make a woodland garden of epic proportions. And furnishing and overlaying each part of the composition is a plant collection to excite expert and layman alike.

The estate was bought by Henry Pochin, the late Lord Aberconway's great-grandfather, in 1874. There was little garden here then, apart from lawns and shrubberies, but when the house was built in 1792, a large number of native trees – in particular, beech, oak and chestnut – were planted. With the help of landscape architect Edward Milner, Pochin began laying out a 'reposeful garden' comprising a spacious terrace, grass banks and spreading trees. On the valley floor, he planted the conifers which are now one of Bodnant's chief delights, and in succeeding years continued to expand the bounds, adding features such as the Mausoleum and the Laburnum Arch in 1878.

The leap of imagination that transformed Bodnant into the garden we see today was made by his grandson Henry, 2nd Lord Aberconway. It was he who, in 1902, with his mother's encouragement, conceived the great terraces and supervised their construction, and who, in 1908, encouraged a then sceptical head gardener called Sanderson to try his hand with Chinese rhododendrons. Subsequently, he subscribed to many plant-hunting expeditions and, after 1920, engaged Bodnant in an extensive programme of rhododendron hybridisation, under his skilled head gardener Frederick Puddle. The evolution continues today under the Hon. Michael McLaren, whose father, Charles, 3rd Lord Aberconway, guided the garden from 1953 to 2003, and was a former President of the Royal Horticultural Society. The garden has also benefited from a remarkable partnership between the family and their head gardeners, since the post was handed down through three generations of Puddles.

A tour of Bodnant traditionally begins with the East Garden and terraces, where the emphasis is on a summer show to succeed the woodland shrubs. Hot-coloured herbaceous plants in the broad entrance border hold the eye before it is carried off by the sweep of smooth lawns. Among the many trees and shrubs to admire in this area are some fine paperbark maples, *Acer griseum*, one of which has its flaking chestnut trunk memorably backlit by orange azaleas.

The drama of the view greets you as you approach the front of the house, though the scale and contents of the terraces below are cleverly concealed. Each is intended as a revelation. You descend alternately by the sides and the centre to savour the full size of the composition, and each set of steps opens onto a vast empty stage of grass or water, edged and flanked by a range of plants and architectural ornament.

LEFT The Pin Mill seen across the flower beds of the lowest terrace.

The top Rose Terrace – its beds now refurbished with modern shrub roses in an array of colours – leads down to the Croquet Terrace, the connecting staircase hung with white *Wisteria brachybotrys* 'Shiro-kapitan' and *W. floribunda* 'Alba' and curving around a Baroque sandstone fountain; the water flows underground and through basin and rill into each of the platforms below. The high, grey-blue retaining walls of the Croquet Terrace are home to many slightly tender shrubs, including *Crinodendron hookerianum*, *Eucryphia lucida*, *Buddleja colvilei*, *Ceanothus* × *lobbianus* 'Russellianus' and scented white rhododendrons. Carpenterias, blue hydrangeas and wall-trained *Magnolia grandiflora* 'Goliath' and *M. delavayi* ensure later colour.

The great cedars on the next terrace, the Lily Terrace, are a legacy of Henry Pochin, and the fact that the terraces were designed around them accounts for the asymmetry of the entire composition in relation to the house. A large reflecting pool occupies the centre of the Lily Terrace, while behind are recently refurbished borders that display their range of pastel-tinted flowers among Pennisetum grasses and the swaying heads of pink Dierama.

To adorn the Canal Terrace below, the 2nd Lord Aberconway had parts of an eighteenth-century mill, once used for the manufacture of pins, dismantled and transported from Gloucestershire. The rebuilding was completed in 1939 and makes another romantic reflection between the rafts of waterlilies. A series of smaller terraces, decorated with painted wooden pergolas, urns and obelisks in Beaux Arts style, sits above the main terrace, lavishly planted in roses and perennials in mainly romantic pink and white colour schemes.

The tree and shrub borders to the north and west of the terraces provide the first hints of the spectacle awaiting you in the Dell. Here are camellias and tree magnolias, including *M. sargentiana* var. *robusta*, *M.* × *veitchii*, *M. campbellii* 'Charles Raffill' and *M. sprengeri* var. *diva*; and a host of rhododendrons, including cream 'Penjerrick', blue *R. augustinii*, the deciduous *RR. albrechtii*, *quinquefolium* and *schlippenbachii*, and some of the famous blood-red Bodnant hybrids. In August, the large group of *Eucryphia glutinosa* in the North Garden is a vision of white.

Behind the Pin Mill, a path leads past further banks of camellias and rhododendrons and through a stream-fed rockery before arriving at the famous vantage point over the Dell. More than 15m (50ft) beneath you is the River Hiraethlyn, the haunt of dippers and wagtails, lushly edged by ferns, blue hydrangeas and large-leaved bog plants and studded by moss-covered boulders; to your right is the old stone mill; and ahead, a long linear prospect of woodland shrubs, speared by rocket-shaped conifers and bare-trunked pines. In spring, it is a riot of colour; in summer, a valley of cool greens.

The conifers on the east side of the river were planted ten years before those on the west, in 1876. They include immense specimens of fir, cedar, hemlock and redwood, and from the shrub borders above the valley you gain the rare opportunity of viewing their cone-studded tops. The rich alluvial soil and moist atmosphere of the Dell suit the larger-leaved rhododendrons well, though frost can be trapped here and plants can be lost in severe winters. Accompanying them are belts of Japanese and deciduous azaleas, the fruity scent of the latter pervading the valley in early June. Magnolias, including the Bodnant-raised *M. sprengeri* var. *diva* 'Claret Cup' and the potently fragrant *M. obovata*, are also a feature. In recent years large additional areas of woodland garden, previously private, have been opened up, allowing exploration beyond the Mausoleum and above the Waterfall Bridge to the Skating Pond and its boathouse and weeping willows. As elsewhere, these are atmospheric reaches, home to otters and kingfishers, with soaring hemlocks, cypresses, pines and other conifers, gulleys of azaleas, banks of old-established rhododendrons, and richly planted streamsides. Furnace Hill, and its accompanying wildflower meadow, will also soon be open, giving fine views back to the house as well as a prospect of the Conwy River.

The shrub borders above the Dell provide an additional tier of entertainment. Japanese cherries, viburnums and shrubby magnolias

ABOVE Blue lacecap and mophead hydrangeas are a feature of the Dell in August.
RIGHT Below the waterfall bridge, the River Hiraethlyn flows beneath the banks of evergreen azaleas.

are succeeded in May, in spectacular fashion, by the suckering stands of Chilean fire bush, *Embothrium coccineum* var. *lanceolatum* 'Norquinco'. The hardiest form, this was collected in the wild by Harold Comber in an expedition organised and part-financed by the 2nd Lord Aberconway (see Nymans). The flame red of the flowers has few rivals among woody plants. Later performers here include *Cornus kousa* var. *chinensis* and the handkerchief tree, *Davidia involucrata*. At the end of the year there is a panoply of autumn colour from birches, rowans, liquidambar and Japanese maples, with a new Winter Garden further up the garden ensuring a concentration of interest through coloured tree barks, bulbs, and flowering shrubs such as *Daphne bholua* at the quietest time of year; snowdrops are also massed on the fringes of Old Park meadow.

Visitors to Bodnant at the end of May have an additional treat, the Laburnum Arch, where saplings of *L.* × *watereri* 'Vossii' – which have been replaced many times since the arch was first planted – are forged into a long, glowing tunnel of brilliant yellow. As a feature, it epitomises the spirit of Bodnant: generous in concept, stunning in decoration, and, with its raised sides and twisted passage, ingenious in design.

Buckland Abbey

YELVERTON, DEVON

AREA 1.2ha (3 acres) • **SOIL** acid/heterogeneous mixture, shale • **ALTITUDE** 76m (250ft)
AVERAGE RAINFALL 1,016mm (40in) • **AVERAGE WINTER CLIMATE** moderate

The approach to Buckland is across the edge of Dartmoor National Park, through a landscape of gorse and bracken, wind-shaped thorn trees and damp sheep and ponies. From this you descend into a green pocket of the Tavy Valley, presided over by the great, golden-grey Cistercian Abbey, which was the home of Sir Francis Drake.

A vast thirteenth-century barn is the gateway into the garden and the intimate tracery of the herb enclosure beyond is a surprise. A herb garden was suggested by Vita Sackville-West, a member of the Trust's Gardens Committee, after a visit in 1953. She disapproved of the serpentine path, convinced that 'everything at Buckland should be as straight and geometrical as possible, to conform with the severity of the house'. In fact, the wavy theme was expanded into an irregular web of 52 compartments, each with a different herb, and the pattern is a great success – although unfortunately the box hedging that formed the compartments has succumbed to blight and has been replaced with *Ilex crenata*.

This informal mood extends into the main abbey gardens over the wall, where specimen trees, evergreens and groups of flowering shrubs edge the sloping lawns and frame the views of the Devon hills. Rhododendrons, azaleas, camellias and magnolias provide the colour, punctuated by curiosities including a handkerchief tree, devil's walking sticks and an old mulberry that has collapsed and now rests one giant limb on the ground and another on the wall behind.

In spite of being exposed to wind and frost, the south front of the abbey hosts huge plants of *Magnolia grandiflora* and the larger-leaved *M. delavayi*, while the adjacent wall shelters *Callistemon citrinus* 'Splendens', a half-hardy Australian shrub with curious red bottlebrushes in summer. The chief talking point, however, is invariably *Aristolochia macrophylla*. This hardy North American climber scrambles over a box bush near the north-west corner of the garden. Its large leaves are impressive enough, but in summer they are accompanied by bizarre brownish flowers, bent like an ear trumpet and flared at the mouth, which prompted its common name of Dutchman's pipe.

To the north of the abbey a new garden, inspired by Tudor precedent, has now sprung up to replace a walk of ancient yews that fell victim to disease. From a granite monument, set in a flowery mead, stone steps descend to an orchard and knot garden, centred on a fountain pool and softened by an assortment of herbs and old-fashioned flowers in sympathy with this tranquil place.

LEFT The Herb Garden displays over forty different herbs, each in its own box-edged bed.

ABOVE Hollyhocks and agastache flower in the Elizabethan Garden in summer.

Buscot Park

FARINGDON, OXFORDSHIRE

AREA 25ha (62 acres) • SOIL acid, alkaline/clay, sandy, loam • ALTITUDE 100m (328ft)
AVERAGE RAINFALL 762mm (30in) • AVERAGE WINTER CLIMATE cold

Towards the end of the nineteenth century, the great gardens of
Renaissance Italy began once again to exert their influence on garden
designers. Buscot boasts one of the finest designs from this period, by
one of its leading exponents, Harold Peto. He was commissioned in
1904, and again in 1912, by the financier and connoisseur Alexander
Henderson, later 1st Baron Faringdon, to create a water garden that
would connect his Neo-classical house to the 8ha (20 acre) lake
below. It was meant to appear suddenly between two elm trees to
the north-east of the house, but sadly one of the elms fell almost
immediately and the other died some years later. Nevertheless, the
drama of first seeing the long, narrow vista cut through the tall,
dense woods framed by box hedges and terminating in the temple
on the other side of the lake remains intense. The stone steps lead
first to a circular pool containing a statue of a dolphin embracing (or
strangling) a boy, and the water then flows off, via canals, rills, still
pools and rushing cascades until it reaches the lake. Much of this is
revealed only as you descend, which you must do on a serpentine
line, skirting the different shapes of the basins, with the invitation to
cross sides by means of a small hump-backed bridge. Roman herms
and other statues embellish the design, and Irish junipers and yews
furnish sharp verticals.

The theme of dynamic formal avenues slicing through the
woods below the house was pursued further by the 2nd Lord
Faringdon. A *patte d'oie*, or goose foot, of avenues, constructed
of fastigiate oak and beech, cherry and poplar, is centred on the
Theatre Pavilion arch. Along one of these rides is a sunken garden,
where citrus trees are set out each summer.

Always there is the backdrop of the park. It was the first
owner of the house, Edward Loveden Townsend, who landscaped
the grounds with two lakes and dense belts of trees, but many more
trees were planted subsequently. The ravages of Dutch elm disease
necessitated an extensive programme of replanting and thinning by
the present Lord Faringdon, and many young oaks and beeches are
now swelling into position for the future.

A second, distinct portion of garden lies to the west of the
house. This centres upon Townsend's walled kitchen gardens, which
have been redesigned and replanted over recent years as formal
flower, fruit and vegetable gardens. The powerful contrasts of the
Parent's Walk borders were devised by Peter Coats in 1986. The
path, like the avenues on the other side of the garden, plunges and
ascends dramatically. It leads to the orchard, where many old
varieties of apple and pear are assembled, some espaliered on the
walls. The main section of walled garden has a formal groundplan,
revolving around a central fountain and quartered by alleys of
Judas tree and hop hornbeam. The walls are concentric, to take

full advantage of the sun's warmth, but although fruit and vegetables are still grown here, the emphasis is now on shrubs and old roses. Statues of the Four Seasons by Frank Forster, cast in fibreglass, set the theme, and the planting of each corner, designed originally by Tim Rees, is anchored in winter, spring, summer or autumn flowers, with roses, potentillas, hellebores and rosemary acting as unifying links. The entrance to the walled garden is guarded by fifteen life-size terracotta warriors, while opposite the descending stairway Buscot's Italianate water features have a contemporary echo in a new water feature by David Harber, comprising panels of highly polished stainless steel.

ABOVE The water garden created by Harold Peto.

RIGHT Terracotta warriors guard the entrance to the walled garden.

Calke Abbey

TICKNALL, DERBYSHIRE

AREA 8ha (20 acres) • **SOIL** acid, alkaline/clay • **ALTITUDE** 91m (300ft)
AVERAGE RAINFALL 635mm (25in) • **AVERAGE WINTER CLIMATE** cold

In 1985, the Trust lifted Calke's veil and exposed an estate that had hardly been disturbed for a hundred years. The grey Baroque house is well sited for seclusion, concealed between deep folds of a large and hilly park, and a succession of idiosyncratic and reclusive members of the Harpur Crewe family, owners of the estate since 1622, ensured it remained a private, self-contained world. The Trust's restoration has been unusual, for the temptation to spruce up the house and garden has been vigorously resisted. Rough grass and the colonising activities of wild yellow mimulus between paving and walls preserve the air of a house lost in time and shrouded in mystery.

The walled flower and kitchen gardens are hidden. They were moved up the hill from the house in the late eighteenth century, following the conversion of the park to a more natural landscape. You can still see vestiges of the earlier formal layout, such as sections of avenues that used to carry the geometry of the house into the park and fragments of the former walled orchard, but the house's present tranquil setting of trees, pasture and lakes is one of curves and undulations. The heart of the woods is ancient, confirmed by the rich population of beetles associated with an unbroken continuity of decaying trees stretching back many centuries.

A shady Pleasure Ground of trees and evergreen shrubs has been renovated after years of damage by Calke's herds of red and fallow deer, which have now been fenced into the north-east section of the park. The plantation is lightened by wildflowers and bulbs, and in one of the secret hollows there is a grotto with its brick walls hidden by minerals such as quartz and satin spar.

The invisible rebuilding of the gate piers that lead into the walled gardens has left the old rust stains on the brickwork. Between the piers, the path leads past summer borders of sweet peas and dahlias to the fruit store and gardener's bothy, still with its old tools and seed cabinet leaning against walls washed a surprisingly opulent blue. The back sheds and stove houses tell a fascinating story of the working of a garden of the period, with early heating systems still in existence. There is also a mushroom house, an ice-house dating from 1810, and a gardeners' tunnel, used by the gardeners to move around out of sight of the family.

The flower garden to the west has been reconstructed as a rare example of a mid-nineteenth-century villa flower garden and given the same polish as the best-kept rooms in the house. The basketweave ironwork that encircles the pond is a typical feature of the period, as is the elaborate, labour-intensive and, to modern eyes, rather eccentric pattern of small beds cut out of the lawn. There are 23 of these, each bedded out brightly with wallflowers in spring and a mixture of annuals and exotic feature plants, such as cannas and Chusan palms. The herbaceous planting that laps the surrounding walls is in Loudon's 'mingled style', with climbers smothering the walls. There are also the remains of an aviary and a Show House, once heated and now full of ferns.

However, the most exciting feature, for garden historians and plant enthusiasts alike, is in the north-west corner. Here, along from the Show House and aviary, is a theatre for displaying auriculas and summer pot plants, possibly the last original structure of its kind in existence. Auriculas, cousins of the primrose, have enjoyed waves of popularity since Elizabethan times, and the idea of showing them

off on covered staging, which exposes them to the air but protects them from rain and midday sun, was recommended as far back as 1717. The Calke gardeners have now built up a large and fascinating collection, with pelargoniums following on for summer.

To the east of the bothy is the Physic Garden, which has been restored as a working kitchen garden. As far as possible, old varieties are grown here, and its 0.6ha (1½ acres) are divided into rotating beds for many old varieties of brassicas, legumes, potatoes and root crops; permanent beds for globe artichokes, rhubarb and soft fruit; borders of medicinal and culinary herbs; strips for cut flowers; and an orchard of local and heritage apple varieties including 'Newton

Wonder' and 'Beeley Pippin'. In addition, there are frames and old hot beds, productive glasshouses and a vinery. The 1.6ha (4 acre) Upper Kitchen Garden over the wall, once a model Victorian working kitchen garden, is now a paddock, mown with the ghostly outlines of the old beds still visible, while the glass-domed Orangery elegantly moulders next to the sole remaining peach house.

ABOVE *Erysimum* 'Persian Carpet' flowering under *Trachycarpus fortunei* in the Walled Gardens.

LEFT In summer, a collection of pelargoniums is displayed in the Auricula Theatre.

Planting Soft Fruit

Steve Biggins, Former Head Gardener
CALKE ABBEY, DERBYSHIRE

Few gardening experiences can match the sheer delight of picking fresh fruit you have grown and guzzling it as you go. Sure, it takes an age even to cover the bottom of the punnet, let alone fill it, but why take the fun out of gardening? However, if you have a more controlled approach to the job and some of the yield does make it back to base, transforming it into your favourite dessert is pretty good too. A summer pudding, a cream tea or just a bowl of fruit – things don't get much better!

On the other hand, there can be few more forlorn sights than a neglected fruit plot where forgotten bushes are choked by brambles and perennial weeds, with mildew and mould in place of succulent fruit. To minimise the chances of this, just follow a modicum of good practice that will ensure you have a sizeable annual crop for years to come.

A little market research around the kitchen table will soon identify your family's preferences and growing a couple of bushes of each fruit type is a good place to start. Pick some for eating fresh and keep the remainder for processing. Most soft fruit is self-compatible (pollinates itself), but evidence suggests that cropping is improved when cross-pollination is possible.

Strawberries are always popular, but I recommend you plant gooseberries instead. A plump gooseberry left to ripen is syrupy sweet and a gooseberry bush makes for less work than a strawberry patch, which will need renewing quite often. Strawberries are the mainstay of pick-your-own farms and can be found everywhere in summer, which is not the case with gooseberries. Whitecurrants and redcurrants are a rarity in the shops and you can pay a lot of money for a punnet not much bigger than a matchbox, so consider allocating space for these as well.

Healthy eating is now recognised as a vital constituent of a healthy lifestyle, and with fresh fruit being a rich source of vitamin C, not to mention fibre, a small fruit plot in the back garden should be a priority for most gardeners.

Making a start

Shop around before you buy: bare-rooted plants of a named variety obtained from a reputable fruit nursery are a must. This is a long-term project, so it is worth investing a little time and effort. If you have decided to grow strawberries, they should be certified virus-free stock; in other words, avoid the plants potted in yogurt tubs from the bring-and-buy stall at the school fête.

Fruit bushes and canes should be planted during their period of dormancy, say between December and January, in well-prepared, clean, open ground. Ideally, soft fruits prefer a slightly acid soil (about pH 6.5), but soil treatment is not necessary unless your soil is very acid (about pH 5.5), in which case you will need to add lime. Similarly, very chalky soils can cause mineral deficiencies that need to be counteracted by the addition of minerals. As soils will always

revert to type and your treatments will need repeating, it is handy to keep a soil-testing kit in your potting shed.

Planting with a trowel will suffice for strawberries, but bush fruit needs a little more effort. Dig a generous-sized hole and spread the roots of the plant in all directions. While gently shaking the plant, gradually backfill the hole, incorporating copious amounts of garden compost, and firm the plant into position. Mulching with the same material is vital to keep in the moisture of the winter throughout the drier summer months. Leave a space of about 1.5m (5ft) between plants.

After planting, pruning is key to strong growth during the first season and that means strong growth in the correct position. Get it right now and you are well set for the future. Blackcurrants need pruning to 5cm (2in) to encourage all shoots to come from ground level. With redcurrants, whitecurrants and gooseberries, the aim is to produce an open goblet-shaped bush on a section of bare stem (or a 'leg'). Commence this by reducing the existing framework by half to an outward-facing bud.

Maintenance

In mid-February, when the days are lengthening and the soil has warmed a little, apply a potash-rich top-dressing to the base of the plant and top up with mulch. This is the most effective form of weed control and will negate the need for watering.

Look out for and pick off any small green gooseberry sawfly caterpillars that might invade in April and combat mildew by keeping a nice open bush. If the birds appear to be enjoying more than their share of the spoils once fruiting time begins, erect a temporary cage with 1–2m (3¼ –6ft) of netting supported by hazel canes or bamboos.

Tips

- Always pick soft fruit in dry weather.
- If you want to grow raspberries, try the autumn-fruiting varieties.
- If your growing space is limited, train cordon gooseberries and whitecurrants or redcurrants up a fence or trellis.

Canons Ashby

CANONS ASHBY, DAVENTRY, NORTHAMPTONSHIRE

AREA 1.4ha (3¼ acres) • SOIL neutral/loam over clay • ALTITUDE 140m (459ft)
AVERAGE RAINFALL 559mm (22in) • AVERAGE WINTER CLIMATE cold

In the decaying house, derelict gardens and priory church of Canons Ashby, the Trust acquired an unspoilt piece of ancient rural England, home to the deeply conservative Dryden family from 1551 to 1981. The exterior of the house looks much as it did in 1710, when Edward Dryden replaced the Tudor brickwork of the south front with golden-brown ironstone. It is neither grand nor ornate, but a solid, masculine residence, with a squat, square pele tower commanding views over the rolling Northamptonshire countryside.

The structure of the garden dates from 1708, the pattern of sheltering walls, terraces, formal axes, statues and grand gateways being in the then fashionable style of the royal gardeners George London and Henry Wise. Thanks to the family characteristically ignoring the eighteenth-century swing in taste towards naturalistic landscaping, we thus have a rare glimpse into a lost era of garden-making. By the end of the nineteenth century the garden had acquired a further overlay of topiaries and Victorian 'Old English' planting, which the Trust has re-created.

The 'extreme simplicity of its design' delighted H. Inigo Triggs, who included it in his book *The Formal Gardens of England and Scotland*, published in 1902. Indeed, it is thanks to the garden's inclusion in Triggs' book, Alicia Amherst's *History of Gardening* (1895), and *Country Life* articles of 1904 and 1921, as well as family plans and photographs, that the Trust has had the benefit of clear guidelines for restoration. The first stage was to grub out tree stumps, brambles and ivy and carefully lift areas of turf to expose the walls and uncover the gravel paths in front of the house.

The main vista from the house's south-facing garden front is down a series of grass terraces, concluding in the Lion Gates and the finest of a series of Baroque gate piers. Circular, diamond-shaped and other geometric flower-beds have now been cut out of the lawns of the upper terraces, and are planted with an array of spring and summer bedding plants, including yellow calceolarias (a Dryden favourite) partnered with purple heliotrope. The four great cedars that once flanked the steps between the top two terraces, that were not part of Edward's original design, came down in storms in the 1950's and have been replaced by four topiary yews in keeping with the original plans.

In the lower two terraces, ribbon bedding has been replicated using lavender and nepeta, which accompanies beds of soft fruit and traditional vegetables, the latter flanked by pear trees and set in a wildflower meadow. The vista used to extend beyond the Lion Gates into the parkland by means of a double elm avenue, reinstated with English elms propagated from trees shown to be disease-resistant to fatal beetle attack. This avenue is one of several that carries the garden's axes into the landscape, connecting it to the church, the former approach road and the lake – one of them being of an unusual zigzag design, switching trees from lime to hornbeam to oak as it runs into the countryside, possibly following old field boundaries. Visitors to Canons Ashby have often remarked on its romantic character, and this relaxed country spirit is being nurtured in the rough grass and area of wildflowers through which you approach the property and in the surrounding landscape.

A 250-year-old cedar tree still stands on the west side of the garden, the lawn here fringed by hardy perennial plants that pick up the exotic theme of the summer bedding, such as crinum, eucomis, agapanthus, *Geranium palmatum* and *Kniphofia caulescens*, given a period backdrop by grey, purple and autumn-tinting vines, roses and clematis. In the lawn below, a black mulberry is accompanied by a border of culinary and medicinal herbs.

Eight topiary yews, planted in the early eighteenth century and restored into obelisks, form the centrepiece of the Green Court opposite the west front. This modestly sized enclosure was once the main entrance for the house, but was turfed down in 1880 by Sir Henry Dryden and now serves as a tranquil sanctuary and home of a lead statue of a shepherd boy, attributed to John van Nost. Against the surrounding walls old varieties of pear have been espaliered, including 'Catillac', 'Beurré Alexandre Lucas' and 'Louise Bonne of Jersey', and under the shadiest wall there is a border of shade-loving ferns, bulbs and herbaceous plants. It is a complete and perfect example of a small formal garden, and a convincing example of the virtues of restraint and symmetry in garden design.

LEFT The phormium border on the top terrace at Canons Ashby.

Castle Drogo

DREWSTEIGNTON, DEVON

AREA 4.9ha (12 acres) • **SOIL** acid/stony shale over rock • **ALTITUDE** 263m (862ft)
AVERAGE RAINFALL 1,143mm (45in) • **AVERAGE WINTER CLIMATE** cold, wet

Castle Drogo – the name sounds a bass note of foreboding, which reverberates when, from the road, you first catch sight of the granite fortress sprouting from its rocky spur, high above the bleak expanses of Dartmoor. Even as you climb towards it, it stretches out no welcoming hand; the long drive has no entrance lodges or banks of flowers, only dark clumps of yew and evergreen oak, and belts of beech trees framing dramatic views of the wild Devon landscape. And when you finally arrive, you are confronted by hostile, defensive walls, with battlements and few windows, silhouetted starkly against the sky. Edwin Lutyens entered fully into the spirit of his unusual brief when he designed this Norman fantasy for Julius Drewe, founder of the Home and Colonial Stores.

The contrast with the wilderness behind is intentionally abrupt. Drewe wanted his castle to appear to rise directly out of the moors and the suggestion by Gertrude Jekyll for elaborate terraced gardens directly below the house was rejected in favour of untamed vegetation lapping the precipice. The only garden connected to the house is the small, draughty Chapel Garden, planted with patio roses and wall shrubs, including a cordon-trained *Viburnum plicatum*. Julius Drewe decided to locate his main flower gardens beyond the drive, to the north-east. Echoing the castle, they are potently architectural, generous in scale and solidly walled in yew, but it is likely that they owe more to the Kent-based garden designer George Dillistone than to Lutyens. The centrepiece is the Rose Garden, planted as a series of square and rectangular beds chequered into a velvet lawn. The soil being naturally poor, hungry and stony, rose cultivation here is a labour-intensive business, but both old and modern Shrub roses and floribundas feature in a variety of colours.

The highlight of the composition is on the terrace above, where the contributions of both Dillistone and Lutyens are clearly defined. The paths follow an intricate Indian motif that Lutyens, then at the height of his international career, imported from Delhi, and conclude in yew pavilions, roofed originally in weeping elm but now in Persian ironwood, *Parrotia persica* 'Pendula'. Into this crisp pattern, Dillistone, a knowledgeable plantsman, wove gorgeously hued and textured plantings of tree peonies, agapanthus, crinums, daylilies, phlox, delphiniums, bearded irises and the glaucous-leaved *Kniphofia caulescens*. The result is as imaginative a herbaceous garden as you are likely to see.

In the centre of the terrace, steps rise between spiky yuccas and dripping wisterias to a fragrant garden, and thence via a gravel corridor between shrub borders, foaming with azaleas, cherries and magnolias in spring and hoherias, eucryphias and lilies in summer, to a further flight of steps guarded by erect cypresses. Here is the greatest surprise of all, for you enter into a huge circle of yew, empty of all but a smooth expanse of shaven grass – a silent counterweight to the bulk of the castle and busy detail of the flower gardens below.

The ever-present backdrop to all this is the trees: beeches marshalled into avenues and flooded in spring by wood anemones and daffodils, and woods of oaks, beeches, Scots pines, tree magnolias and birches, with their understorey of ferns and bluebells. Among these, on the steep slope north-west of the house, meandering paths entice you down into a rhododendron valley,

created by Basil Drewe, second son of Julius Drewe, and now in a lively phase of redevelopment. Blue *Rhododendron augustinii* 'Electra', pale yellow 'Lionel's Triumph', pink *R. racemosum* and rose-magenta *R. albrechtii* pull the eye this way and that, while tactile snakebark maples tempt the fingers and heavy lily scents of 'Loderi' rhododendrons excite the nose. Nearby, a new orchard of Devonian apples and plums, underplanted with snowdrops and daffodils, is also being developed. Like the rest of the grounds, these areas simultaneously defy the raw, windswept terrain and merge scenically with it, comfortably adding to what is one of the most extraordinary flights of fancy of the last century.

ABOVE The Terrace Garden has paths on an Indian motif, designed by Edwin Lutyens, with textured plantings by George Dillistone.

Castle Ward

STRANGFORD, DOWNPATRICK, CO. DOWN

AREA 16ha (40 acres) • SOIL acid • ALTITUDE 24m (80ft) • AVERAGE RAINFALL 864mm (34in)
AVERAGE WINTER CLIMATE frost-free

The setting for this, one of the most eccentric houses in the British Isles, is exceptional, with broad, soft views down over Strangford Lough, a glistening stretch of sea water fringed by misty and lush woods. Into this scene, Bernard Ward, later 1st Viscount Bangor, placed what seems at first to be a straightforward Palladian residence, but at its north and east fronts, suddenly transforms itself into an ornate Gothic structure. The gardens also betray sharp changes in style, through the evolving fashions of several centuries.

Lord Bangor set his new house in an informal, parkland landscape, in the style that was capturing the imagination across the Irish Sea. His planting was considerably enriched after 1841 and the slopes are now well-wooded with oak, beech and sycamore, and with numerous exotics in the lawns around the house. The mild, damp climate seems not only to promote tremendous growth but also to encourage trees to develop a multi-stemmed habit, the most extraordinary example here being *Thuja plicata*. Indeed there are many notable conifers here, including firs and wellingtonias, supplemented by massive evergreen shrubs of *Griselinia littoralis*, yew and, most dramatically, scarlet-flowered *Embothrium coccineum*.

The nucleus of the Victorian gardens is the formal sunken lawn and terraces, studded with tall cabbage palms and sheltered by walls, a young hedge of Chilean yew, *Prumnopitys andina* (syn. *Podocarpus andinus*) and a screen of fastigiate Irish yews. In the flower-beds, the Trust has taken advantage of the climate to pursue the subtropical theme to the full and the beds now bristle with exotics, including glaucous-leaved *Melianthus major* and *Kniphofia caulescens*, red-flowered *Lobelia tupa* and *Acca sellowiana* syn. *Feijoa*

sellowiana, *Sophora macrocarpa*, watsonias, cordylines, phormiums and spiky-leaved *Beschorneria yuccoides* and *Fascicularia bicolor*. The two magnificent stone eagles that feature in Mary Ward's fine painting of 1858 have been restored and returned to preside over the garden on 1.2m (4ft) pedestals.

As complete as this upper garden is, it is only half the story – for as you crunch down the shady paths below the house towards the farmyard and Elizabethan tower house, the parkland begins to reveal further formal touches: a three-tier terrace of ancient yews; a lime avenue, recently replanted; and, the biggest surprise of all, a great rectangular lake, fringed by trees and shrubs. These are the legacy of the early eighteenth century, and accompanied the family's second residence, which once stood on the rise above the lime avenue. It is a picturesque composition that absorbs, as its focal point, Audley's Castle, the fifteenth-century fortification guarding the entrance to Strangford Lough, and signals the coming of more civilised times by answering the castle with the serenity of a Doric Temple, erected in about 1750 on top of the lakeside hill.

The Trust has restored the formal shape of Temple Water, but the scene remains soft-edged, with long grass peppered with wildflowers, clumps of gorse and dogwood, and the edge of the lake broken by weeping ash and *Gunnera manicata*. It has long been a favourite haunt of wildfowl, and swans and dabchicks nest on the small island near the west side.

LEFT The statue of Neptune in the Sunken Garden.
ABOVE The Doric Temple looks over Temple Water, dug in 1728.

Charlecote Park

WELLESBOURNE, WARWICKSHIRE

AREA 2ha (5 acres) • SOIL neutral/light well-drained gravel • ALTITUDE 52m (170ft)
AVERAGE RAINFALL 635mm (25in) • AVERAGE WINTER CLIMATE moderate to cold

A weathered palisade of split oak runs around most of the park, and you look across from the Warwick road to see an expanse of low-lying meadow, furnished with oaks and other trees and grazed by groups of fallow deer and Jacob sheep. The entrance drive carves a straight channel to an Elizabethan gatehouse and then across a balustraded court, newly planted with topiary shapes, to the east façade of a red-brick house, appointed with gables, cupolas and dressed white stone.

Stately and sleepy though it seems, Charlecote – the seat of the Lucy family since the twelfth century – has passed through tremendous swings of fashion. A painting hanging in the Great Hall shows the house in a seventeenth-century setting of splendid parterres, formal water gardens and great avenues. Little of this, except the gatehouse and the long procession of limes that comes in from the south-west, survived beyond 1760, when George Lucy engaged Lancelot 'Capability' Brown to landscape the grounds in the new style. Even the River Avon, curving beside the house's west front, was remoulded, its channel widened and its banks given a 'natural and easy level', while the River Dene (formerly the Hele), joining just to the south, was brought closer and made to enter the Avon via a cascade. The eye wanders freely over the open meadowland, the only architectural eye-catcher being the church tower and adjacent rectory of Hampton Lucy village. In winter, the flooding can be comprehensive.

The nineteenth-century Elizabethan revival brought a return to formal order in the garden. The terrace giving on to the river was re-created, together with its flower parterre; grassed over in the 1950s, this was remade, for a third time, by the Trust in 1995. A croquet lawn was laid opposite the house's north front. The new formal Green Court Garden has recently been created by Sir Edmund Fairfax-Lucy in the entrance court, using geometrically spaced trees to make up the design.

North of the entrance court, steps lead to the cedar lawn, part of the raised section of garden that rides ship-like above the park. A small Victorian orangery, a replacement for George Lucy's 'frightful' Grecian temple, and a thatched garden house stand under the trees, the latter inspired by a visit by Mary Lucy to the Ladies of Llangollen at Plas Newydd.

Beyond, 'Capability' Brown's Ladies' Walk offers a gentle circuit around the prow of the garden, which opens onto lawn shaded by gnarled and ancient mulberries and a fine prospect of park and river. The centre ground was planted as a contrasting Wilderness, and you plunge through gaps in the hedge into a small labyrinth of dark passages, shaded by Scots pine and chestnut, thick with yew, box, ivy, evergreen honeysuckle, butcher's broom and periwinkle, and in spring coloured by snowdrops, aconites and, later, daffodils. Close by, a new herbaceous border has been made and, in front of the summer-house, a planting inspired by roses, herbs, fruit trees and cottage perennials mentioned in Shakespeare's plays. According to

legend, in about 1583 the young William was caught stealing a fallow deer from the park and was brought before Sir Thomas Lucy, the resident magistrate, to be fined or flogged. He took revenge by immortalising Sir Thomas as the pompous Justice Shallow in *Henry IV (Part II)* and *The Merry Wives of Windsor*. If this is true, how Sir Thomas would now react to seeing Shakespeare's flowers in Charlecote's garden, and his bust in the Great Hall, we can only guess.

ABOVE Overlooking the river, the parterre was re-created for the third time in 1995.

Chartwell

WESTERHAM, KENT

AREA 33ha (82 acres) • **SOIL** acid-neutral/sand, loam • **ALTITUDE** 137–168m (450–550ft)
AVERAGE RAINFALL 737mm (29in) • **AVERAGE WINTER CLIMATE** moderate to cold

'The ground falls away steeply below the house into a quiet combe'

From November 1922 until his death in January 1965, this was the family home of Sir Winston Churchill. The great man lived here as Chancellor of the Exchequer, Leader of the Opposition and Prime Minister, and it is hard to view the house and garden today without straining to hear his voice and smell the smoke of Havana cigars. The house is packed with paintings and mementoes, uniforms and letters, while in the garden his chair stays as he left it, empty beside the golden orfe pond. 'I bought Chartwell for that view,' he once declared. Blasted though the old beechwoods were in the hurricane of October 1987, the prospect remains beautiful. The ground falls away steeply below the house into a quiet combe; a series of rock pools and channels, fed from the seven springs of the Chart Well, carry water around the northern edge of the garden down into a pond-like swimming pool and on into the first of two lakes. The construction of these features, which are being restored by the Trust so that they run and recycle water properly, was one of Churchill's preoccupations, and they would have been very expensive to install. He built the swimming pool three times in different locations. Indeed, he worked on the garden tirelessly, and enjoyed the recreation of being a hands-on labourer.

Beyond the lakes, the land climbs to woodland and on towards the Weald of Kent. There is a panorama from nearly every window of the house, and six doors connect the airy rooms with the garden. The series of terraces and walks, anchoring the house on its hillside, was elaborated for the Churchills by their architect, Philip Tilden, who was responsible for transforming and modernising the gloomy residence into the bright and comfortable family home we see today. The planting and overall design of the garden were the province of Lady Churchill, ably assisted by Victor Vincent, head gardener from 1947 until 1979. Although inevitably much replanted, the walled rose garden beneath the north front of the house, awash with pink and white Floribunda and Hybrid Tea roses, indicates immediately her penchant for simple, soft, eye-catching effects. In the water garden, the combination of white foxgloves grown from seed in summer, and royal blue anchusa propagated from root cuttings in April, is repeated each year.

Churchill himself was passionate about wildlife, especially butterflies, which he collected as a young man. In the 1940s, he created a house for breeding and releasing them in a brick summer-house at the head of one of the terrace walks, with advice from the butterfly expert L. Hugh Newman, and this has recently been re-created. It is accompanied by a border of butterfly-attracting plants such as buddleja and lavender. Also, the lake once again sports black swans, which he used to keep here; he stocked the lake with brown trout, bought from Harrods.

On Churchill's death, Chartwell passed to the Trust and Lanning Roper, then a gardens consultant to the Trust, suggested improvements to the structure and planting in consultation with Mary Soames, Sir Winston's youngest daughter. To cope with the large numbers of visitors, many of the grass paths had to be surfaced in stone, gravel or tarmac. Borders had their flowering season extended and other areas of the garden were altered to allow for plant growth and the shaping of views for the future.

The walled garden to the south-east of the house has recently been converted back to the kitchen garden that it was in Churchill's day, when its produce was also sent up to London. The stony soil is not ideal for root crops, but a broad range of vegetables and soft fruit, including asparagus, rhubarb, strawberries and currants, grow here, ornamented by cut-flower beds and edgings of nasturtium. Peaches and kiwi fruit grow on the walls, and there are some nice mulberries. The centrepiece for this area is the Golden Rose Walk, part of the present given to the Churchills on their golden wedding anniversary by their children. Backed by a beech hedge and lapped

by catmint and *Stachys byzantina*, it is a dazzling sight from the terrace above throughout the summer and early autumn, when the tones of the 32 yellow and golden roses are taken up by the fruits of *Malus × zumi* 'Golden Hornet'. The adjacent Wendy house, built for Mary Soames, and much of the lower wall were constructed by Churchill himself.

ABOVE The south front of Chartwell, with spring daffodils in the foreground.

Chastleton House

CHASTLETON, MORETON-IN-MARSH, OXFORDSHIRE

AREA 1.4ha (3½ acres) • SOIL alkaline/loam over limestone • ALTITUDE 244km (800ft)
AVERAGE RAINFALL 635mm (25in) • AVERAGE WINTER CLIMATE cold

'We lost our money in the War,' Irene Whitmore-Jones used to tell visitors to Chastleton in the 1920s. She meant the Civil War. Among the golden, lichen-encrusted walls and tapestry-hung interiors of this Jacobean manor, the presiding century has always been the seventeenth. Her family's genteel poverty served to protect the house from change, while their deep attachment to it ensured it was never once sold from the time it was built in the 1610s until 1991, when it was bought by the National Heritage Memorial Fund and passed to the Trust.

I first encountered Chastleton enveloped in winter mist, and feared the period spell would be broken when I returned in spring sunlight. But remarkably, considering the panorama of rolling Cotswold countryside revealed, its setting remains wonderfully sleepy; the only jarring sound I could hear was the hammering of a green woodpecker. The woods still sport the wild yellow tulip *Tulipa sylvestris*, known locally as the Catesby lily after the owners of the previous house here. It was Robert Catesby, Guy Fawkes' co-conspirator in the Gunpowder Plot, who sold Chastleton estate to the lawyer and politician Walter Jones in 1606.

You walk downhill to the house through the small park and your first sight of it is behind the trees, flanked by the medieval St Mary's church and the park's handsome stone dovecote. It sits high and square on its site and, in typical Jacobean style, walls project from it to create a series of enclosed garden courts. Originally, these were not connected to each other, to allow private access from the house, but over the years openings were made, and some of the walls lowered to give views of the landscape beyond. Seventeenth-century

visitors would have arrived exactly as today, walking under the finial-capped arch and down the gravel forecourt. There are no records of what the various parts of the garden looked like then, the present design having been shaped by successive generations nostalgically reinstating, and reinterpreting, Jacobean features. In the 1840s, a large kitchen garden, part-walled and hedged in yew, was added, and naturally over the years plants have arrived to soften the architecture – roses, cottage perennials, even a paperbark maple.

The Best Garden, below the east wall of the house, is the major delight. Here, a pair of grass terraces, one of them original, descends onto a lawn taken up by a great circle of yew, entered through arches covered in roses and clematis, and ringed inside with an eccentric

parliament of topiaries. Though they are now agelessly amorphous, nineteenth-century photographs show them to be recognisable shapes – teapots, a crown, a horse, a lyrebird, even a ship in full sail. In Jacobean times, the topiaries may have been similarly eclectic, though Walter Jones's interest in astrology may equally have suggested a Copernican theme.

Staunch Royalists, the family had a tradition of political planting. There is a Jacobite stand of Scots pines, as well as a mulberry. (James I asked his subjects to plant mulberries in order to establish an English silk industry. It was a hopeless project, especially since it was the black mulberry that was widely planted; silkworms eat only the white.) Royalist oaks were also planted in the 1660s to celebrate the restoration of the monarchy, and in the 1850s, acorns were taken from the Royal Oak itself, the Boscobel tree in which Charles II concealed himself from the pursuing Parliamentarians. One of the resulting trees stands in alignment with the topiary garden.

The lawn on the north side of the house is celebrated for its association with Walter Jones-Whitmore, who codified the rules of croquet here, and won the first croquet championship in 1868. From the lawn, the grass runs down into a small, meandering wild garden in the Victorian style of William Robinson, comprising naturalised wood anemones, daffodils, martagon lilies and other bulbs, growing around stands of hazel, holly, elder and philadelphus.

In the kitchen garden, espaliered fruits, vegetables and cut flowers are cultivated, with the chequered snakeshead fritillary colonising prettily under the apple, pear and quince trees of the small orchard.

In keeping with Chastleton's long history of straitened circumstances, the garden, like the house, has not been smartened up. The lawns are left slightly rough, weeds pop up in the gravel and the planting is somewhat ad hoc. On the right day, it is like stumbling upon a well-kept secret.

LEFT Typically Jacobean in style, the gardens were divided into enclosed courts with doors added later for access.

ABOVE View of Chastleton House looking over the kitchen garden in June.

Chirk Castle

CHIRK, WREXHAM

AREA 2.2ha (5½ acres) • SOIL neutral-acid/sandy loam • ALTITUDE 213m (700ft)
AVERAGE RAINFALL 1,016–1,143mm (40–45in) • AVERAGE WINTER CLIMATE cold

The gentle folds of oak-studded pasture through which you climb to reach Chirk Castle lull you back into the luscious decades of the eighteenth century. It comes as quite a shock when a massive medieval fortress rears up on the horizon, its high walls joined to heavy drum towers and topped with battlements. For Chirk, completed by 1310, is one of the chain of great border castles built at the command of Edward I to survey the defeated Welsh tribes. It is the transition from military stronghold into a comfortable and splendid home, and the fact that the changes – sometimes subtle, sometimes dramatically abrupt – have been effected since 1595 by a single family, that give Chirk such powerful character. Add to this its stupendous hilltop views, topiary and richly planted shrub borders, and you have one of the Trust's most exciting little-known gardens.

It is an exposed site and the great oaks help to filter the wind through the gardens. As the late Lady Margaret Myddelton once explained to me, 'Without them it would be impossible to stand up.' The yew hedges and shrubberies provide further barricades. However, a hilltop location has many advantages. The panorama from the Terrace, looking out over the Ceiriog Valley towards the hills of Shropshire, is said to encompass fourteen counties; there is a pavilion by William Emes, who landscaped the park after 1764, from which to savour it. The falling ground also accentuates shapes. This is a garden of spectacular silhouettes, cast against a broad sky. Among the most striking is the long topiary hedge beneath the castle, whose black-green battlements create a further defensive courtyard beyond the grey walls. On the terraced lawns within them are many

more yew specimens, a double row of large cones and 'Welsh hats', and a magnificent giant crown resting on a cushion. These were all planted in the late nineteenth century, but allowing them to grow to their present size and plumpness was the suggestion of the celebrated garden designer Norah Lindsay, a close friend of Lord and Lady Howard de Walden, who leased the castle from 1911 until 1946. The task of pruning the Chirk yews takes three gardeners from mid-August until mid-October.

The sunken Rose Garden, filled with old Hybrid Tea and Floribunda varieties, is a softening influence on the scene, as is the lavish assortment of shrubs and climbers against the castle walls, including *Hydrangea anomala* subsp. *petiolaris*, roses, clematis, and, for its autumn colour, *Celastrus orbiculatus*. The climate being relatively mild here, half-hardy plants such as *Luma apiculata* can also

be risked in the more sheltered niches. Alpines such as lewisias and campanulas grow in the dry-stone walls.

Pass between two hefty yew buttresses and their accompanying graceful bronze nymphs – yet another disarming juxtaposition – and you step onto a long, linear sweep of lawn, flanked by fine trees and flowering shrubs. In spring, sheets of daffodils swirl towards the great larch and cedar in the rough grass; and in early summer, it will be the scarlet flowers of *Embothrium coccineum*, backed by the purple leaves of beech, that catch your eye.

The undulating, 274m (300yd) border on the north side has recently been refurbished, its four bays planted for the four seasons with a cast including magnolias, azaleas and Shrub roses interplanted with hellebores, peonies, heleniums and other herbaceous plants.

The luxurious planting of the rock bank, flanking Lord Howard de Walden's thatched Hawk House and the Shrub Garden opposite, is by Lady Margaret Myddelton. In late spring, the fiery trusses of rhododendrons and azaleas blaze against the whites and pinks of pieris, magnolias, dogwoods and the handkerchief tree, *Davidia involucrata*. Later, near the newly extended waterlily pond, white-flowered *Eucryphia glutinosa* glows above pools of blue hydrangeas. February sees a sheet of snowdrops under the woodland canopy, and May a haze of bluebells.

ABOVE Gateway to the upper lawn with silver weeping lime and cedar.

Clandon Park

WEST CLANDON, GUILDFORD, SURREY

AREA 3ha (7½ acres) • **SOIL** alkaline to neutral/heavy • **ALTITUDE** 76m (250ft)
AVERAGE RAINFALL 686mm (27in) • **AVERAGE WINTER CLIMATE** cold

The park and pleasure grounds at Clandon have been subjected to abrupt swings in taste over the years, resulting in a green landscape of contrasting features. At its heart is the imposing Palladian mansion, with its high red-brick walls, sparsely dressed in white stone. In April 2015 it was devastated by fire, leaving its interior a shell – though happily some of the most important contents were saved.

The mansion was built in the early 1720s for Thomas, 2nd Lord Onslow, and originally stood within the grand geometric pattern of avenues, parterres, formal walks and canal that accompanied the previous Jacobean house. By the 1750s a new, naturalistic landscape was replacing it, with Lancelot 'Capability' Brown brought in to complete the project in 1781. In the late nineteenth century the tide again turned. The 4th Earl Onslow divided the flowing composition into fields, reinstated a double avenue of trees west of the house to celebrate the birth of his heir, and laid out extensive ornamental gardens.

The shrubberies that lap the lawns and furnish the Wilderness behind the house recall some of its Victorian past, with plants that would have adorned the early eighteenth-century garden, such as yew, laurel, holly and mock orange, supplemented by coloured foliage including purple Japanese maples, purple beech, hazel and smoke bush, together with golden philadelphus and variegated dogwood. Among the specimen trees are a wellingtonia, an old Chusan palm, and a splendid *Magnolia acuminata*, known as the cucumber tree because of the shape and colour of its young fruits. In spring, large areas of rough grass are yellow with daffodils.

In addition, there are several architectural surprises. An eighteenth-century shell grotto stands opposite the south front,

and three Corinthian capitals, flanked originally by a double row of Lawson cypress, sit deposed on low brick plinths in the grass. Even more disarming is the sight of Hinemihi, a Maori meeting-house, among the trees and shrubs, brought back by the 4th Earl after serving as Governor of New Zealand. Some distance to the east there is also a sunken Dutch garden, created after 1897 and based on the Number One Pond Garden at Hampton Court; this is currently being returned to a high standard of presentation.

Some of the grandeur of the earlier Georgian garden was restored to the property in 1976, when the Trust remodelled the area beside the south front into a small parterre, incorporating bedding plants within box-edged beds. They stand between *palissades à l'Italienne* – stilt hedges of hornbeam – which reflect the origins of the mansion and its architect, the Venetian Giacomo Leoni.

LEFT The parterre garden at the south front of the house.
ABOVE The Dutch Garden in winter.

Claremont

ESHER, SURREY

AREA 20ha (49 acres) • SOIL acid/sandy loam • ALTITUDE 30m (100ft)
AVERAGE RAINFALL 635mm (25in) • AVERAGE WINTER CLIMATE moderate

The restoration of this landscape garden, once praised as 'the noblest of any in Europe', began in 1975, thanks largely to a generous grant from the Slater Foundation. The task facing the Trust was monumental, since 20 years of neglect had turned the entire site into an impenetrable evergreen jungle.

Today, you can see just how much the clearance revealed: contributions by a succession of the eighteenth century's greatest gardeners, each building on (and only occasionally destroying) the work of his predecessor, the whole encapsulating the early evolution of the English landscape movement. A place of varied beauty was awoken, a composition of framed views, dramatic eye-catchers, open arenas and meandering lakeside and woodland walks; the greens complemented by the changing trees and seasonal surges of colour from bluebells, daffodils, purple rhododendrons and yellow azaleas.

The Belvedere Tower, crowning the ridge above the garden, is the obvious place from which to embark on the historical tour, though it stands just a few metres outside the Trust's boundary; the adjoining part of the estate still belongs to the house, now a school, with limited opening since 1995 in conjunction with the Trust. Equipped with a banqueting room and viewing platform, the Belvedere, designed by Sir John Vanbrugh, was the place from which the landscape was to be surveyed, and was the first building erected in 1715 by the garden's creator, the Duke of Newcastle (then Lord Clare: hence, Clare Mount). From this battlemented pavilion, a long grass corridor channels the eye downhill, over Vanbrugh's accompanying bastions (reconstructed by the Trust) and between beech hedges to a rectangular bowling green. The corridor extends into a lime avenue introduced in the 1730s, and replanted by the Trust. Following this around to the left, you suddenly arrive at the vantage point over the next feature to be installed by the Duke, the 1.2ha (3 acre) grass amphitheatre – Claremont's masterpiece.

The designer of this stupendous earthwork, a reference to ancient Rome and, perhaps, an idea borrowed from the gardens of Renaissance Italy, was Charles Bridgeman, the foremost landscape gardener of the time, and a colleague of Vanbrugh at Stowe. The Duke had been consulting him since 1716, and he is thought to have built the amphitheatre not long after the *Vitruvius Britannicus* plan of 1725 was drawn.

Scenic rather than thespian drama was the amphitheatre's purpose, and from the vantage point you have a fine panorama of trees and water. The view below, however, is not of circular pond and plantations, but of informal lake and woods. This change took place in the early 1730s, under the supervision of a second celebrated gardener, William Kent, who would now use the natural contours to create scenes evocative of landscape painting, complete with curving lines and architectural eye-catchers.

The next architectural structure you come upon as you round the south-west corner of the lake is the grotto. Constructed of sandstone and chalk conglomerate, it is probably the work of Joseph and Josiah Lane, the builders of the splendid grotto at Painshill. Behind the lake, the path entices you up a mound, thickly covered in beech, chestnut, oak and bracken. This land, formerly severed from the garden by the main Portsmouth road, was landscaped and brought into the composition after 1768, when, on the Duke of Newcastle's death, the estate was bought by Clive of India.

The bold, sweeping style of Lancelot 'Capability' Brown was now the prevailing fashion, and Clive turned to Brown to build him a crisp new Neo-classical house in place of Vanbrugh's low-lying, castellated palace and to expand and further deformalise the garden. Part of this work involved the smothering of Bridgeman's amphitheatre (which had become far too artificial a feature for contemporary taste) with cedars, deciduous trees and evergreen shrubs. Skirting the north side of the lake, past the laurel shrubberies, through the rhododendron tunnels, and following the line of Brown's brick ha-ha, you come to open meadow, sheeted with native Lent lilies (*Narcissus pseudonarcissus*) in spring and spangled with other wildflowers in summer, and then back up the ridge to the sites of the nineteenth century's architectural additions.

In 1816, the estate was purchased as a home for Princess Charlotte, the only daughter of the Prince Regent, and her husband

Prince Leopold of Saxe-Coburg, and it remained a royal residence until 1922. Several buildings were erected in this period, but apart from the Thatched House (a replacement for the thatched building put up by William Kent, and now a dovecote), they survive only as foundations. Above the amphitheatre you can see the vestiges of Princess Charlotte's Gothic tea house, which became a mausoleum after her death in childbirth. Just below the Belvedere, framed by an ironwork balustrade, are the remains of the camellia house, built in 1824. The bushes of *Camellia japonica*, hardier than the Victorians suspected, now grow in the open.

ABOVE The informal lake and surrounding plantations, devised by landscape architect William Kent in the 1730s.

Clevedon Court

CLEVEDON, SOMERSET

AREA 3.2ha (8 acres) • SOIL alkaline • ALTITUDE 30m (100ft) • AVERAGE RAINFALL 813mm (32in) • AVERAGE WINTER CLIMATE moderate

This is an ancient habitation, for the Great Hall and Tower were already standing when Sir John de Clevedon built the present manor house with its thick, buttressed walls in about 1320. Its south-facing position on the side of Court Hill gains it some protection from the west wind whipping across the Bristol Channel and the high water table of Clevedon Moor, while above the house a dense woodland of evergreen oak, planted in the nineteenth century, lends a southern European air to the backdrop. The grounds do, however, have to contend with the rumble of the M5 a short distance away.

Pines and beeches, and a massive oriental plane beside the short drive to the house, rise high above the roofline. There are also good tulip trees and robinias, a splendid catalpa, and a black mulberry, recorded as being ancient as far back as 1822. Magnolias are a feature in spring, and around the plane tree the grass is flushed with bluebells and camassias.

However, the garden's chief delights are concentrated on the slope between the house and the wood above. Here is what Gertrude Jekyll described as 'one of the noblest ranges of terrace walls in England'. There are no records of when they were constructed, but a painting of about 1730 outside the State Bedroom shows the Pretty Terrace complete, with espaliered fruit trees against the wall. Later in the eighteenth century, Sir Abraham Elton had the space behind the wall backfilled to create the Top or Wild Terrace, while the Pretty Terrace was adorned with an Octagon pavilion and, at the end of the long grass walk, a rustic summer-house to balance the composition. Below the Octagon, a handsome double flight of steps was also added.

The terraces offer fine views over the house and out across the moor to the Mendip Hills, and the mild climate and sunny, well-drained ground allow adventurous planting. The style has swung dramatically with the pendulum of fashion. In the nineteenth century, there were elaborate formal patterns of small beds, annuals and subtropical perennials, popular at the time. The schemes were praised by *Country Life* Illustrated in 1899, but not by Gertrude Jekyll, who lamented in *Wall and Water Gardens*, published in 1901, that the terraces were 'given over to the most commonplace forms of bedding'.

Today a more relaxed style prevails, much refreshed in recent years, with bold associations of shrubs, climbers and perennials and 'the noblest plants' for which Miss Jekyll pleaded. *Magnolia grandiflora*, strawberry trees (*Arbutus*), *Photinia serratifolia* (syn. *P. serrulata*), hardy palms, tree ferns, banana, agapanthus, crinum, *Buddleja colvilei* 'Kewensis', *Heptacodium miconioides* and pollarded foxglove tree (*Paulownia tomentosa*) are among the exotic cast, together with large numbers of peonies and alliums. Foxgloves and other wildflowers blend the planting with the wider landscape, and in 2009, a new rose arbour was erected to celebrate the Elton family's 300 years here.

ABOVE The path to the summer house, flanked by the exotic foliage of cannas and magnolias.

Cliveden

TAPLOW, MAIDENHEAD, BUCKINGHAMSHIRE

AREA 73ha (180 acres) • SOIL neutral-alkaline/gravel overlying chalk • ALTITUDE 75m
(246ft) • AVERAGE RAINFALL 686mm (27in) • AVERAGE WINTER CLIMATE moderate

'Spring sees bright, ever-changing mixtures of forget-me-nots, tulips, bellis and pansies'

An opulent marble fountain by Thomas Waldo Story, which has water pouring from a giant shell between female figures intoxicated by the elixir of love, meets you in the drive; you turn to the south to find yourself looking down a long, broad lime avenue at an ornate Italianate palace. It is a grand, theatrical opening scene. The house, one of the masterworks of Sir Charles Barry and now a hotel, was built in 1850–1 for the 2nd Duke and Duchess of Sutherland. As you approach it, you pass between two forecourt borders of herbaceous plants laid out by the Trust. Planned primarily for seasonal colour rather than for textural contrast, they reach a climax in high summer – after displays of tulips, geraniums and early daylilies – with massed phlox, Japanese anemones, macleaya, achillea, rudbeckia and much else. The scale is suitably impressive and the colours are founded in one border on the yellow end of the spectrum and the other on the pink.

Cliveden's two earlier houses were both destroyed by fire, but when you emerge beside the garden front you discover the first has left a magnificent legacy, a brick terrace of French and Italian inspiration (now undergoing major repair) with arcades, balustrades and a central double stairway. It stands as a podium below the house, and from it you look out over a sweeping platform of lawn and parterre, and a landscape of plunging beechwoods and still largely pastoral valley, centred on a glistening stretch of the Thames. There are miles of hill and riverside walks to explore in this panorama, the eastern route taking you through a landscaped valley, much admired by the influential Victorian garden writer William Robinson, and offering superb views back to the house.

The first house and the terrace, both designed by William Winde for the 2nd Duke of Buckingham, were built in the 1660s and 1670s. The plateau of lawn, levelled for the Duke, was extended and given its terminating raised circle after 1695 by his successor, the Earl of Orkney, and then, in the early 1850s, decorated with the present pattern of wedge-shaped parterre beds. The gardener at the time, John Fleming, is credited with being the first to use spring-flowering bulbs and other plants, bedded out in the autumn, to follow up the summer annuals and tender exotics (earlier gardeners relied upon evergreen bushes), and he wrote an account of his experiments in Spring and Winter Flower Gardening, published in 1870. This historic scheme has been restored by the Trust and spring sees bright, ever-changing mixtures of forget-me-nots, tulips, bellis and pansies, followed in summer by salvias, petunias, begonias and marigolds. Groups of hot-coloured Ghent azaleas are also included, as they were by Fleming, whose varied plant palette also embraced hollyhocks, foxgloves and gladioli.

The Baroque balustrade beneath the terrace was brought from the Villa Borghese in Rome, and was installed by William Waldorf (later 1st Viscount) Astor, who bought Cliveden in 1893. So, this south garden composition was shaped over many years and has involved a succession of owners. Much of the framework, however, is due to Lord Orkney, and the early eighteenth-century mood becomes strong as you turn to the north-west and exchange the open plateau for the shady, wooded bank that runs high above the river. Here, you come to an octagon temple with a copper-domed roof, designed for Orkney by Giacomo Leoni – later transformed into a chapel

garden as an enveloping and organic shape – circular and enfolding like a cabbage – with the colours in a warm sequence from yellow and orange to red and crimson. Modern and more disease-resistant varieties have been used to achieve this, including on the freestanding metal arches that span the paths. Nearby, there is also a memorial garden to the soldiers who died in the Canadian Red Cross hospital on the estate.

The Astors have contributed two further gardens. To the north of the woodland, the 1st Viscount set out the Long Garden, a formal garden echoing the parterre below the house. A great collector of classical and Renaissance art, he introduced the many urns, well-heads, statues and sarcophagi you encounter in various parts of the grounds, and here you find a group of eighteenth-century figures, placed within a linear composition of box-edged beds. Topiary, including of peacocks, adds additional characterful verticals, and within the box is a scheme of 200m (656ft) long borders filled with colourful spring and summer bedding. Flowering shrubs such as lilac, magnolia and laburnum grow in front of the yew trees behind, and a ribbon of perennials, including kniphofias, agapanthus, echinacea and monarda, runs along the south-facing brick wall on the other side, accompanied by roses, sweet peas, and interesting shrubs including *Umbellularia californica*, *Dipelta floribunda* and *Calycanthus occidentalis*.

The other Astor garden is in complete contrast. It is an informal water garden, begun by the 1st Viscount and developed by his son and latterly the Trust into a rather magical landscape with an oriental flavour. This has also recently undergone comprehensive restoration. The centrepiece is a pagoda painted green and gold; it was made for the Paris Exhibition of 1867 but bought later from Bagatelle. This is set on an island amid a pool of waterlilies and golden orfe, and reached by stepping stones. The marginal plants and ornamental trees and shrubs, arranged for contrast and decorative impact, are mainly Chinese, and include primulas, water irises, azaleas and rhododendrons, witch hazel, white cherries, and wisteria grown as shrubs. Nearby is the yew maze, replanted in 2011 and now well thickened. Occupying a third of an acre, it was created by Lord Astor in 1894 but taken out in the mid-twentieth century. There are scenes and diversions at Cliveden for every taste.

and mausoleum by Lord Astor – and pick up traces of the earlier landscape. Orkney's garden designer, probably recommended by their mutual friend Alexander Pope, was Charles Bridgeman, the leading practitioner of the day and a key figure in the transition towards the more naturalistic gardening style shortly to come into fashion.

The combination of straight walks, many bordered by large yew trees, and prospects of the countryside beyond give the flavour of Bridgeman's work, even if much of it has evolved subsequently. In the north-west corner, you come upon the most remarkable remnant, a turf amphitheatre (c.1723), a miniature version of that at Claremont (qv), carved into the slope. Further straight drives cut through the woods, one leading to a triumphal pedimented pavilion, also by Leoni, commemorating the Battle of Blenheim (Lord Orkney was one of Marlborough's brigade commanders), and another leading to a stone urn, said to have been presented to Orkney by Queen Anne.

These enclosed spaces play against the views out over the countryside, and much work is taking place at the moment to re-create them. At the same time, *Rhododendron ponticum* is being removed, and light welcomed in. The short grass swards, especially in the Blenheim Lawn, supports an array of chalkland wildflowers. In one of the glades, the swirling lawns are filled with clouds of evergreen oak, *Quercus ilex*, probably planted by Lord Orkney. In another, you enter a Rose Garden, recently re-created by the Trust to the original 1959 design by Sir Geoffrey Jellicoe. To create a secret and peaceful refuge for Viscount Astor, Jellicoe planned the

ABOVE LEFT The Chinese pagoda presides over an island in the water garden.

RIGHT Gladioli and other colourful parterre bedding in summer evening light.

Clumber Park

WORKSOP, NOTTINGHAMSHIRE

AREA 11ha (26 acres) • SOIL acid/sandy • ALTITUDE 30m (100ft)
AVERAGE RAINFALL 610mm (24in) • AVERAGE WINTER CLIMATE cold

Enter the park under the Apleyhead arch, and you will drive through one of the most impressive lime avenues in England, over 3.2km (2 miles) in length; the grease bands on the trunks are to fend off egg-laying moths, whose caterpillars have ravaged the foliage in the past. The avenue is purely a landscape feature, planted in the 1830s by W.S. Gilpin, the pioneer of Picturesque gardening, to enliven an otherwise featureless stretch of approach road and to indicate the magnitude of the domain through which it leads.

At its heart is the great serpentine lake created in the mid-eighteenth century by damming the River Poulter. This provides the setting for a long terrace walk, adorned with specimen trees and shrubberies, urns and a temple. The transformation of the site was effected from about 1760 by successive Dukes of Newcastle, to whom the estate, then adjacent to Sherwood Forest, had been granted some 50 years earlier. Although 'Capability' Brown was working nearby and may have contributed, it seems most likely that the principal influence on the landscape was Joseph Spence, a tutor and man of letters who was widely consulted on garden matters by northern landowners.

The surprise is that there is no great mansion to give the park its *raison d'être*. The first house burned down in 1879, and its replacement, by Sir Charles Barry, was demolished in 1938 as a drastic tax-saving measure. Adjoining estate buildings, including the stable block and clock tower, however, remain. The treatment of the ground fronting the vanished house poses rather a dilemma for the Trust, since evocation of the earlier formal garden by intricate horticulture only emphasises the void, but as you move away from the buildings, along the lakeside walk, this sense of absence gradually wanes. The entire scene is framed in oaks, limes and other broad-leaved trees, sheltering the garden from the north wind, shading the lawns, furnishing the distant banks and reflecting in the water.

The paths meander through stands of willows, past dense island beds of conifers and Hardy Hybrid rhododendrons, and under some impressive specimen trees. Mediterranean species, in particular cedars, sweet chestnuts, Turkey and Algerian oaks, prove themselves well suited to Clumber's poor sandy soil. Quite a diverse collection of rowans (*Sorbus*) is also growing here. The mood is strongly Victorian, and the design is likely to be the work of Gilpin. In the late 1880s, the ornate Gothic chapel, by G.F. Bodley, was added to the Pleasure Ground and, in the absence of the house, now serves as the core of the garden.

The formal path leads to the Lincoln Terrace, designed by William Eden Nesfield in 1861, a promenade ornamented with splendid stone seats, and concluding in a narrow dock where a pleasure boat was once moored. North of the chapel, an avenue of cedars leads to an absolutely magnificent 1.6ha (4 acre) walled garden, dating from the 1770s and now almost fully restored.

The range of produce grown is mind-boggling, including no fewer than 90 varieties of rhubarb. The lower section is subdivided by numerous additional walls for fruit production, and pre-1910 varieties of peach, nectarine and apricot, together with other crops such as pears, gages, cherries and damsons, are once again being cultivated on them. The grass orchard plots feature apple varieties associated with Nottinghamshire and the north-east Midlands. Soft fruit sections include marionberry, black raspberry, Siberian kiwi fruit and 'Mara des Bois' and 'Cambridge Late Pine' strawberries, while in the vegetable beds grow countless heritage seed varieties such as 'Prince of Prussia' pea and 'Major Cook's Bean'. There are beds for asparagus and Mayan potatoes, and for curious herb and salad crops such as golden purslane, saltwort, red spring onion, and the lettuce 'Drunken Woman'.

To enhance the garden's decorative quality, a double herbaceous border runs 122m (400ft) down its central axis, and this has been planted in graded colours to give a *trompe l'oeil* effect. Beginning with plants such as crambe, cardoon, pale sweet peas and white cosmos, the scheme warms through delphiniums, alliums and phlox to reach a sweltering climax among dahlias, daylilies and crocosmias. Here you are outside the central door of an impressive range of Edwardian glasshouses, the thirteen sections of which lead you past peaches, aubergines, melons, vines such as 'Madresfield Court' and 'Foster's Seedling', and an array of ornamental plants from palms and pelargoniums to fuschsias and tender scented rhododendrons. Beyond them, you gain a glimpse into the range of fruit stores and potting sheds, one of which presents a collection of early garden implements such as a cucumber-straightening jar and a pair of leather horse slippers to prevent hoof prints on the lawns.

This restoration has made Clumber Park a truly fascinating horticultural destination and given it something of its soul back.

RIGHT Allium heads amongst the herbaceous borders in the walled kitchen garden.

LEFT The spire of the gothic chapel, seen in the distance, over the serpentine lake.

Colby Woodland Garden

AMROTH, PEMBROKESHIRE

AREA 8ha (20 acres) • SOIL acid/mineral rich over coal seams • ALTITUDE 15–46m (50–150ft) • AVERAGE RAINFALL 1,143mm (45in) • AVERAGE WINTER CLIMATE mild

The wooded slopes of this hidden Pembrokeshire valley are dotted with small, open-cast mine-workings, and it was this iron ore and anthracite that attracted the industrial entrepreneur John Colby to settle here and commission his Nash-style villa in 1803. Before you plunge into the garden proper, it is worth a wander through the oaks and beeches on the eastern flank of the valley, especially in spring when the ground is white with wood anemones. The climax is a pale obelisk, a monument to Peter Chance, a former chairman of Christie's, who owned and developed much of the garden from 1965 until his death in 1984, when he left it to the Trust.

From here, to the sounds of the birds, including sometimes the wood warbler, you can survey the shape of the garden. Its heart is the meadow, which rolls down the valley bottom in front of the house to, a mile or so away, the sea and the village of Amroth. Bisected by a meandering trout stream, and colonised by violets, primroses, buttercups and meadowsweet, it is a rich habitat for butterflies, dragonflies and damselflies.

On the opposite flank of the valley, the woodland displays a quite different character – a confection of flowering trees and shrubs, especially rhododendrons. This exotic planting began in the late nineteenth century, when Colby was bought by Major Samuel Kay. This was continued by his daughter, Mrs Crosland, and her husband, and then really gathered momentum in the hands of his niece, Miss Mason. By recent times, the planting had become somewhat overgrown and congested, so a programme is under way to marshal the shapes and colours into more scenic thickets and glades, to expose the natural contours and to open up breathing spaces for the

bluebells, daffodils, ferns and other wildflowers. It has been dramatically ravaged by recent plant disease.

Periodic storms have done some damage in the past, but generally this is a mild, moist, sheltered site that is ideal for the cultivation of Chinese and Himalayan plants. As you follow the paths up the hillside, an extensive collection of species and hybrids presents itself, from magnolias and camellias to red-bracted pieris and drifts of blue and white hydrangeas. Among the panoply of rhododendrons, you will find everything from towering pink *R. arboreum*, pale yellow *R. lutescens*, blood-red *R. thomsonii*

ABOVE Japanese azaleas in one of the woodland's sunny glades.

LEFT The walled garden with its gothic gazebo built by Peter Chance.

and some luxuriant, giant-leaved *R. sinogrande* and *R. maccabeanum* to a vast assortment of hybrids, from the pastels of 'Alison Johnstone', 'Lavender Girl' and 'Moonshine Bright' to deep yellow 'Crest', scarlet 'The Hon. Jean Marie de Montague', white 'Peace', wine-crimson 'Moser's Maroon' and hot pink Japanese azaleas.

From South America comes monkey puzzle, the scarlet bottle brushes of embothrium, white-saucered eucryphia and the red lanterns of crinodendron. And it is South Africa we can thank, or curse, for the orange montbretia (*Crocosmia*), which has naturalised itself along the grassy fringes of Colby's pathways, as it has done all along Britain's western seaboard. Here and there you pick up the sound of water splashing down mossy rocks, and at one point it collects into a contemplative pool. The reward for climbing to the top of the woods is the view from the summer-house, out over the sea to the Gower Peninsula, but equally absorbing is that from Pamela Chance's memorial on the lower path, back over the meadow to the house and its adjacent walled garden.

The walled garden has been leased out to the Trust's tenants, Anthony and Cynthia Scourfield Lewis, who open it to the public. They have redesigned it as an intricate plantsman's garden, with sinuous paths, lawns and island beds, and a formal fuchsia garden. Yellow New Zealand *Sophora tetraptera*, crimson *Acca sellowiana* syn. *Feijoa sellowiana* from South America and South African *Melianthus major* are among the original cast savouring the warm micro-climate, supported now by numerous other shrubs and perennials, from indigo-berried *Dichroa febrifuga* to the scintillating blue domes of *Scilla peruviana*. The white gothic gazebo in its top corner, built by Chance and with a trompe-l'oeil painted interior, is a landmark across the garden, and below it, a rill has now been constructed to bring the sound of water to another part of Colby.

RIGHT Pink hybrid rhododendrons bloom along a shady pathway.

C

Coleton Fishacre

KINGSWEAR, DARTMOUTH, DEVON

AREA 12ha (30 acres) • **SOIL** acid/shaly loam; pockets of silty clay • **ALTITUDE** 100m (328ft) • **AVERAGE RAINFALL** 914mm (36in) • **AVERAGE WINTER CLIMATE** frost-free, mild

'The house and garden maintain a strong bond with their Devon setting'

The plunging sides and deep bowl of this south-facing valley garden offer near-perfect growing conditions. Cold air flows away quickly through the combe, and the shelter belts of Monterey pine and holm oak limit the impact of the salt-laden winds. Humidity is high, thanks to the proximity of the sea, while the abundance of underground springs, coupled with the shaly soil and precipitous terrain, provide that ideal but elusive combination of constant moisture and sharp drainage.

Rich and extensive as its collection of rare and tender plants may be, the mood at Coleton Fishacre is not, however, exotic. Rather, true to the spirit of the Arts and Crafts Movement, the house and garden maintain a strong bond with their Devon setting. Walls and terraces are built of stone quarried on site, and their vernacular construction, incorporating steeply pitched roofs and curved walls, enables them to blend easily with the contours of the land. The spirit of Edwin Lutyens is pervasive, though this is the work of his pupil Oswald Milne, commissioned by Rupert D'Oyly Carte, son of Gilbert and Sullivan's business partner, and his wife Lady Dorothy, soon after they purchased the estate in 1924.

A generous leavening of native and traditional plants also helps to mellow the impact of rarified horticulture, but between the cherries and chestnuts, rosemary and wisteria, banks of daffodils and wild garlic, there is rich fare indeed to be discovered. Following a long period of inactivity, the golden opportunities the site offers have again been seized as the Trust advances its programme of restoration and improvement.

As you walk into the garden past suede-trunked *Luma apiculata* and various *Prunus*, you are immediately diverted by the Seemly Terrace. Early in the year it will be hellebores, euphorbias and scented daphnes, such as *Daphne bholua* and *D. acutiloba*, that catch your eye and draw your nose, as you pass the polished mahogany trunks of *Prunus serrula*; later, perhaps, it may be brightly hued crocosmias and hedychiums.

The Rill Garden below, with its canalised stream and horizontal patterns of stone, is strongly redolent of the great formal gardens of the Lutyens-Jekyll partnership. Originally planted with roses, which struggle to thrive in the humid maritime atmosphere, it is now bolstered with unusual and tender perennials in pink and other pastel shades, including salvias and rehmannia. Beds near the house, and along the walk to the Gazebo, shimmer in the richer colour of plants from the hotter and drier parts of the world, such as kangaroo paw, cuphea and king proteas. While fascicularia, aloes and aeoniums contribute an array of spiky and succulent foliage.

The views from the Gazebo out towards the jagged outcrop of the Blackstone rocks and the wide expanse of sea allow a brief pause from this intensive horticulture. But then, taking a deep breath, you must choose your descent into the combe. The open sunny terraces now give way to the dappled shade of woodland, and formal stone-edged rill and basins become burbling stream and natural pools. In spring and early summer you are submerged in colour from camellias, magnolias, rhododendrons, embothriums and dogwoods, with azaleas and tender white-flowered rhododendrons, including *RR. maddenii ssp. crassum, burmanicum, johnstoneanum* and *lindleyi*, providing pools of scent. Hydrangeas, eucryphias, orange-flowered *Lomatia ferruginea*, melon-scented *Magnolia × wieseneri* and self-seeding *Cornus capitata* extend the season through the summer, while providing the backdrop, and a host of subtle green delights, are bamboos and tree ferns, nothofagus and *Pinus radiata*, glossy-leaved *Gevuina avellana*, a large tree of heaven (*Ailanthus altissima*) and a magnificent tulip tree (*Liriodendron tulipifera*).

A multitude of paths snake their way between the shrubs and trees, and as you swing sideways up the combe's high flanks, the scale and drama of the terrain becomes thrillingly apparent. The reward for this slow descent is the sheltered, rocky inlet of Pudcombe Cove, and in late spring your arrival is sweetened by thickets of scented *Elaeagnus umbellata*. No lover of plants will be disappointed by this garden.

LEFT A corner of the bluebell wood where a small gate is almost hidden by the luxuriant spring growth.

RIGHT The stream in the Rill Garden. The clear water is bordered by hostas, azaleas and bluebells.

Compton Castle

MARLDON, PAIGNTON, DEVON

AREA 2.4ha (6 acres) • **SOIL** neutral/heavy loam • **ALTITUDE** 107m (350ft) **AVERAGE RAINFALL** 660mm (26in) • **AVERAGE WINTER CLIMATE** moderate

An armillary sphere in the garden commemorates the 400th anniversary of the acquisition of Newfoundland for Elizabeth I in 1583. Leading the fleet was Sir Humphrey Gilbert, half-brother to Sir Walter Raleigh, whose family lived here from the early fourteenth century to 1800, rescued it from neglect in 1930 by buying it back, and continue to reside here today.

Seafaring history pervades the house, and is a subliminal echo through the garden too. The Camelot-like assembly of high walls and towers sits at the edge of the village in a quiet combe, a couple of miles from the sea, and you enter behind a large walnut tree between the lawns of an Outer Court. The planting here is kept simple – evergreen *Magnolia grandiflora* (introduced from North America in the early eighteenth century), lavenders assembled around a stone cider press, and cordon pears on the wall of the barn, which is still used as a lambing shed for Jacob sheep.

The main garden enclosure is through a stone arch, up a flight of steps, and is being developed by the Trust and the present Mr and Mrs Geoffrey Gilbert, building on the work of Commander Walter Raleigh Gilbert, who restored the castle. Designed in formal segments, it is sandwiched between the defensive wall of the house and the rising ground of a cider-apple orchard, in which the rare cirl bunting may be spotted.

The armillary sphere terrace, the fringes of the lily pond garden below and the long pergola are the preserve of roses, which enjoy the heavy soil. The ancient soft pink Shrub rose 'Maiden's Blush' was found here in the 1930s, but to provide a long summer season it is mainly the newer varieties that hold sway – climbers such as scarlet

'Parkdirektor Riggers' and 'Danse du Feu' alternating with the pink and yellow Hybrid Tea 'Peace', white 'Iceberg' and the modern pink Shrub rose 'Sir Walter Raleigh'. Clematis and white wisteria are among the supporting cast.

The herbaceous border running below the high wall features different colour forms of shrub hibiscus, *H. syriacus*, introduced into Britain in the sixteenth century. Opposite is a small orchard of mixed apple varieties and, below a stone dais, a new knot garden, with a topiary squirrel as its centrepiece – an animal that features on the family crest and after which one of Sir Humphrey's ships was named.

Within the castle walls are further courtyards and passageways. Damp, cold and heavily shaded, they nevertheless support an impressive array of magnolias, rhododendrons and especially camellias, from the more familiar red 'Adolphe Audusson' and pink 'Lady Clare' to plants originating on Roanoke Island, North Carolina, which colonists under the direction of Raleigh attempted to settle in 1585. The colonists were not seen again, presumed killed by Indians.

ABOVE The long rose pergola is planted to provide summer-long colour.

Cotehele

ST DOMINICK, SALTASH, CORNWALL

AREA 6.9ha (17 acres) plus 4.9ha (12 acres) of orchard • SOIL acid/loam • ALTITUDE 76m (250ft) • AVERAGE RAINFALL 1,143mm (45in) • AVERAGE WINTER CLIMATE mild

'Daffodils grow in their hundreds between the well-spaced trees – simple, old varieties'

Here is an estate full of Cornish character. The approach is along narrow, plunging, high-banked lanes, affording sudden views across the Tamar Valley over the hilly expanse of Dartmoor. Below is the tidal river itself, punctuated by Cotehele Quay, once busy with traffic transporting copper and other minerals downstream to Plymouth, but now the tranquil mooring for the last of the Tamar barges, *Shamrock*. Cream teas are served in a former hostelry, the Edgcumbe Arms.

The house and its outbuildings are at the head of the wooded combe high above. In spite of the towers and battlements, they are a snug and welcoming collection of buildings, low-lying and warmly constructed of brown and grey slate. Of medieval origin, the property was remodelled and enlarged in Tudor times by Sir Richard and Sir Piers Edgcumbe, whose family were to own Cotehele estate for nearly six centuries.

The garden, divided into a series of intimate enclosures and sheltered walks, is equally inviting. An avenue of young sycamores opposite the old barn take up the colour of the walls in their clean grey trunks, and in spring this opening scene is cheered by a swathe of daffodils growing on the bank. Later in the year, there will be autumn crocuses and cyclamen flowering under the sycamores. Beyond the two cobbled courts, one with walls hung with wisterias and *Rosa bracteata* and lapped with Algerian iris, and the other flaunting myrtle and camellias, is a gateway leading into an enclosed acre of sloping meadow. Here daffodils grow in their hundreds between the well-spaced trees – simple, old varieties, in clumps that are seldom disturbed. The grass is not cut until the middle of June,

by which time orchids and other wildflowers have completed their cycle. It is a timeless picture.

A white-painted gate leads into the Upper Garden, a large enclosure of sloping lawns with, as its centrepiece, a pool of pink and white waterlilies. Scattered trees, including tree of heaven (*Ailanthus altissima*), a superb tulip tree (*Liriodendron tulipifera*) and a fine yellow-twigged ash, *Fraxinus excelsior* 'Jaspidea', preserve an informal character, while on the south side, a border of tall shrubs screens the garden from the estate cottages and the old orchard. Through a yew arch, you come into a small garden that reflects Cornwall's long history of horticultural commerce. The traditional crops – daffodils, irises, strawberries and eucalyptus – grow in a series of raised and sloping borders, and in one corner stands a replica of one of the corrugated metal packing sheds that were once a common sight in this area. Apple trees also have a long association with the Tamar Valley, and in the winter of 2007–8 the 'Mother Orchard' was planted up with 270 traditional varieties, the trees widely spaced to allow them to grow large and the grass between them managed as hay meadow.

Accompanied by a burbling rill, the Upper Garden's beds and borders are at their most colourful in summer and autumn. On one side, a striking scheme of silver and gold, designed to counteract the many overcast Cornish days, consists of cardoons, daylilies, kniphofias and an assortment of daisy-flowered plants. Elsewhere, tulips and peonies are succeeded by fuchsias, agapanthus, *Eucomis bicolor* and tender perennials, while from the cut-flower garden nearby some 30,000 flowers are harvested and dried for use in the Cotehele Christmas Garland displayed in the Great Hall.

Early in the year, as you walk back into the daffodil meadow along the top path, you will catch the scent of *Acacia pravissima*, foaming with bright yellow flowers. It vies for attention with one of the garden's young cork oaks, standing in the grass above the squat grey tower of the house. To the left, another path beckons, leading you through a gate and over parkland to the three-sided Prospect Tower and its panorama of Plymouth and the rolling fields, woods and moors of the Cornish-Devon border.

The top path now descends between camellias and aucuba, through a bowl of Japanese maples, under the drooping branches of *Erica arborea* var. *alpina*, casting vanilla scent in spring, and across the gravel drive, past crimson *Rhododendron russellianum* and a weeping silver lime (*Tilia tomentosa* 'Petiolaris') to bring you out onto the stone terraces below the east front of the house. This is the most formal part of the garden, constructed in 1862 to complement the house's rebuilt façade, but even here the character is modest and mellow, with cool pink, white and silver-leaved perennials presented

against a relaxed and varied backdrop of magnolias, white wisterias, green-tasselled *Itea ilicifolia*, a bower of *Robinia hispida* and a spectacular pink *Clematis montana* scrambling up a laurel.

The views over the stone balustrade, down into the combe and across to Calstock village and the railway viaduct, were opened up by the severe gales of January 1990. This is not the first time a storm has blasted the woods; Calstock and Cotehele were also rudely revealed to each other in 1891. But although privacy has been lost from the terraces, the gales did not disturb the sense of secrecy within the combe itself, a feeling heightened by the dark stone tunnel that serves as its entrance.

The slopes and fringe woodland, boosted by the Trust, provide the shelter required to exploit Cornwall's mild maritime climate to the full. The tree and shrub planting is exciting and diverse, but so interwoven with the native trees as to appear natural and homely. Self-sowing bluebells, primroses, foxgloves and red

campions form an unpretentious carpet, and on the shady slopes, ferns, especially lady ferns, grow in abundance.

Presiding over the valley is the handsome domed dovecote and stewpond, relics of medieval days when they would have provided meat and fish for the house. From this pond, water splashes down the combe in a series of pools and runnels, increasing the humidity and supplying damp ground for primulas, marsh marigolds, wild mimulus, *Darmera peltata* (formerly *Peltiphyllum peltatum*) and giant-leaved *Gunnera manicata*. The ornamental tree and shrub planting appears to have begun at the head of the valley in 1867, while the building of the viaduct in 1907–8 may have prompted the addition of screening conifers. Much of the present planting, however, is the work of the Trust, including the establishment of a new arboretum on the land known as Nellson's Piece.

Early in the year, rhododendrons are prominent, including large stands of *Rhododendron arboreum* and *R. Smithii* Group ('Cornish Red' as it is known in Cornwall, 'Devon Pink' over the border) and an extensive range of azaleas. But they are not grown to the exclusion of other shrubs: camellias, enkianthus, kalmias, embothriums and magnolias are also well represented, with eucryphias, hoherias, hydrangeas and Japanese maples providing later colour. Hemlocks, firs and the unusual *Sciadopitys verticillata* are among the comparatively modest conifer population. Striking an exotic note is the Chusan palm, *Trachycarpus fortunei*, which produces panicles of yellow flowers in early summer, followed by great bunches of black fruits that persist throughout the winter and spring. Towards the bottom of the combe, the vegetation reverts to native woodland and a footpath leads to Sir Richard Edgcumbe's chapel and the River Tamar.

LEFT The terrace and east front of Cotehele are the most formal parts of the garden.
ABOVE The former stew pond in the Upper Garden blooms with water lilies.

Coughton Court

ALCESTER, WARWICKSHIRE

AREA 11ha (26 acres) • SOIL alkaline/limy, gravel • ALTITUDE 61m (200ft)
AVERAGE RAINFALL 635mm (25in) • AVERAGE WINTER CLIMATE cold

In recent years, some lavish flower gardens have sprung up at Coughton (pronounced 'coaton'), instigated and designed by the Throckmorton family, who have lived here since 1409. They partner the towers and castellations of a magnificent Tudor house, rearing up beside the Alcester road across an expanse of flat parkland. Behind the house, the landscape becomes picturesque and undulating, ornamented by a lake and spliced by the River Arrow. The circuit walk takes you alongside the river, past drifts of hostas, ferns and wild garlic, via a bog garden of native marsh plants and a boardwalk fringed with bulrushes. Further upstream, you can walk across the field to a bluebell wood.

The first of the new formal gardens is directly below the house walls, where a box-edged parterre has been created around a pool of quatrefoil design. The Polyanthus rose *R.* 'Little White Pet' syn. *R.* 'White Pet' is the principal ingredient here, together with alchemilla, penstemon and, in spring, several varieties of tulip. Behind them, the evergreen climber *Clematis armandii* and evergreen shrub *Itea ilicifolia* flourish unexpectedly well in the permanent shade.

Avenues of pollarded red-twigged limes – one of them alongside a very fine dawn redwood, *Metasequoia glyptostroboides* – flank the view down the lawn to a pair of small sunken gardens, planted with a contrasting gold and silver theme. In spring, the scene is lively with the blossom of thorn and crab apple trees, and with daffodils – varieties raised by Dr Tom Throckmorton, an American relative and noted daffodil expert, being grouped in the grass around an armillary sphere.

Away to the south, the path leads to the L-shaped Walled Garden, where the main summer display takes place, and which Trust members are asked to pay a small supplement to see. Designed by Christina Williams, daughter of Clare Throckmorton, this is now a sequence of enclosures, subdivided by hedges and arbours, of exuberant and romantic character. In one area, lavenders are massed around a painted pavilion; in another, standard wisterias drip over beds of pink, white and crimson hybrid peonies. There is a fountain garden, ringed with pots of white lilies; a pair of herbaceous borders in contrasting hot and cool colours; and a seductive Rose Labyrinth, stuffed with accompanying perennials, which flaunts some 200 old and new Shrub, Climber and Rambler rose varieties. Memorable planting combinations abound. Beyond is an orchard and vegetable garden, in which numerous local varieties are cultivated, including the ancient 'Black Worcester' cooking pear.

ABOVE Lily-flowered tulips and clipped box in the Courtyard.

RIGHT Mediterranean style planting with silver santolina, verbena and kniphofia around topiary yews at The Courts.

The Courts

HOLT, BRADFORD-ON-AVON, WILTSHIRE

AREA 2.8ha (7 acres) • **SOIL** alkaline/loam • **ALTITUDE** 61m (200ft)
AVERAGE RAINFALL 762mm (30in) • **AVERAGE WINTER CLIMATE** moderate

This is a garden in the Hidcote tradition, full of charm and variety, and deserving to be far better known. The house, described by Christopher Hussey as 'an early Georgian gem', was built for one of the area's prosperous cloth manufacturers, and had a mill adjacent, powered by the stream that flows from Great Chalfield Manor. The mill was demolished in the third quarter of the nineteenth century.

The bones of the present garden were set out by Sir George Hastings, who owned The Courts between 1900 and 1910, and the design was elaborated and given its rich overlay of plants by Lady Cecilie Goff after 1921. It is a compartmented garden, not as severely delineated as Hidcote, but each section has a formal structure and its own rather imaginative blend of colours. Generally, it is a quirkier composition: Lady Cecilie loved springing surprises. You enter from the village along a walk of pleached limes (formerly of pollarded poplars), emerging opposite the east front of the house onto wide lawns, framed by assorted hedges and topiaries. Though planted symmetrically, each seems to have its own idiosyncratic bulging or lopsided shape, immediately setting the relaxed mood. Pillars and cones of common yew, fringes and slabs of green box, domes of holly and giant buns of golden yew are part of the scene, supported by a backdrop of fine trees.

Into this are inserted the self-contained planting schemes. There are hedged semi-circles of pink, lilac and white (limonium, galtonia and pink old-fashioned roses among them); a pair of blue and yellow borders featuring thalictrum, asters and achillea; a long fuchsia border, brightened with white Japanese anemones; and a small fernery. The most exciting colouring is in the Mediterranean-style walk, flanked by sentinel yews, down which scarlet, orange and pale yellow flowers (zauschneria, crocosmia, cephalaria and others) crackle among the silver mounds of santolina, artemisia and the perennial wallflower *Erysimum* 'Jacob's Jacket'. It is a superb piece of planting. All is in contrast to the pale stone of the house and its loggia, the terraces and paths (the slabs gleaned by Lady Cecilie from the demolished Devizes gaol), and the various ornaments – a large dog, a column surmounted by a Roman bust, pillars hung in vines and much else – many of the grander pieces being copied by Sir George Hastings from those at Ranelagh House, Barnes.

The greenhouse, kept frost-free and stocked with exotics like aloes, tender nerines and *Passiflora* × *exoniensis*, is similar to the pastiche Georgian orangery Sir George created at Ranelagh. And at the head of a long, straight grass walk below the house, now flanked by borders with a pink and yellow colour scheme (phlox, crinums and Japanese anemones, partnered with golden-leaved *Cornus alba* 'Spaethii' and physocarpus, and the curious evening-opening daylily, *Hemerocallis citrina*), he installed a classical temple.

We are now in the lower garden. Water sets the theme here, and at various points you cross the trickling stream by little bridges. A large rectangular pool, created by Lady Cecilie and restored by the Trust, is framed by beds of Siberian iris and dierama and covered by vast rafts of pink, crimson, yellow and white waterlilies. It lies parallel to the temple walk, and below it is the informally shaped Dye Pool, fringed with giant gunnera and other bog plants. Everywhere, there

are thickets of trees and shrubs. The range should inspire all visitors who share a heavy, limy soil, especially in autumn, when the leaf colours are quite as brilliant as those to be seen in acid woodlands. Paperbark and Nikko maples (*Acer griseum* and *A. maximowiczianum* syn. *nikoense*), *Viburnum carlesii*, cotinus and Sargent's cherry (*Prunus sargentii*) are among those contributing reds and oranges, and there are major displays from the various cultivars of guelder rose (*Viburnum opulus*), the native wayfaring tree (*V. lantana*), and the thorn *Crataegus persimilis* 'Prunifolia', all of which partner their tinted leaves with coloured fruits.

There is more drama in the arboretum, an extensive area of pasture developed by Moyra Goff in 1952, and a welcome change from the intimacy and formality of the rest of the garden. Pink-candled horse chestnuts, limes, walnuts, a fine cut-leaved beech, Turkey oak and catalpa are among the contents, with daffodils appearing beneath them in spring, followed by snakeshead fritillaries – a native plant that once carpeted many an English water meadow. The recently restored Kitchen Garden includes herb borders, an apple arch and an apple orchard framed by espaliered pears.

ABOVE Autumn reflections across the Dye Pool, interspersed with rafts of water lilies.

RIGHT Trees are complemented by formal evergreen shapes to striking sculptural effect.

Cragside

ROTHBURY, MORPETH, NORTHUMBERLAND

AREA 405ha (1,000 acres) • **SOIL** acid/sandy moorland • **ALTITUDE** 152m (500ft)
AVERAGE RAINFALL 813mm (32in) • **AVERAGE WINTER CLIMATE** cold

Here is the rugged and mystical landscape of the Gothic novel and
Wagnerian opera, a landscape of dark conifer forests, boulder-strewn
hillsides, lakes and waterfalls. The estate encompasses over 688ha
(1,700 acres), 405ha (1,000 acres) of which are owned by the Trust,
and in its midst, on a site blasted from the cliff face, stands the
massive frame of the Victorian *schloss*. It is all the work of the 1st
Lord Armstrong, inventor and armaments manufacturer, who, from
1864, began harnessing in earnest his great wealth, ingenuity and
engineering skill to create an extensive picturesque retreat out of the
empty moorland. The transformation involved much of the male
population of Rothbury and included the planting of seven million
trees and shrubs, the laying of 50km (31 miles) of road and pathway
and the digging of four large lakes.

There is no tame garden around the house. The stupendous
rockery that anchors it to the steep, west-facing slope running down
to Debdon Burn looks as if it has been created by an avalanche.
Before the Trust began its restoration, there was hardly a rock
showing; gaultheria had run rampant, and *Rhododendron ponticum*
swept in from the surrounding woods. Now, thanks partly to the
help of volunteers, the giant stones are again revealed. Alpine
and moorland plants, including saxifrages, sedums, *Hypericum
olympicum*, heathers and vacciniums, have been reintroduced into
the crevices and bays, with phormiums and hebes in the hotter
spots. A gentle transition from wilderness into garden has been

RIGHT The steep valley running down to Debdon Burn divides the garden in two,
linked only by the recently restored footbridge.

allowed by planting a range of shrubs and trees that furnish splashes of contrasting colour without being overly ornamental. These include a wide range of Hardy Hybrid rhododendrons, evergreen and deciduous azaleas, brooms, berberis and some beautiful Asian rowans, including orange-berried *Sorbus sargentiana*, pink-berried *S. hupehensis* and the seldom-seen whitebeam *S. vestita* syn. *S. cuspidata*.

This same transition takes place rather more dramatically nearer the burn. Here, on the lower banks and floor of the valley, the black woods of pines and firs break into an open arboretum of conifers. The cool, moist atmosphere promotes tremendous growth, especially in North American species, and many trees have reached champion size. There are soaring specimens of Douglas, Caucasian, and noble fir, western hemlock and Nootka cypress, and, as at Bodnant, the terrain allows you both to stand among their trunks and to view their crowns from above. Dippers and grey wagtails can often be seen braving the fast-flowing water, and beyond the arched iron footbridge the paths entice you into many more acres of wooded pleasure ground, through plantations of autumn-tinting trees, past drifts of foxgloves and rustic bridges, and on towards Tumbleton Lake, which you can now walk around.

In 1991, the Trust acquired the missing part of the picture, the terraced formal gardens, 800m (½ mile) from the house, the restoration of which is almost complete. The Orchard House,

with its quirky system of turntables for rotating the pots in order to promote balanced growth, has survived intact and is once again filled with figs, grapes, peaches, citrus and other fruits. Early crops of vegetables are cultivated in front of it, with other produce such as tomatoes and broad beans grown in pots nearby. Other houses have disappeared, but exotic-looking hardy plants and summer bedding are being cleverly used to convey their former character. *Lobelia tupa* is a feature in what was once the Palm House; unusual shrubs grow in the Display House; and an assortment of hardy begonias and crested and fancy ferns filter in between the boulders in the Temperate Ferneries.

A display of Victorian carpet bedding – one of the most intricate examples in the Trust's gardens – is part of the colourful fringe to the lawns, which also includes a walk of double-flowered dahlias. The Italian Terrace has also been restored: centred on a quatrefoil pool and water spray, the borders have been replanted with striking foliage, scented flowers, and plants considered half-hardy in Victorian times, such as fuchsias, nerines and kniphofias. The fine clematis collection mentioned in the *Gardener's Chronicle* of 1880 has also been reassembled. It is all in striking contrast to the rest of this wild estate.

ABOVE Fruit trees and vegetables line the shelves in the greenhouse at Cragside. They are grown in large pots before being planted out on the estate.

Croft Castle

LEOMINSTER, HEREFORDSHIRE

AREA 2ha (5 acres) • SOIL lime-free/light loam • ALTITUDE 167m (550ft)
AVERAGE RAINFALL 635mm (25in) • AVERAGE WINTER CLIMATE cold

Far-reaching views over unspoilt border countryside, ancient trees and a rare taste of the Picturesque phase of English landscaping are the principal draws to this remote property. The fortress of grey-brown limestone, built some time around the fifteenth century, stands on a ridge above parkland and woods, with a prospect south to the Black Mountains. You climb to the castle under avenues of great oaks and young beeches, and there are further avenues off to the west, which you can trudge to across the park – passing more venerable oaks on your way, including one with reputedly the largest girth in the country.

The celebrated avenue of sweet chestnuts is some distance away and something of a mystery. Some of the trees are huge, gnarled and with characteristic fissured, twisted trunks. They are arranged in one and then three ranks over a distance of 800m (½ mile), and, according to legend, represent battle lines of the Spanish Armada. Otherwise, the avenues are presumed to be part of the larger formal composition of garden and park which, as in so many properties, was swept away in the eighteenth century. However, at Croft the landscape that replaced it was not flowing parkland adorned with Neo-classical temples, but a more rugged, romantic style as championed by Richard Payne Knight, who may have tendered advice here.

You taste it at the head of the oak avenue, where you are met by a neo-medieval curtain wall; around the castle, Gothicised inside and out, and fringed by a battlemented terrace wall; and in the narrow Fish Pool Valley that runs beside the approach drive. This is a steep-sided glen, heavily wooded with ash, oak, birch, alder, poplar

and willow, its stream dammed to form a chain of nine ponds, and appointed with a rough stone pump house and grotto. Currently under restoration, it is a mysterious and tranquil place, echoing to the sounds of songbirds and woodpeckers; goshawks, which can be almost buzzard-sized, are also seen here.

Over the centuries, the fortress has evolved into a welcoming home, and there are many eruptions of flowers to soften the impact. The giant white Rambler roses, *Rosa filipes* 'Kiftsgate' and *R. brunonii* 'La Mortola', cloak the curtain wall, and as you continue down the curving drive, you pass between a border of rhododendrons and other shrubs and a lawn where pretty primroses and daffodils appear around the boles of the trees in spring, followed by elegant cyclamen in late summer.

The castle walls shelter roses, clematis and a variety of flowering foliage and flowering shrubs, including aralia, *Itea ilicifolia* and purple smoke bush, *Cotinus coggygria* (strikingly partnered with blue-leaved *Kniphofia caulescens*). The small-flowered pink nerine, *N. flexuosa*, is among the bulbs and perennials in the small secret garden below the west wall; given protection from the wind, this is a fairly benign climate, with good frost drainage. There are also beds of roses in front of the adjacent St Michael's church, which pre-dates the castle, and a 1.2ha (3 acre) walled flower garden and vineyard, owned and developed by the Croft family, who are still in residence. Myriad house martins swoop about the turrets and battlements in summer.

ABOVE Purple wallflower and variegated comfrey among a medley of flowers in the Walled Garden.

Croome

HIGH GREEN, SEVERN STOKE, WORCESTERSHIRE

AREA 295ha (730 acres) • SOIL neutral/silty loam, some clay • ALTITUDE 20–33m (65–108ft)
AVERAGE RAINFALL 635mmn (25in) • AVERAGE WINTER CLIMATE moderate

From high ground beside the church of St Mary Magdalene, you look down onto a wide bowl of open park and farmland, scattered with trees. A river curls across the valley, leading the eye to the presiding ornament, a large, pale Palladian house. It is an uncluttered scene, rising in the middle distance into a ring of hills. The confident hand of Lancelot 'Capability' Brown is unmistakable. Brown was still at Stowe, and just establishing an independent design practice, when he was approached by George William Coventry, later 6th Earl, to undertake the grand and expensive transformation of Croome. He worked here for over 30 years, intensively between 1751–6 and 1762–6. It was his first complete landscape, and cemented his reputation, while Croome itself became hugely influential as the first landscape in which the existing topography was harnessed and perfected in the new 'natural' style.

However important Croome has been in the history of gardening, it has not been spared from indignity. In the 1940s there was an RAF base here, with attendant runways; in 1948 the house was sold off; and in 1962 the M5 motorway sliced through the estate. Over the years, grazed parkland turned into arable farmland, the river silted up, and there was even a proposal for a golf course. So the Trust, which acquired the heart of the park in 1996 with the help of a grant from the Heritage Lottery Fund, has embarked upon a major restoration project. While the buildings and contours are emerging again in pristine order, the extensive replanting now gives the sense of a landscape in the making, much as it was 250 years ago

– the accuracy of the project assisted by comprehensive historical records.

The Gothic exterior of the church, like the exterior of the house itself, was designed by Brown, and both form part of the succession of architectural eye-catchers, changing views and set-piece scenes that are revealed on the circuit tour. There was no river here before the 1740s. This was one of Lord Coventry's first projects, which he undertook with advice from a friend, the architect and landscape gardener Sanderson Miller, before Brown's arrival. Brown curved it – echoing the course of the River Severn on the boundary of the estate – and extended it into a lake, as well as completing the extensive network of drains required to convert the marshy ground into fine grassland.

Following the paths down the hill, you exchange the unimpeded prospect of the house – to which the grass is intended to flow seamlessly, across an unusual inward-facing ha-ha – for meandering shrubberies. By the church, the shrubbery is sombre and melancholy, thick with evergreens such as box, yew, privet and ruscus growing under pines and ash; concealed among them is a thatched ice-house. But the area is carpeted with snowdrops and bluebells early in the year, and elsewhere, the shrubberies are cheery with shrub roses, philadelphus and much else besides, for Croome was at the forefront of new plant introductions in the eighteenth century, its collection said to be rivalled only by Kew's. Some of the most prized

BELOW The statue of Sabrina in the Grotto.

RIGHT The lake at Croome has been extensively dredged as part of the ongoing restoration of the landscape.

plants would have been grown in the Home Shrubbery near the house, which now sports young catalpa, mulberries, hollies and viburnums.

Continuing downhill, you are led through a long mingled thicket, called the Evergreen Shrubbery, which is filled with shrubs for winter interest, including daphne, rosemary, variegated holly, viburnum, and wintersweet – each variety often represented by a single specimen, which is very strange to modern eyes. A restored statue of Pan, dating from about 1800, presides over a glade where snakeshead fritillaries, wild tulips, anemones and dog's tooth violets are naturalised, and here and there are small island beds, or flowering studs, of shrubs, roses, and herbaceous plants such as monkshood, astrantia, verbena, daylilies and cardoons.

The route now takes you to the magnificent Temple Greenhouse, designed by Robert Adam, who joined Brown in producing buildings and interiors for Lord Coventry after 1760. Protected by glass in winter and warmed by a furnace, it provided the opportunity to display a rich assortment of tender plants behind its Doric portico, and is again home to plants such as agapanthus, oleander, agaves and olives. After this diversion, the path continues under oaks and chestnuts, past a Coade stone statue of a druid and under a stone bridge – designed by Brown and sporting the Coade stone heads of river gods between vermiculated decoration

– to the lake. Here, a grotto, also designed by Brown, is encrusted with shells, fossils and crystals, and features Sabrina, goddess of the Severn, pouring water from her urn. This stands in contrast to Adam's elegant temple, presiding over one of the lake's two islands, supported by Corinthian columns and decorated with Coade stone reliefs. Collections of trees including planes, thorns and cedars of Lebanon provide the sylvan setting.

A further array of architectural eye-catchers draws the eye into the wider reaches of the park and landscape, blending the garden with the countryside and rewarding the eighteenth-century visitor who took the longer tour. To the south, 1.6km (1 mile) away, is Dunstall Castle, built by Adam as a Gothic ruin, while another sham castle, Pirton Castle, to the north and the Panorama Tower to the west were completed some years later by James Wyatt. The Rotunda, sitting on high ground close to the house and ringed by 250-year-old cedars, offers a fine view out, and from the windows of the house itself you get a prospect of the newly rebuilt Chinese bridge spanning the river.

The debt owed to Brown is expressed in the monument by the lake, erected by Lord Coventry some years after Brown's death in 1783, which bears the dedication 'To the Memory of Lancelot Brown Who by the powers of His inimitable and creative genius formed this garden scene Out of a morass'.

ABOVE The lakeside urn designed by Robert Adam.

Dudmaston

QUATT, BRIDGNORTH, SHROPSHIRE

AREA 3.6ha (9 acres) • SOIL acid/sand • ALTITUDE 76m (250ft) • AVERAGE RAINFALL 889mm (35in) • AVERAGE WINTER CLIMATE cold

A short walk across the park from the mansion at Dudmaston, the sheep-grazed pasture drops into a wooded dell. It is a dark place, cool, green, and silent but for the birdsong and the splash of water at the bottom of the high-sided banks. You descend, cross the stream and climb, your nose treated to the damp scents of ferns and moss and your eyes to the beauty of the trees and the drama of the rock, until finally you emerge into daylight to be greeted by a long sheet of still water, edged by trees, wildflowers and rafts of waterlilies.

This valley wilderness, known as the Dingle, is a romantic piece of late eighteenth-century landscaping, and of considerable interest to garden historians as the best surviving example of the Picturesque style of William Shenstone. It is the creation of one of his former gardeners, Walter Wood, in collaboration with his employers at Dudmaston, William and Frances Whitmore, and it reflects closely Shenstone's influential ideas that a landscape should offer 'scenes of grandeur, beauty or variety' and that, to paraphrase his friend Dr Johnson, its walks should be entangled and its water winding.

By contrast, the William and Mary hall has a deliciously lush setting of grass, woods, hills and water. The terraces connecting the house to the Big Pool, the largest of the string of lakes, were constructed soon after 1816 by Whitmore's son, William Wolryche Whitmore, and marked the arrival of more formal gardening at Dudmaston. His gravel paths and island beds were later grassed over, but the flowers are preserved around the brewhouse and the small paved terrace beside the house, added in the 1920s. Three of

the most eye-catching plants here were introduced after 1952 by Lady Labouchère: daisy-like *Erigeron karvinskianus*, which has now extensively colonised the cracks between paving slabs and steps, and two opulent roses, the cream 'Lorenzo Pahissa' and the bright pink 'Gava', brought from Spain where Sir George Labouchère was the British Ambassador.

The prominent outcrop of red sandstone nearby – a rugged feature that must have delighted his parents – was tamed by William Wolryche Whitmore with walls and steps. Topped by a big cedar and a stand of amelanchiers, it is now home to a variety of rock plants, including helianthemums and broom. The American Garden to the east of the house, a popular feature in gardens of the time, was also his creation, though its design has since been made less formal and the planting extended. *Kalmia latifolia* and *K. angustifolia* thrive on the sandy soil here, together with magnolias, Japanese cherries, azaleas and old hybrid rhododendrons.

Of particular interest in the house is the large collection of botanical art, ranging from work by P.J. Redouté to John Nash, collected by Lady Labouchère. Outdoors, Sir George introduced some fine modern sculpture, including the abstract *Watcher* beside the Big Pool, and the dynamic steel gates near the stable block, where a new vista has recently been opened up. Thus Dudmaston enriches itself from another passing century.

ABOVE The west front of the house can be viewed from across the lake.

Dunham Massey

ALTRINCHAM, CHESHIRE

AREA 10ha (25 acres) • **SOIL** severely acid/loamy sand • **ALTITUDE** 25m (82ft)
AVERAGE RAINFALL 889mm (35in) • **AVERAGE WINTER CLIMATE** mild to moderate

Thanks to the bequest of the 10th Earl of Stamford, one of the most generous in the Trust's history, these 1,214ha (3,000 acres) of farmland and woods will be a permanent green oasis between the conurbations of Manchester and Liverpool. At their heart is a predominantly early eighteenth-century brick mansion, tactfully described by the landscape architect Dame Sylvia Crowe as one of 'beautifully proportioned austerity', richly planted gardens and a wooded park of great historic and scientific interest.

Dating back to medieval times and still roamed by a large herd of fallow deer, the park was formalised by George Booth, 2nd Earl of Warrington, in the fashionable French style. The first avenues were already installed by 1697, and the final, all-embracing landscape of radiating rides, allées, circular, triangular and oval plantations, canals, formal ponds and architectural eye-catchers (the whole bounded by brick wall) is depicted in the series of fine bird's-eye paintings by John Harris the Younger hanging in the Great Gallery; they date from about 1750. Very few such landscapes survived the change in eighteenth-century taste towards a more flowing, naturalistic composition, but at Dunham this informal style was practised in a new park to the east, leaving much of the old framework intact. The Trust has now repaired and replanted a number of these tree lines, so that from the south front of the house you can have the rare prospect of a triple row of lime trees either side of the forecourt, leading to a grand *patte d'oie* (goose foot) of six long avenues centred on a grass semi-circle.

An obelisk, dating from 1714, survives as a focal point for one of these. It is the only ornamental monument to remain, but as you explore the park, you come upon other handsome functional buildings, notably a two-tiered, brick deer barn. The garden also has its ancient features. Your first view of the house is across the moat belonging to the previous medieval and Elizabethan house. It appears as a broad, lake-like swathe of water, curving around the north and west walls. In one direction, the water runs from the garden as a narrow canal, while in the other, a channel leads past the cupola of the stables and coach house to a seventeenth-century saw-mill. Just to the side of the house, a semi-circle of ground extends into the lake, and here, behind the trees, are the remains of a mount. The core may be Norman, but it was built up in the Elizabethan period to form a garden vantage point, a favourite feature, complete with circling terraces and a crowning pavilion; the garden then extended to the west of the house, where the service range now stands. The mount survives today as a mysterious hummock of grass under a grove of robinias. The remainder of the garden is, likewise, many-layered, thoroughly restored after years of gradual and almost terminal decline to convey the pristine flavour of a Victorian pleasure ground, but one founded on a late eighteenth-century layout of meandering lawns and shrubberies, and including some formal Edwardian touches and inspired contemporary planting.

You enter through a slice of woodland, brought into the garden in the last century and bordered by a stream. This area was

totally overgrown in 1976, but clearance revealed some good trees, including two forms of sycamore, the rare *Acer pseudoplatanus* 'Corstorphinense', and 'Brilliantissimum' with eye-catching shrimp-pink leaves in spring. Moisture-loving perennials such as persicaria, shuttlecock fern and a mesmerising display of the blue Himalayan poppy, *Meconopsis × sheldonii*, in an intense turquoise form, appear in drifts above the water, and there is a good stand of the giant lily, *Cardiocrinum giganteum*.

Since 2007, the plant display here has been embellished significantly by the additional 2.8ha (7 acres) that have been carved from the overgrown former pony paddock and turned into Britain's largest winter garden. Meandering paths take you past a meadow of blue-flowered bulbs including chionodoxas, scillas, crocus and the dwarf iris 'Harmony' and lead you on between carpets of other

bulbs, such as daffodils, muscari, cyclamen and species tulips, all in myriad forms. There is a huge range of snowdrops, with a large number of additional bulbs planted annually. These are joined by hellebores, pulmonarias and epimediums; trees and shrubs offering handsome winter barks, such as snakebark maples, willows, birches and dogwoods; winter flowers such as cherries and camellias; and winter fruits such as crab apples. There are scents from sarcococca, viburnums, daphnes and wintersweet, and variegated foliage from hollies and eleagnus. The season begins in autumn with the tinting leaves of Japanese maples, amelanchiers and cercidiphyllum (which turns pink here) and the berries of rowans, and it extends well into spring with magnolias and rhododendrons.

ABOVE A sea of bluebells surges under the foliage of rheum and chestnut trees.

The acid sandy soil and high water table make good azalea ground, and those in the woods here belong to a notable strain, being seedlings raised by an amateur Cheshire-born plantsman, Denny Pratt. His main purpose was to carry the colour and scent of the tribe into midsummer by crossing various Knap Hill azaleas with the late-flowering American species *RR. viscosum, arborescens, prunifolium* and *bakeri*; seedlings were also produced from *R. atlanticum*, and from crossing *R. occidentale* with the common yellow azalea, *R. luteum*. So far, only a few have been named and widely propagated – 'Summer Fragrance' and 'Anneke' being the best known – but a June visit to Dunham is a revelation.

Hardy hydrangeas are also well represented here, with various forms of white-flowered *H. heteromalla* and *H. arborescens*, and the large, felted-leaved *H. aspera*, growing on the wood's fringe with the contrasting foliage of bamboos and grasses. Others, forms of *H. serrata* – more tolerant than the common lacecaps of the late frosts to which the garden is prone – grow in the dappled shrubbery along the boundary wall, with lilies, *Rhododendron yakushimanum* and a collection of skimmias.

You then emerge into spacious open lawn, studded with large specimen trees such as mature Lucombe, cork and red oaks; beside the house, a tall swamp cypress; and elsewhere, rarities such as tropical-looking (though bone hardy) *Magnolia tripetala*. Further plant riches are revealed as you break through the shrubbery, following a meandering grass path between birch and purple beech, north to the canal. First you pass low beds of *Geranium macrorrhizum*, bergenia, tiarella, iris, astrantia and other ground-cover subjects – the pastel schemes finely tuned for textural contrast – and then, on the sunny banks by the canal itself (cleared and rebuilt by the Trust), there are lush waterside plantings; the panther lily, *Lilium pardalinum*, does especially well here, the orange Turk's cap flowers leaping out of the borders in high summer, and there is a memorable leaf partnership between two invasive colonisers, the purplish hearts of pink *Clerodendrum bungei* and the grey, feathery foliage of the Californian tree poppy, *Romneya coulteri*.

The main lawn, however, also has architectural attractions. Tucked into the shrubbery is an early nineteenth-century rustic arbour, made of robinia bark, and a fine eighteenth-century orangery. In the Edwardian era, the orangery was incorporated into elaborate formal gardens, set out when the house was restored. These had mostly fallen into disrepair during the Second World War and were removed afterwards, but traces do remain. The grove of purple beeches evolved from hedges that once enclosed the rose garden.

This has recently been re-created, not as a copy of the 19th-century original but drawing inspiration from it. Some 160 rose varieties, including soft pink 'Dunham Massey', have been arranged as a vibrant and scented colour wheel around an airy central rotunda, accompanied by lavenders and other nectar-rich perennials (there are bee hives nearby).

A small parterre of 1905 lies between the north front and the lake, contained by hedges of golden yew and coloured with spring- and summer-bedding schemes on a yellow and blue theme. Permanent structure comes from short, clipped evergreen domes – not of box, but, interestingly, of an unusual bushy oak, *Quercus phillyreoides*. Iron railings give an open view across the water down the north avenue into the park, and if you penetrate it, you will find a long line of dogs' graves, beginning with that of a pug, Old Vertue, dated 1702; his portrait, by Knyff, hangs in the house.

Below the east front, there are blowsy borders, planted in dark rich shades to combat the strength of the red brick; they include salvias, dahlias, delphiniums and daylilies, with the grey-bloomed Dusty Miller vine, *Vitis vinifera* 'Incana', as a backing. Within the house, you come upon a courtyard hung with climbing plants and set around a central fountain.

ABOVE Skunk cabbage and other leafy plants border the canal.
RIGHT Dahlias in the walled Dream Garden at Dunster Castle.

Dunster Castle
and Gardens

DUNSTER, MINEHEAD, SOMERSET

AREA 6.9ha (17 acres) within parkland • SOIL acid to alkaline/sandy loam

ALTITUDE 0–85m (0–280ft) • AVERAGE RAINFALL 838mm (33in)

• AVERAGE WINTER CLIMATE mild to moderate

The picturesque vision that greets you from the Taunton to Minehead road is, in large part, a Victorian fantasy. There has been a castle on this precipitous outcrop of rock since Saxon times, when the sea, now 1.6km (1 mile) away, lapped the base of the hill. But in 1617 a mansion was built within the fortifications, and by the end of the Civil War, when Dunster was besieged for 160 days, little of the castle, though a surprising amount of the house, remained. The present assembly of warm sandstone towers, turrets and battlements was grafted onto the Jacobean mansion by Anthony Salvin between 1868 and 1872.

The slopes that link the water meadows to the castle shelter a wealth of plants. They were already thickly wooded by 1733, and by 1830 evergreens and flowering shrubs had joined the company. This planting has been considerably enriched both by the Luttrell family and latterly by the Trust. The climate here is windy but very mild, offering scope for adventurous gardening. Furthermore, the hill provides slopes facing in every direction, encompassing a range of habitats from sun-baked terrace to moist, shady dell.

This potential has long been exploited on the South Terrace beside the castle, where a row of tall Chusan palms strike the subtropical note much enjoyed by the Victorians. New plantings of agapanthus, eucomis, cannas, bananas and alocasias provide a supporting cast and, to cap them all, a lemon tree grows by the castle wall. This celebrated plant, guaranteed to astonish all who see it, is protected in winter by a cold frame, and was already well established by 1830.

A small, bow-fronted conservatory, refurbished and replanted by the Trust, connects with the Drawing Room and Library. This building, with its cool green and Indian red colours, is as redolent of the Victorian age as anything at Dunster. A variety of pot plants jostle on stands and clothe the back wall.

Out on the slopes, the mild climate has promoted some very bold effects, and as you walk along the labyrinth of paths and drives that spiral their way steeply up the hill, your eyes will frequently be on stalks. This is not from encountering exotic plants of giant height, for the tree cover is essentially native, but from meeting shrubs that you are used to seeing in ones and twos luxuriating in monstrous drifts. *Viburnum tinus* has colonised freely to envelop huge chunks of shady slope; philadelphus, spurge laurel and common laurel, periwinkle and *Rubus tricolor* have spread likewise. On the sunnier banks, hypericum and buddleja have taken control of sizeable areas, together with self-sowing holm oaks. Accompanying these are massive groupings of, among many others, *Brachyglottis* (formerly Senecio) 'Sunshine', hydrangeas, escallonias, deutzias, *Lonicera syringantha*, yew, fuchsia, ivy and Virginia creeper. On the southern side is an entire wood of strawberry trees (*Arbutus unedo*). This is ground-cover planting on the largest scale.

At the bottom of the hill, the River Avill, a winding walk, an old mill, a rustic Lovers' Bridge and a rocky cascade provide the picturesque setting for a more intricate garden. Here there is moisture and shelter enough for a full-blooded plantsman's paradise,

in which *Bupleurum fruticosum*, rhododendrons, azaleas, camellias, eucryphias and large-leaved hydrangeas grow in the company of shuttlecock ferns, hostas and giant-leaved *Gunnera manicata*. Specimen trees, including wellingtonias, cryptomerias, magnolias, styrax and a large handkerchief tree (*Davidia involucrata*) add to the scene, and a *Celastrus orbiculatus*, spectacular in autumn, scrambles to quite a height up into the canopy of its host.

In recent years a winter border has been added near the garden's main entrance, featuring shrubs with coloured stems or attractive winter flowers, berries and leaves, set among drifts of bulbs. The walled Dream Garden, overlooking the village church and previously used as a nursery, is currently undergoing a major restoration, taking it back to the original parterre design that was created by Alys Luttrell and landscaped by Treseders' Nurseries of Truro in the 1920s. Its peak season comes in summer and early autumn, when it stages a

tremendous show of dahlias together with cottage garden perennials and cut flowers across numerous large and small, formal and informal beds of assorted linear and circular shapes. The box edging to the beds is being added gradually, as cuttings are raised.

I have not mentioned the views out over the countryside, which are among the chief rewards for making the ascent to the castle. They encompass moorland, hills, deer park and sea, and, at the foot of the hill, the cluster of Dunster village. From the keep they are panoramic, vying for attention with the myrtles, pittosporums, nandinas, *Acca sellowiana* syn. *Feijoa sellowiana*, aralias, abelias and romneyas that grow on the tor's windy summit.

ABOVE Dahlias and cosmos in the Dream Garden with the tower of St George's church behind.

Dyffryn Gardens

ST NICHOLAS, VALE OF GLAMORGAN

AREA 22ha (55 acres) • SOIL acid loamy clay • ALTITUDE 52m (170ft) • AVERAGE RAINFALL 1,000–1,250mm (32–49in) • AVERAGE WINTER CLIMATE wet and mild

'We felt at liberty to indulge in every phase of garden design which the site and my client's catholic views suggested,' wrote the designer Thomas Mawson. His client was Reginald Cory, one of the early 20th century's leading amateur gardeners, and together they transformed a staggering 22.25 ha (55 acres) of secluded Welsh valley into a landscape of lawns, an arboretum, pools, terraces, outdoor rooms and architectural flights of fancy, overlaid with most eclectic and expansive planting. Newly acquired by the Trust, Dyffryn Gardens are once again on their way to becoming a major horticultural showcase.

The estate, a few miles from the sea, was bought by John Cory, a wealthy local colliery and ship owner, in 1891. After having the house remodelled and enlarged into the present mansion, he turned his attention to the grounds, retaining the existing walled kitchen gardens and wooded pleasure ground to the sides of the house, but adding a balustraded terrace and sunken tennis lawn to the front and creating a small lake in the park beyond.

Meanwhile, his son Reginald had been developing a deep interest in both architecture and plants, much inspired by the Botanic Garden in Cambridge, where he had gone to read law, and much encouraged by his supportive parents. Perhaps it was he who suggested Thomas Mawson to his father, initially to design a model village on the edge of the estate (which was only partly realised) and then, in 1903–4, to produce a plan for their substantial Dyffryn gardens.

By this time, Mawson was well established. His Windermere landscaping business was a large nationwide practice, with a string of prestigious newly moneyed clients. He had also published his landmark book, *The Art and Craft of Garden Making*, in 1900. This featured many of his own projects (a later edition would include Dyffryn) and extolled his favoured approaches to formal design: strong architectural structure (often with decorative, grand or even grandiose detailing), axial lines, and compartmented, patterned spaces. These elements were to be the basis for Dyffryn too, but with the scale and intricacy of the design heavily influenced by Reginald Cory.

Overly attentive clients can be an irritant to designers, but here the two protagonists developed great mutual respect, even travelling to southern Europe together to gather ideas. 'Mr Reginald Cory is a typical example of the English enthusiast for horticulture and arboriculture at its best,' Mawson wrote. Indeed, Cory's expertise – and clearly very personable, if private, character – would later take him deep into the upper echelons of gardening society and onto the Council of the Royal Horticultural Society. The Reginald Cory Memorial Cup is still presented annually by the RHS to the grower of the best new hybrid plant.

That Dyffryn's gardens have survived to this day so remarkably intact is thanks first to their falling into the benign ownership of Sir Cennydd Traherne, who remained resident on a neighbouring estate, and latterly into the care of the Vale of Glamorgan Council, which applied successfully for substantial Heritage Lottery grants to repair and restore their fabric. In 2013, the Trust took over the stewardship with a 50-year lease from the Council, and layer by layer the work is continuing and the planting is being enriched.

Entering through the new Visitor Centre brings an immediate enticement up the slope and through the limestone fernery into the 8.9 ha (22 acre) Arboretum. Groves of old yews and scattered native trees – including the remnant of a circle of oaks and a fastigiate hornbeam of breathtaking size and spread – pre-date the Corys, and are a reminder of the former wooded pleasure grounds, which Reginald Cory developed first into a nursery area for trees and later absorbed into the main garden.

As you walk along the mown grass paths – bordered by sheets of daffodils and chionodoxa, and here and there by patches of ancient wildflower meadow, rich in orchids and butterflies – you are met by a succession of Cory's more exotic specimens, many now of champion stature. Among them are a wonderful *Magnolia × veitchii* and cucumber tree, *M. acuminata* var. *subcordata*, a Chinese elm, *Ulmus parvifolia*, and a splendid paperbark maple, *Acer griseum*. This

last came from seed collected in China by Ernest Wilson in 1901, and is accompanied by a host of younger paperbark maples, planted by the Council together with collections of hawthorn and pear to enhance the middle storey. Between 1917 and 1927, Reginald Cory sponsored plant-hunting expeditions to China by George Forrest and to Chile by Harold Comber, sharing in the spoils on their return.

Along the western edge of the Arboretum and its rockery spur, crowned by a black pine and matted with dianthus, pulsatillas and other alpines, are wide views over the house and its ocean of lawn. Mawson proposed formal gardens on both sides of the house, but the Corys decided to keep the drive and entrance approach contrastingly simple, as parkland, and to focus their energies on the south front. Here, Mawson set out his great lawn, 'the object being to gain a sense of scale, a restful base to the house and a compensating expanse of view from the principal rooms, to make up for the lack of more distant landscape views,' he explained. 'To secure variety, we formed a long central canal and lily pond, extending from the second balustrade to a small lake, to receive which we made use of a natural depression. The end of this canal is to be completed in due course by the erection of a water pavilion overlooking the lake.'

This enlarged lake proved disastrous, the restriction to the water flow by the dam causing serious flooding in the house's cellars, and it was abandoned and drained soon after it was finished in the early 1920s. (Dyffryn's high water table continues to cause periodic floods, as well as making the grounds an ideal habitat for great crested newts). The water pavilion was also never built. So, the canal vista did end in rather an anticlimax. In a bold gesture, the Council subsequently addressed this by creating a vine walk on the cross axis, consisting of a pair of small pavilions and a vine-clad colonnade. The empty lake area beyond still awaits an imaginative solution.

The surrounding trees, and the specimens on the lawns themselves – among them limes, walnuts, copper beeches and a venerable Lucombe oak – have now grown up to create a handsome, self-contained setting for Mawson's canal garden. From the house's upper terrace, you look down on it over lines of Irish yews – two of them, in a quirky Mawson detail, sprouting golden yew centres to create 'torches' – while under and around the house itself, in both beds and containers, are elaborate and ever-changing bedding displays, centred in spring on hyacinths, forget-me-nots, pansies and tulips of every hue, and in summer on dahlias, cordylines and various tender exotics. There is also a swashbuckling succulent border, bristling with agaves and barrel cactus, purple-leaved aeoniums and blue-leaved echeverias.

Experimental and ever-changing horticulture was a hallmark of Reginald Cory's garden, and he had a particular penchant for the new and the bold. Dahlias were a passion, and in 1913–4 he and his head gardener, Arthur Cobb, conducted national trials at Dyffryn which involved growing some 1,000 varieties. He also brought interesting and exotic plants back from his travels, most notably in 1927, when he went plant-hunting in South Africa, accompanied by, among others, Lawrence Johnston of Hidcote.

In its evocations of the past, the Trust is assisted by black-and-white photographs taken by Neame Roff in 1910 and 1920 and, more particularly, by a series of vibrant watercolours painted in 1923 by Edith Adie, which present luxuriant and romantic scenes of foaming roses and dripping wisteria, borders and pots overflowing with floral delights, peacocks strutting through yew arches and white doves drinking from fountains. Sadly and surprisingly, Cory instructed that other garden records in his possession were to be destroyed on his death in 1934. His large horticultural library was given to the Royal Horticultural Society.

West of the house you plunge into a veritable maze of garden rooms. At their head, beside the bothy, are the old walled kitchen gardens (perhaps dating back as far as the mid 17th century), together spanning around 0.5 ha (1.25 acres) and each with a central dipping pond. As in the Corys' day, the smaller garden is filled with soft fruit, including cordon apples, currants, rhubarb and strawberries, and the larger garden sports an array of vegetables from asparagus to globe artichokes. But these were always decorative gardens too, and to complement the produce are banks of sweet peas and beds of flowers for both eating and cutting, while along the entire back wall of the larger garden is a compartmented glasshouse. This impressive structure was built by the Council in 2011 to evoke the range in which Reginald Cory grew his collections of orchids, palms, ferns, hippeastrums and pelargoniums, and it incorporates a vine house, a central landscaped cactus display, and a tropical house full of orchid curiosities.

Below the walled gardens' south wall – where there is the architectural flourish of a little stone-arched Italian terrace – are a pair of herbaceous borders of stupendous length and richly mingled colours. Among the company are daylilies and peonies, phlox and

ABOVE The herbaceous border with its rose-covered arches in July.

geraniums, agapanthus and shasta daisies, while the walls are cloaked with unusual shrubs and curtains of climbers including aristolochia, loquat, fiery campsis and white crinodendron. Mawson's decorative touch is the web of ironwork arches that frame the borders, which explode with roses of bright and dashing pink hue such as 'Blush Rambler' and 'American Pillar'. In full summer bloom, it all makes for a heady, redolently Edwardian picture.

From here you descend into a series of more recently conceived gardens: a courtyard, which in the Corys' time was a Dutch garden but which is now cushioned in Mediterranean sub-shrubs – silvery lavenders, santolinas and helichrysums – partnered with dianthus and a forest of irises; a mixed border themed by the Trust to reflect the collecting of Ernest Wilson and other plant hunters; a Physic Garden with drifts of medicinal and edible herbs (it is unclear what Cory grew in this area); and a kaleidoscope of annual native wildflowers, backed by impressive lime, gingko and dawn redwood trees (*Metasequoia glyptostroboides*).

Now come Mawson and Cory's themed architectural rooms: a paved and stepped Theatre Garden, with stage wings of yew, which was built to be a setting for Reginald's collection of bonsai, then the best in Britain (since it featured a number of Japanese maples, and was accompanied by much Japanese ornament, together with large wisterias, this area was also known as the Japanese Garden); a yew-walled Cloister Garden; a Bathing or Reflecting Pool Garden, its large water tank encased within a stone terrace and paths adorned with more bonsai, purple Japanese maples and standard white wisterias; a Paved Court, set out below a latticed brick balustrade with canopied pool, its paths edged in lollipops of privet and a lavish confection of hot-coloured flowers including tulips and crown imperials for spring and fuchsias, marigolds, lilies and heliotropes for summer; and, perhaps the *pièce de résistance*, the Pompeiian Garden, directly inspired by Mawson and Cory's trip to Italy, which conjures up the fantasy of a Roman garden with colonnades, loggia, pedimented temple and central fountain pool, but one richly adorned with roses, wisteria, clematis and cascades of annuals, and with a viewing platform to savour it all from above.

This last garden bears a date of 1909. By 1911, some 12.14 ha (30 acres) of the garden are thought to have been developed. After the interruption of the War, Reginald Cory continued expanding and enhancing the grounds until his marriage in 1930, when he moved to Wareham in Dorset, Dyffryn having been left to his older sister Florence on the death of his father.

From here, you saunter on into a circular rose garden, its assorted colours displayed in a box-edged pattern of wedge-shaped beds; a large and meandering tree and shrub garden, with maples, dogwoods, eucryphias, magnolias, standard wisterias, and tall Trachycarpus palms among its highlights; a Lavender Court, framed by a white trelliswork screen, Italianate arched walls and a viewing tower of warm brick, and incorporating small waterlily pools which house the overflow of Cory's big waterlily collection in the canal; a lily allée; and a heart-shaped garden, pumped with red dahlias in summer, which was created possibly as a memorial following the First World War.

'It is true there are startling contrasts and surprises, but as each garden is enclosed in its own screen or architecture or foliage, it seldom clashes with its neighbour,' declared Mawson. This design of planted rooms and architecturally themed spaces invites comparison with Biddulph Grange and, of course, Lawrence Johnston's Hidcote that was being created at much the same time. But with its contrasts of scale and horticultural intricacy, its elements of grandeur and Italianate/Beaux Arts flourishes, its avoidance of Arts and Crafts rusticity and of Jekyll-inspired colour scheming, Dyffryn sets its own mood. It is fascinating both as one of the best-surviving works of a prominent garden designer and as an insight into the world of an idiosyncratic and clearly insatiable plantsman.

ABOVE Dianthus and sedums in the Rockery at Dyffryn.

Dyrham Park

DYRHAM, BATH, GLOUCESTERSHIRE

AREA 2.4ha (6 acres) within parkland • SOIL alkaline/sand, loam • ALTITUDE 137m (450ft)
AVERAGE RAINFALL 762mm (30in) • AVERAGE WINTER CLIMATE moderate to cold

'One of the grandest Dutch-style gardens of the late seventeenth century'

Neptune, landlocked in Dyrham's deer park, now gestures down at the mansion like a madman. Armed with a trident, he once presided over a spectacular cascade of 224 steps and one of the grandest Dutch-style gardens of the late seventeenth century, extending from both sides of the house, complete with fountains and a canal, and an elaborate and extensive pattern of terraces and parterres, avenues and formal walks. But fashion changed, the cost of upkeep was too great, and the Bath to Gloucester road was improved behind his back. He was left, as it were, high and dry.

It is hard to regret the garden's passing, for the present setting is nothing short of stupendous. From the entrance, you plummet down the Cotswold escarpment and suddenly, between muscular folds of green hillside and splendid beeches, horse chestnuts and cedars, the handsome Baroque house is revealed in the valley. If the sun is drawing out the gold in the Bath stone and illuminating the distant mountains of Wales, so much the better.

The Tudor manor house was transformed into the present mansion by William Blathwayt, Secretary of State to William III, between 1692 and 1704. George London, the most celebrated contemporary designer of formal gardens, was consulted on the landscaping. The garden, though not wholly complete, was already impressing visitors by 1700. At that time, the main entrance was opposite the west front of the house, the carriageway leading from the west gate to the impressive Italianate double stairway adjoining the terrace. The rectangular ponds on the west side were part of the original formal design, fed by water channelled discretely under the stable block.

The long terrace above the church still exists, and the old limes are likely to be those shown in Kip's engraving of 1712. In the park, radiating avenues of elms were also spared, only to succumb, ironically, to Dutch elm disease. They have been replaced mainly with limes by the Trust. Little else remains of the formal garden, which had fallen into disrepair by 1779, after which it was extensively remodelled.

William Blathwayt IV engaged a Bath surveyor, Charles Harcourt Masters, to 'mark out plantations' and 'dispose and plant trees', and Humphry Repton visited in 1800, contributing for several years and probably rebuilding the niched wall below the ponds. In turning the east garden into a deer park, Blathwayt made a connection with the past, for the name Dyrham is derived from the Saxon *deor hamm*, meaning 'deer enclosure'. The pale-coloured strain of fallow deer that graze the slopes is of great antiquity.

Today, the only detailed horticulture to be found on the east side of the house is pursued inside the greenhouse. Built in 1701, this is one of the earliest examples in the country to be given architectural importance, and was used to overwinter the pots of citrus fruits, bay trees and aloes that adorned the formal walks and parterres. Now partly re-created, it reprises this role.

A ten-year development plan is now under way on the west side of the house to recapture a late seventeenth-early eighteenth century

mood. The west terrace will be relandscaped as gravel and grass parterres combined with topiary and pots of citrus, and the borders in the church court will be gradually restocked with period plants: the layout, with its long central driveway, reflecting that shown in the Kip engraving, and adorned with topiary and espalier fruit. Beside the stables, the formal fruit walks are bordered by a low wall and railings, giving a glimpse over the water gardens.

The garden was subjected to considerable change in the Victorian era, and some of this overlay is being retained, not least in the rockwork fernery uncovered at the head of the west approach drive and around the main pool, where mixed ornamental trees and shrubs are grouped in the company of old mulberries. Trees are one of Dyrham's chief glories, and in the parkland arc numerous North American species such as tulip trees, red oak and black walnut, reflecting the first William Blathwayt's position as administrator of the American Colonies. Many plants were sent from Virginia in 1694. Beyond the cobnut walk, there is also a traditional perry pear orchard, its meadow grasses infiltrated with daffodils, fritillaries and other wildflowers.

LEFT St Peter's Church is reflected in the Lower Pool at Dyrham Park.

RIGHT Standard robinia trees in the walled garden at East Riddlesden Hall.

East Riddlesden Hall

BRADFORD ROAD, KEIGHLEY, WEST YORKSHIRE

AREA 4.9ha (12 acres) • SOIL slightly acid/loam • ALTITUDE 76m (250ft)
AVERAGE RAINFALL 952mm (37½ in) • AVERAGE WINTER CLIMATE cold

Standing on the north-western edge of the Bradford-Leeds conurbation, this mid-seventeenth-century property preserves a small pocket of rural charm. The soot-darkened walls of the hall, part-framed by a fine stand of beech trees, are revealed as soon as you turn off the main road – but first you must pass the large pond. Reeds and willows soften its sides, and mallard and farmyard ducks ripple the still water. In spring, the grass is studded with wildflowers and bulbs, including primroses, campions and the native Lent lily, *Narcissus pseudonarcissus*, and in late summer you will see elders on the rough banks leading down towards the River Aire.

The walled formal garden, reached through the house, was designed by the Trust in the early 1970s. It is not a period piece, but plays on traditional themes to provide an appropriate and colourful accompaniment to the house. Box hedges and avenues reinforce the linear framework. From the rose window on the south front, there is a procession of pyramidal fruit trees, including the apples 'James Grieve' and 'Lane's Prince Albert' and the pears 'Winter Nelis' and 'Doyenné du Comice'. And beside the relics of the gabled façade of the Starkie wing, demolished in 1905, runs a double line of mophead acacia, *Robinia pseudoacacia* 'Umbraculifera' (syn. 'Inermis'), so compact in growth that it needs to be clipped only every other year.

A double border of herbs and soft fruit also helps to establish a link with the past. Camphor, the prostrate borage *Borago pygmaea* (*syn. B. laxiflora*) and alecost (*Tanacetum balsamita*), used to flavour ale in the Middle Ages, are some of the curiosities. The garden also boasts a large number of varieties of sweet violet, a plant that has

been cultivated for many centuries. The nucleus of the collection was donated by a Lancashire enthusiast, and includes singles and doubles, pinks, reds, whites, blues and purples. They form an intricate and absorbing cast. Richer splashes of colour come from beds of 'Dusky Maiden' roses in the sunken garden and the frothing array of shrubs, climbers and herbaceous plants that fringe the lawn. Improved with generous quantities of organic matter, the light soil produces good displays of hardy geraniums, including magenta *Geranium psilostemon* and the tireless and exquisite *G. pratense* 'Plenum Violaceum'. Shrub roses, sweet-scented philadelphus, lavender and clematis are also here, accompanied by daylilies, irises, peonies and ever-popular bellflowers.

The view across the valley over the low east wall is rather marred by the proximity of the gasworks, but they are screened by the hedge of *Ilex × altaclerensis* 'Hodginsii', a handsome green holly valued in the Midlands from the nineteenth century for its tolerance to industrial pollution.

Beyond the walls, a new orchard is maturing. Planted with old Yorkshire varieties of apple, such as 'Ribston Pippin', 'Cockpit', 'Catshead' and 'Yorkshire Beauty', it takes its mood from William Robinson's *The Wild Garden*, first published in 1870. Backed by roses, honeysuckle, clematis and ivy, the grass has been infiltrated by numerous bulbs, wildflowers and garden perennials to give a changing tapestry of colour from early spring to late summer. In recent years, a new cut-flower area, grass maze and children's playground have also been added.

Emmetts Garden

IDE HILL, SEVENOAKS, KENT

AREA 2.4ha (6 acres) • **SOIL** acid/greensand ridge over stone • **ALTITUDE** 198–220m (650–720ft) • **AVERAGE RAINFALL** 889mm (35in) • **AVERAGE WINTER CLIMATE** cold

'In spring, the grass is patched yellow with daffodils and below the South Garden the path leads off enticingly into bluebell woods'

Emmetts is one of Kent's highest gardens. After the 1987 storm, the views became panoramic: north to the North Downs, east towards Ide Hill village, and south and west over the great sweep of trees that lead towards Crowborough Ridge. Now the native trees have grown up again, though a fine view is preserved south to the Kentish Weald.

The garden is largely the creation of Frederic Lubbock, a banker who bought the property in 1893, but in its design and planting it owes much to the influence and advice of his friend William Robinson, the gardening writer, who lived not far away at Gravetye. Part of the rock garden was illustrated in Robinson's *Alpine Flowers for the Garden* (1903). The only touch of formality is the Italianate rose garden, in which purple 'Cardinal Hume', pink 'Escapade' and white 'Iceberg' roses, Hybrid Musk roses and catmint (*Nepeta*) are arranged around a central fountain pond. Following the discovery of photographic slides taken from before the First World War, swags for Climbing roses have recently been reintroduced, with Rosa 'Climbing Cécile Brünner' trained along them. The rock garden, with its cascade, pond and outcrops of Westmorland limestone, has also recently been invigorated with 95 tonnes of Kentish ragstone. This has created a montane scree for the cultivation of a diverse range of unusual alpines.

Otherwise, the garden follows a relaxed pattern of lawns, glades and meandering paths – an informal Edwardian design that evolved in response to a straightforward passion for plants displayed in a natural way, a mood that the Trust is actively fostering. The conditions are not perfect for a collection of trees and shrubs, the soil being light and fast-draining, but thanks to copious quantities of mulch, many Asian species flourish. Among the notable plants in the upper garden are *Eucryphia glutinosa*, showered in white blossom in August, *Magnolia denudata* and the heavily scented summer-flowering *M. × wieseneri*. These are accompanied by generous plantings of azaleas, including the white-flowered *Rhododendron quinquefolium*, while *Nyssa sylvatica*, *Enkianthus perulatus* and seed-raised *Berberis wilsoniae* give a panoply of rich berry and leaf colour in autumn.

Lower down the slope, across the former drive, the collection takes on the flavour of an arboretum, with individual trees and stands of shrubs displayed in grass. The tall Dawyck beech withstood the 1987 storm, and there are still good examples of *Cercidiphyllum japonicum*, *Davidia involucrata* var. *vilmoriniana* and *Stewartia pseudocamellia*, together with an enormous clump of *Pieris japonica* and a number of good rhododendrons, including *R. ferrugineum* and *R. smirnowii*. In spring, the grass here is patched yellow with daffodils and below the South Garden the path leads off enticingly into bluebell woods.

RIGHT The Bluebell Bank in May.

Erddig

RHOSTYLLEN, WREXHAM

AREA 5.3ha (13 acres) • SOIL slightly acid/loam and clay • ALTITUDE 61m (200ft)
AVERAGE RAINFALL 889mm (35in) • AVERAGE WINTER CLIMATE moderate

*'The banks of the canal are colonised
by the wild Welsh Lent lily'*

'We call this the State Bedroom,' announced Philip Yorke III as he showed his television audience around Erddig, 'because it is always in such a state.' It is hard for me to maintain a proper perspective on this property, whose wooded park and minnow-filled brook was my childhood playground, and whose squire, frequently seen cycling around Wrexham on his penny-farthing, was the stuff of local legend. The bedroom was not the only part of Erddig to have fallen into disrepair. The garden was all but lost in a jungle of nettles, brambles, overgrown shrubs and seedling sycamores, with sheep as the only gardeners. After what has been described as 'a heroic holding operation', Philip Yorke eventually passed his beloved estate, tenaciously held by his family since 1733 and comprising nearly 809ha (2,000 acres), to the Trust in 1973.

There is no hint today of the monumental task of restoration that was faced in 1973. Spread out before the east front of the hall is a crisp pattern of straight paths and mown grass, avenues of pleached limes, groves of pyramid fruit trees, yews and variegated hollies, lines of Portuguese laurels clipped to mimic orange trees in white Versailles tubs and a broad, smooth-edged canal. Remarkably, the bones of the design had been unaltered since the early eighteenth century, and thanks to the bird's-eye view drawn in 1740 by Thomas Badeslade, the Trust was given the opportunity to reconstruct fairly accurately this rare example of a formal garden in the Dutch style.

Fruit trees, marshalled into quincunxes and espaliered on walls, were then especially valued as part of the formal structure. Lists were made in 1718 detailing Erddig's wall fruits, and varieties still in existence have been reintroduced. Apples, now the most numerous wall fruit, were not, in fact, mentioned, suggesting they were grown only as free-standing trees. Today the collection includes some 180 varieties, including 'Nonpareil' and 'Fenouillet Rouge', supplemented by pears such as 'Bon-Chrétien d'Hiver' and 'Windsor', and plums 'Blue Perdrigon' and 'Red Magnum Bonum'. All these were in cultivation before 1700. An annual apple festival is held here each October complete with cooking displays and cider tasting.

The borders are strewn with climbing and herbaceous plants, and beneath each fruit tree there are bulbs: in the orchard are strips of pheasant's eye narcissus (*Narcissus poeticus* var. *recurvus*), and in the borders, a number of old varieties of daffodil dating from before the First World War. 'Lord Kitchener', 'Will Scarlett', 'Saint Olaf', and 'Bonfire' are among the many unfamiliar names. The banks of the canal are also colonised by the wild Welsh Lent lily (*Narcissus pseudonarcissus*), followed in summer by thousands of common spotted orchids which were able to gain a foothold during the garden's long period of neglect. It is a fascinating collection.

Fruit trees were not merely decorative; their crops were an important part of the garden's utilitarian function. The pond, north of the canal, would also have been stocked with fish for the table, and it seems likely that the strange yew niches beyond were designed

RIGHT A view across the Victorian parterre, with orange crown imperials.

for bee skeps and honey production. This same productive theme is evoked by the squadron of plump, egg-laying farmyard ducks waddling across the lawns, and the new border of culinary, medicinal and strewing herbs against the south-facing wall of the former vegetable garden.

Powerfully rooted in the early eighteenth century though they remain, Erddig's formal gardens continued to be embellished by the Yorkes, most notably in the late nineteenth century. The parterre is decorated with mossy, stalagmitic fountains, and the Trust's bedding schemes of cheerful annuals reinforce the Victorian flavour. The adjacent walled rose garden is being developed in the Gardenesque style; it houses, apart from Shrub roses, a large black mulberry (once a single stick in the undergrowth), pampas grass in the lawn, and a silver birch, whose trunk was at one time tapped for sweet sap to be used in wine-making.

The nineteenth-century mood is even stronger in the small Victorian Flower Garden, which was described in detail in the *Journal of Horticulture* of 1909. Here, pink 'Dorothy Perkins' roses and deep violet *Clematis* 'Jackmanii' are strung along swags of rope, around specimens of variegated *Acer negundo* against geometric plantings of Bush roses and annuals. Specimen trees, including a magnificent swamp cypress, date from the mid-1800s. *Taxodium distichum*, at the head of the fish pond, and the avenue of wellingtonias beyond the south wall of the garden also date from this period. Against the shadiest walls is a National Collection of ivy, that plant so popular with the Victorians.

The west front offers a quite different prospect – an abrupt drop into woods and undulating parkland. The landscape was moulded by William Emes, a contemporary of 'Capability' Brown who also worked at nearby Chirk Castle and Powis Castle in the dominant naturalistic style of the late eighteenth century, but the pastoral scene is now interrupted by the looming silhouettes of Hafod and Bersham collieries in the middle distance, binding Erddig firmly to its locality. Emes' most wonderful feature can be seen between trees to the north-west: an extraordinary circular weir, known as the Cup and Saucer, into which the waters of the Black Brook – no longer darkened by passing through coal seams – are flushed; at times of flood, it becomes a whirlpool in the meadow and, to an impressionable child, a vision that stamps itself forever on the mind.

LEFT A stone column with gargoyles decorates the garden at Erddig.

Farnborough Hall

BANBURY, WARWICKSHIRE

AREA 3.2ha (8 acres) • SOIL neutral • ALTITUDE 76m (250ft) • AVERAGE RAINFALL 686mm (27in) • AVERAGE WINTER CLIMATE cold to very cold

A Grand Tour to complete his education, followed by much travelling to and from Italy, turned William Holbech into a connoisseur of Italian art and architecture, and in about 1745 he set about reconstructing the manor house inherited from his father. The result is an elegant Palladian-style villa of golden ironstone which stands among trees at the edge of the village, slightly elevated above the patchwork of meadows in the Warmington valley.

The broad grass terrace walk ascending the ridge to the south-east of the hall is Holbech's other great legacy. Beginning steeply, it follows a leisurely S-shaped line to terminate in a soaring obelisk, 1.2km (¾ mile) distant. En route are his 'viewpoints' – an Ionic temple and an unusual oval pavilion with open loggia and an upper-storey Prospect Room, its ornate blue and white interior recently restored to full Rococo glory. There was a third temple in the park, but it was demolished about 1820. Probably completed in 1751 and pre-dating the great Rievaulx Terrace by a few years, it thus gives an insight into eighteenth-century landscape gardening at a period when the last touches of formal design were giving way to the Picturesque. The amateur architect and landscape gardener Sanderson Miller, a friend of Holbech, almost certainly assisted in the remodelling of Farnborough and was probably the designer of the temples.

The walk is flanked on one side by a dense belt of trees and evergreen shrubs, and on the other by a curving laurel hedge, broken by 33 projecting bastions along its length, which provide views out over the surrounding countryside. The views between these trees and those on the bank below are panoramic, looking out over the Warwickshire plain and across to Edgehill and the Malvern Hills, with the glistening stretch of Holbech's river pool directly below. Sadly, the scene has now been disturbed by the arrival of the M40 in the middle distance. Broken belts of trees have been planted in the valley to lessen its impact but the former tranquillity will never quite be regained.

The return walk takes you through the wood behind the terrace to the Game Larder, a handsome hexagonal building that looks back towards the village across seventeenth-century stewponds. These feed into the large Sourlands Pool over the road from the hall and then into the river pool. This last, topped by a cascade, is reached by a path leading from the spacious, cedar-shaded lawns, and as you skirt the field, a flowery surprise is sprung in the form of a parterre of Bush roses, framed by box and cubes of golden yew. The site of the old eighteenth-century orangery (pulled down in 1960) is threaded with thyme and backed by wisterias; its alcove seat (the terracotta-pink wall well matched by 'The Fairy' roses foaming over the stones) offers another green prospect for contemplation.

ABOVE Steps leading to the parterre, with box hedging, roses and cubes of golden yew, known as 'Granny's Garden'.

Felbrigg Hall

CROMER, NORFOLK

AREA 2.9ha (7¼ acres) • **SOIL** alkaline/light loam • **ALTITUDE** 61m (200ft)
AVERAGE RAINFALL 635mm (25in) • **AVERAGE WINTER CLIMATE** cold

A short walk from the hall, across the donkey paddock, is one of the Trust's best walled kitchen gardens, 1.6ha (4 acres) in size and now returned to a high level of production, conjuring up the luscious atmosphere of a decorative potager in its country-house heyday. The south-facing slope is divided into three compartments, with a handsome octagonal dovecote, probably dating from the eighteenth century, crowning the central axis. As they were in the past, the birds are a source of manure and meat, being used in the restaurant to make pigeon and rabbit pie. Borders of herbs fringe this northerly path, accompanied by espalier pears, ancient fig trees, cardoons and grapevines, including 'Madeleine Royale', 'Léon Millot' and the Strawberry Grape, grown on timber obelisks. The pyramid apple trees lined in front of the dovecote are 'Norfolk Royal Russet', one of the many varieties growing here associated with East Anglia; they are flanked by 'Norfolk Beefing'.

A range of produce from onions, carrots, courgettes and marrows to strawberries, asparagus, artichoke and sweet corn is cultivated in the large vegetable plots, intermingled with flowers for both decorative and practical effect, to distract and deter predatory insects and attract beneficial ones. The bright displays include seed-raised annuals such as nasturtiums, marigolds and cosmos and also dahlias and gladioli. Along the east-facing wall, the espaliered fruits, including the dessert pear 'Baronne de Mello', are joined by a ribbon border of dianthus, alliums, ixias and pink lavender. Morello cherries ripen on the north-facing wall, near to a fine old medlar tree.

The long double borders which cross the width of the central section of the garden are a magnificent sight in their rich summer livery that spans oranges, purples, reds and acid greens. Apricot 'African Queen' lilies and red bottlebrush are among the highlights, together with great bushes of grey-leaved, lilac-flowered *Buddleja crispa*. The adventurous and exotic planting in these and other borders of the walled garden is indicative of the mild maritime influence – the sea is only 3.2km (2 miles) away. Tender *Dasylirion*, looking like a fibre-optic lamp, appears in the garden's gravel beds among sedums, euphorbias and kniphofia, and olive trees have been planted in the lawns of the garden's lowest compartment. The lean-to glasshouses are kept just frost-free to support spiky agaves, aloes, blue plumbago and citrus fruit.

Beyond the dovecote, a new orchard has been planted with fruit trees known to have been grown here in the nineteenth century. This area also holds a National Collection of colchicums, whose goblet flowers appear in early autumn. The uncommon *Colchicum tenorei* has long flourished along the walled garden's central cross-walk, and its presence and obvious liking for the compacted sandy soil prompted the Trust to build up the collection. This now comprises more than 60 varieties in all shades of lilac, mauve, carmine and white, single and double, plain and chequered. *Amaryllis belladonna*, another autumn-flowering bulb, is also long established, producing its pink funnels beneath the apricots and peaches on the central compartment's south-facing wall.

The Walled Garden has always been Felbrigg's main flower garden, but there is a small garden featuring yucca and lavender beside the hall and, on the rising ground below the Great Wood,

a Victorian overlay of ornamental trees and shrubs around formal lawns. This pleasure ground was originally set out by William Broderick Thomas, who also landscaped for the future Edward VII at Sandringham, and has recently been renovated and replanted with camellias, rhododendrons, azara, drimys and other interesting plants. Many of the fine trees, including red oaks and wellingtonias, are North American. The centrepiece is the early eighteenth century Orangery. Given its glass roof in the nineteenth century when it became a conservatory, it is filled with old camellias, underplanted with the giant-fronded *Woodwardia* fern.

The hall's Jacobean south front looks onto open parkland receding towards Norwich. William Windham III, the great-great-grandson of the hall's builder, Thomas Windham, was landlord and patron to the young Humphry Repton from the mid-1770s, and it is likely that the Felbrigg landscape was

the first sizeable project to which this great designer contributed. The woods and stands of oak, sweet chestnut, beech and sycamore are welcome breaks to the bleak horizontals of the Norfolk countryside, and give vital shelter to the hall and gardens from the bitter North Sea winds. The many trees felled for timber during the First World War were replaced in subsequent decades by Robert Wyndham Ketton-Cremer, who bequeathed the estate to the Trust; it was he who added the Coronation group of beeches and the Victory V rides to commemorate VE Day. In its turn, the Trust has done much replanting in the wake of the 1987 storm.

LEFT The kitchen garden, with plants and vegetables growing in carefully tended rows.

ABOVE Purple geraniums, climbing hydrangea and clouds of *Crambe cordifolia* in July.

Fenton House

WINDMILL HILL, HAMPSTEAD, LONDON

AREA 0.6ha (1½ acres) • SOIL neutral/sandy loam • ALTITUDE 122m (400ft)
AVERAGE RAINFALL 635mm (25in) • AVERAGE WINTER CLIMATE moderate

The discovery of mineral springs on the slopes of the hill at the turn of the eighteenth century began the transformation of the village of Hampstead into a fashionable place of residence, eventually to be absorbed into London. Just a short distance from the arterial roads and shopping streets, the warm brick merchant's house, built in 1693, and its gardens are now a reminder of the village's quiet past.

The narrow walk that leads from the ornate ironwork entrance gates to the south front is now a redolent, though not slavish, period piece, with an avenue of false acacias (a tree that became popular soon after its introduction from the eastern part of North America in the early seventeenth century) shading the gravel path. The fresh green of its foliage, and of the lawn, is set off by a heavy backdrop of ivy, holly, arbutus, bay, aucuba, holm oak, evergreen viburnum and acanthus – the last echoing the motif of the gates.

Behind the house, the garden opens out into a series of sunny terrace walks, which the Trust has enlivened with flower borders in the Old English style. Tubs of agapanthus reinforce the formal framework of the narrow upper terrace, while across the lawn below are pyramids of variegated holly and columns of Irish yew. Around these spill shrubs and perennials for every season.

The changing levels and visual blocks allow many surprises. At one point, sunken cross borders are suddenly revealed, planted as a late season medley of reds, pinks, violet-blues, silvers and whites, including sedum, persicaria, Japanese anemones, perovskia, aster, phlox, ballota and *Fuchsia magellanica*. A little further along, you come to a sunken rose garden of mixed modern and old-fashioned varieties in pastel tints, such as 'Buff Beauty', pink 'Sydonie' and creamy-white 'Jacqueline du Pré'.

The greatest surprise is the sight of the lower garden, a relaxed country orchard and vegetable garden, reached down steps overhung with an enormous strawberry tree, *Arbutus unedo*. 'It's like a supermarket down there,' London children have been heard to exclaim. In spring, the scene is more poetic, as you look at trees in blossom and grass sheeted with bulbs, from daffodils and snakeshead fritillaries to exotic blue *Scilla peruviana*. The vegetables and cut flowers are at one end of the orchard, behind varieties of espaliered apple including 'Beauty of Bath' and 'Devonshire Quarrenden'. At the other end is a working greenhouse, an adjacent herb garden and even a beehive.

ABOVE The kitchen garden is a sunken oasis with orchard, glasshouse and herb border.
RIGHT A view across the kitchen garden to the stables.

Companion Planting

Danny Snapes, Former Gardener-in-Charge
FENTON HOUSE, HAMPSTEAD, LONDON

The term 'companion planting' means selecting plants that can benefit their neighbours in many different ways, from providing a support for climbing plants to attracting insects that prey on pests. This system can be used by organic and non-organic gardeners alike.

Companion planting has been used since at least Roman times and it has notably been practised by Native American peoples in a technique known as the Three Sisters, where maize (corn), a climbing bean and squash are all planted together; the maize is used as poles for the beans to climb, while the squash is used as a ground-cover mulch to help retain moisture under its large leaves. Today, combination plants are often used for their capacity to:

- Give off a scent or chemical that repels insects, or disguises the smell of the crop.
- Attract beneficial insects, such as ladybird larvae, parasitic wasps, hoverfly and lacewings.
- Leave a residual chemical in the ground that repels nematodes or benefits the companion plant.
- Fix nitrogen into the soil via the roots, which are dug in after harvesting (such as members of the legume family).
- Create shade for other plants that need shelter from the sun.
- Act as sacrificial plants that will attract harmful insects away from certain plants or crops.
- Provide a windbreak for other plants.
- Attract pollinating insects to improve the yield of crops.

One of the most common combinations is that of roses underplanted with garlic, which gives off a scent that is said to repel aphids. In the vegetable garden, golden feverfew (*Tanacetum parthenium* 'Aureum') is often used to ward off onion and carrot fly.

When you thin out either of these vegetables, rub the feverfew to give off the strong scent, both before and afterwards, to confuse the flies and disguise the smell of the plants. Another bonus of planting the feverfew is that it makes the vegetable garden look good as well.

I have often used Mexican marigold (*Tagetes minuta*), which is around 1.2m (4ft) high, to ward off aphids but have found that it is useful for root crops too as it gives off a chemical that repels nematodes. It also gives good protection to other plants as a windbreak and to plants that need shade.

I regularly use broad beans as a sacrificial crop as they readily attract aphids early on in the season (though the crop from the beans is not destroyed). This allows me to destroy the aphids by cultural methods, reducing the numbers early on and giving a benefit to the garden for the rest of the season. I use part of the Native American Three Sisters technique by planting sweet corn and squash in adjacent rows, which helps to keep the moisture in for the corn and also keeps weeds down. In the future I plan to try beans climbing up the stems of the sweet corn as well.

Plants used for companion planting

Common fruit, herbs and vegetables

PLANT NAME	COMPANIONS	INCOMPATIBLE
apple	chives, mint, nasturtiums	
beetroot	beans, onions	runner beans
beans	carrots, cauliflower	onion family, peas
broccoli	broad beans, caraway, dill, potatoes, rosemary, thyme	
cabbage	beans, herbs, celery, beetroot, spinach, Swiss chard	mustard species, onion family
carrots	peas, lettuce, onion family, sage, tomatoes	
courgette	borage, fennel, nasturtium	
garlic	carrots, beetroot, roses, lettuce, tomatoes	beans, peas
leek	celery, carrots, apples, pears	lettuce, parsley
lettuce	carrots, celery, radish, kohlrabi	
onion	tomatoes, parsnips, carrots	beans, peas
pears	mint, nasturtiums	
peas	beans, carrots, radish, turnips, sweet corn	onion family
potato	lavender, horseradish*	sunflowers, sweet corn
sweet corn	squash, beans, pumpkins, sunflower	tomatoes
strawberries	beans, lettuce	rosemary, thyme
tomato	basil, onion family, nasturtiums, marigold, carrot, parsley	potatoes, cabbage family

Flowers and herbs

PLANT NAME	COMPANIONS	INCOMPATIBLE
allium	vegetables, fruit trees, peppers	peas, beans
basil	tomatoes, parsley	tansy, rue
borage	strawberry, squash, tomatoes	
catmint	aubergine, swede, thyme	
coriander	all vegetables, attracts bees	
feverfew	roses, onions, carrots	
geranium	roses, grapevines	
hyssop	cabbage family, grapes	radish
lavender	potatoes, thyme	lettuce, parsley
marigolds	most plants, especially beans, basil, roses, tomatoes	
mustard	cabbage, cauliflower	
nasturtium	apples, pears, radish, cabbage, tomatoes	broad beans
oregano	brassicas	
parsley	asparagus, tomatoes, roses, basil	lavender
rosemary	beans, cabbage, sage, carrots	marrow family
sage	cabbage family, rosemary	cucumbers
thyme	cabbage, beans, roses	marrow family
wormwood	cabbage family, some aromatic herbs	sage, basil
yarrow	most aromatic herbs	

Tips

- When planning a new border, think about diversity and companion planting to make it difficult for harmful insects to find the plants that they need for food or reproduction. One example is planting vegetables and herbs in your decorative borders to confuse the pests and make it more difficult for them to find their food source. This can be very attractive too, as some of the new vegetable plants can look really good.

- Ensure that the plants are growing in the best possible conditions available as this will assist them in fighting off any pests and disease.
- Remember to mulch regularly, weed when needed to stop competition from other plants and fertilise at the right time to ensure that your plants take up the nutrients when they are most beneficial.

Florence Court

ENNISKILLEN, CO. FERMANAGH

AREA 8ha (21 acres) within parkland • SOIL acid/clay • ALTITUDE 91m (300ft) AVERAGE RAINFALL 610mm (24in) • AVERAGE WINTER CLIMATE moderate

'The Situation has a Majestic Wildness,' wrote the Rev. William Henry in 1739, and though many acres have been tamed by park and pleasure grounds, the encircling hills, mountains, peat bogs and lough continue to instil a sense of remoteness. The first view of the Palladian house is across open, rising pasture, speared by rushes and grazed by sheep, with the mass of the Cuilcagh range looming behind. Mixed woodlands, managed by the Forest Service, provide a lush frame. The house was built in the mid-eighteenth century for John Cole, Governor of Enniskillen, and the park was landscaped for his son around 1778 by a Mr King, who also worked at Castle Coole, in the smooth 'Capability' Brown manner.

The copper beech beside one of the flanking octagonal pavilions indicates the start of the Pleasure Grounds, and after the house's simple parkland setting, the panorama of exotic trees and shrubs that confronts you is electrifying. Beeches and maples, silver pears and whitebeams, rhododendrons and conifers are clumped or scattered between the glades and paths. In spring, the sharp tints of the new leaves add to the contrasts, none more impressively than those of the celebrated weeping beeches, represented here in a tall rather than wide-spreading form. The lime green stands out crisply against the dark woodland belts and the brooding bulk of Benaughlin behind. After the massed display of 'Cornish Red' rhododendron (*R*. Smithii Group), flowering highlights are furnished by azaleas, dogwoods, *Rosa rugosa*, eucryphias, hydrangeas and naturalised drifts of the giant montbretia, *Crocosmia paniculata*.

The dark Irish yews punctuating the planting have a very special association, for it was on the slopes of Cuilcagh Mountain that the original plant, one of two seedlings of markedly erect habit, was found. Mr George Willis, a farmer from Aghatirourke, made the discovery while coursing hares, but in exactly which decade of the mid- to late-eighteenth century is disputed. One seedling he took to his own garden, and the other, a free-berrying female type, was transplanted here and propagated. The mother of all the millions of Irish yews around the world, it grows near the bank of the Larganess River, west of Kerrshill Wood, and is passed on one of the woodland trails.

The Pleasure Grounds were laid out for the 3rd Earl and Countess of Enniskillen some time after 1844, probably under the direction of the landscape gardener James Frazer. The thatched summer-house, recently rebuilt by the Trust, overlooks the grounds and gives outstanding views to the surrounding mountains. The sawmill and hydraulic ram below were built in the same period and, now restored by the Trust, accompany the birdsong with trundling and splashing sounds. The air down here is infused with the grapefruit scent of giant firs, and you can follow the course of the little stream, past stands of large-leaved gunnera and darmera and pockets of meadow grasses, rich with orchids and other wildflowers, to Lady Kathleen's Garden, where hostas, daylilies and astilbes fringe the shrub beds.

From the late eighteenth century, fruit and vegetables were grown in the Walled Garden beside the entrance drive. Overgrown when

the Trust leased it in the mid-1970s, this has now been cleared and restored to a simplified plan that includes a rose garden and new orchard of traditional and rare Irish apple varieties. Vegetable beds are also gradually returning. Like the Pleasure Grounds, the Walled Garden is bordered by water in the form of two narrow ponds, spanned by a rustic bridge rebuilt by the Trust to a traditional design. The accompanying trees and waterside plants provide a relaxed wilderness setting; in spring, there is a fine show of Irish daffodil cultivars on the grass banks. Groups of cherries, amelanchiers and cercidiphyllum contribute to spring and autumn colour, but most

remarkable of all to many visitors from across the sea is the luxuriant growth of mosses and lichens growing on the branches – evidence of the sweetness of Fermanagh's air and an extremely high rainfall.

ABOVE View through the pillars of the summer-house, over the verdant garden and surrounding countryside.

Fountains Abbey and Studley Royal

FOUNTAINS, RIPON, NORTH YORKSHIRE

AREA 296ha (731 acres) • **SOIL** alkaline-neutral/limestone, boulder clay • **ALTITUDE** 80–100m (262–328ft) • **AVERAGE RAINFALL** 508mm (20in) • **AVERAGE WINTER CLIMATE** cold

This remarkable landscape garden, in an advanced state of restoration, has become one of the Trust's most popular properties. Nature's gift was a narrow, wooded gorge and the tumbling water of the River Skell. In the early eighteenth century, these features were seized upon and manipulated to create a sinuous garden of formal pools, canals and shady walks, adorned with classical temples, Gothic eye-catchers, grottoes and rustic bridges, and later, annexed as its climax, was the stupendous prospect of the great Cistercian abbey itself, its massive tower surprisingly intact and its ruined walls still standing high and pale against the hanging woods.

Excavated and planted over a period of some 65 years from 1716, the garden unfolds the early chapters in the story of Georgian landscaping, though none of the famous names of landscape gardening were involved here. The designer was its owner John Aislabie, who immersed himself in the project after his expulsion from Parliament for his role, as Chancellor of the Exchequer, in the South Sea Company scandal. After Aislabie's death in 1742, his son William completed the garden by acquiring the abbey. The nucleus of John Aislabie's design, and the oldest section, is the formal water garden, a serene composition of lawn-lapped moon- and crescent-shaped ponds, in which the golden Temple of Piety and statues of Bacchus, Neptune and Endymion are reflected as in a mirror. Beside them, the canal channels the river over a cascade between two fishing pavilions into the lake.

In this spot is most memorably captured the turn from French- and Continental-inspired gardening to the new classical English landscape. The symmetry and order of the water garden is set against the billowing curves of the wooded hillsides, where meandering paths lead you to discover a series of garden buildings and prospects down across the valley. On the west is the Banqueting House, at the head of a coffin-shaped lawn; on the east, the Octagon Tower, Temple of Fame and Anne Boleyn's Seat, from which you obtain that famous surprise view, across the Half Moon Pond and up the river, to Fountains Abbey.

The layers of trees and shrubs on the slopes are full of interest, with the beeches, oaks and limes capped with larch and Scots pine, and underplanted with predominantly native shrubs, with a generous complement of yews to furnish winter colour and permanent frames for views. The area is noted for its limestone flora, with fine displays

of primroses, cowslips, common spotted orchid and field scabious (*Knautia arvensis*).

Below the lake is the sharpest contrast to the formal water garden. Here, William Aislabie indulged in the new taste for the wildest landscapes. Instead of taming this stretch of gorge, he emphasised its plunging contours and exposed rocks by judicious tree planting and a zigzag series of bridges to highlight the twists of the river. Originally he followed an oriental theme, with pagodas and pavilions, but this was later exchanged for a raw, rustic mood. It is one of the earliest examples of the Picturesque style in England.

A final surprise awaits you if you leave through the deer park at the eastern end of the estate. A sweeping avenue of limes carries your eye in one direction up towards St Mary's church, the Victorian masterpiece by William Burges. Looking the other way, you find, framed in the gateway, the distant towers of Ripon Minster. To have two noble medieval structures on his doorstep was an extraordinary stroke of good fortune for John Aislabie: for his landscape, they are borrowed eye-catchers that few other gardens can match.

ABOVE The River Skell, a natural landscape feature of the garden, provided the basis for much of its design.

NEXT PAGE The Temple of Piety with its pediment and Tuscan columns, seen over the canal and Half-Moon Pond, with the statue of Bacchus in front.

Gawthorpe Hall

PADIHAM, BURNLEY, LANCASHIRE

AREA 12ha (30 acres) • SOIL acid • ALTITUDE 76m (250ft) • AVERAGE RAINFALL 1,143mm (45in)
AVERAGE WINTER CLIMATE cold

The Burnley-Padiham conurbation has advanced on Gawthorpe, but at the end of the drive you find yourself in an amphitheatre of greenery, enclosed by layers of beech, oak, lime, chestnut and sycamore, and presided over by a high, square house of yellow sandstone. Above the hall, an avenue of young limes carries the eye up to the woods; below, the ground plunges into the meadows of the Calder Valley. The Victorian mood is pervasive. In the early 1850s, Sir James Kay-Shuttleworth engaged the architect Sir Charles Barry to restore and embellish the hall, built for the Shuttleworths at the turn of the seventeenth century. The tower, parapets and opulent interior, the last recently refurbished, are the result.

You must walk around to the north front in order to see Barry's reinterpretation of Elizabethan garden design reproduced in full. Here, using the waste from the excavation for the South Parterre, he extended the ground to make a broad semi-circular bastion, fringed with a parapet wall. Obelisks and, at the end of the terrace walk, armorial seats, designed by Barry's son Edward, reinforce the Elizabethan flavour, and filling the composition is a geometric pattern of radial flower-beds, edged in stone and separated by gravel paths. All Barry's work is in sympathy with early seventeenth-century style; the strong Victorian mood comes from the planting. In the North Parterre, the present scheme, installed in 1978, is a simplified labour-saving version of the original. But the colour scheme of purple and gold – for modern eyes, a spectacular affront to the optic nerve – and the use of exuberantly hued and exotically shaped foliage sets the composition squarely in the

nineteenth century. Berberis, privet, yucca and the shrub honeysuckle *Lonicera nitida* 'Baggesen's Gold' are the plants employed.

Other parts of the garden display the Victorian fashion for sombre evergreens, which at the time were flooding into Britain from the Americas and the Far East. Rhododendrons filter through the woods, their purple and pink trusses of flowers in sharp contrast to the yellows of laburnum, azalea, spotted aucuba and golden privet. The hall is fringed with mahonias, berberis, laurels, bergenias and *Yucca recurvifolia*. By contrast, the small rose garden, opposite the east front and on the site of another of Barry's parterres, has a lighter Edwardian air. It was planted in 1987 using pink 'Petit Four', 'White Pet' and 'Sander's White Rambler' as standards, the original design taken from a photograph in the hall, dated around 1900.

In winter, the church spire of Habergham is visible between the limes that rise above the South Parterre. The path leads to the pond, sited on high ground, with its banks raised. It is a tranquil spot, with oaks and birches furnishing shade, ferns and bluebells colonising the ground, and pheasants calling; buttercup fields provide the backdrop.

ABOVE View across the circular Rose Garden to the east front of the hall.
RIGHT The Long Walk towards the Column to Liberty, which rises above the Gibside estate.

Gibside

ROWLANDS GILL, GATESHEAD

AREA 214ha (528 acres) • SOIL neutral/clay, with some sand • ALTITUDE 115–130m (377–426ft) • AVERAGE RAINFALL 838mm (33in) • AVERAGE WINTER CLIMATE moderate to cold

A fiery-tempered coal baron, sportsman and *bon viveur*, George Bowes had an equal appetite for the arts. In 1722, in his early twenties, he inherited this wooded estate on the steep, southern slopes of the Derwent Valley, and within a few years was embarking on an ambitious landscape garden.

This was a time when the English landscape movement was gathering momentum, and by 1730 Bowes had made contact with one of the leading architects of the changing style, Stephen Switzer. With the resulting plan (now lost) for guidance, he then spent a further 30 years developing the garden. Today Gibside stands as a rare survivor – all the more remarkable for its proximity to the ravenous Tyneside conurbation – from a period of transition in gardening taste from the formal to the naturalistic: a fusion of straight axes and meandering rides, enclosed compartments and panoramic views, pleasure ground, field and forest.

Gibside has suffered intermittent periods of neglect, for after 1874 there was no resident family here, the estate having reverted to the Earls of Strathmore, whose home and seat was at Glamis Castle in Scotland. The house and land were leased out, and following fellings in the 1930s and '40s, the woods were let to the Forestry Commission from 1953 and restocked with conifers. Since 1965, the Trust has been securing the historic core of the estate piece by piece, repairing its features, opening up views, creating gardens, and replacing conifers with deciduous trees.

The Gothick Banqueting House, owned and restored by the Landmark Trust, commands one of the principal axes through the woods. Constructed in the early 1740s from the local golden sandstone, its circular wall lifted into castellated points, it sits like a crown on its high ground. Below, the ground plunges to a formal basin of water, the Octagon Pond, originally set in a wide lawn with statuary, below a formal amphitheatre, the earthworks of which survive. Manicured in its heyday, it is now a wilder habitat and home to wildflowers, grass snakes and great crested newts. Bowes' entrance drive curves around the pond and on past the Stables, built in Palladian style by the same architect as the Banqueting House, Daniel Garrett.

At the round point known as the Top of the Hollow Walk, the three main axes connect. To the north is the circular Lily Pond, itself the hub of further radiating rides. To the south-west is the impressive Long Walk, a broad corridor of grass 800m (½ mile) in length, now with a mixed avenue of Turkey oaks, planted in the nineteenth century. A ha-ha raises the ground above the contrasting informality of the adjoining fields, which are like a giant glade, surrounded by pleasant woods.

At each end of the Long Walk is a major monument. The Column to Liberty, a Doric column 43m (140ft) high, proclaims Bowes' liberal Whig principles and was completed under the supervision of James Paine in 1757. The opposite eye-catcher is Paine's Chapel, a Palladian gem, complete with Ionic columns and a drum and domed roof, swagged in flowers.

Bowes' daughter, Mary Eleanor, finished the Chapel and is also responsible for the Orangery, built in the 1770s, which now stands glassless and gutted, awaiting restoration, along the old river terrace from the house. Fronted with an arcade of Tuscan columns and sliding sash windows, it housed not just orange trees but many palms and other exotic plants, for Mary Eleanor – later dubbed 'The Unhappy Countess' for her disastrous marriage to the Irish rogue Andrew Robinson Stoney – was a keen botanist.

The adjoining Victorian shrubbery has recently been restored, guided by the 1857 Ordnance Survey plan. The period shrubs are dispersed in bold groups, with evergreens, such as *Mahonia aquifolium*, *Daphne pontica* and *D. laureola*, contrasting with decorative scented Shrub roses such as 'Queen of the Bourbons' and 'Reine Victoria'. Large beds have also been planted with early Hardy Hybrid rhododendrons including 'Cynthia', 'Sappho' and 'Prince Camille de Rohan'.

The walled garden too is coming back to life, with volunteers and community groups raising produce in the central plots and young apples, pears, gages and plums replanted along the walls, to be trained into espaliers and fans. A double row of apples divides the garden as in the past – the original trees having sandstone flagstones around them to restrict root growth – and there is an unusual D-shaped fish pond in the corner.

Beyond the heart of the garden are more extensive circuit walks and carriage drives. Snipes Dene is especially atmospheric, a narrow ravine through a piece of ancient woodland (this mood of a Scottish glen being much savoured by the Victorians). It brings you out close to the river, which is still quiet enough for kingfishers, dippers and even otters, despite being just a few miles west of Gateshead.

ABOVE Pink diascias growing in the ruined Orangery at Gibside.

RIGHT Glendurgan's paths follow the contours of the landscape between towering trees and lush foliage.

Glendurgan

MAWNAN SMITH, FALMOUTH, CORNWALL

AREA 10ha (25 acres) • SOIL acid/sandy loam • ALTITUDE 10–70m (33–230ft)
AVERAGE RAINFALL 1,016mm (40in) • AVERAGE WINTER CLIMATE mild

The woodland gardens of Cornwall's southern coast are a world apart. Glendurgan, wedged between folds of hillside, with grassy, stream-fed banks rolling down to the Helford estuary, has a site as snug as any to be found in this mild corner of Britain. Gales are the main enemy, and as soon as Alfred Fox, a Quaker businessman from Falmouth, bought the property in 1823, he set about erecting shelter belts of native deciduous trees, strengthened with Scots and maritime pines, silver fir, Norway spruce and holm oak. In the three valleys, the early emphasis was on fruit trees – this previous history being evoked in the recent re-creation of a small orchard. However, fruit production began to wane as the possibilities for growing the more flamboyant and tender trees and shrubs were exploited by successive members of this prominent Cornish gardening family and, latterly, by the Trust with the family's continued involvement. As shipping agents, the family were well placed to request seed and plants from abroad, and there was much exchange of material between their own gardens and those of friends.

Rhododendrons luxuriate in the warmth and humidity. *R. arboreum* and the Loderi hybrids create huge domes of scarlet, pink and white, supplemented by the blue of *R. augustinii*, the sulphur of 'Saffron Queen' and the fiery tints of Exbury azaleas. Additional lily fragrance comes from the white-flowered *maddenii* clan, including *R.* 'White Wings' and *R.* 'Fragrantissimum'.

In the Camellia Walk, there is a concentration of camellia blossom from numerous forms of *C. japonica*, including 'Debutante', 'Nobilissima' and 'Adolphe Audusson', complemented by 'Captain Rawes' and other of the more tender variants of the Chinese

C. reticulata. Elsewhere, drama comes from a stand of white-tiered *Cornus kousa*, a glade of white magnolias and cherries, Chilean fire bushes (*Embothrium*), and a handkerchief tree (*Davidia involucrata*).

Yet in spite of the luxury of such scenes, the flavour of Cornwall is pervasive. There are the views of woods, estuary and fields; the rough paths that saunter gently down the slopes; the open sweeps of meadow that bring light and warmth into the garden, providing a simple backdrop to so many of the exotic displays; and there are the wildflowers. Primroses, violets and native Lent lilies (*Narcissus pseudonarcissus*) spangle the meadows and woodland fringe in early spring; further on, there are bluebells, campions and naturalised columbines, and, in the damper sites, ragged robin, early purple orchids, and naturalised *Primula prolifera* (syn. *helodoxa*).

Halfway through the tour, having descended into the lower portion of the valley, you take a deeper draught of rural Cornwall by stepping out of the garden altogether. Crossing the old cattle rush, through which the animals were brought to the stream to drink, you find yourself in the hamlet of Durgan, consisting of some 20 cottages clustered around the cove. Refreshed by the sound of the lapping water and the tang of seaweed, you re-enter the garden by the kissing gate up the lane.

As the spring tide of colour ebbs away, a patchwork of greens is left in the valley. Many belong to evergreen plants: *Michelia doltsopa*, *Drimys winteri*, ferny-leaved *Lomatia ferruginea*, bamboos,

self-sowing myrtles and *Cornus capitata*, with clotted cream bracts in early summer, are among the broad-leaved cast. Further contrasts of shape and texture come from conifers, including *Cunninghamia konishii* and *C. lanceolata*, *Pinus patula*, *P. bhutanica* and a massive *Thuja plicata*. The collection has been boosted by a gift from the Royal Botanic Garden, Edinburgh, of tender conifer species seldom seen in British gardens, and by other wild-sourced plants. In spring, these are joined by the ephemeral greens of beech, sweet chestnut, oak and a host of other species, among which the two fine tulip trees planted by Fox and the weeping *Taxodium distichum* with its exposed knuckle-shaped roots lodge in my mind.

Following the line of pools and streams down the centre of the valley is some of the most startling greenery of all. On the shallow, well-drained banks near the house, the sight of gigantic, spine-tipped succulents, *Agave americana*, has everyone rubbing their eyes; the flower spikes rise over 6m (20ft). This unreal theme is continued by tall Chusan palms, and, in the deeper, damper ground, by Japanese bananas (*Musa basjoo*), giant-leaved *Gunnera manicata* and self-sowing tree ferns (*Dicksonia* and *Cyathea*). Hydrangeas, eucryphias, hoherias, streamside plantings of pink *Persicaria campanulata* and white *Zantedeschia aethiopica*, and an impressive specimen of *Rhododendron* 'Polar Bear' add summer flower.

Generally, this is a lush valley of woods and meadows with natural plantings and pastoral views, rather than expressions of self-conscious design. However, in the middle of the garden, on the west-facing slope, is an entirely unexpected leap into formal gardening: an asymmetrical cherry laurel maze. It was laid out by Alfred Fox in 1833. The entrance and exit routes are 1.2km (¾ mile) in length, and the hedges take two gardeners a full week to prune. The maze underwent a major restoration to mark the centenary of the National Trust in 1995, and the thatched summer-house was reinstated at the centre. The Christian symbolism of mazes may be contemplated on the Holy Bank above, where plants with Biblical associations are assembled, among them tree of heaven (*Ailanthus altissima*), *Colletia paradoxa* (syn. *C. cruciata*) and Judas tree (*Cercis siliquastrum*).

LEFT The thatched gazebo in the centre of the laurel maze at Glendurgan.
RIGHT The terraces in front of the Goddards House.

Goddards Garden

YORK, NORTH YORKSHIRE

AREA 1.2ha (3 acres) • SOIL sandy, silt loam • ALTITUDE 19m (62ft) • AVERAGE RAINFALL 483mm (19in) • AVERAGE WINTER CLIMATE cold

The tower of the old Terry's chocolate factory can still be glimpsed behind the stands of York Racecourse, a convenient walking distance from Goddards, which is perched on the hill above. Noel and Kathleen Terry bought this site in the prosperous Dringhouses suburbs – then an open field at the edge of the village – in 1925, and commissioned the leading Yorkshire architect, Walter Brierley, to build their house. It is a homely sprawl of mellow brick and tile in the Arts and Crafts manner, with vernacular rooflines and leaded windows; from the road, you are led to it through a Tudor-style gatehouse and an avenue of pollarded horse chestnuts. Since its acquisition by the Trust in 1984, the house has been used as a Regional Office and is not open to the public.

The series of shallow, formal, flagstone terraces beside the house, incorporating a circular brick basin which feeds rainwater from the roof down into a cruciform lily pond, is likewise a potent Arts and Crafts period piece. It was set out by the Sussex-based landscape architect George Dillistone, who contributed designs here from 1926 and on into the 1930s. Dillistone worked alongside Edwin Lutyens at Castle Drogo and it is possible he was introduced to the Terrys by their mutual friend Edward Hudson, the editor of *Country Life* magazine.

In the Terrys' time, these terraces contained myriad beds of roses and other flowers and a profusion of colours and scents even in the paving, which was studded with alpine plants. The Trust has grassed over and simplified much of this for ease of maintenance, although since 2006, when the decision was taken to open the garden, a programme of improvements has been under way. Today, the top terrace once again sports much the same planting schemes as those devised by Dillistone, who as a former nurseryman was knowledgeable about plants. The cast centres on catmint and the red *Penstemon* 'Newbury Gem', interplanted with bedding such as pink, purple and ivory tulips for spring and annual blue asters and pink lavatera for summer.

The middle terrace, edged in lavender, leads off to a pair of herbaceous borders. There are no records of their original content, but they are being refurbished more or less in the style of Gertrude Jekyll, the leading influence on border design at that period, with the present purple smoke bushes (*Cotinus*) retained as punctuation. Jekyll designed Walter Brierley's own garden, Bishopsbarns, in 1905.

There was clearly much interest in horticulture at Goddards, and at the bottom of the garden there is a substantial greenhouse by W. Richardson & Co. of Darlington, which has recently been restored. As you walk down the hillside, you also come to a bowling green and a grass tennis court, both contained within yew hedges, for this was also a relaxed family garden, intended for recreation. Indeed, Noel Terry liked a fairly wild and natural mood, especially around the formal garden's fringes. From the terraces it is not at all obvious how much garden there is below, and once you start following the winding paths and steps you soon become disorientated. The site is generously planted with trees, the many fine specimens including ginkgo, pine and robinia, and a sycamore that pre-dates the house. In the lower garden, the trees are underplanted with shrubbery beds of mixed evergreen and deciduous species such as mahonia, berberis, viburnum, escallonia and exochirda. The slightly acid soil, which promotes good growth in the conifers, also supports camellias. It

is all rather overgrown and mysterious, and so makes an excellent habitat for birds from owls to treecreepers.

The heart of this lower section is the large rock garden, constructed with tonnes of weathered limestone presumed to have come from Malham Tarn, at the foot of the Yorkshire Dales. Rock gardens were in their heyday in the early twentieth century, and the naturalistic treatment of the rock at Goddards accords with that advocated by the most famous rock gardener of the time, the Yorkshire writer and plant hunter Reginald Farrer.

The layered outcrops and sections of pavement are a plausible presence here on the hillside, and over the years have become fused into the surrounding vegetation. They encase two pools, well colonised by rushes and other water plants, and are shaded by substantial junipers, yews and spruces, many of which were no doubt acquired as 'dwarf conifers'. The sudden view out from this tangled and introspective world into the adjoining open expanse of the racecourse is quite a surprise.

LEFT Lutyen's Arts and Crafts house is the perfect backdrop to the period design of Goddards Garden.

ABOVE Poppies and foxgloves, planted to encourage wildlife.

Godolphin

HELSTON, CORNWALL

AREA 1.6ha (4 acres) • SOIL rich, sandy loam • ALTITUDE 65m (213ft) • AVERAGE RAINFALL 787–991mm (31–39in) • AVERAGE WINTER CLIMATE mild

An air of sleepy antiquity pervades this estate, of which the fields, woods and walls harbour the bones of many centuries of human activity, together with one of the very earliest gardens in England. At the summit of Godolphin Hill, with its panoramic views south to St Michael's Mount and north to St Ives Bay, the heathland, pasture and granite outcrops are crowned by a ceremonial stone enclosure thought to date from the Neolithic period; near the river below, the oaks and sycamores shade the legacy of mounds and depressions from the tin and copper mining which from medieval times onwards would bring wealth and status to the Godolphin family and fuel their rise from Cornish gentry to ennobled courtiers.

A winding lane, bordered by woods and mossy, fern-encrusted walls, leads to the house and accompanying farm buildings. The house – low, solid and soberly grand with its castellations and colonnaded loggia – was begun some time in the late fifteenth century and embellished over the following 150 years. It replaced the family's smaller, fortified medieval manor, which stood close to the same site, its new garden enclosures overlapping with the old manor's precinct. This opens up an intriguing possibility, for the archaeology appears to suggest that Godolphin's Side Garden, with its compartmented design and raised perimeter walk, may well relate back to the medieval fortified manor which pre-dated the present house, with which it is strangely disconnected and out of alignment. This would provide a unique insight into the very deepest fourteenth-century recesses of English garden history.

But any pre-Renaissance garden is a rare and remarkable survivor, and Godolphin's principal enclosures are thought to date from at least before 1520. Verification and exact dating here is invariably problematic, for there is a gaping absence of records, many of which were probably lost in the house fire of 1667.

The garden's survival stems largely from the fact that from the early eighteenth century this was no longer the family's permanent home, and although the grounds were periodically worked on, and the house subsequently tenanted and sold, the property became a quiet backwater, out of the eye of fashion. It was saved from modern development and rescued from disrepair by the Schofield family, who owned it from 1937 to 2007, when it was bought by the National Trust, which already owned the wider Godolphin landscape.

From the road, there is a glimpse down the small straight drive, shaded by evergreen oak and sweet bay, to the entrance forecourt, set out as a turning circle between buttressed walls and with a curious stone column and water basin in the centre of the lawn. Through the colonnade is another simple walled lawn space, forming an inner

LEFT Forget-me-nots and scented white stock by the path east of the house.

ABOVE A path winds through the bluebell wood.

green court within the wings of the house and the romantic ruins of the Great Hall, demolished in the early nineteenth century. But the visitor route is through the part-cobbled farmyard, and on past the piggery and the chickens scratching in their run.

Here, behind the stable block and below the house's first-floor state apartment, is the high-walled privy (private) garden, later called the King's Garden to commemorate a visit in 1646 thought to have been made by the future Charles II on his escape to France via the Scilly Isles, of which Sir Francis Godolphin was Governor. Today, it presents a quartered design with four pads of lawn, edged in stones and set among straight gravel paths. While the walled framework is early sixteenth century, the raised terrace walks that would probably have been here have long since disappeared, for in about 1800 the garden was filled in with soil and used for vegetable growing.

Gnarled and knobbly box bushes run down the central pathway, and they are joined by more recent additions including a run of old lavenders (among which ferns have naturalised, as they invariably do in Cornwall), *Magnolia × soulangeana*, and a border of herbs and other nectar-rich herbaceous plants, for the stable wall has cavities for bee skeps. On sunny days these plants infuse the sheltered space with warm aromas.

On the other side of the entrance forecourt, you are led through the orchard, with its cider house dating from around 1700 and backdrop of old chestnut trees; this is now being replanted with fruit varieties associated with south-west England. The raised perimeter walk of the adjacent Side Garden, with its retaining earth walls faced with stone and rubble, gives views into this area. The walk is shaded by lines of wonderful veteran sycamores, which were introduced into Britain in the sixteenth century and widely planted at Godolphin. They are interspersed with wild holly in a medley of wildflowers, including primroses, polypody ferns and bluebells, the last of which also flood through the woods.

The estate map of 1786 shows the Side Garden and Garden Paddock, contained within hedges and raised walks and subdivided into nine square or rectangular compartments, each quite large and further subdivided by formal plantings and pathways. It has been suggested that the surviving framework of the compartments in the Side Garden could represent the eastern side of a nine-compartment enclosure around the earlier house. The additional six compartments of the Garden Paddock were developed on a new site extending into former fields, probably after the house was rebuilt on a new alignment from the late fifteenth century. It was fashionable for early gardens, such as Lord Burghley's Great Garden at Theobolds

in Hertfordshire, to have this nine-compartment design. Some of Godolphin's compartments were functional but others would no doubt have been decorative, perhaps incorporating pleached arbours, topiaries, knot gardens and heraldic or symbolic decoration, all conveying the high social status of the family.

The six newer compartments then disappeared back into the field in the nineteenth century – their outlines still visible in the mown strips cut into the garden paddock – while the remaining three compartments closest to the house appear to have survived both the fifteenth- and nineteenth-century phases of destruction. They could, in fact, date as far back as 1300, though they now have many later overlays of planting, including that carried out by the Schofields.

Throughout, their topography is varied by terraces and banks. The northern compartment comprises lawns contained by relaxed borders of shrubs, herbaceous plants and accompanying trees, including some large sentinel yews. The run of tall box hedging which forms one of its subdivisions may be very old indeed. The central compartment has fruit trees and wild flowers while the southern compartment, the most historically evocative, is taken up by the ancient depressions of two large rectangular fish ponds which would have produced a good supply of food for the household.

The task of repairing Godolphin and returning some of its lost features without disturbing the bewitching atmosphere of antiquity and quiet decay is the challenge faced by the Trust. The temptation to over-restore and over-tidy is being resisted, for much of the charm comes from the weed-bedecked cobblestones and crumbling, ivy-topped grey walls, which are home to an exceptional diversity of rare lichens. With the King's Garden and Side Garden listed as ancient monuments by English Heritage, even routine gardening requires careful deliberation. Meanwhile, continuing research and archaeology should provide a stronger factual basis for our conjectures about the ancient origins of this remarkable place.

ABOVE Godolphin's compartmented design and raised walk are thought to be relics of a medieval layout.

Great Chalfield Manor

MELKSHAM, WILTSHIRE

AREA 2.8ha (7 acres) • **SOIL** alkaline, limestone • **ALTITUDE** 46m (150ft)
AVERAGE RAINFALL 711mm (28in) • **AVERAGE WINTER CLIMATE** cold

The collection of honey-coloured buildings sits secluded above low-lying pasture at the end of an oak avenue. The manor, rebuilt in the second half of the fifteenth century, was restored between 1905 and 1912 for the engineer Robert Fuller, who then purchased the property from his father and whose family continues to live here. With gables, oriel windows, gargoyles and other figures, it is splendidly decorative. Architecturally, the north front is the finest, for which the fourteenth-century parish church and the defensive moat, fed by a medieval leat 823m (900yd) long, provide picturesque accompaniments.

However, it is the south front and adjacent half-timbered wing, clad with wall shrubs and climbing plants, including Moroccan broom and yellow Banksian rose, that enjoy the most romantic views of the garden. From here, you look out over the sunny and sheltered Inner Court, where scented Bush roses surround a well and *Campanula pyramidalis* self-sows between stone paving slabs, down to the lower moat or fish pond. It is a timeless scene. Meadowsweet, rushes and scarlet-stemmed dogwood (a striking partnership in winter, when the rushes turn parchment-tan) soften the division between grass and water, and in spring the far bank, backed by a copse of tall trees, is a ribbon of daffodils. Moorhens and dragonflies enliven the picture, and the fortunate will catch sight of kingfishers.

South-east of the house, a rough orchard slopes down to the fish pond. The grass is cut once a year for hay, and in spring it too is stained yellow with daffodils. Wildflowers, including snakeshead fritillaries, anemones, cowslips, primroses and wild asparagus, are in abundance here, as elsewhere in the grounds; roses, including 'Rambling Rector', 'Wedding Day' and 'Sander's White Rambler', scramble up the apple trees.

It is this combination of old, mellow architecture, meadows and wildflowers, trees and water, that sets the mood at Great Chalfield, and it is respected in the unpretentious treatment of the more formal parts of the garden. The grounds were renovated by Robert Fuller at the same time as the house, with advice from a Mr Partridge and the watercolourist and garden designer Alfred Parsons RA, who lived at Broadway. East of the house are a lily pond, old and new mulberries, yew topiaries, and a huge sweep of enclosed lawn concluding in a handsome gazebo. Along the retaining wall below the lawn are softly coloured herbaceous borders.

ABOVE Roses cling to the mellow stone walls of the Gatehouse wing.

RIGHT A beautiful blue and white border with hardy geraniums and irises.

Greenway

GALMPTON, BRIXHAM, DEVON

AREA 12ha (30 acres) • SOIL neutral/shillet • ALTITUDE 30m (100ft)
AVERAGE RAINFALL 991mm (39in) • AVERAGE WINTER CLIMATE mild

*'The impression is of a jungle of exotics
and rarities rather than of carefully
composed scenes'*

Legend has it that the stone wall of the overgrown camellia glade, which you meet amid the maze of woodland paths above the river at Greenway was built by Spanish prisoners of war from the Armada of 1588. Greenway was then owned by John Gilbert, half-brother of Sir Walter Raleigh, and a member of the seafaring family of Compton Castle. Such layers of history romanticise a property already charged with the heady atmosphere of a 'lost' garden, cut off from the modern world inside a large estate, on its own private wooded promontory over the Dart, and with its design overwhelmed by the luxuriance of a mild, humid climate.

'An ideal house, a dream house,' wrote the crime writer Agatha Christie, who bought Greenway as a holiday home in 1938 and featured it in two of her novels, *Dead Man's Folly* and *Five Little Pigs*. The Elton family, who owned Greenway until 1832, seem to be responsible for much of the framework of the present garden – the sweeping curves and picturesque views, decorative outbuildings and enclosed flower gardens. Although the style reflects that of Humphry Repton, the designer is not known. Following the Eltons came a series of plantsmen owners, including Agatha Christie's son-in-law Anthony Hicks, who described the garden as 'on the verge of going wild'. Today the impression is of a jungle of exotics and rarities rather than of carefully composed scenes.

Down the long, winding entrance drive, the hanging beech woods and fields of Devon Red cattle soon give way to the first exotics, set around grassy dips and knolls of ferns and wildflowers: Chusan palms, handkerchief trees (*Davidia involucrata*), cedars and large-leaved oaks alternating with eucryphias, variegated osmanthus,

a large *Michelia doltsopa* (a tender magnolia-like tree with sweetly scented, cream flowers), and a host of rhododendrons and azaleas.

This eclecticism sets the tone for the enclosed gardens above the former stone barn and stable block. On one side of the drive a doorway leads into an old tennis court, overhung with *Rhododendron arboreum*, Judas tree, another handkerchief tree, and a pink-flowered *Magnolia campbellii*. On the other, a giant Chinese wisteria lures you into a large kitchen garden, its walls buried behind the most esoteric planting imaginable. The longer history of plantsmanship is signalled by the presence of the vinery on the north wall, where tropical stove plants would have been nurtured in Victorian times. Now fully restored, it houses passionflowers, ginger lilies and tender tree ferns, as well as grapevines.

The Victorian influence intensifies in the garden beyond, where a cast-iron Coalbrookdale fountain splashes onto a rockery backdrop of limestone and quartz, interplanted with giant-fronded Woodwardia and other ferns. It connects to another period piece, the Putting Green, a clock-golf course installed in the 1940s, fringed by white-flowered Judas tree (*Cercis siliquastrum*), smooth-barked *Cornus kousa*, and a bed of assorted dahlias, planted by Agatha Christie and not lifted since.

Next, the garden dissolves into woodland again, the paths leading you on a leisurely traverse of the steep riverbank at several parallel levels, each joined to the next by steps or serpentine passageways. It is easy to get lost. The upper Plantation takes you past pines and southern beeches (*Nothofagus*), yew-like *Podocarpus* and its relative *Dacrydium*, and old plantings of camellias,

rhododendrons and red-lanterned *Crinodendron hookerianum*. From *Michelia yunnanensis* to *Azara uruguayensis*, it is full of delights and curiosities.

On the next level are tree magnolias and foxglove trees (*Paulownia*), a giant monkey puzzle and a huge Californian black oak (*Quercus kelloggii*). The far end of this path is the warmest part of the site, and a brick wall surviving from the Victorian era shelters a border of herbaceous exotics. At the opposite end of the path is a balancing piece of formality, in the form of a box-edged walk, planted with hydrangeas and scented white *Rhododendron maddenii*.

Spring-flowering, carmine-pink *Cyclamen repandum* has colonised here among the grass and primroses and around a modern sculpture, *Mother and Child* by local artist Bridget McCrum. Nearby, bluebells surge in their thousands under the trees. This next path leads past coniferous *Cryptomeria*, *Cornus capitata*, *Magnolia virginiana* and white-flowered *Rehderodendron macrocarpum*, under a sunny slope of acacia and eucalyptus, and on to a pair of pools. In Victorian times, there was a more extensive water garden here, but most of it is now engulfed in vegetation.

Here and there along the circuit, between the tree trunks, you get glimpses of the River Dart, its yachts and river boats, wooded banks and settlements – Dittisham across the water, and Kingwear and Dartmouth 1.6km (1 mile) or so downstream. The paths now take you right to the river's edge, first to a late eighteenth-century Boat House, complete with plunge pool, and then to the Battery, with its castellations and canons. The picturesque route takes you home along a path edged in cherry laurel, past sweet chestnut, cork oak and, of course, ever more trees and shrubs to confound the most expert botanist.

ABOVE The Fernery at Greenway, with creeping saxifrage and bergenia.

Greys Court

ROTHERFIELD GREYS, HENLEY-ON-THAMES, OXFORDSHIRE

AREA 1.2ha (3 acres) • **SOIL** limy • **ALTITUDE** 76m (250ft) • **AVERAGE RAINFALL** 686mm (27in)
AVERAGE WINTER CLIMATE moderate

This garden has an almost mystical atmosphere. Cut off from the outside world by folds of Chiltern downland and hills capped with beechwoods, the gabled Elizabethan house and its accompanying medieval towers present their own reality. To this has been added the sensitive touch of Sir Felix and Lady Brunner, who bought the property in 1937. The result is a blend of ancient flint walls, dappled walks, fountains, scents and mellow colours which engulfs the senses. The house stands on the western edge of the fourteenth-century courtyard, surveying the Great Tower and its adjoining ruined walls across an expanse of lawn. Scots pines add their craggy shapes to the scene, and north of the house a venerable European larch rests its branches on the grass.

On both sides of the house the grass merges quietly with the park, assisted by the encircling ha-ha, but to the north the view is partly interrupted by a grove of strawberry trees, planted on the bank at the suggestion of the Brunners' friend Humphrey Waterfield, a painter and gardener. The Killarney strawberry tree, *Arbutus unedo*, carries bountiful crops of white pitcher-shaped flowers and red fruits simultaneously in late summer and autumn, while *A. × andrachnoides* contributes peeling branches of cinnamon and chestnut-red.

Slip through the gateway beneath the Great Tower, past the warm aromas of sun-loving Mediterranean cistuses and rosemaries growing in the rubble, and you find yourself surrounded by white flowers and grey foliage, in the first of a disorienting series of irregular-shaped enclosures. A new loggia in the White Garden, built in 2002, houses pots of citrus fruits, and by the entrance are two

impressive Japanese bitter orange, *Poncirus trifoliata*, flaunting vicious spines. In spring, they bear fragrant white flowers. Later, there are heady scents from roses, honeysuckles and the pineapple-flavoured *Philadelphus microphyllus*.

The rosarian Hilda Murrell advised the Brunners on the planting of the Rose Garden, reached through the next gateway. Here, the lawn is shaded by a spreading foxglove tree, *Paulownia tomentosa*, and at midsummer the central beds are awash with old-fashioned roses. The surrounding borders are planted with herbaceous plants in colour schemes of pink and purple, yellow and orange.

The principle that if a plant is worth growing, it is worth having a decent show of it is followed happily at Greys Court. In the Wisteria Arbour, which connects the Rose Garden to the Kitchen Garden, there is a display of *Wisteria sinensis* such as you will never have seen. You duck right under it, weaving between the gnarled and part-rotten stems, under an enormous canopy of twisted branches and, in spring, dripping flowers. The gardeners refer to it as 'The Beast'. The Kitchen Garden is designed as a matrix of straight paths infilled with fruit trees, bushes and espaliers, as well as vegetables and unusual salad crops. Companion plantings of flowers and herbs among the beans and asparagus peas, gourds and pumpkins, make a lively display, and in front of the plums and greengages there is a long cut-flower border of cornflowers and other country favourites. A hedge of striped 'Rosa Mundi' (*R. gallica* 'Versicolor'), an avenue of 'Ballerina' crab apples, a sumptuous peony border, and a circle of fastigiate Irish junipers, with philadelphus, box, myrtle and lavender, arranged around a Roman-style fountain, complete the scene.

Equally striking is the tunnel of pink and white blossom in the adjacent Cherry Garden, through which a rustic path of stone and cobbles curves enticingly past another fountain, found on a farm in Switzerland and installed to mark the Brunners' 40th wedding anniversary. This grove, recently replanted, was another of Humphrey Waterfield's inspirations, and, like the other cherry highlights, comes into its own again in autumn when the leaves turn orange and russet. A soaring tulip tree (*Liriodendron tulipifera*) and ancient weeping ash over the wall enhance this scene, and provide part of the backdrop for the little knot garden, redesigned by the Trust, beside the Cromwellian stables; the building was reputedly commandeered by soldiers during the Civil War.

The garden has not been anchored in any single historical period, and modern additions have been welcomed. Furniture, fountains, ironwork and statuary have all been commissioned from contemporary local artists, and in 1980, inspired by the enthronement sermon of the Archbishop of Canterbury, in which Dr Robert Runcie drew an analogy between people searching for life's secret and being lost in a maze, Lady Brunner conceived the idea of a pavement maze at Greys Court. It was realised in brick and grass by Adrian Fisher, and, with its wealth of Christian symbolism and allegory, adds yet another contemplative layer to a timeless and tranquil garden.

LEFT Lavender lines a stone-flagged path leading to the Kitchen Garden.
BELOW Looking past a hedge of roses to the fourteenth-century Great Tower.

Gunby Hall

GUNBY, SPILSBY, LINCOLNSHIRE

AREA 2.8ha (7 acres) • SOIL alkaline/clay, loam • ALTITUDE 30m (100ft)
AVERAGE RAINFALL 635mm (25in) • AVERAGE WINTER CLIMATE cold

Roses galore; that will be your lasting impression of Gunby if you visit during the summer months. They foam against walls, scramble up trees, spill into water, fling themselves across pergolas and billow from flower-beds, creating welcoming scenes of carefree opulence that defy the inhospitable climate and featureless landscape.

The unreal quality here is set by the William and Mary house, built in 1700 for Sir William Massingberd, from a Saxon family long established in the neighbourhood. An impossibly pretty building of orange brick with limestone dressings, it is entirely unexpected in the midst of this Lincolnshire farmland, 13km (8 miles) from the North Sea. Numerous handsome outbuildings accompany the house, including coach houses, a clock tower, and a pigeon house, pre-dating the present hall and surmounted by an ornate weathervane.

Succeeding generations of Massingberds have left their mark on the garden, but its present character can be attributed largely to Margaret Massingberd, who undertook a thorough overhaul in the early years of the twentieth century, and to the former tenants Mr and Mrs John Wrisdale, who, in collaboration with the Trust, restored the garden with imagination and gusto over a 40-year period. Lawn sweeps around three sides of the house, interrupted by ornamental trees and some formal planting beside the tennis court and in front of the house. The grass is peppered with early spring bulbs, and roses make their first appearance. Against the hall are 'Alister Stella Gray', 'Climbing Lady Hillingdon', the richly scented 'Climbing Madame Butterfly', 'Breeze Hill' and the extremely rare Rambler 'Elisa Robichon'. On the east side are crimson 'Etoile de Hollande' and, in box-edged beds, the unusual Hybrid Tea 'Mrs

Oakley Fisher', which, with its coppery flowers and plum-tipped foliage, is particularly associated with Gunby Hall.

The older trees on the lawns, including the great cedar, were planted by Peregrine Massingberd, a friend of Sir Joseph Banks, the naturalist and traveller, in the early nineteenth century. He is also responsible for considerable park and woodland planting, as recorded in the Gunby Tree Book, which has been kept since 1670.

At the eastern edge of the garden, the vista from the house is terminated by rose shrubberies, where, on my first visit to Gunby, I recall watching a family of stoats playing in the midday shadows. Yellow-flowered *Rosa* 'Cantabrigiensis', white 'Nevada', pink 'Constance Spry' and ferny-leaved *R. multibracteata* are part of the cast, underplanted with hardy geraniums. At midsummer, a cascade of white roses of 'Wedding Day' illuminates the sombre evergreens behind; a second cascade, in pink, is furnished later by 'Minnehaha'.

The ghost of one Miss Massingberd, searching for her lover, is said to haunt the walk beside the rectangular pond, possibly a stewpond for the earlier manor house. The planting of slim, swaying Irish junipers and luminous white flowers, including

those of *Rosa* 'Albéric Barbier' tumbling down the bank, is intended to spook those foolish enough to stroll at or after dusk.

Mellow brick walls and arched entrances beckon you towards the walled garden. Even the herbaceous borders that front them, lavish with a succession of plants from anchusas to asters, fail to prepare you for the sight ahead: massed displays of dazzling and extrovert flowers assembled in great belts and blocks beside long, straight paths. Here is a colony of yellow Floribunda roses, including 'Chinatown' and 'Arthur Bell'; there, 'Orange Triumph' and the bright reds of 'Frensham' and 'National Trust'. Lavender, dianthus and bearded irises stream beside them, while hefty Climbing roses such as pink 'Léontine Gervais' and 'Madame Isaac Pereire' furnish spectacular backdrops. There is also a herb garden, a temple summer-house, cutting borders, a sundial lawn and jam-packed greenhouses.

It is the same story in the adjacent Kitchen Garden, though in recent years more ground has been given over to fruit and vegetable production with a diverse range of produce cultivated, from asparagus and sweet corn to root vegetables and salad crops. Here there are hydrangeas, rivers of catmint and creamy *Sisyrinchium*

striatum, and further extravagant plantings of Bush roses such as pink 'Madame Caroline Testout' and scented Hybrid Musks. For me, the most entrancing performance is by the Rambler *R. multiflora* 'Grevillei', the Seven Sisters rose, which presents its huge trusses of flowers, comprising every shade from white and soft pink to lilac and crimson-red, against the pigeon-house wall. Experts are also quick to spot 'Reine Marie Henriette', a rare Victorian Climbing rose with highly fragrant blooms in cherry-red.

I have not mentioned fruit trees. A survey of 1944 listed 228 varieties, probably planted by Margaret Massingberd. There are still at least half that number remaining, lining paths, espaliered on walls, and filling the orchard, with recent plantings of old and local varieties in the East Garden. In spring and autumn they are a fine sight, and the produce is safely stored in the garden's handsome apple house.

LEFT Chives in flower in the herb garden.

ABOVE This path in the Kitchen Garden is edged with many colourful flowers, including poppies and irises.

Ham House and Garden

HAM, RICHMOND, LONDON

AREA 7.3ha (18 acres) • SOIL lime-free/sandy • ALTITUDE 15m (50ft)
AVERAGE RAINFALL 635mm (25in) • AVERAGE WINTER CLIMATE cold

'To see the House and Garden of the Duke of Lauderdale, which is indeed inferior to a few of the best Villas in Italy itself; the House furnished like a great Prince's; the Parterres, Flower Gardens, Orangeries, Groves, Avenues, Courts, Statues, Perspectives, Fountains, Aviaries, & all this at the banks of the Sweetest River in the World, must needs be surprising,' wrote the diarist John Evelyn, after walking to Ham on a summer's evening in 1678.

What strikes the visitor as most remarkable today is that so much of it is still here, little ruffled by centuries of change and the burgeoning of London. Its avenues of trees still stretch out towards Ham Common and the Thames – the most comfortable and convenient means of getting to the City in the seventeenth century. The house itself is still almost exactly as it looked in the 1670s when it was enlarged: a tall, compact building of reddish-brown Jacobean brick dressed in white stone, and its rooms still with their original furnishings. Even better, the architectural bones of the formal seventeenth-century garden have also survived, making this one of the earliest and rarest garden layouts in the Trust's hands. The inspiration at the time came from the Baroque gardens of Europe, and Ham's style is a simple form of the typical Dutch garden, referred to by contemporaries as the New Mode. Sadly, the identity of the designer is unclear.

The clipped greens and statuary of the entrance forecourt set the mood. The topiary planted by the Trust comes as hefty drums of bay and, against the flanking walls, cones of yew and squares of box, planted with bulbs. All these are kept sharp-edged and tight, the dark colours contrasting with the central circle of closely mown

lawn, in which the large frame of a river god reclines. Thirty-eight busts, some representing Roman emperors and senators and others unknown, look over the scene from niches in the house and garden walls. Originally the court was completely enclosed, with a straight path leading to the front door, but alterations were carried out at the end of the eighteenth century and now the park is separated only by an ironwork screen and a ha-ha.

The adjacent East or Cherry Garden, redesigned by the Trust after a plan of 1671, is the most intimate part of the composition. Fruit was integral to the formal Dutch garden, and the cherries may have been either trained in situ or grown in containers. Now the garden is purely ornamental, with the central diamond-pattern box parterre – filled with Dutch lavender and dwarf cotton lavender, clipped as silver domes – held in a *berceau*, or cradle, of hornbeam tunnels. It is a simple but striking treatment. Likewise, figs, vines and other espaliered fruits adorn the walls of the main enclosure, part of the green, expansive scene surveyed from the broad gravel terrace. In the foreground are the plats – eight large squares of close-mown grass, separated by paths – which were remade out of the existing lawn in 1975. Beyond, an avenue of limes carries the eye past the garden gates, deep into Ham Common.

Occupying the middle ground is the Wilderness, a fashionable contemporary adjunct to the formal garden offering a taste of mystery and solitude. The Trust has reimposed its geometric pattern with hedges of hornbeam, speared by field maples, and the grass paths once again radiate, as in the 1671 plan, in a *patte d'oie* (or, more recognisably, an early version of a Union Flag design) from a central circle. Each compartment is planted as a thicket of deciduous and evergreen trees and shrubs – with scented plants next to the grass paths – and lead statues are being commissioned as centrepieces, as illustrated in the painting attributed to Henry Danckerts which hangs in the house. The narrow borders around the garden are planted in seventeenth-century style, with rows of plants in front of wall-trained fruit trees. The Vine Border, directly below the South Terrace, has been replanted with old-fashioned pinks (*Dianthus*), columbines and lavender.

In 2003 work began on the furthest compartment, in front of the Orangery, reached through an avenue of evergreen oak, *Quercus ilex*. The 1671 plan shows this as the kitchen garden, divided into 32 plots, and as the restoration advances, these are being filled with an assortment of fruits, vegetables, herbs, roses and flowers for cutting, displayed within box hedges. Peaches, plums, apricots and cherries are trained as espaliers and fans on the walls. The Orangery itself, built in 1674 and one of the oldest to survive in Britain, is draped in eleven wisterias and overlooks a terrace furnished with olive trees and citrus fruits in wooden planters.

LEFT The kitchen garden is being restored to the 1671 plan and grows produce for the restaurant.

RIGHT The East Garden, with its box-hedged compartments filled with santolina and lavender, after a design of 1671.

ABOVE Wisteria smother the Orangery in May.

Hanbury Hall

DROITWICH, WORCESTERSHIRE

AREA 8ha (20 acres) • **SOIL** neutral/clay • **ALTITUDE** 66m (216ft) • **AVERAGE RAINFALL** 635mm (25in) • **AVERAGE WINTER CLIMATE** moderate

Before 1993, you would have found this decorative William and Mary squire's house, built in red brick, with hipped roof, cupola and pavilions, somewhat stranded in well-treed but flat parkland. Now, one of the rarest and most curious forms of English garden has sprung up beside it – a sunken parterre, fruit garden, vegetable garden, and Wilderness in the style of the 1700s.

The restoration, financed by two generous private legacies and a heritage award from the EU, is based on the original scheme installed by the celebrated lawyer Thomas Vernon to accompany his new mansion. The designer was the leading garden designer of the day, George London, since the plans are endorsed 'Mr London's Draughts'. This is exciting, for London's elaborate, labour-intensive gardens were immediate victims of the abrupt swing in eighteenth-century taste in favour of naturalistic landscapes, and not one has survived to the present day. At Hanbury, this destruction happened in the 1770s.

In the Victorian era, formality was back in fashion and a forecourt in front of the Hall was created, even using copies of the original ironwork gates, which had been sold in 1790 to the owners of nearby Mere Hall. Surrounded by brick pillars (and, formerly, ironwork panels), the forecourt sports a lively pair of Moorish pavilions decorated with Minton tiles.

Had its creator, another Thomas Vernon, not died at the age of 27, he might well have set to work re-creating a parterre on the lawn to the west. As it is, this was left to the National Trust. Other than a dip in the lawn there was not a trace remaining, so the starting point was the existing plans and illustrations, especially the bird's-eye drawing of 1732 by James Dougharty. The exact layout and dimensions were then established by archaeology. There are some peculiarities: the garden is not properly aligned with the house; the sunken parterre is not a true square; and the twin pavilions at the northern end are not at right angles to the garden.

Equally odd, to modern British eyes, is the arrangement of plants. In the Sunken Parterre, you look down on four giant grids of green and gold-tipped box, each with a large central topiary, and punctuated with further cones of box and corner-posts of 'gilded' (golden-variegated) hollies, topped with golden balls. Inserted into this pattern is a colourful array of annuals and perennials, drawn from lists used by the royal gardener Henry Wise, with whom London ran the celebrated Brompton Nursery. Further planting information has been gleaned from *The Retir'd Gardener*, the French work translated by London and Wise in 1706.

Separated by neatly tilled bare earth, each plant is treated individually and set out, jewel-like, in strictly regimented rows: French, African and English marigolds, London pride, pasqueflower, snapdragons, carnations, armeria, *Aster amellus* and, of course, Brompton stocks. There is some repetition, but no attempt at a unified scheme of colour or form. This is a highly formalised, manicured composition, revealing the sophisticated mastery over nature that was the essence of the prevailing French- and Dutch-inspired fashion. A ribbon border of bulbs, running along the yew hedges above the parterre, contributes spring colour, with terracotta pots – tulips in spring and citrus fruits in summer – adorning the path edge.

On axis with the Sunken Parterre is a decorative fruit garden, featuring 'Black Worcester' pears and 'Ribston Pippin', 'Golden Pippin' and 'Ashmead's Kernel' apples in the grass, framed by narrow, box-edged beds of lavenders and topiary bay trees. A re-created pair of trellis timber 'green houses' flank the iron railings of a clairvoyée, through which you have a view down over a mirror pond into the park beyond.

There is no relaxation of formality in the adjacent Wilderness, speared by a timber obelisk, where Damask, Gallica and wild roses, philadelphus, hazel, hibiscus and evergreen phillyrea, rhamnus, ruscus and Italian cypress are marshalled into lines and rigorously pruned. Their arbitrary arrangement within the goose-foot pattern, however, gave the desired taste of wild disorder to the eighteenth-century visitor. Behind, great blocks of clipped beech enclose a circular pool which is another re-creation of the original London garden design.

Reinstated in 1988 were the Bowling Green, with another new pair of garden pavilions crowned with golden balls and The Grove. This combines order and disorder within an oval pattern of box and upright English juniper, its compartments comprising a mix of rowan and service tree, guelder rose and the elm *Ulmus* 'Dodoens', which is so far proving resistant to disease.

The pots of lemons in the formal gardens come from a handsome brick Orangery to be discovered between lawn and trees west of the Bowling Green. It was probably built a few years after Thomas Vernon's death in 1721. An assortment of oranges, lemons, pomegranates, agaves and oleanders are displayed outside in summer, while clipped cones of evergreen *Phillyrea angustifolia* stand all year round between the high windows.

Tucked into the adjacent spinney is a Victorian mushroom house, now used to force rhubarb and as an apple store. The nearby orchard, an addition to the late eighteenth-century walled kitchen garden, is reached along a primrose walk – a straight ride between yew and holly – which is still sulphur yellow in spring. Other formal elements to survive here are an oak avenue and a cedar walk, the latter dating from London's garden, and leading to an exceptionally fine mid-eighteenth-century ice house.

ABOVE The Sunken Parterre, re-created from James Dougharty's original plans and illustrations.

Hardwick Hall

DOE LEA, CHESTERFIELD, DERBYSHIRE

AREA 7ha (17½ acres) • **SOIL** alkaline/light sandy loam • **ALTITUDE** 178m (584ft)
AVERAGE RAINFALL 660mm (26in) • **AVERAGE WINTER CLIMATE** cold

'A woman of masculine understanding and conduct, proud, furious, selfish and unfeeling. She was a builder, a buyer and seller of estates, a moneylender, a farmer and a merchant of coals and timber; when disengaged from those employments, she intrigued alternately with Elizabeth [Tudor] and Mary [Stuart], always to the prejudice and terror of her husband.' So wrote Edmund Lodge in 1790, describing Bess of Hardwick, Countess of Shrewsbury. It was she who, in the 1590s, built this awe-inspiring house; the initials ES, carved above the high, square towers and topped by a coronet, proclaim her name and status across the estate, and the entire property pulsates with her forceful personality.

The Old Hall, now a ruin, was once her childhood home and was extensively rebuilt by Bess in about 1585; but on the death of her estranged fourth husband, Lord Shrewsbury, she had control of her fabulous wealth, and, although in her early sixties, embarked on a second, grander residence a short distance away. There have been gardens around the New Hall since its completion, and the spacious courts that we see today, with their decorative gateways and garden houses, finial-capped walls and banqueting house, were set out at that time. However, the smart hedges and colourful plantings within them are the creation of the last two centuries.

Colour is concentrated in the surrounding borders, and what triumphant colour schemes they are. The Trust redesigned them in the mid-1980s, basing the planting on a Jekyllian sequence of lively harmonies. Variegated aralias, flowering grasses and cimicifugas furnish creamy highlights, while dahlias, argyranthemums, penstemons, crocosmias, purple heuchera and cotinus progress through the hottest shades, and sedums, verbenas, asters and buddleja through the warm reds and purples. There is a generous complement of half-hardy perennials. I recommend a trip to Hardwick in late summer purely to savour them.

Running along the other side of the south wall is a long border of cooler, pastel colours, at its brightest in spring and early summer. Clematis, vines and roses cloak the walls, accompanied by hardy perennials such as euphorbias, asters and agapanthus and supplemented by half-hardy plants such as salvias, osteospermums and gazanias for later in the season. This border is part of the largest court, the South Court, which covers an area of 3ha (7½ acres) and was laid out in its present pattern of four quarters, divided by allées of yew and hornbeam, by Lady Louisa Egerton, daughter of the 7th Duke of Devonshire, in 1861. The Devonshires are direct descendants of Bess, and the fact that Hardwick has changed so little over the centuries is due in large part to its being owned by a family whose principal seat was elsewhere, at Chatsworth, whence came the statues in the central *rond-point*. At one time, this entire court was given over to fruit and, probably, vegetable production. Today two of the quarters are orchards replanted by the Trust, and in the third, *Magnolia × soulangeana* and other specimen trees grow in the grass.

The fourth quarter contains the *pièce de résistance*, one of the largest herb gardens in Britain, accompanied by a nuttery. Installed by the Trust in the mid-1970s, this has recently been redesigned to incorporate a box 'snake' and taller, pyramidal plantings in the centre. Wigwams of golden and green hops echo the gilded posts that were a favoured ornament in Elizabethan gardens. The great array of

culinary and medicinal plants on show here would all have been familiar to gardeners of the time, and in constant demand for the house.

The scale and crispness of this court can be appreciated fully from the upper landing of the house, where you can see it set out against a broad backdrop of Turkey oaks, sycamores, limes, beech, estate buildings and farmland. From the adjacent long gallery, there is a fine view out over the East Court, with its lawn, roses and central pond, across the ha-ha, and down the lime avenue, planted in the 1920s. The limes curve to embrace the field opposite the house, giving the effect of an upturned wine glass with an 800m (½ mile) stem. This courtyard highlights the work done in the garden by Dowager Duchess Evelyn, the last member of the Devonshire family to live at Hardwick.

Among the many fine tapestries in the house is a series of 32 octagonal panels embroidered with botanical subjects, with accompanying aphorisms. They are a further reminder of the delight the Elizabethans took in flowers and another happy link between house and garden. Many carry Bess's monogram. The initials ES are likely to haunt you long after you have departed this extraordinary place, so rich in history.

LEFT The herb garden, with tripods for hops.

BELOW View across red valerian and golden hop to the south front of the New Hall.

Hardy's Cottage

HIGHER BOCKHAMPTON, DORCHESTER, DORSET

AREA 0.8ha (2 acres) • **SOIL** rich • **ALTITUDE** 107m (350ft) • **AVERAGE RAINFALL** 610m (24in)
AVERAGE WINTER CLIMATE cold

'So wild it was when first we settled here.' Thomas Hardy quotes his grandmother in his poem *Domicilium*, written when he was sixteen. The thatch and cob cottage, where the novelist and poet was born in 1840 and spent most of the first 34 years of his life, is still secluded, framed by Thorncombe Wood, through which you walk to reach it and which is still home to nightjars – though 'untamed and untameable' Egdon Heath is now largely forestry plantation. To modern eyes the cottage and its garden are a chocolate-box picture, with roses and honeysuckle around the windows and door and a profusion of traditional shrubs and perennials spilling onto the grit paths and daisy-covered lawn, but it was a hard and impoverished life here in the nineteenth century.

Fruit and vegetables from the garden would have been greatly valued, and the small plot includes rows of currants and the old potato varieties 'Lumper' and 'Portland Black'. Elsewhere, lupins, columbines, Solomon's seal, peonies, foxgloves, shasta daisies and asters – 'such hardy flowers/As flourish best untrained' – rise above the primroses, lily of the valley, pinks and woodland ferns. Lilac and mock orange add their scents, and the formal pattern of beds and paths is reinforced by clipped box, holly and bay, though the mood is kept authentically relaxed, even slightly unkempt. Old varieties of apple tree grow in the orchard, while the wood is peppered with bluebells and other wildflowers.

RIGHT Thomas Hardy was inspired to write *Far From the Madding Crowd* and *Under the Greenwood Tree* here.

Hare Hill

OVER ALDERLEY, MACCLESFIELD, CHESHIRE

AREA 4ha (10 acres) • SOIL slowly permeable fine clay loams subject to seasonal waterlogging • ALTITUDE 120–150m (394–492ft) • AVERAGE RAINFALL 813–991mm (32–39in) AVERAGE WINTER CLIMATE moderate

There is the option of walking to this estate along the 3.2km (2 mile) path from the red sandstone ridge of Alderley Edge. The rolling dairy farmland makes Manchester and its conurbation seem a world away. You arrive to find a garden set into a wood, a walled enclosure surrounded by a web of meandering pathways and glades of exotic shrubs. There is no house visible. The planting is centred on the detached former kitchen garden, and the Georgian mansion was sold by the Trust in 1978 to help finance the running of the remainder of the estate. Thus, there is some sense of a garden stranded, and of exploration and discovery. The whole garden is quiet, wrapped in its oaks, beech and conifers, with dappled light, mossy scents and the sounds of woodpeckers and other forest birds. There is an especially mysterious area to the north, where the trees open onto an old marl pit, filled with peaty water, which you cross by bridge and grass causeway between dark evergreens and bamboo.

From midsummer onwards, the greens predominate. In spring, the wood is quite a different place. The moist, acid loam and westerly location make this prime rhododendron land. Colonel Charles Brocklehurst, the Trust's benefactor, was a great enthusiast and, with advice from the plantsman James Russell, introduced them steadily from the 1960s until shortly before his death in 1981. There are no colour schemes or specialisations. You pass from colourful banks of Hardy Hybrids and richly scented Knap Hill and Exbury azaleas to drifts of white, red and pink *Rhododendron williamsianum* and specimens of yellow *R. wardii,* purple *R. × edgarianum,* orange *R. cinnabarinum,* pink *R. loderi* and white *R.* 'Polar Bear'. The foliage colours, shapes and sizes are equally magnificent, ranging from glaucous-blue *R. lepidostylum* and *R. cinnabarinum* subsp. *xanthocodon* to elephantine *R. maccabeanum* and the staggeringly beautiful cinnamon growths and soft, rust-red undersides of *R. rex* subsp. *fictolacteum* and *R. bureavii.*

Accompanying them are *Pieris formosa* var. *forrestii, viburnums, Magnolia sprengeri* var. *elongata,* hostas, bluebells, Himalayan poppies and a notable carpet of the creeping, white-flowered *Cornus canadensis.* The Trust continues to enrich the scene, progressively replacing the thickets of old purple *R. ponticum* with fresh assortments of colour. The season is also being extended. The early colour was already provided by snowdrops, daffodils, a massive *Clematis montana,* yellow-flared skunk cabbage and the pink chalices of *Magnolia campbellii.* The later interest came principally from roses, most impressively a huge pink Rambler 'Paul's Himalayan Musk'. Now, there is a boost from lacecap and other hydrangeas, and from the white-flowered 'Nymans' eucryphia, grouped in a line outside the Walled Garden.

The garden inside is a curiosity: at its head, a white trellis pergola draped in clematis; a flanking pair of equestrian wirework sculptures set in beds of 'Pearl Drift' roses; surrounding orange brick walls cloaked in an array of blue and yellow shrubs and climbers; and, at its heart, an empty lawn of such vastness that it throws everything out of scale. The contrast of light and scale is exciting, but the absence of an impressive centrepiece, such as a sweep of waterlily pool or an imaginative modern sculpture, is sorely felt.

There is one further feature to mention: the hollies. The wood is home to an extensive collection, from rare forms of the green Highclere holly (*Ilex × altaclerensis*) such as large-leaved 'Atkinsonii'

and dark 'Nigrescens', to curious forms of the common holly (*Ilex aquifolium*), such as the delicate 'Ovata' and the spineless, twisted-leaved 'Scotica'. With them come an assortment of silver and golden, yellow- and orange-berried varieties, providing the material for an absorbing visit. The garden is closed in winter to conserve the woodland paths.

LEFT View of the central lawn from the Walled Garden.

BELOW Rhododendron and skunk cabbage at the edge of the old marl pit.

Hatchlands Park

EAST CLANDON, GUILDFORD, SURREY

AREA 4.9ha (12 acres) within parkland • **SOIL** alkaline-acid/heavy soil • **ALTITUDE** 91m (300ft) • **AVERAGE RAINFALL** 686mm (27in) • **AVERAGE WINTER CLIMATE** cold

'In spring, snowdrops, daffodils and bluebells abound'

The curving path from the old orchard, now the car park, brings the eighteenth-century mansion into view at an oblique angle between the trees. In its restored state, it is a striking block of red brick and white paintwork, contrasting sharply with the parkland grass that sweeps almost to the door. The Reptonian flavour of the scene is intensifying as the Trust's new plantings mature. Humphry Repton was at the height of his career when engaged by the estate's owner, George Sumner, to improve the park and garden, and his recommendations of 1800 alterations seem to have been carried out. The London road was diverted, a new carriage drive and gravel walks were constructed, and an area of lawn was set out around the house, complementing features already planted by Fanny Boscawen, the wife of Admiral Edward Boscawen, who built Hatchlands in the 1750s.

These lawns are endowed with some fine trees and shrubs, notably cedars, arbutus, a huge stone pine and a magnificent London plane, which casts its resinous scent far and wide. New shrubberies frame the stone temple, brought here in 1953 from nearby Busbridge Hall, and in spring, snowdrops, daffodils and bluebells abound. Fanny Boscawen's Walk, edged in lilac, laburnum, holly, yew and philadelphus, is currently being restored.

In 1913, Gertrude Jekyll submitted plans for a south and west parterre garden. Only the first was executed, and this has been reinstated, the pattern of beds planted with Shrub and old Bush roses, in the company of peonies, geraniums and irises. It is a pretty scheme at its summer peak, but does sit somewhat oddly in the flowing parkland. Reconciling the conflicting styles and contours is one of the Trust's tasks, together with elevating the overall standard after the decline seen between 1959 and 1980, when the property was let as a finishing school – but slowly the garden has become a fitting accompaniment to the house.

LEFT Roses and peonies in full bloom, looking out to the parkland.
ABOVE Red valerian and pink lupins.

Hidcote Manor

HIDCOTE BARTRIM, CHIPPING CAMPDEN, GLOUCESTERSHIRE

AREA 4ha (10 acres) • **SOIL** alkaline • **ALTITUDE** 183m (600ft) • **AVERAGE RAINFALL** 635mm (25in) • **AVERAGE WINTER CLIMATE** cold

An encounter with England's most influential twentieth-century garden begins softly. The high, twisting lanes of the Cotswold countryside lead into a courtyard only slightly more distinguished than those accompanying the other large houses that pepper the hilltops. It takes an eagle-eyed plantsman to notice that the sober plantings against the golden walls are a little out of the ordinary – *Schizophragma hydrangeoïdes*, *Magnolia delavayi* and *Mahonia lomariifolia* are among the cast.

In a recent change of the visitor route, you now enter the garden through the house, emerging through the door into the tiny front garden, decorated with variegated shrubs and bedding plants. Immediately, your eye is carried across the farm lane down an avenue of lime trees; at its head is a statue of Hercules, cleverly illuminated by the gap left in the tree line for the afternoon sun to penetrate. This juxtaposing of grandeur with Cotswolds vernacular is typical of Hidcote.

Then, walking beyond the corner of the house and the old cedar of Lebanon shading the lawn, you turn to find another exciting vista is upon you. This one, far more varied and colourful, runs down the heart of the whole garden, through half a dozen different spaces. Hidcote is now revealed as a patchwork of passages, open spaces and flower-filled enclosures, a network of private gardens each gaining impact from the garden before it, with changes in scale, design, colour and atmosphere at each turn.

Within the walled garden by the house there is a tiny White Garden, surveyed by a thatched cottage, animated by topiary doves, filled with 'Gruss an Aachen' roses in a wash of dianthus, phlox and other plants, and contained by yew hedges afire in early summer with blood-red flame flower. There is also a garden of Japanese maples, a corridor of acid-loving plants such as meconopsis and rhododendrons growing in peat imported many years ago to reduce the PH and, either side of grass walkways, a series of large mixed borders stuffed with the pink, purple, white, blue and magenta colours of tulips, geraniums, peonies, campanulas, roses, deutzias, salvias and dahlias.

Slightly giddy from all this intensive plantsmanship, you step out into the Circle, an enclosure so intimate in size that there is scarcely room to pass the other visitors, but with the refresher of a roundel of lawn, surrounded by lilacs and other cool-coloured shrubs, and beyond, the crisp symmetry of the grass vista between the Red Borders. Turn right, and in a great *coup de théâtre*, the world expands; the Great Lawn is revealed. It is vast, incomparably bigger than you would expect in such a garden. Rather – with its immaculate sward, crisp surround of dark yew, and elevated stage containing three beech trees – it seems to have strayed from an early eighteenth-century landscape park.

Turn left from the Circle, and you find yourself in a succession of green gardens: a brick parterre; a dark garden filled with a huge,

ABOVE Topiary in The White Garden.

RIGHT View down the Long Walk to the gate, designed to lead the eye into the landscape.

circular stone basin; and then a small, empty circle of lawn. Rough, meandering paths lead on into the Stream Garden, a large, loose, shady area of ditches and spinneys. Here, the sticky banks and gulleys are furnished with fat clumps of leafy perennials, including comfreys, darmera, *Rodgersia pinnata* 'Superba' – splendidly partnered with blue-leaved hostas – and colonies of *Lysichiton americanus*, which illuminate the garden in spring with yellow, sour-smelling flares. These grow among a choice collection of trees and shrubs, including magnolias, hydrangeas, daphnes and *Osmanthus yunnanensis*.

Now, another *coup de théâtre*. From the wooded wilderness, you step directly into the grand, open sweep of the Long Walk. Really, it needs to be viewed from the gazebo above to savour the full drama of the plunging and ascending hornbeam hedges, but from this intermediate point the climb to the empty horizon is thrilling enough. And so the garden goes on, varied and enticing, through 4ha (10 acres) of compartments. Hidcote's linear patterns recall earlier, Continental styles of gardening. The Great Lawn, Fuchsia Garden and Bathing Pool Garden are part of this, as are the pillars of yew in the Pillar Garden, the umbrellas of sweet bay in the Pine Garden, the avenue of Irish yews through the Long Borders, and, famously, the stilt hedges of hornbeam, or *palissades à l'Italienne*, which flank the last section of the main east-west axis. The abundance of evergreen oaks also adds to the Continental flavour.

It was an Anglicised American, born in Paris and brought up in France, who had the vision to pull these disparate threads together. When Lawrence Johnston and his mother, Mrs Winthrop, came to live at Hidcote in 1907, the present garden was exposed farmland. It does not appear that Johnston ever had a master plan; rather, land for the garden was snatched piecemeal from the farm over a number of years. The design draws on many contemporary themes, but he moulded and fused them together with triumphant originality. The sequence of terraces, lawns and flower gardens seen in larger country houses he reduced to a chain of intimate rooms; Gertrude Jekyll's art of arranging plants with one eye on nature and the other on associations of texture, form and colour he carried to new levels of romantic informality, with shrubs, climbers, self-sowing perennials and bulbs spilling into one another in carefree style. He owed a large debt to his close friend Norah Lindsay, a gifted gardener who designed and planted with great panache.

Plants at Hidcote are assembled principally by colour, texture and flowering season. Mrs Winthrop's Garden blends acid green euphorbias, glaucous-leaved thalictrum, blue salvias and copper cordyline, while in high summer the Red Borders swelter with dahlias, verbenas, red salvias and Floribunda roses, supplemented by the sombre leaves of purple berberis, heuchera, plum and sloe.

Vita Sackville-West believed Johnston would want to be remembered principally as a botanist and plant-hunter, and at heart Hidcote is, of course, a plantsman's garden. The plant collection is huge; at every turn there are choice and rare subjects, and the garden offers the maximum diversity of planting sites. Johnston participated in two notable plant-hunting expeditions: to China with George Forrest, and to South Africa with 'Cherry' Ingram. To the former, we owe *Mahonia lomariifolia* and the pot jasmine, *Jasminum polyanthum*. Johnston's sharp eye for a superior garden variant is evident in the number of excellent plants bearing his or Hidcote's name, including a lavender, hypericum, verbena, campanula, penstemon and rose.

At present, Hidcote is undergoing a great renaissance, in the wake of a major historic survey carried out in 2000 which revealed just how much of its original character had been lost – for when it was taken on by the Trust in 1948, as the first property accepted on the merits of its garden alone, there was limited expertise within the Trust, no garden records and a serious shortage of funds. Vita Sackville-West's 1949 description of the garden as a 'jungle of beauty' captures the spirit of Johnston's Hidcote. Its high content of tender and exotic plants, over-wintered both in temporary glasshouses and a heated Plant House, gave 'a general impression of dripping luxuriance'. There were even humming-birds, macaws and flamingos. The planting was very loose, almost wild. 'Plants grow in a jumble . . . spilling abundance.' And the plant content extended into comprehensive collections of alpines and other rarities.

Already Mrs Winthrop's Garden has taken on this more relaxed and mingled style, and reflects more of a Mediterranean flavour. The Rock Bank, previously planted up by the Trust in labour-saving shrubs, has been cleaned and restocked, with the help of the rediscovered notebooks of both Johnston and Jack Percival, who worked here as a gardener in the 1920s and '30s. Johnston intended the effect of walking up this western flank of the garden to be like climbing up the maritime Alps through bulb and boulder fields, across scree and past glacial meltwater pools. His more formalised Alpine Terrace below the pleached hornbeam hedges has also been reinstated; it has a glass roof in winter to counter excess rain, allowing the survival of plants such as aeoniums, aloes and even Chilean puya.

Perhaps the most dramatic change has been beside the lily pool to the north of the house, where Johnston's large Plant House has been reintroduced. A copy of its predecessor and with much the

same exotic plant content, it has glass panels which are removed in summer. In winter, its lemons, plumbagos and tender jasmines are kept just frost-free.

The kitchen garden has recently been revived, with vegetables, flowers for cutting and new apple and pear espaliers grafted from the original trees. Johnston's yew-enclosed tennis court has also been reinstated, complete with thatched pavilion; he employed a tennis professional through the summer because his friends were not of a sufficient standard to give him a proper game. Whether the Italianate Bathing Pool will revert to its original clear blue, accompanied by lounger cushions, remains to be seen.

LEFT Dahlias in September in the Old Garden, with the manor house beyond.
ABOVE Alliums and poppies in May in the Pillar Garden at Hidcote Manor.

Lawn renovation and maintenance

Glyn Jones, Garden and Countryside Manager
HIDCOTE MANOR, GLOUCESTERSHIRE

'Grass is green and covers the ground, that's all you need to know,' was the advice I was given many years ago as a trainee gardener – not the best advice I have ever heard, but if you can manage the 'green' bit then you are halfway to a decent lawn.

I think that to succeed in having a good-quality lawn, you have to be prepared to spend time on some simple cultivation tasks.

Letting the soil breathe

This is important, otherwise you will end up with anaerobic conditions in your lawn. To let the soil breathe, you need to ensure that the build-up of thatch is not excessive. This can be done by reducing the amount of clippings that are left behind after mowing, but it is still also advisable to scarify on a biannual basis. On small lawns this is best done by using a wire rake for 20 minutes at a time; if you can do more than 20 minutes then you are probably not raking vigorously enough! On large lawns it is preferable to hire a petrol-driven scarifier with a collection box, otherwise you will still have to rake up all the thatch that arises. Scarifying is best done either in September or into spring, perhaps in March once the grass is actively growing again. After scarifying you will be able to scatter seed over any bare patches.

To ensure the soil remains healthy, aeration is recommended, especially on those areas that are frequently walked on. This is best done with a garden fork on small areas and a hired machine on large areas. After spiking, if your budget allows you can top-dress with a good lawn top-dressing available from garden centres; this will improve both drainage and soil condition.

As a side benefit, if you want to improve your own fitness both scarifying and aeration are really excellent cardiovascular exercises if done manually.

Helping the grass grow

Once you have improved the condition of the soil, the next important thing is gently encouraging the grass to grow strongly. One of the best ways of doing this is to mow regularly, but never in the same direction for more than two or three cuts, as changing direction prevents stalky grass establishing. In spring, as mowing begins, set the mower on a high setting, gradually lowering the height as the season progresses towards summer; for ornamental lawns never cut closer than 1.5cm (¾in), and during dry periods be prepared to raise the height to 2.5cm (1in). As autumn approaches, raise the height again in order to allow the grass plants to strengthen up before winter sets in. During mild winters you may need to top off the grass to prevent it becoming too long; this should be done on a high setting.

Collecting the grass clippings by means of a grass box on the mower removes plant growth and nutrition, so this needs to be replaced by using fertilisers. There are some very good non-chemical ones available these days, especially those made out of poultry manures, but they do smell for a week or two after application.

Controlling weeds

If you keep your soil healthy and your grass strong this should reduce the need to control moss and weeds, as the grass will out-compete these. However, after a while you may get some weed species coming into the sward and these are best knocked out with a proprietary moss or weedkiller. I recommend against using the combination feed and weed type product, as it is best to either kill the weeds or feed the grass.

Tips

- Grass is one of the highest-maintenance areas of the garden so if you find you do not have time to care for a lawn, consider creating a new border. In the long run, borders require less work than grass if they are well designed and planted.
- A rotary-type mower with a rear roller as opposed to wheels at the rear gives a closer cut and is far more durable than a traditional cylinder-type mower.
- Always ensure you have enough time to relax and enjoy your garden, with a G&T to hand!

Hill Top

NEAR SAWREY, AMBLESIDE, CUMBRIA

AREA 0.2ha (½ acre) • SOIL acid/loam • ALTITUDE 90m (295ft) • AVERAGE RAINFALL 1,524mm (60in) • AVERAGE WINTER CLIMATE moderate

Anyone familiar with Beatrix Potter's stories will feel immediately at home in her village farmhouse and cottage garden, since the scenes are just as she painted them. We have seen Mrs Tabitha Twitchit brandishing her toasting fork in this same rose-covered porch, and watched Jemima Puddle-Duck try to hide her eggs in this same rhubarb patch. Indeed, it was the royalties from *The Tale of Peter Rabbit* and other early works that enabled her, at nearly 40, to escape the stifling atmosphere of her parents' house in London and buy Hill Top.

Restored by the Trust, the garden is planted and maintained in the neat but muddled style of an old-fashioned cottage plot, its contents and arrangement loosely based on old photographs, Beatrix Potter's paintings and journal notes. The long borders accompanying the sloping path up to the front door undergo an imperceptible transition from currant bushes and herbs to traditional annuals, perennials and flowering shrubs, and generous applications of farmyard manure give the hungry, slaty soil good heart.

Spikes of foxgloves, mulleins and hollyhocks rise between clumps of lady's mantle, lamb's lugs and sweet william, while lilac and sorbaria foam and violets, snapdragons and poached-egg plants self-sow merrily. Sweet peas are trained up hazel poles, and the trellis that screens the apple-tree paddock is festooned with Rambler roses, clematis and honeysuckle. Scent wafts from *Rosa rugosa*, *Lilium regale* and summer jasmine, while a white Chinese wisteria on the house and a *Eucryphia glutinosa* in the border add unexpected notes of sophistication. Gooseberry 'Whinham's Industry', which entangled Peter Rabbit in its protective net, still occupies the

right-hand side of the border. Opposite the front door, over the dry-stone wall, is the small vegetable garden, its businesslike rows of potatoes, carrots, cabbages and onions complemented by colourful bursts of ruby chard, runner beans and raspberries.

Beatrix Potter was a great supporter and benefactor of the National Trust, and a close friend of its co-founder, Canon Hardwicke Rawnsley. Concerned by the growing threat to the Lake District of insensitive development, she began buying farms and tracts of land with the ultimate aim of giving them to the Trust. By the time of her death in 1943, she had ensured the preservation of over 1,618ha (4,000 acres) of pasture and fell.

ABOVE Beatrix Potter's vegetable patch.

RIGHT A herbaceous border with vermillion *Lychnis chalcedonica* prominent and alliums standing tall behind.

Hinton Ampner

BRAMDEAN, BRAMDEAN, HAMPSHIRE

AREA 5.3ha (13 acres) • SOIL alkaline/clay, chalk • ALTITUDE 122m (400ft)
AVERAGE RAINFALL 838mm (33in) • AVERAGE WINTER CLIMATE moderate

Ralph Dutton, the 8th and last Lord Sherborne, inherited this estate in 1935 at the age of 37, and devoted the following 50 years to improving and embellishing it. A deeply cultured man, a connoisseur of art and architecture, author of *The English Garden*, and with the wealth and leisure to indulge his tastes, he produced as elegant a composition of house, park and garden as the last century can show.

The Georgian house stands on a ridge of chalk above well-treed farmland. You pass through a series of gentle transitions as you climb to it, curving through parkland, and then, across a cattle grid, through ornamental shrubberies speared by conifers and specimen trees. There is a pocket of deep acid greensand here on the northern fringe, which allows rhododendrons, azaleas, camellias, blue hydrangeas, *Magnolia × soulangeana* and various Japanese maples to accompany the more chalk-tolerant species like *Magnolia wilsonii* and *Parrotia*, but the colour scheme is kept soft, as it is throughout the grounds, with the richer tints of yellow and orange confined to a few highlights.

As the house looms between the trees, the drive straightens and the grounds become more formal. On one side is the walled kitchen garden belonging to the original house, demolished in 1793. In recent years, this has been brought back into the Trust's management, having previously been leased out, and after much restoration it is now producing a range of fruit and vegetables. Ralph Dutton extended its path-line to turn the area on the other side of the drive, backed by a Norman church, into a formal cherry orchard. Its trees – pink- and white-blossomed, and in a meadowy carpet of early bulbs, daffodils and then cow parsley – stand inside four box-edged

enclosures, making an unusual and very effective combination of the natural and the ordered. This pattern of simply designed, rectangular compartments and strong long axes connecting them provides the framework for the many flower-filled scenes to the south, in classic mid-twentieth-century style. A lily pond, partnered by a bed of 'Iceberg' roses and magenta *Verbena rigida* (syn. *V. venosa*), aligns with the east front of the house, while the main, sunny façade looks onto a sweeping grass terrace, inherited by Dutton and retained as the necessary quiet counterbalance to the surrounding colours.

Before the Second World War, Dutton created further terraces below, using the lines and proportions of the Georgian façade to set the parameters of the central space and carrying the cross-path east and west to form another long axis, running one way through an avenue of Irish yews and the other between ornamental shrubberies; both views conclude in a classical ornament, one backed by trees and

the other by open park. It is a beautiful passage of design, further enhanced by a flight of steps providing a graceful change of level *en route*. Later, he cleverly connected the lime avenue, dating from the eighteenth century and cutting across the park in alignment with the original house, by extending and connecting it, via a straight walk, to this axis, and erecting a temple at the intersection.

As well as valuable lessons for the design student, there is much to absorb the plant-lover. Shrubs are the principal source of colour. Evergreens, including *Magnolia grandiflora*, pittosporums and bay grow against the house's south wall, and, below the stone terrace, they are joined by lower-growing subjects, including lavender, caryopteris, perovskia, escallonia and seams of Headbourne Hybrid agapanthus, all appreciative of the hot, dry conditions. Crisply partnered for foliage contrast, larger shrubs also flank the many grass walks fringing the terraces, especially those to the east, around the

tennis court lawn. The smoke bush, *Cotinus coggygria*, is prominent in its purple and green-leaved cultivars, together with lilacs, various viburnums (especially evergreen *V. davidii* and *V. rhytidophyllum*, and the deciduous wayfaring tree, *V. lantana*), scented philadelphus, berberis, cotoneasters, buddleias, weeping silver pear and many different Shrub roses.

At one point, the ground suddenly plunges into the basin of a chalk pit – giving the garden a strong sense of locality – and you find yourself looking up at steep banks clad in yew, rampaging Rambler roses and paulownias. They are joined, in the damper pockets, by foliage plants such as spotted lungwort, hostas, rheum and giant hogweed, and in the drier parts by euphorbias and Corsican

ABOVE Thirty clipped Irish yews line the Long Walk.

hellebore. It is a peaceful and atmospheric place in which to linger, especially in June.

Around the house, the shrubs also give way here and there to other plants. Delicately blended bedding plants fill the small, yew-hedged room, east of the main lawn terrace, while to the south you descend to a lawn appointed with topiary figures, where dahlias traditionally follow a spring show of bulbs, to the accompaniment of a border of pastel perennials and silvery foliage. I remember striking partnerships here between Regale lilies and blue shrubby euphorbia, pink helianthemum and the trailing *Convolvulus altheoides* (hardy here), and, best of all, magenta *Allium cernuum* and *Artemisia schmidtiana* 'Nana', the former's magenta heads sprouting through the rug of grey leaves. But schemes like this are being tended creatively, with new plants and combinations of plants allowed to play variations on the themes, and they do not remain static.

An opening in the hedge, directly opposite the house, gives an interlude in the garden tour, bringing you out above the ha-ha and to a grass bastion. Ahead, the park rolls away into the Hampshire countryside, past the stands and belts of trees, rigorously thinned by Dutton to ensure the development of good, spreading specimens. Trees were his favourite plants, and the large specimens of beech, lime, oak and pine shading the garden's drives and neat lawns contribute to the sense of history, spaciousness and tranquillity he so valued, as well as supplying the much-needed shelter against the wind.

LEFT A bank of pastel colours, including silver-leaved ballota and helianthemum.

ABOVE Pink and white foxgloves border the terrace, overlooking the parkland beyond.

The Homewood

ESHER, SURREY

AREA 3.2ha (8 acres) • **SOIL** acid/sand • **ALTITUDE** 30m (100ft) • **AVERAGE RAINFALL** 635mm (25in) • **AVERAGE WINTER CLIMATE** moderate

'A fascinating composition, highlighting a little-recorded period'

While Vita Sackville-West was ensconcing herself in Sissinghurst's Elizabethan tower, others were seizing on twentieth-century technological and social changes and reflecting them in a new type of architecture and design. The Homewood, built in 1937–8, is a period piece of the Modern Movement, its glass and white concrete box exterior, supported on columns, an essay in clean geometry and its open bright interior a machine for modern living, complete with sprung dance floor. Its architect was its owner, Patrick Gwynne, who, at the age of 24, managed to persuade his parents to let him build this new house for the family in the corner of their woodland garden. Gwynne went on to live here all his life, continually refining the house and, from the 1960s onwards, developing the grounds around it until he died in 2003.

You enter off the busy Portsmouth Road down a curving drive, and the principal excitement of the composition is almost immediately sprung: the dramatic contrast of the bold horizontals of the house seen through the verticals of tree trunks, silver birches echoing the white concrete, pines the dark wood. The trees were thinned by the storm of 1987, which Gwynne thought an improvement, and the effect today is of a play of thicket and glade, mass and void, sunlight and shadow, with the views of the house presented down gently meandering lawns, across sunny pools and heather beds, framed by trees and evergreen shrubbery.

The Homewood is at its most successful when it is echoing the Surrey woods and heathland that surround it. The pink and white heathers (a favourite basking ground for snakes), daffodils, bluebells, scented yellow azaleas and rhododendrons follow attractive swathes,

the curves picked up by the stream that Gwynne dammed to create a series of ponds. Crossed by concrete stepping squares and bridges, the water is bordered by big architectural stands of gunnera, together with yellow lysichiton, bamboo and, around the lower pond, a ring of pollarded willows. Japanese maples give a dashing foreground to the house when in red autumn livery. But within this informal woodland are some more self-consciously ornamental touches – a formal flight of steps edged in grey and yellow plants, a purple and variegated foliage walk, and a garden of blue and white plants set in herringbone brick paths.

Outdoor entertainment was provided by a tennis court and a small swimming pool, attractively associated with some formal lily ponds and connected to the front of the house by a concrete terrace. Here, further formal squares are cut out in geometric grid patterns (a recurrent motif in modernist design) for the display of bedding plants – tulips in spring and begonias in summer. Gwynne enjoyed vivid colours. Further along is an oval pool, designed by the architect Sir Denys Lasdun as a house-warming present for the family, which Gwynne later jazzed up with blue glass mosaics. Altogether, this is a fascinating composition, highlighting a little-recorded period, both in domestic architecture and garden-making.

RIGHT The south front of the house was strategically placed to provide views over much of the garden.

Hughenden Manor

AREA 1.9ha (4¾ acres) • SOIL alkaline • ALTITUDE 152m (500ft) • AVERAGE RAINFALL 711mm (28in) • AVERAGE WINTER CLIMATE cold

'Wisteria, clematis, ceanothus and jasmines flower against the house'

The Gothic house, sitting on its chalky hilltop among the steep-sided combes and beechwoods of Buckinghamshire, today cuts as exotic a figure in the landscape as did its former owner in the Tory establishment. For Hughenden was the country home, from 1848 until his death in 1881, of Benjamin Disraeli, statesman, novelist and Prime Minister.

The trees were among Disraeli's chief delights. Singly and in groups, they soften the lower reaches of the park and shade parts of the curving drive and churchyard, where Disraeli is buried; on the hillside, they thicken to screen and shelter the house, and on the escarpment and hills beyond, they unite into full-blown woods. Whitebeam, ash, oak, lime and hornbeam accompany the beeches, and old man's beard (*Clematis vitalba*), snowdrops, wood anemones and bluebells enliven the picture; here and there are patches of Disraeli's favourite flower, the primrose. The scene was already set when the Disraelis came to Hughenden, but over the years they undertook much new planting. Mary Anne Disraeli developed part of the wood as a 'German Forest', adorned with rustic seats and with rides edged in laurel and yew, and on the banks and lawns around the house numerous conifers were installed.

The sight that greets you as you walk into the forecourt is triumphantly Victorian, with an assortment of dark and decorative cedars, firs and spruces set against the pinnacles and red and blue brick of the Gothic façade. This area, in common with much of the rest of the garden, has been restored and replanted by the Trust over recent years, following contemporary photographs. The trees in the oval lawn make an interesting assembly of lime-tolerant species, and

include Chilean yew (*Prumnopitys andina*, syn. *Podocarpus andinus*), Brewer's weeping spruce (*Picea breweriana*) and Cyprus cedar (*Cedrus brevifolia*). The main garden is reached by skirting the east wall of the house, from where there is a carefully framed view down over the ha-ha into the parkland – this 'landscape window' being an eighteenth-century feature preserved by the Disraelis.

You now step out onto a wide terrace with broad views over the valley, neighbouring hills and an advancing High Wycombe, partially screened by trees. 'We have made a garden of terraces, in which cavaliers might roam and saunter with their ladye-loves,' wrote Disraeli to his friend Mrs Brydges Williams. Today the main terrace comprises an expanse of lawn, edged in gravel paths and statuary, with the original bedding schemes restored. Wisteria, clematis, ceanothus and jasmines flower against the house, fronted by a formal planting scheme incorporating ivy pillars to evoke the pergola that was here previously. The Italianate ambience and outdoor living that the Disraelis enjoyed under it is likewise echoed in the presence of olives and clipped box, woven into a serpentine pattern with *Hebe* 'Red Edge', the Victorians being very fond of coloured foliage.

Like this bed, the row of stone Florentine urns that flank the flight of steps are filled each spring and summer with annuals in gaudy Victorian colours, as is the large cast-iron basket below and the fountain bowl at the southern extremity of the plateau, which stands in the centre of the small formal rose garden, soon to be reinstated. Marigolds, pelargoniums, petunias and cineraria are among the ever-changing cast, following wallflowers and tulips. This is a windy site, and plants have to be chosen with care. The only missing

element is peacocks. 'You cannot have a terrace without peacocks,' was Disraeli's dictum. Unfortunately, peacocks and flowers do not go happily together.

By the old driveway, on sloping ground below the plateau, there is a change of mood in the form of a wild, meandering pleasure ground, with trees, shrubberies and oval beds, newly created and stocked with pampas grass and perennials. Daffodils and primroses carpet the grass here in spring.

In recent years, the walled Kitchen Garden, dating from the 1750s, has also been brought back to sparkling life and is now a hub of organic gardening education, with plots run experimentally by volunteers and interactive displays for children. Vines, figs, pears,

plums and Morello cherries are trained against the walls, and the vegetable, soft fruit and cut-flower beds are structured by 57 varieties of apples associated with Buckinghamshire, including the local variety 'Arthur Turner', all grown on semi-dwarfing rootstocks. The orchard was renovated in the 1980s, and in 2008 an additional cherry orchard was established to accommodate varieties of cherry tree that used to be grown commercially in the Chilterns.

ABOVE The South Front of the Manor, showing the annual bedding schemes. The gardens have been restored in recent years to period styles.

Ickworth

HORRINGER, BURY ST EDMUNDS, SUFFOLK

AREA 28ha (70 acres) • SOIL very alkaline/clay • ALTITUDE 76m (250ft)
AVERAGE RAINFALL 533mm (21in) • AVERAGE WINTER CLIMATE cold to very cold

A fairly cold climate, level ground and heavy clay soil are not an ideal combination for an Italian garden. However, the light is good and the rainfall low, and here, in the gently undulating Suffolk countryside, there is one of the finest examples in Britain, a garden of evergreen plantations, where Mediterranean scents hang in the air and slim conifers cast pointed shadows across the grass. It was started in 1801 as an accompaniment to the astonishing Italianate house begun a few years earlier by the 4th Earl of Bristol and Bishop of Derry, and was developed by his son, the 1st Marquess of Bristol, in the 1820s. It is thus one of the first properties to have re-embraced geometry and the plants and patterns of European gardens after the long supremacy of Lancelot 'Capability' Brown and the English landscape garden.

The proportions of the house demand large-scale effects, and generous stands and belts of trees set the mood of the garden. You approach the vast rotunda, the centrepiece of the entire composition, past towering evergreens, including redwoods, Crimean and Pyrenean pines (*Pinus nigra* var. *caramanica* and *P. n.* var *cebennensis*), Lucombe oaks and a young grove of cedars, planted at 14m (15yd) spacing. Many of the original cedars were nearing the end of their lives when the hurricane of October 1987 struck, enabling the Trust to undertake comprehensive replanting. Eighteen varieties of deodar, Lebanon, Atlas and Cyprus cedar have been installed, using an interesting technique widely favoured on poorly drained soil in the nineteenth century; instead of being planted in a hole, the trees were planted on the surface and earth mounded over their roots. Fast-growing cypress and hemlock have been employed

as a nurse crop and will be removed in time. In spring and early summer, the plantation is spangled with bulbs and wildflowers. The herbaceous border on this north side of the house is very generously proportioned, but the bulk of the rotunda behind does it no favours.

The main part of the garden is to the south, reached through a gateway beside the Orangery. Here, a pair of large, wing-shaped lawns, echoing the architecture of the house, meet on the central axis of the rotunda. A procession of young *Phillyrea angustifolia*, a bushy Mediterranean evergreen with sweetly scented flowers in early summer, reinforces the symmetry, and framing the scene are two plantations of majestic holm oaks, supplemented by a wealth of evergreen shrubs and contained by box hedges.

The assortment of outlines and leaf shapes is fascinating. The slim verticals so characteristic of the Italian landscape were originally authentically furnished by extensive plantings of Italian cypress, *Cupressus sempervirens* 'Stricta'. However, the majority were badly damaged in a series of severe winters around the turn of the last century, and over the years they have been generally replaced with hardier species that have a similar outline – in particular, *Chamaecyparis lawsoniana* 'Erecta', 'Wisselii' and 'Kilmacurragh'. Textural contrasts are provided by shrubs such as *Phillyrea latifolia*, mahonias, photinias, osmanthus, hollies, *Viburnum tinus* and large-leaved *V. cinnamomifolium*, choisyas, privets, *Arbutus unedo* and a National Collection of box, which includes bushes in all shapes and colour variants from gold and fresh green to deep green and blue. Olives have been successfully tried in the more sheltered spots, but in the open garden the hardier sea buckthorn, *Hippophaë rhamnoides*, serves as a silvery substitute; the females bear heavy crops of bright orange berries.

The overall formality belies the variety of detail in this part of the garden. There is a secret glade of bluebells and silver leaves; a sinister Victorian 'stumpery', where ferns grow on upturned roots; a glade of golden foliage, boasting a fine specimen of half-hardy *Olearia solandri* with heliotrope-scented flowers in late summer, and a little garden of floribunda roses presided over by a temple. The trees include a large cucumber magnolia (*M. acuminata*), a range of evergreen oaks and a spectacular golden rain tree, *Koelreuteria paniculata*. Further colour is provided by the rich blues of *Agapanthus africanus* set out in tubs on the Orangery steps. Inside the Orangery, ivies are grown on tripods.

The southern boundary of the garden is marked by a raised gravel terrace, 320m (350yd) long and separated from the lawns and plantations by a tapestry hedge of seedling box; this, and the

fact that it seeds freely in the woods, was the inspiration for the box collection. From here, there are broad views over the park, encompassing Ickworth church and, in the distance, the Obelisk, erected in memory of the Earl Bishop by the people of Derry. 'Capability' Brown advised on the park in the mid-eighteenth century, when the family were living in Ickworth Lodge, and he may well have suggested the idea of a walk encircling the present deer park, to the west of the existing house, though it was not laid out until the early nineteenth century. The path leads you through alternating areas of dappled sunlight, created by groves of oak, beech, ash and maple, and deeper shade cast by yew, pines and evergreen oaks. The woods are a haven for wildlife.

ABOVE The Rotunda and Italianate Garden, looking towards the west wing.

Ightham Mote

IVY HATCH, SEVENOAKS, KENT

AREA 5.7ha (14 acres) • **SOIL** acid to neutral • **ALTITUDE** 85–115m (279–377ft)
AVERAGE RAINFALL 584mm (23in) • **AVERAGE WINTER CLIMATE** moderate/cold

'On entering … you seem at once transported into the home of some powerful landowner of the sixteenth century … and when you enter the courtyard you quite expect some of the grand dames of the period to be seen at the windows.' So the *Gardeners Chronicle* reported in 1889. Even today, the house is a dreamy sight, a varied assortment of russet stone and half-timbered walls, tiled roofs, gables, high chimneys and a gatehouse, guarded by a moat. With additions and restorations from every century, it has been woven together by its various owners with remarkable sensitivity to its medieval origin – and this respect for the past has also encompassed the garden, whose linear medieval design has been little altered.

Much of the tranquillity and sense of mystery is owed to water. Its low-lying position makes Ightham a damp and misty place, and in nearly all parts of the garden there is the sight or sound of a pool, fountain or rivulet. Indeed, water features occupy much of the main north-south axis. At the upper end of the garden, a stream flowing through the Victorian pleasure grounds collects in a small lake. From here, the water drops down a cascade into two catchment pools and is carried, via culverts under the lawn, into the moat around the house, and down into a second lake below.

In contrast to the moat's mellow formality, the two lakes are edged with rough grass, wildflowers and trees. The south lake, in more recent times divided from the house by a country lane, is also accompanied by two cobnut coppices and a London plane of enormous dimensions. Happily, this was spared by the 1987 hurricane, which tore down so many of the garden's best trees, and in spring it is the backdrop for a sheet of daffodils; in autumn, its own

leaves deliver another spectacle of yellow. Adding to the romance is the knowledge that, buried under part of the lawn, are the remains of a medieval stewpond. In the early eighteenth century it was converted into a bowling green and became the green foil for a more ornamental garden.

The magazine articles of the late nineteenth and early twentieth century revelled in Ightham's 'quaint old-world look' and relaxed plantings. This new nineteenth-century taste for evocative design and poetic planting is clearly expressed in the Trust's restoration of the more ornamental areas on the west side of the lawn and house. The long border running beside the lawn has the swaying heads of plume poppies (*Macleaya*) and tall grasses (*Miscanthus sinensis* 'Silberfeder' and *Stipa gigantea* among them) repeated down its length; *Gypsophila paniculata* and varieties of *Aster ericoides*, geranium and veronica froth between them, in the company of a range of other soft-toned shrubs and perennials.

Beside the group of Scots pines at the north-west corner of the house, a circular water basin, surrounded by decorative bedding, makes a striking feature. A gateway leads into a small walled garden, where a pond, scented philadelphus and tobacco flowers and a host of silvery plants are set against the beautiful early Tudor stable range. As the entry in *Gardens Old and New* (*Country Life*, 1900) relates, 'There seems to be no jarring note here, and Ightham is a place where the sweetness of the garden and the country reigns.'

ABOVE The Cutting Garden, with hedged beds and cane tripods for training climbers
RIGHT The West Front and circular basin.

Kedleston Hall

DERBY, DERBYSHIRE

AREA 4.9ha (12 acres) • SOIL acid/clay • ALTITUDE 100m (328ft) • AVERAGE RAINFALL 686mm (27in) • AVERAGE WINTER CLIMATE cold

Pass through the arched gateway at North Lodge and you enter one of the great eighteenth-century Arcadias, a serene and sweeping composition of trees, lake and pavilions, presided over by Robert Adam's Neo-classical palace. The 'swelling and sinking' contours of the land are nature's gift; the rest is art. Adam was commissioned from 1758 by Sir Nathaniel Curzon, 1st Lord Scarsdale, and the composition offers an insight into his skill as a landscape gardener, for as well as being given sole responsibility for the hall by Lord Scarsdale, Adam had, as he wrote to his brother James, 'the intire Managdement of his Grounds … with full powers as to Temples Bridges Seats and Cascades' – although William Emes also worked here from 1756 to 1760.

The open pasture in front of the house is framed by generous belts of trees, which fill the hilltop horizon and embrace the furthest stretches of lake. The eye-catcher in the middle distance is the bridge, somewhat grander than Adam envisaged, with three arches spanning the cascade. His finest piece of garden architecture, the Fishing Boat house, is just upstream.

The garden, or Pleasure Ground, is on the south side of the house. Bounded by a ha-ha, the expanse of lawn and accompanying trees carry the eye across the rising parkland to the woods above. To the west, the informal shrubberies, adorned with a fine urn and Medici lion installed by the 1st Lord Scarsdale, are in the process of major renovation, in the wake of attack by *Phytophthora ramorum* disease. Infected plants are being removed, and others hard pruned, and gradually beds will be restocked using pre-1800 plants considered to have resistance to the disease. Still standing sentinel,

however, are some fine trees, including wellingtonias, Corsican pine, Turkey oak, and, near the Orangery, a superb fern-leaved beech, *Fagus sylvatica* 'Aspleniifolia', a variant worth planting in large gardens purely for the hiss of its leaves in the wind.

Behind this beech, you turn, through wrought-iron gates, back into Adam's landscape. You are now at the start of the Long Walk, a 4.8km (3 mile) circuit that takes you up into Vicarwood, directly opposite the south front of the hall, and back down to the lakes on the other side of the house. Such belt walks were a popular feature of eighteenth-century gardens, and the changing moods instilled by alternating evergreens and deciduous trees and flowering shrubs, by heavy shade and dappled sunlight, and by tunnels of foliage and breaks in the canopy, are gradually being restored by the Trust. Adam proposed a series of buildings along the path, but the tiny Hermitage seems to have been the only one constructed.

ABOVE Looking over the parkland towards the Palladian bridge, designed by Robert Adam.

RIGHT *Osteospermum* 'Whirligig'.

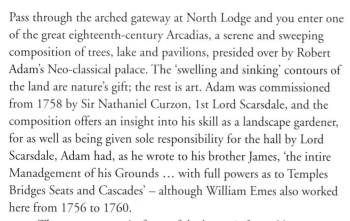

Killerton

BROADCLYST, EXETER, DEVON

AREA 8ha (21 acres) • SOIL acid/sandy loam • ALTITUDE 50–107m (164–351ft)
AVERAGE RAINFALL 914mm (36in) • AVERAGE WINTER CLIMATE mild

'It offers an arboretum of the highest calibre, with a dramatic and distinctive skyline'

It takes little effort to imagine the excitement of gardening in those decades of the nineteenth and early twentieth century when exotic and untried woody plants, collected in far-flung corners of the world, were flooding into Britain. Killerton was one of the first gardens to indulge, and for a period of over 130 years the enthusiasm only briefly waned. Today it offers an arboretum of the highest calibre, with a dramatic and distinctive skyline of trees, and a springtime spectacle that few gardens can equal.

The garden lies on the slopes of Killerton Clump, a volcanic outcrop that rises several hundred feet above the flood plain of the River Exe. The soil is free-draining, deep, fertile, acidic and a rich, Devon red; coupled with the southerly aspect and comparatively mild climate, it provides excellent growing conditions. The foundations for the collection were laid in the 1770s, when Sir Thomas Dyke Acland decided to create a landscape park to accompany his new house; the present flat-topped, pink-washed building was originally intended as a temporary residence, but a grander mansion was never built.

Acland chose as his gardener and land steward John Veitch, who soon proved an exceptional landscaper. With Acland's help, he also started a nursery at nearby Budlake. It was to become the most celebrated of its day, and in 1840, under the direction of his son James, was the first to dispatch plant-hunters into the wild. The association between the Acland and Veitch families held until 1939, and, apart from a 30-year period following Sir Thomas's death in 1871, Killerton received batches of new plants with regularity. Old specimens of *Thuja plicata* and *Sequoiadendron giganteum* in the

garden are almost certainly from seed brought back from the west coast of America by Veitch's collector, William Lobb, in the 1850s. A great many other trees and shrubs are either original plantings or direct descendants from seed collected in South America, China, Japan and the Himalayas during the nineteenth and early twentieth centuries.

From the house, the view up the hillside is of mown grass, specimen trees and flowing shrub beds, capped by an exotic woodland of mixed conifers and broad-leaved trees. Fine specimens of the erect Japanese walnut, *Juglans ailanthifolia* var. *cordiformis*, and the wide-spreading *Zelkova serrata* are some of the highlights among a cast that includes *Nothofagus obliqua*, Indian horse chestnut, blue

Atlas and incense cedars, golden Monterey cypress, wellingtonias and redwoods. Early in the year, the banks are peppered with daffodils, the flowers of magnolias and rhododendrons, and the blossom of Japanese cherries.

The hillside paths reveal countless treasures: a stand of cork oak, with thick, rugged bark; the evergreen, acid-loving *Quercus acuta*; a magnificent *Stewartia pseudocamellia*, with patterned trunk and fiery autumn colour; *Ehretia dicksonii*, with fragrant flowers in June, and *Taiwania cryptomerioides*, a rare and tender conifer, both from seed gathered in China by Ernest Wilson from 1899 to 1905; *Cornus kousa*, producing a cascade of white flowers in June; and *Cryptomeria japonica* and its variant 'Lobbii', grown from Thomas Lobb's Javanese seed.

This is only scratching the surface. Drifts of scented azaleas and further hummocks of *Rhododendron arboreum*, in red, pink and white, colour the glades between trees. Early in the year, crocuses and *Cyclamen coum* create pools of lilac and carmine; later come *Cyclamen repandum*, primroses, violets and bluebells; later still, campions and Queen Anne's lace; and finally, in the autumn, *Cyclamen hederifolium*. At every turn, there are fresh surprises and framed vistas.

In the early part of the twentieth century, two significant features were added to the garden, enabling the vast plant collection to expand still further. In about 1900, the great garden writer William Robinson was asked to advise on the garden, which over the previous 30 years had fallen into a sorry state. His legacy is the Great Terrace, west of the house. Originally planted with roses, which did not succeed, the generously proportioned beds here now contain an assortment of low-growing Mediterranean shrubs and other plants in soft, pastel tones, their shapes contrasting with stands of yuccas and the heavy verticals of Coade stone vases. Over the terrace wall, there are broad views of the gently undulating park. The herbaceous border that runs alongside the parterre was originally planted by John Coutts, who became head gardener as this part of the garden was being completed. The present Jekyllian colour schemes of pastel tints, blending into a hotter core of reds and oranges, is more recent. It has a long season, beginning with crown imperials in spring, reaching its climax at midsummer with peonies, irises and Shrub roses, and continuing into autumn with buddleias, dahlias and other late perennials.

The second significant feature installed by Coutts is the rock garden, sited beyond the thatched summer-house, known as the Bear's Hut (it once housed a Canadian black bear). This precipitous

composition is a superb period piece, busily intricate in rockwork, and capped by a stand of Chusan palm, *Trachycarpus fortunei*. It has recently been replanted with Asian plants introduced in the Edwardian era. A cool and private part of the garden, the silence is broken only by the stream that trickles softly into the rock pool, edged in ferns, primulas and astilbes. Following exposure to all this colour and variety, there is refreshment to be had in the green shadows around the Victorian chapel, where you can walk among oaks, chestnuts and conifers, and search for the lime-yellow flowers on the two great tulip trees planted in 1808 by John Veitch.

LEFT William Robinson's Great Terrace, looking towards the exotic woodland.
RIGHT One of several Coade stone vases positioned at intervals on the Great Terrace.

Kingston Lacy

WIMBORNE MINSTER, DORSET

AREA 13ha (32 acres) • SOIL alkaline, some acid/varied • ALTITUDE 61m (200ft)
AVERAGE RAINFALL 813mm (32in) • AVERAGE WINTER CLIMATE moderate

The high-chimneyed Italianate mansion, remodelled in the 1830s by Sir Charles Barry for William John Bankes, stands pale and elegant in the midst of an open park. Oaks, beeches and other venerable trees, survivors of the gale of January 1990, are dispersed, singly and in clumps, over the level terrain. Animating the scene is a herd of what seems, from a distance, to be bison; at closer range, they reveal themselves as horned, red North Devon cattle.

This relaxed pastoral scene was set in the late eighteenth century as the original linear landscape laid out by Sir Roger Pratt, the builder of the house, was dismantled. But, as in so many of the great country seats, the pendulum of fashion continued to swing, and as you walk around the house, you find the strict formality reimposed on the immediate surroundings in Victorian and Edwardian times in the form of terrace gardens, avenues of trees and axial vistas. Rose and herbaceous borders, and in spring big splashes of red 'Oxford' tulips, lead you around the house's south front to the impressive sunken parterre, studded with topiary 'skittles' and balls of golden yew accompanied by brightly clashing carpets of spring hyacinths and summer begonias.

Kingston Lacy's gardens had their heyday in the early twentieth century under Henrietta Bankes and her head gardener Mr Hill, though near the house much of the panache comes from the architectural ornaments enthusiastically assembled by William John Bankes on his travels. Veronese lions, well-heads and vases – some endearingly supported by tortoises, which were kept here as pets – decorate the terrace, while, in line with the door, a soaring pink obelisk, brought from a temple beside the Nile, casts a crisp shadow across the broad expanse of lawn that recedes to the ha-ha and parkland.

The gardens were in a sorry state when the Trust took possession of the property in 1982, but fortunately the restoration has been aided by good records. The large, box-edged fernery beside the main lawn, which had become buried under seedling sycamores, was one of the first features to be tackled. It is now a bewitching part of the garden, a strange and shady world of meandering gravel paths, horizontally trained yews, stone walls and raised beds, in which some 40 varieties of ferns, so appealing to the Victorians for their eccentricities and Gothic habits, hold court. They are joined by cyclamen, lily of the valley, and a fine National Collection of *Anemone nemorosa*.

Snowdrops are to be found here, too, as they are in much of the garden. They are a particularly memorable sight along Lady's Walk and the Lime Walk, where they are complemented by the glowing red twigs of the limes; there is also a warm glow from the base of the trees, where, unusually, the epicormic growth has been allowed to remain. This avenue, extended by Walter Ralph Bankes in the 1870s, is in fact a vestige of the seventeenth-century formal layout. Beyond the fernery, a long border of blue and white plants, including irises, phlox and crambe, has been recently re-created. Opposite is the patterned sunken garden, enclosed by yew hedging and formally bedded out following the original late nineteenth-century design by William Goldring of Kew. Pampas grass and rodgersia occupy the central bed, and further on you come to an island bed of *Osmunda* fern set into the lawn.

On breezy days, you will hear the distinctive hiss of the cut-leaved beech, *Fagus sylvatica* 'Aspleniifolia', as you enter the Blind Walk, so-called because it is hidden from view by evergreens. Here the Victorian taste for coloured leaves is fully indulged, the thickets of purple and gold shrubs and small trees, underplanted with pulmonarias, leading to a monument erected to celebrate Queen Victoria's Golden Jubilee. Maples, plums, privets, berberis and elders add to the indigestion. The shrubbery extends into the nearby Cricket Walk (so-called because it once led to the family cricket pitch) in the form of cistus and hydrangeas, accompanied in spring by massed daffodils.

Along the wooded Lady's Walk, you come to the newly restored Japanese Garden, spanning 2ha (5 acres) and with an enclosed tea garden as its centrepiece. Inspired by the Japan-British Exhibition of 1910, this is an interpretation rather than an authentic re-creation of a Japanese garden, with a thatched entrance gate leading into a miniature landscaped valley appointed with dry stream, rocks, cut-leaved maples and traditional ornaments including a tea hut and waiting arbour. It is set within extensive plantings of cherries, maples, azaleas and cloud-pruned box.

The path leads across the road to the 2.4 ha (6 acre) kitchen garden, which is currently under restoration. In the nineteenth century, 20 gardeners were employed here, and the standard of cultivation was so high that members of Queen Victoria's own gardening staff came for training. There is a good range of glass and forcing houses, including a fine vinery awaiting repair.

ABOVE The 'Dutch', or parterre, garden designed in 1899 by C. E. Ponting.

There is a further assembly of ornamental trees and shrubs in Nursery Wood, part of the loop walk that takes you out along the camellia grove and lime avenue and back through the Cedar Walk to the house. A pocket of acid soil allows a colourful run of lime-hating azaleas and rhododendrons here, which would not thrive on the chalk and clay elsewhere in the garden. The trees include Hungarian oak, black walnut, ginkgo, tulip tree, and some striking young *Prunus serrula*, with polished chestnut trunks. The Bankes family were meticulous in recording tree planting, and at one time all the trees in the Cedar Walk carried commemorative plaques. Sadly, the cedar planted by King Edward VII fell in a recent gale; that planted in 1907 by the Kaiser remains.

LEFT One of a series of bay trees on the Italian marble well-heads at Kingston Lacy.
ABOVE The Japanese Garden, inspired by the 1910 Japan-British Exhibition.
RIGHT Forcing rhubarb in the kitchen garden at Knightshayes.

Knightshayes Court

BOLHAM, TIVERTON, DEVON

AREA 101ha (250 acres) • SOIL acid-neutral/heavy • ALTITUDE 122–152m (400–500ft)
AVERAGE RAINFALL 914mm (36in) • AVERAGE WINTER CLIMATE moderate

This garden, developed by Sir John and Lady Heathcoat Amory – the former champion golfer Joyce Wethered – is one of the best-displayed plant collections in the country, comprising formal gardens, conservatory, alpine beds, naturalised bulbs and hectare upon hectare of exotic woodland and glade, stocked with the choicest trees, shrubs and perennials. Neither had any experience of gardening when they began married life here in 1937, but Sir John became a dedicated collector, Lady Heathcoat Amory a gifted plant arranger, and they worked with a small staff of gardeners, turning for outside help to some of the best contemporary designers and landscapers – Lanning Roper and Sir Eric Savill – and plantsmen, including Graham Stuart Thomas, Norman Haddon and Miss Nellie Britton, who ran a well-known alpine nursery near Tiverton.

The setting is potently Victorian. The red sandstone house, standing high on the eastern flank of the Exe Valley with open views across the Devon countryside towards Tiverton, was designed by William Burges and built between 1869 and 1874. The long, curving entrance drive through the park takes you past its western flank, uphill between Burges's stable block with its fairytale tower and the walled kitchen garden, and onwards to the car park. Favourite Victorian trees, including Scots pine, cedar, wellingtonia and purple beech join the parkland oaks (English and Turkey), and beyond the walled garden is a suitably sombre plantation of fine Douglas firs, offering a hushed, cool walk through the box and bracken understorey.

In front of the house, the scene is livelier. The terraces here were set out by the garden designer and writer Edward Kemp in the 1870s, but they are no longer the scene of swashbuckling bedding schemes. Instead, you look down upon clean patterns of lawn, clipped yew, paving and stone ornament, fringed by pastel schemes of rosemary, cistus, lavender, iris, agapanthus and other sun-lovers.

Restraint and profusion: these two themes interplay throughout the garden, the contrast heightened here by the tension between the crisp, formal groundplan and the curves and spill of the flowers and foliage. It is felt still more intensely in the yew-hedged compartments, up the short flight of steps to the east. Here, you come to a small paved garden, patterned with low silver and ice-blue perennials, a lead cistern and flanking pair of standard wisterias; and formal terraces of alpine (in a lowland setting, far more harmonious a feature than an eruption of rock), including scented daphnes, dianthus, dwarf iris, zauschneria and bulbs.

These are placed in contrast with an empty lawn, around which topiary hounds chase a topiary fox – a much celebrated touch of whimsy added by Sir Ian Heathcoat Amory, a keen huntsman, in the 1920s; and a larger space (formerly the bowling green) framed by Victorian battlemented hedges and backlit by *Acer pseudoplatanus* 'Brilliantissimum', where a circular pool, the solitary statue of a bather, stone benches and a weeping silver pear are the only ingredients: a charming piece of modernist composition, simple and complete.

Another few steps and you are inside Knightshayes' most famous planting, the Garden in the Wood. This area was gradually annexed from about 1950 and now encompasses some 10ha (25 acres) of ornamental walks and glades, under the canopy of the thinned and high-pruned nineteenth-century oaks, beeches, limes and conifers. It begins with a straight grass walk, bordered by Shrub roses and rhododendrons (not a partnership often encountered in gardens), underplanted with geraniums, pulmonarias and electric blue omphalodes. As the walk breaks into curves and glades, you come upon traditional woodland raised beds colonised by mosses, ferns, wood anemones, violets and much else. Larger grass glades open up, speared by the trunks of the tall pines and native trees. At the edges are herbaceous schemes – perhaps shrubby euphorbias,

their lime-yellow cylinders of flower matched with purple-leaved violet and Bowles's golden grass, or, later in summer, a flush of yellow, apricot and orange crocosmias. Sword-leaved phormiums and silver astelia punctuate views, and in one spot, a purple thundercloud looms, created by massed *Rhododendron augustinii* hybrids.

Gravel paths meander through a grove of larches and lead into an area of distinctive character where waves of creamy-white and pink erythroniums break against outcrops of bronze *Polystichum* ferns; later, white Excelsior foxgloves and white gentian filter between the conifers. Naturally, spring and early summer see the main flowering of the wood – the former a magical time when the chalices of tree magnolias are lighting a largely leafless canopy, and hellebores are blooming in thick carpets under their shrubby cousins

denied to many inland gardens. There is a concentration of them on the grass slope below the wood. These 1.6ha (4 acres) also support a collection of southern beeches (*Nothofagus*), as well as cherries, magnolias and ever more hardy rhododendrons; crimson-red rhododendrons blooming in front of white-trunked birches create a striking picture. Elsewhere, an area of native woodland plants has recently been developed.

Momentously, in 2003 the Victorian Walled Kitchen Garden also opened to the public for the first time. Just over 0.8ha (2 acres) in size, with stepped, tile-capped stone walls and decorative conical-roofed corner turrets, this was designed by William Burges very much as a showcase garden and, enhanced by its backdrop of trees, is one of the most handsome in the Trust's hands. But having been grassed over in the 1960s, it has required much work to bring it back to a high standard of presentation and production. It slopes from north to south, with, ingeniously, a little slatted gate at the lowest point to allow the frost to drain away. The long, buttressed upper wall shelters double borders of exotic plants appreciative of the warm micro-climate, including giant *Dahlia imperialis*, *Rosa bracteata*, *Tetrapanax papyrifer*, *Leptospermum myrtifolium* and *Fitzroya cupressoides*. There are also herbaceous and cut-flower borders, and beds for culinary and medicinal herbs.

Vegetables and fruit, however, take centre stage. Unusual and heritage varieties abound in the large permanent and rotational plots, among them 'Purple Dragon' carrot, 'Fat Lazy Blond' lettuce, walking stick cabbage, oca (*Oxalis tuberosa*), skirret, and Taunton Deane cottager's kale, a variety that doesn't produce seed and crops all year. Gages, damsons, cherries and plums grow on the north-facing wall behind the rhubarb varieties, and elsewhere there is an array of soft fruit, pears and Devon and Cornish apples. Pumpkins and squash grow in hot beds, there are mulberry trees in little roundels, and there is even a vineyard plot – the red 'Regent' and white 'Orion' grape varieties being blended to make rosé. The walled garden is a major addition to a tour of the grounds, and for the visitor completes the experience of a country house garden in the round, seen in its heyday. Its produce can be tasted in the restaurant opposite, a fine example of 'plot to plate'.

– but hypericums, hydrangeas, clethras, tricyrtis, clerodendrums and Japanese anemones keep the colour flowing into high summer and autumn, when the large colonies of cyclamen, growing on the dry banks and around the boles of trees, are performing their pink and white butterfly dance.

Mahonias are a favourite tribe, and ferns are ubiquitous – delicate maidenhair ferns beside the discs of *Cyclamen repandum*, and the creeping, rust-coloured *Blechnum penna-marina* picking up the suede undersides of *Rhododendron falconeri*, among the many memorable associations. Knightshayes cannot support the more tender trees and shrubs encountered on the Cornish peninsula, but the soil is rich and the climate is still warm and wet enough for some of the early-flowering and more exotic-looking trees and shrubs

ABOVE Looking down the Pool Garden towards distant fields.

Lacock Abbey

LACOCK, CHIPPENHAM, WILTSHIRE

AREA 4.4ha (11 acres) • **SOIL** alkaline/loam • **ALTITUDE** 45m (150ft)
AVERAGE RAINFALL 635mm (25in) • **AVERAGE WINTER CLIMATE** cold

'The setting is of open water meadows, belts of trees, rough shady lawns and a series of walled enclosures given over to fruit and allotments.'

The vaulted chapter house and cloisters of the former Augustinian nunnery are preserved behind the mellow walls of this great house, a cool and silent refuge from the outside world. Of the former medieval and later gardens, there is now little trace.

The setting is of open water meadows, belts of trees, rough shady lawns and a series of walled enclosures given over to fruit and allotments. One of the enclosures has now been re-created as a botanic garden, evoking that made by William Henry Fox Talbot, the pioneer photographer, whose home this once was. A keen botanist, he collected plants himself on trips to the Mediterranean, grew many untried species from seed, and delighted in experimenting with the new introductions made by plant hunters such as David Douglas in North America. The borders mix annuals and vegetables with perennials to extend the season, while the reinstated greenhouse displays the more exotic species he grew.

Early in the season is a good time to visit Lacock, when snowdrops, winter aconites, sweet violets and spectacular sheets of wild *Crocus vernus* are covering the ground, soon to be followed by drifts of daffodils, dog's tooth violets and snakeshead fritillaries. But for much of the year, there are scattered plants in bloom. Roses, mock orange, wild cranesbills and martagon lilies give summer colour in the grassy glades, while the Abbey walls lend a golden backdrop to a range of shrubs and climbers.

The hot, dry conditions of the south and west façades suit yellow Banksian rose, Judas tree, figs, rosemary and lavender, together with ceratostigma, *Geranium renardii* and myrtle. Against the east wall grow hydrangeas, ferns and Virginia creeper, a fine sight in its autumnal scarlet, and the rose garden, based on a photograph of 1841, has recently been refurbished with mixed modern and shrub roses and climbers growing up wrought-iron arches.

Yet these can only be incidents in the large-scale scene of abbey and meadow. Behind the house, the mood is more intimate, set by the canopy and fringe of trees. Beeches hang over the old stewpond, with its rushes, sweet flag and dragonflies. Nearby there are tall oaks and limes, a group of huge London planes and a suckering wing-nut tree, *Pterocarya fraxinifolia*, with fissured bark; elsewhere, fine specimens of black walnut, a young tulip tree, swamp cypress and catalpa, with late trusses of highly scented white flowers.

RIGHT Lavender surrounding the entrance to the cloisters at Lacock Abbey.

Lamb House

WEST STREET, RYE, EAST SUSSEX

AREA 0.4ha (1 acre) • SOIL neutral/loam • ALTITUDE 15m (50ft) • AVERAGE RAINFALL 762mm (30in) • AVERAGE WINTER CLIMATE moderate

'The quite essential amiability of Lamb House only deepens with age,' wrote Henry James, who lived here from 1898 until his death in 1916. The Georgian house stands at the turn of one of Rye's cobbled streets, and behind it is a walled garden with a central expanse of grass, gravel and stone paths, cherry trees and box-studded borders packed with plants. The American novelist was not a gardener, but as his last secretary, Theodora Bosanquet, noted: 'It never failed to give [him] pleasure to look out … at his English garden where he could watch his English gardener digging the flower-beds or mowing the lawn or sweeping the fallen leaves.'

James was advised by Alfred Parsons, the painter and garden designer, on a new garden layout. No plan exists, however, and the garden continues to evolve. Periodic gales, a hazard in coastal gardens, have also brought changes. But on most days, the garden is kept snug by its walls and trees and by the surrounding houses; the principal view is over the spikes of acanthus flowers to the spire of St Peter's church.

The borders that flank the perimeter paths are narrow and full of surprises. Flame-coloured *Campsis radicans*, an ancient specimen here in James's time, grows against the south wall of the house. In the sunny beds, among violets, lavenders and irises, you will come across stands of eucomis and scented hybrid lilies; in the shady corners, camellias, hellebores, montbretia and white impatiens. In spring, bluebells and grape hyacinths are ubiquitous; in autumn, Japanese anemones, nerines and hardy plumbago create pools of pink and blue between the amber curtains of the cherry branches. There are no sophisticated planting themes here, and the mood is relaxed. A trellis, hung with roses, conceals the kitchen garden. There are more roses beyond – bushes of 'Paul Shirville', 'Peace' and others – for cutting, with alyssum and, in spring, chionodoxa and jonquils growing beneath them.

Lamb House's literary association did not end with James's death: the property also became the home of E.F. Benson, whose Mapp and Lucia novels were written and set in Rye.

ABOVE July in the herb garden at Lamb House with santolina, lavender, thyme, rosemary and fennel.

RIGHT Magnolia in full bloom near the River Fowey at Lanhydrock.

Lanhydrock

BODMIN, CORNWALL

AREA 12ha (30 acres) • SOIL acid/good loam • ALTITUDE 122m (400ft)
AVERAGE RAINFALL 1,524mm (60in) • AVERAGE WINTER CLIMATE moderate

Hanging beechwoods, plunging entrance drives and tree-studded parkland rolling down to the River Fowey provide a dynamic setting for this low, labyrinthine house of silver-grey granite, with its accompanying church and ornate, obelisk-capped gatehouse. The buildings, part seventeenth-century and part late Victorian, are tucked close into the wooded ridge and face east, down the valley and away from the prevailing wind. For although this is Cornwall, the house stands at 122m (400ft), 11km (7 miles) from the sea and with the south-western edge of windswept Bodmin Moor only 4km (2½ miles) away.

This chillier climate and shadier aspect distinguishes Lanhydrock from the balmy coastal gardens, depriving it of the more tender and earliest-flowering exotics. But the spring display is every bit as spectacular and, as the season advances, colour surges through the woods. Thickets of camellias and enormous specimens of *Rhododendron* Smithii Group ('Cornish Red') become beacons in the landscape, while above, various forms and hybrids of *Magnolia campbellii*, the first in a long succession of tree magnolias, hold their pink and white chalices to the sky. By late April, countless other shrubs are in bloom, together with waves of daffodils and bluebells.

Most of the other great Cornish woodland gardens are made on slopes below their houses, but here the main garden is above, and the flower-framed views down across the rooftops, gatehouse and accompanying lines of Irish yew trees are one of the property's most memorable features. The yews are part of a very different style of garden set out around the house for the 1st Baron Robartes in the 1850s. It was thought that its design emanated from the architect

George Gilbert Scott, who was engaged to work on the house, but pen-and-wash drawings recently uncovered in the archive show the inspiration behind this formal Italianate garden to have come from George Truefitt, a London architect and founder member of the Architectural Association. His design was then condensed and reworked by Richard Cound, Gilbert Scott's Liskeard-based associate, with the planting scheme probably devised by the family in collaboration with their head gardener. The design was further simplified in the 1920s and '30s.

It is a crisp and satisfying composition of lawns, yews, urns, roses and bedding schemes, enclosed and partitioned by the low battlement walls. Floribunda roses – pink 'Octavia Hill', white 'Margaret Merril', yellow 'Bright Smile', the well-scented, rosy-violet 'Escapade' and 'Songs of Praise' – give a long display of colour opposite the east front, while in the parterre, the schemes are usually based on tulips, pansies and forget-me-nots for spring, with begonias later. Fine trees fringe these formal lawns, including cork oak, chestnuts, a towering Monterey pine, and two copper beeches planted by the prime ministers William Gladstone and Lord Rosebery. Behind the Croquet Lawn stands a remarkable field maple, its limbs caked in lichens, mosses and polypody ferns, which flourish in the clean, moist air. It was not until after 1930, when the 7th Viscount Clifden inherited, that the more flamboyant species of trees and shrubs – for decades, the sensation of other Cornish gardens – began to be sampled at Lanhydrock.

As you walk towards the Higher Garden, you get an inkling of the displays to come. In spring the shrubby *Magnolia loebneri* and

its hybrids 'Leonard Messel' and the exquisitely scented 'Merrill' will be in bloom and beyond, the first of the show-stopping trees: among them forms of *M. × veitchii* and *M. dawsoniana*. Rhododendrons, including the crimson-flecked, creamy 'Dr Stocker', pink 'Mrs C.B. van Nes' and *R. arboreum* var. *roseum*, add to the scene. Later, there will be scented Occidentale azaleas, *Magnolia tripetala*, and, in high summer, 'Rostrevor' eucryphias.

The winding paths lead through ever richer banks of blossom, on and on, past a stream up to the Holy Well and thatched gardener's cottage. Everywhere, the magnolias billow and the rhododendrons and camellias surge. *Magnolia sargentiana* var. *robusta*, *M. sprengeri* var. *diva* and hybrids of *M. cylindrica* make spectacular trees, while the shrubby *M. × soulangeana* and its many selections are ubiquitous; at one point, lines of *M. × soulangeana* 'Lennei' form a tunnel of blossom. In late spring, *M. sieboldii* and its relatives, with pendant flowers, enter the stage, followed by *M. ashei*, fragrant *M. thompsoniana*, and *M. hypoleuca* and *M. × wiesneri* (syn. *M. × watsonii*), both carrying the pervasive scent of ripe melons.

Hardy Hybrids make up a large proportion of Lanhydrock's rhododendron collection and they are here in all colours. Massed lacecap and mophead hydrangeas reproduce for summer some of this springtime spectacle, but now attention shifts to the great circle of clipped yew below the woodland banks. Here, beside a barn, is a distinctively designed circular garden of herbaceous plants, the southern half of which was set out by Lady Clifden before 1914. The Trust completed the hedge and added matching perimeter flower-beds in 1971. The foliage of *Yucca recurvifolia*, yellow tree peony, *Melianthus major*, fascicularias, rodgersias, hostas and ligularias set a lush, exotic theme, against which the flowers of agapanthus, penstemons, *Canna iridiflora*, *Cautleya* 'Robusta', and other perennials appreciative of the long, warm, moist s ummers are displayed.

In April, the Higher Garden's Top Walk is bordered by a notable colony of white pheasant's eye narcissi, the bulbs having naturalised luxuriantly since their introduction in the mid-1970s. A new summer-house has been installed here and a gate leads into the wilder Woodland Garden, where ferns and bluebells invade the steep banks, beneath oak and beech. The finest views of the house and park are now revealed, complemented by the dazzling blood-reds of the rhododendrons 'Tally Ho', 'Matador' and Smithii Group ('Cornish Red'), and the elephantine leaves of *R. maccabeanum*, *R. grande* and other giants.

LEFT Summer bedding of begonias in the box parterre.

ABOVE The East Front and forecourt with yew hedging and topiary.

Lavenham Guildhall

LAVENHAM, SUDBURY, SUFFOLK

AREA 0.04ha (¹/₁₀ acre) • **SOIL** neutral/loam • **ALTITUDE** 47m (153ft)
AVERAGE RAINFALL 572mm (22½2 in) • **AVERAGE WINTER CLIMATE** moderate

The timber-striped façade of this sixteenth-century hall, in the market square of the medieval town of Lavenham, is a mesmerising sight. It was built by the religious Guild of Corpus Christi, almost certainly members of the town's cloth-making elite, and the association continues, for the interior is now a museum exploring the craft of cloth-making and dyeing.

The small courtyard garden tucked behind is notable for its mortuary, prison cell and splendid old fire engine, as well as its array of dyers' plants. Yellows were produced from herbs such as agrimony, camomile, goldenrod and tansy; pinks and reds from madder and safflower; greens from cardoon, lily of the valley and yarrow; orange from weld; black from yellow flag iris roots; and blues from wild indigo, elecampane and woad. Mixed with dyer's greenweed, *Genista tinctoria*, woad also produced the famous Lincoln green.

The garden was redesigned in the early 1990s with imported fenland soil after an outbreak of honey fungus, and given a surprisingly modern patio feel, using new bricks and plants of recent origin. But there are plenty of old favourites too, including hellebores, lavender and crown imperials, and a fine young tree of the stewing pear 'Catillac', which has white flowers of outstanding quality followed by fruits with the shape and firmness of cannonballs. Summer sees a great crop of roses, from the Climbers 'New Dawn', 'Zéphirine Drouhin', 'Madame Alfred Carrière' and 'Félicité Perpétue', and the Bush roses 'Gertrude Jekyll', 'Octavia Hill', 'Saint Cecilia' and 'Marguerite Hilling'. An armillary sphere was added to commemorate Queen Elizabeth's Golden Jubilee in 2002.

ABOVE An array of plants previously used to make dye for cloth, part of the history of the Guildhall.

RIGHT Looking towards Lutyens' Lindisfarne Castle on Holy Island from the Walled Garden.

Lindisfarne Castle

HOLY ISLAND, BERWICK-UPON-TWEED, NORTHUMBERLAND

AREA 0.05ha (⅛ acre) • **SOIL** alkaline/free-draining loam • **ALTITUDE** 5m (16½ ft)
AVERAGE RAINFALL 813–1,194mm (32–47in) • **AVERAGE WINTER CLIMATE** cold

The island fortress of Lindisfarne, standing on a steep crag and cut off from the mainland at high tide, is a potent eye-catcher amid the raw beauty of the Northumberland coast. Built in the 1570s to guard against incursion from the Scots, it was in a sorry state when discovered by Edward Hudson, the founder of *Country Life* magazine, in 1901.

To convert it into a comfortable holiday home, and add a cheerful and productive garden, it was natural that Hudson should turn to his famous friends, the architect Edwin Lutyens and the garden designer Gertrude Jekyll, who was changing the face of English gardens with her advocacy of cottage-garden exuberance and painterly plant combinations in place of the stiff artifice of Victorian bedding. The pair had recently worked together on his Berkshire home, The Deanery in Sonning. By the time Miss Jekyll ventured to Lindisfarne, in May 1906, she was in her sixties, extremely short-sighted, and seldom away from home. She was rowed across to the island, accompanied by Lutyens, who was somewhat encumbered by a recuperating raven, given to him by his dentist, which he was carrying in a Gladstone bag. It provided much entertainment. There were also musical evenings in the castle, with Jekyll singing to the guitar.

Initial ideas for planting close to the castle were abandoned, and efforts were concentrated some distance away on flat ground, consisting of a small plot, enclosed by low grey walls. Lutyens drew up a simple formal pattern of flower-beds and stone paths, which defied the irregular geometry, and Jekyll set about devising a planting scheme. Her first plan was for a vegetable garden, jollied up by

sweet peas and other annuals, but this was revised to concentrate on flowers, both annual and perennial, some of which would have been intended for cutting.

The early research and archaeology for the restoration of the garden was carried out by Michael Tooley of Durham University, his wife Rosanna, and volunteer students. Since then, the present scheme by Jekyll expert Richard Bisgrove has been planted, although extensive research has gone into the restoration, which is as faithful as possible to the spirit of the garden.

Banks of sweet peas raise curtains either side of the main axis, framing the view to the castle as well as screening off the vegetables and early flowering roses in the side borders. These last include the dark red Shrub rose 'Hugh Dickson', and the Climbers 'Madame Abel Chatenay' in pink and 'Madame Alfred Carrière' in white. Pink *Clematis montana*, purple *Clematis* 'Jackmanii' (filtering into silver-leaved *Hippophaë rhamnoides*), lavenders and sweet-scented mignonette (*Reseda*) are among the supporting cast.

The principal south-facing border blends the more vibrant reds of hollyhock, bergamot and fuchsia with the yellows and whites of helianthus, santolina and Japanese anemones. Carmine *Gladiolus byzantinus* sprouts from Jekyll's own 'Munstead Red' sedum in the central bed, and in the surrounding beds blues are introduced into the mix, courtesy of *Scabiosa caucasica*, *Centaurea cyanus* and delphiniums. Jekyll used the spent stems of the delphiniums as a support for creamy *Clematis flammula* – one of her trademark touches of genius.

ABOVE Extensive research has gone into the restoration of Jekyll's original planting scheme in the Walled Garden.

Little Moreton Hall

CONGLETON, CHESHIRE

AREA 0.4ha (1 acre) • **SOIL** lime-free/sandy loam • **ALTITUDE** 76m (250ft)
AVERAGE RAINFALL 635mm (25in) • **AVERAGE WINTER CLIMATE** moderate

When the Trust acquired this startling timber-framed house, built for the Moreton family in the sixteenth century, the moated garden was neglected and overgrown. There were no records of the early design, nor many significant features remaining, other than the two grass-covered mounts – one within and one without the garden – so it was decided to reinvent a garden, which, though without the support of direct historical evidence, would be an appropriate setting for the house and would reinforce its domestic Elizabethan flavour. The design of the knot, happily echoing the timber pattern on the house, was taken from Leonard Meager's *The Complete English Gardener* of 1670.

Now, 30 or so years later, the plantings are well established, and the garden has acquired much charm, the only jarring note being the proximity of the busy A34. From the small cobbled courtyard, you are drawn into the orchard, where the older trees have been supplemented by traditional varieties. Quinces, apples and medlars are among them, with one of the mature pears supporting a Rambler rose.

The Elizabethan pattern of formal enclosures has been restored through the planting of hedges. A mixed screen of hornbeam, holly, sweetbriar and honeysuckle surrounds the orchard, and the adjacent knot garden and tunnel have sides of yew. The knot itself is made of dwarf edging box (*Buxus sempervirens* 'Suffruticosa'), with gravel, grass and yew topiaries filling the spaces within. In the sixteenth century, the spaces were often planted with flowers, but to keep the design crisp and uncluttered, these have been confined to side beds. Here, long-grown herbaceous plants such as tradescantia, iris, peony and astrantia are cultivated in neat rectangular blocks, with standard gooseberries (replacements for lavenders, which succumbed to the prevalent cold, damp winters) rising from square mats of sweet woodruff, golden marjoram, thrift, camomile, wild strawberry, bugle and other low perennials.

The narrow walk around the moat brings you to other beds. One pair contains old varieties of vegetable, including 'Carlin' pea, broad bean 'Martock', ruby chard, oak leaf lettuce and the dwarf French bean 'Soldier'; another has culinary and medicinal herbs such as liquorice, rue, borage and summer savory. The ornamental beds within the house's projecting wings are damp enough to support fat clumps of umbrella plant, *Darmera peltata* (formerly *Peltiphyllum peltatum*). But these outlying plantings are simply details beside the tranquil fringe of trees, sweeps of meadow and expanse of dark water. The perch and golden orfe that break the surface are further reminders of the varied produce an Elizabethan household would have expected from its domain.

ABOVE Neatly clipped box hedge outlines the gravelled Elizabethan-style knot garden at Little Moreton Hall.

Llanerchaeron

CILIAU AERON, ABERAERON, CEREDIGION

AREA 4.9ha (12 acres) • SOIL acid/clay • ALTITUDE 43m (141ft)
AVERAGE RAINFALL 1,321mm (52in) • AVERAGE WINTER CLIMATE mild

Since the early nineteenth century, the clocks have ticked slowly in this private and remote estate. Owned by the Lewis family for ten generations, it came to the Trust in 1989, its farm, park, pleasure grounds, and walled fruit and vegetable gardens in poor repair but remarkably intact.

You have your first glimpse as you drive up the wooded valley, away from the sea and the cheery harbour town of Aberaeron. There on the valley floor, sandwiched between trees and meadow grazed by sheep and Welsh black cattle, appears the ochre-washed villa. It was remodelled in the early 1790s for Colonel William Lewis by John Nash, who would later become the presiding architect of Regency London. It is not known who advised on the accompanying landscape, but the influence of Humphry Repton, the leading landscape designer of the day, is certainly felt in the framed views, tree clumps, and the formal separation, by iron railings, of house and park (from the mid-1790s, Repton collaborated with Nash on various English commissions).

The pathways, formerly impenetrable with brambles, have now been opened up; they offer views out into the park and lead you to the lake, where the oval island is a favoured nesting site for herons. A deep stone-walled leat, which once carried water for use in the house, winds through the trees and the pleasure grounds, and at one point you come upon a pair of rockery mounds, a popular feature of the period, adorned with quartz, pumice, and other local and alien stones. Nearby, a series of scallop-shaped beds, edged in stones, supports a collection of eccentric ferns.

You are now met by a closed door in an old garden wall – the paintwork a beautiful cracked turquoise overlaying rusty red. It is an irresistible invitation, and you open it to find yourself in a huge enclosure, the first of two adjoining walled gardens, each 0.4ha (1 acre) in size – this one framed in brick 3m (10ft) high, its sister garden largely of stone. Extracting clay for all the bricks, together with those needed for the house, is likely to have created the pit that formed the lake.

Thanks to grants and a small army of volunteers, this garden has been returned to an impressive level of production. Plums and gages are newly trained on the walls, and historic apple varieties have been planted on the orchard lawns and path fringes to augment the surviving trees, which include a splendid old espaliered 'Northern Greening'. Plots of rhubarb and asparagus, a soft fruit cage, and an extensive range of herbs complement the rows of legumes and root vegetables. While the high rainfall dictates much cultivation in raised beds, continual working and liming of the heavy acid clay over the centuries has produced an excellent crumbly soil.

Flues, incorporated into the south-facing wall, used to conduct warm air from fires in the outhouses behind in order to heat a series of frames and glasshouses, enabling much early and tender produce to be grown. The remains of one of the early nineteenth-century glasshouses can still be seen; in its central beds, fermenting manure was used to heat the soil for pineapples and melons. Later nineteenth-century glasshouses, derelict and engulfed in ivy, have now been restored, and once again grow tomatoes, cucumbers and grapes, as well as pelargoniums, jasmine and passionflower.

A further, twentieth-century, glasshouse, built of concrete, awaits attention, its resident camellias perfectly happy in the open air. Behind the walls loom the grey stone and slate of the farm buildings, and the sounds of cattle, sheep and pigs.

LEFT A summer display of Shasta daisies, purple veronica and magenta *Lychnis coronaria*.

Lyme Park

DISLEY, STOCKPORT, CHESHIRE

AREA 6.5ha (16 acres) • **SOIL** acid/clay • **ALTITUDE** 152m (500ft)
AVERAGE RAINFALL 1,016mm (40in) • **AVERAGE WINTER CLIMATE** cold

The contrasts between the formal elegance of Lyme Park and its gardens, and the wild landscape in which they sit, gives spice to this property. On the edge of the Peak District, the hall surveys wooded slopes and rolling moorland, grazed by ancient herds of red deer. The climate is harsh, with high rainfall, a cool, late spring and a short summer – conditions that have prompted complaints from gardeners at Lyme Park since the late seventeenth century, when the first garden records appear.

The Elizabethan house was given its Italianate grandeur by Giacomo Leoni in the early eighteenth century. The gardens had their heyday in the late nineteenth century, and their present planting and patterns are reminders of that sumptuous era of country-house living. But by 1947, when Lyme Park was transferred to the Trust, the property had declined as a result of high taxation and shortage of staff. Until 1994 Stockport Metropolitan Council was responsible for its upkeep, but funds were not available for the restoration of the hall until the early 1970s and attention was turned to the garden after that.

The starting point was the most spectacular feature, the huge sunken Dutch Garden to the west of the hall, created in the early eighteenth century. In 1973, a violent summer storm caused a torrent of water to flow into the lake above, to which the ancient sluice system proved unequal. The south-east corner of the wall could not support the pressure from the floodwaters, and cracked; the result was a cascade of mud, water and stones across the parterre. Today, however, you look down once more on the pristine scheme as installed by the 1st Lord Newton. Surrounding the central fountain,

the intricate pattern of beds, edged in ivy, are filled with seasonal schemes with a strong period flavour. Daffodils and tulips are the mainstay of the spring display, and impatiens, cineraria, marigolds and calceolaria in their thousands are highlights of the summer show, while among the heavy evergreen and variegated shrubberies that clothe the banks come further bursts of colour from rhododendrons, osmanthus, philadelphus and viburnums.

The smaller sunken garden to the north is set out with trees and shrubs mainly given by or commemorating the Hon. Vicary Gibbs, a renowned gardener and friend of the 2nd Lord Newton. *Malus × purpurea* 'Aldenhamensis', 'Gibbs' Golden Gage' and *Ligustrum* 'Vicaryi' are among the plants carrying Gibbs's name or that of his garden in Hertfordshire.

In the nineteenth century, no fashionable country house was complete without its conservatory. Lyme's grand Orangery was designed by Lewis Wyatt in about 1815, but the interior, with its central fountain and floors in Minton patterned tiles, was remodelled some 50 years later by Alfred Derbyshire, who also added the glazed cupola. Once warmed by the excess heat from the laundry and brewhouse behind, the Orangery is no longer heated, but the fig tree and two great camellias survive from Victorian times, and, together with choisya, pittosporum, *Cestrum elegans*, ferns and scented *Lilium regale*, continue to project the exotic mood.

Terrace beds in front of the Orangery, in summer often displaying the half-hardy, white-throated *Penstemon* 'Rubicundus' raised at Lyme in 1906, a recently reinstated early nineteenth-century geometric garden, and the Rose Garden to the east, planted with

standard 'Sander's White Rambler' and Floribunda roses, are further expressions of formality. Beyond, the garden's lines are more flowing: the eye follows first the sweep up to the Lantern Tower, erected as a folly in the eighteenth century and framed by woods, and then turns to trace the curving path between hedged herbaceous borders.

From Hamper's Bridge, you follow the stream through still more meandering and naturalistic plantings. The area known to the gardeners as 'Killtime' is sufficiently moist and sheltered to suit rhododendrons and azaleas, accompanied by ferns and other pondside plants. Swiss Arolla pine, Bhutan pine and small-leaved lime are among the many good trees. Behind the lake, you walk through rhododendron shrubberies until you are in line once more with the centre of Leoni's south façade. The Lime Avenue to the south, is, together with the lake, one of the four remaining vestiges of the seventeenth-century garden. It was planted by Richard Legh, whose family was associated with Lyme for nearly 600 years.

LEFT The Dutch Garden's central fountain is surrounded by a symmetrical parterre of summer bedding.

ABOVE The formal Rose Garden and Orangery look out onto the parkland to the east of the house.

Lytes Cary Manor

CHARLTON MACKRELL, SOMERTON, SOMERSET

AREA 2ha (5 acres) • **SOIL** alkaline/clay • **ALTITUDE** 61m (200ft) • **AVERAGE RAINFALL** 762mm (30in) • **AVERAGE WINTER CLIMATE** cold

'The house itself is clad in evergreen magnolia, the Climber rose 'Paul's Lemon Pillar' and Banksian roses'

In 1907, the medieval and Tudor manor of Lytes Cary, home of the Lyte family for five centuries from 1286, found its champion in Sir Walter Jenner, son of Sir William Jenner, the eminent physician. As well as restoring and sympathetically enlarging the decaying house, Jenner set out a series of simply furnished, grassed and paved formal enclosures, aptly described by Christopher Hussey as 'a necklace of garden rooms strung on green corridors'. Like the house, Jenner's garden is broad and low-slung, crouching for shelter in its flat, exposed farmland. The yards of yew are important buffers, in addition to giving the garden its patterns and secrets.

Although the bones of the gardens are largely unaltered since Sir Walter's day, a programme of renovation and improvements was begun by the Trust in 1963. This included the replanning and enrichment of the main flower border, which runs along a corridor opposite a buttressed yew hedge. The planting is mixed and follows a deliberate colour sequence, in the Jekyllian manner, warming from the blues and yellows of potentilla, caryopteris, *Hibiscus* 'Blue Bird', achillea, polemonium and *Aster × frikartii*, into the purples and rich crimsons of smoke bush, berberis, self-sowing *Atriplex hortensis* and mats of purple sage. Floribunda roses, including 'Magenta', 'Lavender Lassie', 'Rosemary Rose' and 'Yellow Holstein', together with annuals and dahlias, help to ensure a good succession of flowers, and the wall behind is hung with a range of climbers, including clematis. Beyond is a white garden with 'Iceberg' roses, hebe, philadelphus, tobacco flowers and silver foliage.

Other parts of the garden have their bursts of colour too. The ornamental orchard, planted with crossing avenues and symmetrical pairs of medlars, quinces, crab apples, walnuts and corners of weeping ash, is spangled with daffodils, camassias, cowslips, fritillaries and other wildflowers in spring and early summer. Between the Irish yews on the raised walk above, a stream of *Hypericum calycinum* contributes yellow flowers later in the year.

The house itself is clad in evergreen magnolia, the Climber rose 'Paul's Lemon Pillar' and yellow Banksian roses, with its south façade, around a handsome oriel window, lapped with myrtle, *Teucrium fruticans*, *Lilium candidum*, *Gladiolus byzantinus*, rosemary and a wealth of other Mediterranean herbs. These are some of the plants that appear in the 1578 translation by Henry

Lyte of Dodoen's Flemish text, the *Cruedeboek* (1569), a copy of which – *A Niewe Herball or Historie of Plants* – is on display in the Great Hall.

Recently, the floral display in this area has expanded into what was formerly the tenants' private garden. Here, you are led into a sunken lawn, flanked by beds of richly tinted perennials and Shrub roses, and on into a small parterre. This is presided over by a weeping silver pear and enlivened by box-edged borders of sweet peas and other flowers for cutting, herbs, white flowers, and – following on from tulips and alliums – a bed of summer exotics such as castor oil plants, dahlias and deep red lilies.

However, the predominant colours of Lytes Cary are the greens of trees, lawns, yew hedges and countryside, and the mellow tints of the golden stone walls and dovecote (in reality, a disguised water-tower). From the raised walk above the orchard, from which there are wide views towards Yeovilton and Camel Hill, you descend through a long grass alley into a series of restrained enclosures: a pool garden; an oval of evergreen and variegated shrubs, reached through a hornbeam tunnel; a grass arena quietly washed with box-edged beds of lavender; and a wide sweep of open croquet lawn. They are reminders that the simplest treatments make for some of the most satisfying garden pictures.

LEFT Guarding the path to the entrance are the twelve 'Apostles'.

ABOVE The Pond Garden is surrounded by yew hedging interspersed with statuary.

Lyveden

OUNDLE, PETERBOROUGH, NORTHAMPTONSHIRE

AREA 32ha (80 acres) • SOIL neutral/loam over clay • ALTITUDE 84m (275ft)
AVERAGE RAINFALL 546mm (21½ in) • AVERAGE WINTER CLIMATE moderate

There is quite a story here: religious persecution, imprisonment, concealed papers and, buried in the undergrowth for four centuries, one of the oldest surviving garden layouts in England.

The peaceful, prosperous Elizabethan age saw the building of many great houses and the creation of grand gardens to accompany them – formal, architectural designs, inspired by the Renaissance gardens of France and Italy, and the setting for lavish entertainments. Until Lyveden's emergence from the brambles in the 1990s, every one of these English gardens was thought to have been lost, victims largely of the eighteenth-century's revolutionary new taste for naturalistic parks.

Lyveden's owner, Sir Thomas Tresham, was a courtier and wealthy member of the Northamptonshire gentry. However, his extravagant lifestyle, together with his Catholicism, for which he attracted repeated recusancy fines, meant that he spent fifteen of the last 25 years of his life either under house arrest or in prison, from where much of his garden was planned. The result was that his grand 22ha (54 acre) design for Lyveden proceeded slowly and never reached fruition.

What greets you on this windy hilltop is the lonely, roofless shell of his New Bield (literally, New Building), its unfinished limestone walls and gaping mullioned windows silhouetted against the surrounding meadows and the fringes of Rockingham Forest. Situated about 0.8km (½ mile) up the hill from his main house, Lyveden was intended to be both a private retreat and the banqueting house finale to an expansive garden tour. It was also to be an intricate physical expression of Tresham's Catholic faith, for it is designed in

the shape of a Greek cross, adorned with religious emblems, and constructed in multiples of numbers representing, for example, the Trinity, the wounds of Christ and the Stations of the Cross. Such symbolism – indicative of the Elizabethan delight in puzzles – is also apparent in Tresham's intended design for his garden.

Remote and remarkably undisturbed since Tresham's death in 1605, the New Bield came to the Trust as far back as 1922. But the impetus and funding to tackle the garden was very late to arrive – fortunately, perhaps, since garden archaeology and restoration are now much more advanced arts. Gradually, the invading large trees and scrub were removed; the waterways were cleared of silt and willow, and had their banks repaired; and soil samples were analysed for organic particles and pollen. Meanwhile, Tresham's own papers were deciphered. Hidden away in a secret alcove at Rushton Hall, and rediscovered in 1832, they include a long letter of detailed instructions for setting out the garden. Research continues, and the intention is slowly to re-create more of the composition as Tresham left it, but to go no further.

The lowest part of the garden is the large formal orchard. The original trees were sold by Tresham's widow to assist in settling his debts, but Tresham detailed many of the varieties. Newly replanted, apples such as 'Catshead', 'Green Costard' and 'Winter Queening' and pears 'Windsor' and 'Black Worcester' are once again growing here, along with 'Shropshire Damson', 'Shepard's Bullace' and 'Transparent Gage', set each side of a central avenue of common walnut. The fruits were used for medicinal as well as culinary purposes, and the surplus could be sold off, so an orchard combined pleasure, produce and profit. A rich meadow mixture of wildflowers has been sown between the trees, with swathes of cowslips in late spring. From the orchard, you climb up to a grass terraced walk,

punctuated by a pair of pyramidal mounts, giving you a prospect of the estate.

Below the terrace, a moated garden reveals itself, rising up again in the distance into a pair of spiral mounts. The western side of the moat was never completed, but elsewhere the channels are deep enough for guests to have been ferried by punt. What occupied the large area inside the moat was unknown until archaeological research was undertaken and an exceptionally clear wartime photograph was discovered, taken by the Luftwaffe (there was an RAF airfield nearby). This revealed a series of concentric circles comprising the outline of a large labyrinth. Mirroring the form of the Chemin de Jérusalem in Chartres Cathedral, the labyrinth is currently mown as a pattern into the grass; it would originally have been planted with scented roses and raspberries. Tresham's grand diamond-pattern parterre is similarly mown into one of three well-established wildflower meadows.

All this would have been in perfect alignment with the house below. But the New Bield itself is off on a dog-leg, maintaining its own element of surprise, and sited to command a panorama of the rolling landscape. Indeed, Tresham probably intended to add another floor to it, which would have given a spectacular bird's-eye view of his entire garden. Aptly, this has been called his Unfinished Symphony, but paradoxically, had it been finished and become a desirable property, it would probably have been destroyed by changing fashion as surely as have its contemporaries.

LEFT The mown outline of the circular labyrinth invites visitors to undertake the journey of contemplation and enlightenment intended by Tresham.

ABOVE The spiral mount at the south-east corner of the moat system provides impressive panoramic views of the moats, meadows and New Bield.

Melford Hall

LONG MELFORD, SUDBURY, SUFFOLK

AREA 3.6ha (9 acres) • SOIL limy • ALTITUDE 30m (100ft) • AVERAGE RAINFALL 584mm (23in)
AVERAGE WINTER CLIMATE cold

A turreted gatehouse beside Long Melford village green is the entrance to this Elizabethan mansion. It stands across a dry moat, a sweep of warm red brickwork bristling with onion-domed towers and chimneystacks. Built by Sir William Cordell, a distinguished lawyer who rose to become Speaker of the House of Commons and Master of the Rolls, it was erected on the site of a monastic manor house some time before 1578, for in that year Sir William received his sovereign here. According to one observer, Queen Elizabeth was waited upon by '200 young gentlemen cladde all in whyte velvet, and 300 of the graver sort apparelled in black … with 1,500 servyng men all on horsebacke … and there was in Suffolke suche sumptuous feastinges and bankets as seldom in anie parte of the worlde there hath been seen afore'.

The gardens, contained within the walls and moat, have evolved over the centuries in response to changing tastes. Two fine features, however, remain from early times. One is a narrow, raised bowling green running between the drive and the house, emphasised by the Trust with the addition of flanking pairs of Irish yews along its length. The second is the handsome, and rare, octagonal banqueting pavilion that was added to the head of it in the early seventeenth century. Appointed with gables and finials, it has a heating system worked by a furnace and flues in the wall. Stone stairs lead to a panelled upper room, which was found on restoration to have been sumptuously decorated in green and gold.

To the south is the most sheltered part of this exposed property, and here a tree-studded Victorian pleasure ground replaces the intricate patterns of flower-beds and trained fruits that would have existed in Sir William's time, the trees interspersed with topiary domes of green and variegated box. Aconites and daffodils flood the grass in spring, with pink cyclamen succeeding them in late summer. Sir William Hyde Parker, father of the present baronet, was a keen hybridiser of daffodils and a number of his bulbs are growing here; the hall contains many display vases, a reminder of the times when daffodil parties were held each April. Melford is also noted for its snowdrops and limestone wildflowers, among them the meadow saxifrage, *Saxifraga granulata*. Herbaceous borders run below the high west wall, against which are trained wisteria and Moroccan broom, a maidenhair tree (an unusual use of this plant), and, as an echo of the past, a rich array of ornamental vines. The Victorian Rambler rose 'Blush Boursault' was reintroduced into cultivation from the Melford specimen, which still grows on the west wall of the house.

To the south, fronted by a belt of flowering shrubs and small trees, including suckering *Xanthoceras sorbifolium*, a seldom-seen Chinese species with panicles of white flowers resembling those of horse chestnut, is the most quirky ingredient – a serpentine, or crinkle-crankle, wall. Designed to take maximum advantage of sunshine in order to ripen fruit, such scalloped walls were an eighteenth-century innovation and are more commonly encountered in Suffolk than elsewhere. This example dates from 1793, but was rebuilt in 1990.

In 1937, to give the garden more of an Elizabethan flavour, Ulla, Lady Hyde Parker, set out a small enclosure of yew in the centre of the lawn, and arranged a crisp pattern of herbs around a circular lily pond; this planting has recently been refreshed using salvias and lavenders. The moat border has also been replanted with iris cultivars, trained specimen pears and Suffolk apple cultivars.

The park, rising to the east beyond the hall, is rather bald, but the Trust has put back the converging avenues of oak trees (grown from Melford acorns) in accordance with the estate survey of 1613.

These follow the lines of the medieval pathways that once intersected the fields, and in time will forge a strong bond between the axes of the hall and its rural setting.

LEFT A clump of green-tipped snowdrops, *Galanthus nivalis* 'Viridapice'.

BELOW The hedge bordering the moat looking towards the 17th-century octagonal pavilion, used as a banqueting house.

Mompesson House

SALISBURY, WILTSHIRE

AREA 0.2ha (½ acre) • SOIL alkaline/loam with chalky subsoil • ALTITUDE 46m (150ft)
AVERAGE RAINFALL 737mm (29in) • AVERAGE WINTER CLIMATE moderate to cold

There are few wall plants that could do justice to a façade such as Mompesson House presents to Choristers' Green, in the heart of Salisbury. Really there is only one, *Magnolia grandiflora*. Introduced from North America in 1734, its glossy foliage and cream, waterlily flowers are as bold and opulent as could be expected from any hardy evergreen, and it is no coincidence that it adorns so many of our grandest houses. By 1888, the pair at Mompesson had already reached the eaves; they have since been cut back to reveal more of the limestone front.

The house, built by Charles Mompesson in 1701, is as elegant inside as out. Major repairs were required by 1952, when it was purchased from the Church Commissioners by Denis Martineau, a London architect and connoisseur, but most of the original details survived intact and unaltered. The rear walled garden, however, Martineau had to set out anew, and since the late 1970s the Trust has modified and embellished his design. There has been no slavish adherence to the eighteenth century. The flavour is simply of an old-fashioned town garden, formally designed with a central lawn and a circuit of straight paths between rectangular flower-beds. On the right day it is extremely beautiful, but in winter it suffers from being in the permanent shade of the house, is exceptionally cold and gloomy and is, sensibly, closed to visitors during these months.

The rain shadows from the walls and buildings also cause problems, the shortage of moisture exacerbated by the chalky soil; the lawn had to be relaid following the severe drought of 1976. However, the garden in summer is well stocked with plants, imaginatively chosen and performing splendidly under the adverse conditions.

In shady beds, directly beside the north-facing façade of the house, *Stachys byzantina* and lavenders provide unexpected pools of silver, in the company of hardy geraniums, veronicas and annual tobacco flowers. This theme is reinforced by a fine pyramidal specimen of the seldom-seen silver pear, *Pyrus × canescens*, growing in the south-west corner of the lawn; it was planted in 1977 to commemorate the Queen's Silver Jubilee. Streams of lavender flank the path towards the stone cartouche commissioned by Denis Martineau and bearing the Mompesson coat of arms. Old-fashioned and other Shrub roses, including 'Königin von Dänemark', 'Marie de Blois', 'Comte de Chambord' and 'Buff Beauty', offer a mass of flowers at midsummer.

The north wall adjoins the cathedral close, but the intimacy of the garden is preserved by mophead acacias, clipped every few years to keep them within bounds. In front, the south-facing border offers daffodils, tulips and Canterbury bells in spring, and hollyhocks, peonies, irises, mallows, columbines and delphiniums in summer, all tended in the cottage-garden style, with bulbs and annuals pushed freely into any gaps. The greenhouse nearby is crammed with pelargoniums, coleus and begonias for the house; on its exterior wall grows the jasmine-like *Trachelospermum asiaticum*. The pergola to the east of the lawn provides a contrasting shady walk. Wisteria, evergreen *Clematis armandii*, winter-flowering *C. cirrhosa* var. *balearica*, C. 'Perle d'Azur' and the honeysuckle *Lonicera × americana* give a succession of flowers; there is a striking disparity in leafing and flowering times between the plants of 'Perle d'Azur' at the sunny and shady ends. Fastigiate rosemary fills in the gaps at the base of the stone columns, and the interior glows with the lime-yellow foliage of golden philadelphus. On a warm summer afternoon, the scents are intoxicating. Pots of tender rhododendrons, bulbs and annuals, together with a fig, scented viburnum and ornamental quince decorate the courtyard beyond – and viewed against the sun, through the windows of the garden-room teashop, the red leaves and black grapes of the Teinturier vine are a sumptuous finale.

RIGHT A cottage mixture in one of the borders, featuring foxgloves, campanulas and sweet peas.

Monk's House

RODMELL, LEWES, EAST SUSSEX

AREA 0.7ha (1¾ acres) • SOIL alkaline/loam • ALTITUDE 15m (50ft)
AVERAGE RAINFALL 889mm (35in) • AVERAGE WINTER CLIMATE mild

'Back from a good week-end at Rodmell – a week-end of no talking, sinking at once into deep safe book reading; and then sleep: clear, transparent; with the May tree like a breaking wave outside; and all the garden green tunnels, mounds of green: and then to wake into the hot still day, and never a person to be seen, never an interruption; the place to ourselves: the long hours.' (Virginia Woolf's diary, 1932).

Virginia Woolf and her husband Leonard bought Monk's House as a country retreat in 1919. A modest 'unpretending' building, clad in whitewashed weatherboard and hidden down a lane at the edge of the village, it was to be a source of great happiness for many years. Leonard had fallen for the garden even before he became owner of the house. A cheerful assembly of low flint walls (the remnants of a piggery) and fruit trees, lawns and vegetable plot, it soon began to take on an exotic air – Leonard's choice of plants no doubt influenced by his time in the Colonial Office in Ceylon.

Today, after a period of decline, it is once again full of colour and character. Near the lane, a holm oak presides over a shady little Italian garden, complete with pond, the dark green of yew and ivy, and Florentine ornaments. The main garden is on the sloping ground behind the house. A Chusan palm greets you as you turn the corner, with, to the left, a lushly stocked conservatory, rudely flaunting the terracotta rear of a copy of Donatello's *David*. The frost-free half of the conservatory contains pelargoniums and other pot plants; the unheated section houses an old grapevine, datura, jasmine, camellia and tall white crinums. From here the garden looks small and intimate, a pattern of brick paths, decorated with millstones, punctuated by terracotta jars each containing trailing perlargoniums, and bordered by cottage plantings of mock orange, geraniums and feverfew; bold displays of fuchsia, osteospermum, and Leonard's favourite kniphofias reflect the coastal climate. But as you explore, the site opens out. Another formal section is revealed, where delphiniums, roses, poppies, cosmea and dahlias foam in summer, and in spring, wallflowers and tulips.

Bordering the walled gardens are grassed areas, shaded by fruit and ornamental trees and with a dew pond, made by Leonard.

His and Virginia's ashes were scattered under the two elm trees that once stood in the hedge behind. The path from the southern walled garden leads into the orchard and to the spire of St Peter's church. 'Our orchard is the very place to sit and talk for hours in,' Virginia wrote. In spring, the crocuses are succeeded by massed daffodils.

Beyond the bowling green and the vegetable garden (now run as allotments by the horticultural society founded by Leonard), the landscape opens out into a panorama of downs and water meadows. Virginia's writing-room, a weatherboard outbuilding standing by the churchyard, looks over it, and the views were her greatest delight. At the bottom of the valley flows the River Ouse, into which Virginia stepped, terrified by her approaching madness and with her pockets weighed down with stones.

ABOVE A relaxed, informal mood is set here by species roses, wild geraniums and foxgloves.

Montacute House

MONTACUTE, SOMERSET

AREA 4.9ha (12 acres) • **SOIL** alkaline/sandy silt loam, some clay • **ALTITUDE** 76m (250ft)
AVERAGE RAINFALL 762mm (30in) • **AVERAGE WINTER CLIMATE** moderate

'Flower gardens do not come more richly appointed'

The Elizabethan mansion, ascending through three tiers of massive leaded windows, surmounted by soaring chimneys and high curved gables, dominates its site. Montacute was built of the same golden stone as nearby Tintinhull House for Sir Edward Phelips, at the turn of the seventeenth century. Its west front, which was added in 1785, was in fact a Tudor construction taken from another house, and is an edifice ornate with pillars and balustrades, statues, pinnacles and other carved details. Because the drive dips and rises, it looks deceptively close. In fact, it is a 0.4km (½ mile) from the wrought-iron gates to the door.

Such scale and ornament, designed to impress, is reflected also in the garden, where decorative walls and pavilions, lawns, trees and processions of trim Irish yews (96 in all) make for a stately setting of green and gold courts, terraces and gravel walks. While the framework is largely original the internal design was altered in the eighteenth century, and what you see today is the work of Ellen Helyar, who married into the Phelips family in 1845, and, with her able gardener, Mr Pridham (whom she brought with her from her family home, Coker Court), re-created and reinterpreted the Elizabethan style of gardening here. It is one of the many historic reconstructions prompted by the awakened Victorian interest in the architecture and gardening of the past.

The southern approach walk takes you past cauldrons of golden yew, variegated holly, and curious feathery evergreen tumps – in fact,

giant redwoods transformed into multi-stemmed shrubs after their trunks were felled in the last war – and onward to the North Court, the grandest of the green enclosures. This is the site of the original Elizabethan garden, its shape and probably its raised walks dating from that period. Like many contemporary gardens, it once featured a mount, but this seems to have vanished by 1825 and is now replaced by a substantial balustraded lily pool, in a setting of neat lawns, broad gravel walks, seats and ornaments.

Ellen Phelips had this as an elaborately patterned flower parterre, but today's is a simpler scheme, framed by the Irish yews and a high, contoured yew hedge, and with the flowers confined to those of *Yucca recurvifolia* growing by the entrance to the lower court and, below the terrace, a pair of borders filled with old-fashioned species and Hybrid Musk roses, including the incense-scented Climbing Musk, *Rosa* 'Princesse de Nassau' (syn. *R. moschata* 'Autumnalis') – all quietly underplanted with the bluish-leaved *Hosta fortunei* var. *hyacinthina*. The Orangery, with its fern-covered fountain of stone and tufa, is currently closed for repair.

The main flower garden is now within the East Court, presided over by the house's most decorative front and framed by balustraded, obelisk-capped walls and a romantic pair of pavilions. This was the former Tudor entrance court, and at that time you would have arrived through an outer court and through a gatehouse, and had a better prospect of the high façade, which is rather overpowering at close range. Golden euphorbias and achilleas, orange and red roses and dahlias, and numerous other hot-coloured perennials, in a scheme first devised by Phyllis Reiss

of Tintinhull, now contribute to the summer kaleidoscope in this part of the garden. Claret-leaved vine and smoke bush and an assortment of crimson and deep purple clematis cloak the walls behind. Acanthus and macleaya add some taller structural foliage, and evergreen magnolias, crambe, peonies, yuccas and the highly scented Rugosa rose 'Blanc Double de Coubert' give some contrasting notes of cream and white. Flower gardens do not come more richly appointed.

Next to the car park – formerly the kitchen garden – a spacious lawn, shaded by blue and green cedars and a fine pair of sweet chestnuts, leads to an arcaded garden house and a hedged semi-circle of lawn (added in the twentieth century), adorned with stone columns, yew topiaries and mirror beds of spiky yucca. Weeping silver lime and cut-leaved beech grow nearby, with evergreen oaks, pines, koelreuteria and Judas tree, underplanted with a succession of bulbs, to be found in a small adjunct of rough meadow.

Although the garden is formally severed from the village and park by its walls, hedges and railings, the raised walks allow you to survey the rolling countryside and the lines and scattered clumps of the nineteenth-century parkland oaks. This adds to the sense of space. From various parts of the garden, you also have a prospect of the wooded conical hill above the village and church – the *mons acutus*, which gives Montacute its name – and the folly tower erected on it in 1760.

ABOVE Deep purple clematis contrasts with the imposing honeyed stone frontage.

RIGHT The quarter-mile drive provides a grand approach to the West Front.

Moseley Old Hall

FORDHOUSES, WOLVERHAMPTON, STAFFORDSHIRE

AREA 0.4ha (1 acre) • SOIL acid to neutral/varied • ALTITUDE 76m (250ft)
AVERAGE RAINFALL 686mm (27in) • AVERAGE WINTER CLIMATE moderate to cold

From a distance, there is little to commend this property, a plain brick house set in undistinguished farmland. There are, however, surprises in store. Walk through the studded back door of the hall and you step back two centuries further than you expected; the nineteenth-century brickwork is merely cladding. Panelled and whitewashed rooms are revealed, with low ceilings and exposed timbers, heavy oak furniture, pewter and Royalist portraits. If you are reading the guidebook, an adventure unfolds simultaneously – for in 1651, the hall was a hiding place for Charles II after his defeat at the Battle of Worcester. He arrived, disguised as a woodcutter, and concealed himself two days later beneath a trapdoor in a bedroom cupboard while Parliamentarian troops passed by. He then escaped by night, disguised as a servant, to safety in France. The King's Gate, standing between the sweet chestnut paddock and Nut Alley, marks his entry into the garden.

Whether the present disposition of covered walks and orchards, roses and patterns of box resembles the garden he encountered no one can say, for when the Trust took possession of the hall, the site was derelict. What you see is an educated piece of guesswork, a full-blown reconstruction of a small seventeenth-century garden, its design details drawn from contemporary sources and its plants those known to have been in cultivation before 1700. The red walls that surround the garden do it no favours, and on the wrong day, especially in late summer when flowers are few, the mood is very sober – but at rose and apple blossom time, or in autumn when the vines are turning, there are many outstanding features that will lodge in your memory.

Most celebrated of these is the Knot Garden. Executed in box, the simple geometric design was copied from one laid out in Yorkshire in the 1640s by the Rev. Walter Stonehouse. In his original scheme, ornamental plants were grown inside the beds but, for ease of maintenance, gravels have been used here and the result is satisfyingly crisp. Like all knot gardens, it is best viewed from the upper windows of the house.

The covered walks provide some shade and a contrast in flavour. A succession of bulbs, including snowdrops and winter aconites, snakeshead fritillaries, colchicums and autumn cyclamen accompany the hazels in the Nut Alley, while on the wall behind romps Shakespeare's Musk rose, *Rosa arvensis*. An arbour of hornbeam leads into the most beautiful passage of all, a tunnel of claret vines (*Vitis vinifera* 'Purpurea'), *Clematis viticella* and *C. flammula* edged with old English lavender. Constructed of oak, with arching sides as well as a vaulted roof, it is an absorbing structure in its own right. The design was taken from an illustration in Thomas Hill's *The Gardener's Labyrinth*, published in 1577. With the sun shining through them, the dusky black vine leaves are transformed, and the interior of the tunnel acquires stained windows of ruby red. There is a lesson here in the placing of all purple-leaved plants.

The marriage of the utilitarian and ornamental sets the theme of the garden. The trees that line the central path all provide fruit for the house – medlar, black mulberry and quince. The cherries on the large, spreading Cornelian dogwood, *Cornus mas*, would also have been stewed to make preserves. Herbs fringe the house walls, and there are niches for bee-skeps beside the barn.

But from medieval times, gardeners took delight in growing plants simply for their flowers – sweet-scented roses and eglantine against walls, for example, and wildflowers in meadow grass. Here, the apples and pears stand among narcissi and other spring and early summer perennials, and around the walls there is a varied cast of roses. Against the south façade of the house, above a bed of unimproved marigolds, sunflowers, sweet peas and other annuals, grows the true Musk rose, *Rosa moschata*, an ancient garden plant valued for its late-summer flowering.

There is a concentration of Shrub roses accompanying the tiny lawns and box topiaries in the front garden, reached from the main plot by a wrought-iron gate. The Jacobite rose, 'Alba Maxima', the Red Rose of Lancaster, *R. gallica* var. *officinalis*, and the autumn damask, *R.* × *damascena* var. *semperflorens*, are among the cast. A mixed array of cottage perennials adds to the colour and extends the season, including red and pink peonies, yellow daylilies, madonna lilies, Florentine iris, Solomon's seal and double pink *Saponaria officinalis* 'Rosea Plena', a herb long used for making soap.

LEFT The knot garden, composed of box and gravels, is a re-creation by the National Trust; the entire garden was derelict when it took over.

ABOVE Peonies and Solomon's seal flower in a corner of the garden in early summer.

Mottisfont Abbey

MOTTISFONT, ROMSEY, HAMPSHIRE

AREA 12ha (30 acres) • **SOIL** alkaline/thin loam over gravel • **ALTITUDE** 34m (110ft)
AVERAGE RAINFALL 737mm (29in) • **AVERAGE WINTER CLIMATE** moderate

Push open the white door of Mottisfont's walled garden in midsummer and you plunge into a sea of roses. Not the gaudy roses of today, but the pink and crimson roses of yesterday, eulogised by the classical poets, painted by the Dutch masters, assiduously collected by the Empress Josephine and hybridised by the nurserymen of nineteenth-century France: rounded, petal-packed, drenched in fragrance and giving, in the main, one bountiful, mid-June to early July performance. There is nothing to equal them.

The paths lead you along their ranks, past the Apothecary's Rose and Red Rose of Lancaster, *R. gallica* var. *officinalis*, and its pink-striped sport 'Rosa Mundi'; the Jacobite Rose, 'Alba Maxima', the White Rose of York, 'Alba Semi-plena' and the soft pink 'Great Maiden's Blush', known since the fifteenth century; past damask roses, cabbage roses, moss roses and on to those carrying the inheritance of the autumn damask and, more importantly, of the China roses, conferring the much-desired ability to flower late or continuously: the short Portlands, the open and fragrant Bourbons, the hybrid perpetuals, the China roses themselves and their early Tea rose hybrids.

The collection was assembled over many years by the eminent rosarian and Gardens Adviser to the Trust, Graham Stuart Thomas, and brought here in 1972, when the garden became available. The formal design, echoing the original kitchen garden layout, is founded on four open plots of grass, framed by borders and an outer box-edged walk – a clever piece of geometry, in fact, since none of the walls are parallel or the same length. The centrepiece is a circular lily pool, flanked by pillars of Irish yew and with a low dome of the

pink rose 'Raubritter' spilling into it, providing the enhancing note of asymmetry. It is to this that the sweep of yellow gravel carries the eye as you enter the garden.

The borders either side of the path, also planned by Graham Stuart Thomas and almost entirely herbaceous, are a lesson in planting design, demonstrating the virtue of a restricted palette, of orchestrating the colours in clear bands, of providing vertical shapes to complement the mounds, of repeating key subjects and of much else. They are among the most perfectly schemed borders I have come upon. In 1982, ten years after this garden was planned, the adjacent enclosure to the north became available, allowing a home for a further collection of old roses, acquired by Graham Stuart Thomas from the German National Rose Garden at Sangerhausen.

However, the rose gardens are by no means Mottisfont's only attraction. The abbey itself, a grand and romantic medieval priory remodelled in the Tudor and Georgian periods, lies low amid undulating parkland, sweeping lawns and gigantic plane, cedar, sweet chestnut and beech trees. The prize specimen is a twin-trunked London plane (in reality, two trees melded together), over 40m (130ft) high, with a 12m (40ft) girth and with a canopy covering a 0.13ha (¹/₃ acre); it is possibly the largest tree in the country. But there are also fine old mulberry and crab apple trees; good specimens of hornbeam, walnut and tulip tree; and a short-trunked oak, probably as old as the medieval abbey itself.

The topsoil here is dry and gravelly, but underneath there is water. A tributary of the River Test, famous for its trout, flows just to the east of the house. The adjacent spring, or font, probably gives the abbey its name – mottis being derived from the Saxon moot,

meaning 'meeting-place'. The clear water rises into the deep pool at a rate of at least 909 litres (200 gallons) a minute, and is carried off by a stream. Recently, a richly coloured and scented winter garden has been created nearby, incorporating rivulets of foliage plants which appear to wind through banks of willow and dogwood and spill down into the stream.

Two noted designers have contributed effective formal details to this part of the garden, both commissioned by Mr and Mrs Gilbert Russell, who bought the property in 1934. Geoffrey Jellicoe introduced grass terraces, one bordered by a contrasting run of lavender, speared by clipped Irish yews; an octagon of English yew; and a connecting walk of pleached limes, underplanted with chionodoxa. It is a crisp and simple linear treatment, in his own words, 'muted to leave the existing ethos of place undisturbed'. A couple of years later, in 1938, Norah Lindsay set out a small parterre on the south side of the house, edged in lavender and box, and filled seasonally with bedding plants in a pattern of blue and cream for spring, and yellow and mauve for summer.

Later, Russell Page was asked to recommend shrubs for the garden. Some of these, with later additions, are grouped along the house walls with, on the sheltered, sunny wall behind the parterre, quite tender plants such as *Acca sellowiana* syn. *Feijoa sellowiana*, *Hoheria lyallii*, *Ceanothus thyrsiflorus* and the climbing tea rose ' Lady Hillingdon' picking up the apricot tints in the brick.

Elsewhere, there is a fascinating collection of Prunus varieties, underplanted with crocus and daffodils; recently, the Trust has been enriching the area beyond the river with more bulbs and autumn-coloured shrubs, including shrub roses and viburnums, to enhance the existing display from the red-stemmed dogwood. But none of these interrupts the peace of the garden, induced by the grass, the trees and the sound of bubbling water.

LEFT Topiary pillars and a foundation pool are the centrepiece to the axial borders in Mottisfont's rose garden.

RIGHT *Rosa* 'Raubritter' spills over water, with rose-festooned tunnels behind.

Pruning Roses

David Stone, Former Head Gardener
MOTTISFONT ABBEY, ROMSEY, HAMPSHIRE

Many people find the subject of pruning rather mystifying, but in fact there are no secrets to doing it successfully: sharp secateurs, strong gloves and an understanding of 'why' as well as 'when' and 'how' are all that you require.

When?

Early March is an excellent time to prune repeat-flowering roses such as Hybrid Teas (large-flowered), Floribundas (cluster flowered) and most modern Shrub and Climber varieties. For comfort's sake, choose a mild, dry day if possible, simply to make the work more enjoyable.

Why?

Roses will survive with the minimum of attention, but if they are to thrive a certain amount of careful pruning needs to be undertaken. The aims of pruning are to develop shape; control size; maintain vigour; encourage flowering; and produce a happy and healthy plant.

A well-shaped rose bush is an adornment to any garden, even out of the growing season. Maintain a balanced and open-branched structure by pruning main stems to an outward-facing bud and completely removing any dead or entangling stems at, or near to, ground level. Remember that a naturally tall-growing rose cannot be kept short by hard pruning. However, careful attention at the right time can help to contain strong-growing varieties to within manageable proportions.

How?

Most repeat-flowering roses can be divided into the following pruning groups.
Bush (Hybrid Tea and Floribunda) New plants should be pruned

back hard to within 10–15cm (4–6in) of the ground to encourage the formation of new, strong branches from near the plant's base. In subsequent years, prune away all weak and ageing wood before reducing the remaining stems by approximately one-half to two-thirds of their length. Strong growers, such as the ever-popular 'Peace' (Hybrid Tea) and 'Iceberg' (Floribunda) can be pruned less severely. As a general rule, prune lightly for quantity of bloom or hard for quality of bloom.

Climbers With new plants, the emphasis should be on training new shoots to cover the supporting wall or trellis. Shorter side shoots, which may have flowered the previous summer, are best pruned back to within a bud or two of the main branch. As the plants develop, they may become 'leggy', with flowers held above eye level. To encourage the formation of fresh young shoots from ground level, prune away the occasional older stem completely. If such stems are

stouter than 12mm (½in), you will need long-handled pruners or a small, sharp saw to cut through the stems.

Modern Shrub roses This wide and varied group of mainly repeat-flowering varieties includes the English roses, such as 'Graham Thomas', and the older but ever-popular Hybrid Musk varieties 'Cornelia' and 'Buff Beauty'. In general, it may not be necessary to do more than tip back the leading shoots of established plants, but it never does any harm to reduce all new stems by approximately one-third of their length. According to the habit of growth, some thinning out of the stems may be required in order to avoid overcrowding and hard pruning of older stems may prove necessary from time to time in order to encourage further new growths. Most Shrub roses are best left to form largish specimens, although there are many excellent varieties available for the smaller garden.

Old-fashioned Shrub roses Within this large group of midsummer flowering roses are included Rambling roses such as 'Albertine' and species roses such as *Rosa moyesii* as well as the ancient *R. gallica*, *R.* × *damascena* var. *semperflorens*, *R.* × *centifolia* and *R. alba*. Such roses flower best on the shoots that were produced the previous year, but will continue to bloom on older stems for several years. In general, they are best left to form naturally wide and branching shrubs, but in order to keep them within bounds some formative pruning may be required. Newly planted shrubs will need little in the way of pruning for their first year or two; thereafter selected

thinning of older, already flowered, stems can take place any time through July and August, when the flowering season is finished for the year. Pruning at this time will encourage the rose to produce those all-important new shoots, which will bear the best blooms in future summers. In order to maintain a robust shrub, new shoots of the previous summer should be reduced by approximately one-third in winter and any untidy branches lightly pruned to shape.

Tips

- March: complete all major pruning and mulch with manure or organic (peat-free) compost. Remember, prune lightly for quantity of bloom, prune hard for quality of bloom.
- July: remove the spent blooms from repeat-flowering varieties to encourage the development of a second crop.
- October: tie in new shoots of climbing roses to avoid damage by the autumn gales.

Mottistone Manor

MOTTISTONE, ISLE OF WIGHT

AREA 2ha (5 acres) • SOIL neutral/sandy loam • ALTITUDE 50m (164ft)
AVERAGE RAINFALL 889mm (35in) • AVERAGE WINTER CLIMATE mild

Here is a varied and rather quirky garden, with Arts and Crafts charm and wonderful topography. It occupies the head of a south-facing valley, and from high up its slopes you have a view seaward over the headlands to Brighstone Bay, and inland up the bluebell woods to the downs. The garden flows down the valley bowl, changing from light woodland to terraced compartments, and finally spilling over a low wall to meet the village green.

Two-thirds of the way along, it passes the house, a low, ancient, L-shaped building of dark sandstone tucked into the bank. Engulfed by a landslide in 1703, it was not properly restored and enlarged until 1927, when John Seely, the architect son of the 1st Lord Mottistone, was entrusted with the task; he worked in collaboration with his partner Paul Paget, advised by Sir Edwin Lutyens. One of the unusual features in this garden is the building called 'The Shack', a wooden sea-shanty structure, supported on staddle stones, which Seeley and Paget used as a weekend studio.

You enter the garden through a Tudor barn, and into a courtyard lively with roses, notably pink 'François Juranville'. The light acid greensand soil is not ideal for roses, but they were a favourite of Sir John Nicholson, the 2nd Lord Mottistone's step-brother, a businessman and Lord Lieutenant for the Isle of Wight, who with his wife Vivien developed the garden from the 1960s until his death in 1994. The Bush roses 'Pink Parfait', 'Amber Queen', 'Iceberg' and bright red 'Evelyn Fison' bloom around a staddlestone nearby, the lively mood already set by the terrace plantings of penstemon, agapanthus and other perennials.

A carefree approach to colour is one of the garden's Mediterranean traits, for Lady Nicholson, a passionate and hands-on gardener, was brought up in Sicily. She added terrace walls near the house and injected an exoticism into the planting, which the Trust is fostering and developing. Proteas, aloes and ginger lilies (*Hedychium*) bloom below the entrance gate, and in the lower garden overlooking the sleepy hamlet, around a lawn shaded with a mulberry, tulip tree, and umbrella-shaped holm oak, the beds sport red leptospermums, scented *Pittosporum tobira*, white African agapanthus, and several varieties of banana, all of which prove hardy in this mild climate. Indeed, even oleander survives by the house.

On the slope above the house, the formal touches sit more oddly in the landscape – steps not quite in alignment, parallel hedges ending abruptly and made of different plants, and an avenue of mixed orchard trees that flower and leaf-up independently – but it all adds to the relaxed atmosphere. The double borders, once a blaze of summer snapdragons, zinnias and other annuals, have been converted to perennials. The organic vegetable garden has been kept in full swing, however, producing peppers, aubergines, marrows, sweet corn, Lady Nicholson's beloved basil, and plenty of root crops, which always outperform brassicas here. Nearby, a grove of young olive trees has been planted.

At the top of the garden, these small enclosures are exchanged for an open arena of grass. On the steep, muscular contours of the eastern bank, the grass is peppered with wildflowers, from primroses and daffodils to geraniums and scabious; from the adjacent wood, the bluebells flood out under the pine, oak and beech trees. There are still red squirrels resident, and though more wary than the greys, they are often spotted foraging here on the garden's fringes on quiet days.

March-flowering *Magnolia campbellii* and a small camellia dell prepare you for the more exotic mood on the western bank, where the oaks and bluebells are joined by a large collection of Japanese flowering cherries, many more camellias and, in the gulley below, some discerningly chosen rhododendrons. This makes for a sparkling spring-time scene. Sir John had strong business links with Japan, and in a small bog garden down by 'The Shack', there is further Japanese-inspired planting in the form of massed *Iris kaempferi* syn. *Iris ensata* in an array of imperial colours – a sumptuous sight in June.

LEFT The double borders, formerly a blaze of summer annuals, have now been converted to perennials.

Mount Stewart

NEWTOWNARDS, CO. DOWN

AREA 39ha (97 acres) • **SOIL** acid/brown earth overlying beach deposits
ALTITUDE 0–24m (0–80ft) • **AVERAGE RAINFALL** 889mm (35in) • **AVERAGE WINTER CLIMATE**
almost frost-free

This is an extraordinary place, a flight of fancy on the grandest scale. It is a garden founded on rare and exotic plants, strange and mythical beasts, poetry and symbolism, and only the most sullen of visitors will be able to resist the dreamlike state it induces the moment you plunge into its 39ha (97 acres) of lush woodland. Yet when its creator, Edith, Marchioness of Londonderry, first visited her husband's family home, some years before he inherited in 1915, she thought 'the house and surroundings were the dampest, darkest and saddest place I had ever stayed in'. From 1921, the transformation truly began.

The hillside's south-facing aspect, its all-important sheltering woods, the influence of the adjacent salt-water lough, and above all its close proximity to the Irish Sea and the Gulf Stream create mild, humid, almost subtropical conditions. These, with the help of her gardening mentors, Sir John Ross of Rostrevor, Co. Down, and Sir Herbert Maxwell of Monreith, Scotland, she exploited to the full, joining them to an idiosyncratic design and a theatre of imagery, evoking family history and Irish legend.

The house – set within a large and rare intact domain – opens exotically onto a view of New Zealand cabbage palms and 30m (100ft) high Tasmanian gum trees, *Eucalyptus globulus*, punctuating stone terraces, a grand sunken Italian parterre and, terminating the vista, a Spanish water parterre and tiled garden house. The quantity of architectural and horticultural detail is mind-boggling, and it takes a moment to adjust to it. The cast of plants on the upper terrace alone will provoke a good many gasps: fat clumps of spiky fascicularia, *Puya alpestris* and *Beschorneria yuccoides*, planted in

1922; soaring white and yellow Banksian roses and *Rosa gigantea*; scarlet lobster's claw, *Clianthus puniceus*, above a hummock of China blue Chatham Island forget-me-not, *Myosotidium hortensia*. *Echium candicans* even thrives here. Edgings of purple berberis and white heather frame the herbaceous plants on the parterre below, and in the Spanish Garden, Leyland cypresses are clipped to make an open hedge of tight arches.

Already there are references and allusions in the design – among them coronets and a picture of George and the Dragon (there is a dragon on the family crest) made in cobbles on the terrace. On the adjacent Dodo Terrace, the imagery is at its most playful. Here, cement statues of the Ark and various living, extinct or mythical creatures, including a stegosaurus dinosaur, hedgehog, mermaid, frog and monkey, as well as four dodos, relate to the First World War and Lady Londonderry's Ark Club; members, drawn from the family, politics, the armed forces and other branches of the war effort, were given the Order of the Rainbow (the sign of hope) and an animal name. The dodo represents Edith's father, Lord Chaplin, who was not the most dynamic MP and was satirised as a dodo by the *Westminster Gazette*. Close by is the Mairi Garden, named after Lady Londonderry's daughter, Lady Mairi Bury, overlooked by a summer-house and dovecote, and designed in the shape of a Tudor rose, with a blue and white colour scheme (the family colours); the garden commemorates Edith's creation and running of the Women's Legion, to which she gave the emblem of a Tudor rose. Everywhere there are choice tender and luxuriant plants, grouped for harmony of flower colour and contrast of shape and foliage: among them you will find *Melianthus major*, *Lapageria rosea*, *Camellia japonica* 'Akashigata' (syn. *C. japonica* 'Lady Clare'), *Fuchsia excorticata*, *Pittosporum eugenioides*, *Olearia phlogopappa*, palms, peonies, agapanthus and crinums.

To the west of the house, further compartments are revealed. The large Sunk Garden, divided from the terrace by great domes of clipped sweet bay (like those on the north Front Court, imported fully grown from Belgium), is based on a design sent by post by Gertrude Jekyll; having never commissioned the plan, Edith declined to pay for it. The garden is enclosed on three sides by a stone pergola, hung with vines, yellow and apricot roses (including another superb *R. gigantea*), and blue and violet clematis, ceanothus and solanum. Tender varieties such as *Lardizabala biternata*, *Dendromecon rigida* and *Mutisia oligodon* join them, while borders of the azalea 'Coccineum Speciosum', flame red but peppered with orange- and yellow-bloomed branches that have arisen from the rootstocks, fuel

the colour scheme. In summer, the herbaceous beds below flaunt electric-blue delphiniums and balloons of powder-blue clematis (*C.* × *durandii*, 'Juuli' and 'Prince Charles'). Beyond is the famous garden of Irish symbolism, a hedged enclosure in the shape of a shamrock, containing a topiary Irish harp, and, coloured in seasonal annuals, the Red Hand of Ulster. A massive new topiary figure from Celtic mythology – half-man/half sea monster – is also now slowly taking shape here, a replacement for the giant anteater that died a few years ago.

This lush wooded backdrop, a patchwork of greens and an assortment of silhouettes from oaks and limes, pines and wellingtonias, cypresses and eucalyptus, is highlighted in spring with flashes of colour from rhododendrons. I recall my first foray into this wood on a balmy afternoon in early May, walking through cool glades of emerald ferns and blue Himalayan poppies and, with each breath, tasting the scents of tender, white-flowered rhododendrons. At every turn, there is a plant to amaze or confound you: *Luma apiculata* (syn. *Myrtus luma*), *Rhododendron sinogrande*, *Gevuina avellana*, nothofagus, eucalyptus, magnolias, candelabra primulas, *Dryopteris affinis* (syn. *D. pseudomas*), tree ferns and giant lilies (*Cardiocrinum*).

There is more in the Memorial Glade, planted by Lady Mairi Bury after her mother's death in 1959: scarlet embothriums, yellow azaleas, orange-cupped narcissi, white lilacs, purple hydrangeas and *Prunus sargentii*. Among the towering conifers beyond, huge specimens of *Rhododendron arboreum* and *R. maccabeanum* light up the drive with spring colour; later, the beacons are handkerchief tree, hydrangeas and white-flowered eucryphias, including the tender *E. cordifolia*.

As you return to the green woods and open lawns to the north of the house, you might easily assume that this dream sequence was now reaching its end – but you would be mistaken. A short walk up the hillside, you find yourself looking across a 1.6ha (4 acre) lake, excavated by the 3rd Marquess of Londonderry in the 1840s, fringed by water plants, a new cast of ornamental trees and shrubs, including some superb red rhododendrons such as half-hardy *R. elliottii* and *R. facetum* (syn. *R. eriogynum*), and, in the distance, the towers and walls of yet another formal garden. The larger part of the garden tour is yet to come.

The towers and walls belong to Tir N'an Og (Scots Gaelic for 'The Land of the Ever Young' – the daughter of the Duke of Sutherland, and brought up at Dunrobin Castle, Edith always considered herself a Scot). This is the family burial ground built by Lord and Lady Londonderry in the 1920s. According to a legend with pagan origins, a great white stag bears your soul to the west, and on the east side of the lake you will glimpse it between the

ABOVE The south front and formal garden at Mount Stewart.

trunks of trees, standing in a glade. The burial ground hillside is the sunniest and best-drained part of the garden, and an extensive range of Southern Hemisphere plants has been established here: among them, leptospermums, acacias, corokias, sophoras, callistemons, cassinias, hakeas, watsonias and kniphofias. This esoteric character is taken to extremes on Tir N'an Og's south wall, where the company includes such rarities as *Metrosideros umbellatus* (syn. *M. lucidus*), *Kennedia rubicunda*, *Vallea stipularis* and *Picconia excelsa*. Below are fine stands of echiums.

The eastern return route is through the Jubilee Avenue, planted in 1936 to mark the Silver Jubilee of King George V and Queen Mary. The patriotic theme of red, white and blue is achieved with embothriums, fuchsia, photinia and *Rosa moyesii*; cherries, philadelphus, rhododendrons and white hydrangeas; ceanothus, solanum, blue hydrangeas and *Eucalyptus globulus*. A streamside garden of primulas and complementary plants follows, decorated with ornaments brought back from Japan by Lord and Lady Londonderry. And then, once again, it is headlong into rhododendrons, 6ha (15 acres) of hybrids and species leading you down to the house. In addition to the many with richly coloured flowers, there are choice forms grown for their elephantine foliage, such as *sinogrande*, *magnificum*, *rex* subsp. *arizelum* and *falconeri*; for their fine bark, such as chocolate-hued *genestierianum*; and for their scents, including *RR. burmanicum*, *maddenii* and *johnstoneanum*. Edith loved scent, so these tender Maddenia rhododendrons greatly appealed to her, and many more have now been planted in leaf

litter and on logs along a newly developed Himalayan Walk and streamside, where they are accompanied by rare and interesting ferns.

Indeed, there has been a great deal of new planting throughout the garden – notably along the entrance path above and around the Mairi Garden, where new and exotic trees and shrubs from wild-sourced seed such as schefflera andaralia feature prominently. An exciting project for the future will be the large walled garden, with its orchard, vinehouse and lost rose garden, which can be seen along the newly opened up Lady's Walk. Altogether, Mount Stewart is a garden no one can afford to miss.

LEFT A view up to Tir N'an Og from the lake at Mount Stewart.

ABOVE The fountain centrepiece of the Mairi Garden.

Topiary

Phil Rollinson, Former Head Gardener
MOUNT STEWART, CO. DOWN, NORTHERN IRELAND

As a garden art form, topiary has a long history. In Ancient Rome, the gardening work was done by slaves and the *topiarius* was the slave with the specific job of looking after the ornamental garden, or topia – hence the name, which in due course came to be applied specifically to clipped greenery. Clipped hedging became hugely popular in Renaissance Italy and by the late Middle Ages in Britain a formal style had developed using hedges in elaborate geometric patterns, often forming mazes and labyrinths, as well as shaped forms grown as standards.

However, the golden age of topiary was in the seventeenth century, when it became an essential part of the formal landscape. This culminated in the giddy excess of Versailles in France, whose style spread across the great gardens of Europe. While topiary was largely swept away by the eighteenth-century landscape movement, it was revived by the Victorians and continued to thrive into the twentieth century as part of the Arts and Crafts style, as at Hidcote Manor in Gloucestershire and at Mount Stewart where Edith, Lady Londonderry, created the formal gardens in the 1920s and 1930s.

At Mount Stewart, the parterres are hedged with an unusual choice of species such as heather, berberis, hebe and bay laurel. Huge arches of Leyland cypress and large domed bay trees provide a strong Mediterranean, architectural structure. The Shamrock Garden is enclosed by a yew hedge topiarised to depict a humorous family hunting scene adapted from the Psalter of Queen Mary Tudor. Other iconic images include the Irish harp with two British crowns in the background.

Choosing the right plant

The most common plants used for topiary are yew and box because of their small leaves and dense growth, and their ability to regenerate readily not only from clipping but from hard pruning. However, other evergreens do just as well, such as holly, privet, Portuguese laurel and even ivy. You could try deciduous plants, too, for example beech, hawthorn and hornbeam, and experiment with more unusual species such as Chinese holly (*Osmanthus delavayi*), mock privet (*Phillyrea*), *Escallonia* and *Euonymus* – or, for milder locations, bottlebrushes (*Callistemon*).

Creating your chosen shape

Simple shapes can be cut freehand, but the more complex the design the greater the need for a guiding framework. These are readily available to buy or you can make your own using a variety of materials, such as fencing wire, chicken wire, rods, stakes and bamboo canes. Tie in stems to the framework, pinching back any new shoots to encourage branching out and speedier covering of the frame. New growth will have to be trained to fill in gaps, tying shoots in with something that is biodegradable, such as tarred string. This is best done in the growing season when the shoots are young and pliable.

Topiary does not have to be geometrically accurate to be of interest. Over the years the shapes can become quite wonky, perhaps as a result of bad weather, pests and diseases or human error. You might start with a shape in mind but end up with something totally different – just go with the flow and make a feature of it.

Ideally, once established, topiary should be clipped every four to six weeks in the growing season to retain a crisp finish; from May through to September is a good guide. Once it is mature one trim a year is generally adequate except in an exceptional growing year when two trims would be better to retain crisp, sharp outlines. Always be wary of late or early frosts, which can scorch new growth badly or even kill plants, especially box.

Trimming topiary takes time and patience and lots of standing back to study the shape. For intricate specimens you should use scissors, secateurs and hand shears. Electric hedge trimmers are good for less intricate work and for general hedge tidying. Try to avoid petrol-driven trimmers – they are noisy, smelly and generally also heavy to use.

Don't forget you are using sharp cutting implements. Always wear proper personal protective equipment and keep the blades well clear of the cables when using electric trimmers – residual circuit breakers are a must. Make sure ladders and steps are firmly secure, and always concentrate on the job in hand.

Routine care

Just as for any freestanding shrubs, weeding, watering and mulching are essential to promote healthy, vigorous growth. Feeding during the growing season with a good, balanced fertiliser, twice if possible, is good practice, particularly if any renovation or heavy pruning has to be done. This may be necessary if hedges or topiary have been neglected and have grown badly out of shape. Yew and box are both excellent at regenerating from severe pruning, right back to the trunk if necessary.

Snow building up on topiary can be very damaging because of the extra weight on branches. Gently knock it off any flat surfaces or, better still, use temporary netting over your topiary pieces to alleviate the problem.

Tips

- Smaller plants are best when creating new hedges or specimens – they acclimatize to local conditions much more quickly than larger plants.
- If possible, clip little and often to retain a crisp finish.
- Always use sharp tools and ones you are familiar with.
- Take time to stand back and look when you are trimming – frequently and from a number of viewpoints.

Nostell Priory

DONCASTER ROAD, NOSTELL, WAKEFIELD, WEST YORKSHIRE

AREA 4.9ha (12 acres) • **SOIL** acid to neutral/clay • **ALTITUDE** 61m (200ft)
AVERAGE RAINFALL 635mm (25in) • **AVERAGE WINTER CLIMATE** cold

'Rhododendron belts are edged with foxglove, campion, comfrey and hosta'

Behind this Palladian mansion, built for Sir Rowland Winn in about 1735 by the young James Paine and later modified by Robert Adam, the ground plunges into a self-contained landscape of lakes and trees. It is a welcome oasis at the edge of the Leeds-Wakefield conurbation, and a refreshing sight for drivers as they cross the hump-backed bridge on the Doncaster road. Sir Rowland commissioned the famous gardener Stephen Switzer to prepare plans for this park, though little of it seems to remain, and his clump planting of trees was largely obscured by the introduction of rhododendrons, conifers and other exotics in the Victorian era.

The more ornamental portion of the park is on the west side of the middle lake. Here the rustle of cut-leaved beeches and the scent of mock orange and pine usher you into the shadows, where the rhododendron belts are edged with foxglove, campion, comfrey and hosta. Snowdrops, daffodils and bluebells succeed each other in spring, and in early June the shrubs of *Rosa* 'Paulii' are a magnificent mass of white.

Shortly afterwards you find yourself in the Dell, following a curving path between neatly mown lawns and a grove of *Magnolia × soulangeana*. Beds of azaleas and Japanese maples are backed by the exposed rock face, and *Hydrangea anomala* subsp. *petiolaris* scrambles up a stone column. You are brought back to the lakeside through a stone arch, and you can view the bridge from under the branches of a splendid cedar of Lebanon; the view is enhanced in spring by massed bulbs reflecting in the water. New plantings accompany the new footpath that now encircles the pleasure grounds.

Recently, the productive side of the garden has also been rekindled, with the installation of an orchard of Yorkshire apple varieties and the creation of vegetable beds.

ABOVE Opium poppies make interesting contrast in the Rose Garden.

Nunnington Hall

NUNNINGTON, NEAR YORK, NORTH YORKSHIRE

AREA 3.2ha (8 acres) • **SOIL** neutral/loam • **ALTITUDE** 46m (150ft)
AVERAGE RAINFALL 635mm (25in) • **AVERAGE WINTER CLIMATE** moderate

While an epic landscape of avenues, triumphal arches and obelisks was being fashioned by the Earl of Carlisle and Sir John Vanbrugh at nearby Castle Howard, a more modest formal garden was being perfected at Nunnington. Enough details remain, or have been restored, to give us an insight into the appearance of a country squire's garden of the late seventeenth and early eighteenth centuries. The sandstone house, part Elizabethan and part Stuart, is rather plain, but the assortment of roofs, chimneys and gables, in company with the sycamores, oaks and willows, gate pillars and hump-backed bridge over the river, makes a picturesque first impression.

You approach the house across a wooden footbridge and crunch across a gravel court enclosed by beech hedges. Robinias, *Hydrangea paniculata* 'Praecox', wall-trained Morello cherries, and, quite likely, strutting peacocks draw your eye en route to the main, walled south garden. A generous rectangle of grass, formalised into close-mown lawn, punctuated with topiary yews and with flanking squares of rough orchard, occupies the bulk of the space. The apple trees, reintroduced by the Trust, are all varieties traditionally grown in the locality. For Ryedale, although a frosty valley with a short growing season, had a thriving industry in producing long-storing fruit for the sailing ships: 'Burr Knot', 'Cockpit', 'Gooseberry' and 'Dog's Snout' are among the idiosyncratic names. The grass beneath the trees is managed as a flowering hay meadow.

Fruit, grown in the company of flowers, was a valued ingredient of gardens from the Elizabethan era onwards, and apples and pears are also espaliered on the surrounding walls. Beside the wall to the east of the house are glamorous displays of Hybrid Tea and Floribunda roses, punctuated by standard 'Iceberg' roses and catmint in post-war style.

The hidden garden of tall and dwarf bearded irises is a pretty sight at midsummer. These colourful plantings reflect the gardening of Mrs Ronald Fife, who restored much of the hall in the 1920s and bequeathed it to the Trust on her death in 1952. The entire garden is managed organically, and the composting and other methods used can be thoroughly inspected in the Cutting Garden, formerly the tennis court, where fruit and vegetables are now cultivated together with cut flowers.

ABOVE Cosmos and modern roses bring late colour to the garden.

Nymans

HANDCROSS, HAYWARDS HEATH, WEST SUSSEX

AREA 12ha (30 acres) • SOIL acid/sandy loam • ALTITUDE 152m (500ft)
AVERAGE RAINFALL 762mm (30in) • AVERAGE WINTER CLIMATE moderate

The high, wooded ridges of the Sussex Weald, with their acid, sandy topsoil and excellent frost drainage, offer perfect conditions for many of the trees and shrubs from the world's temperate forests. From the 1860s, the opportunities were seized by stockbroker Ludwig Messel and his talented head gardener James Comber, and subsequently by Messel's son Leonard, with the cast of rare and wild-collected woody plants accompanied by herbaceous and rose gardens, flowing lawns and superb views, and with every habitat fully exploited.

The collection spills over almost all the garden, but each area has its own mood. Below the lime avenue of the entrance drive the parkland plunges into a woodland bowl, lit up in early autumn by the tinting leaves of North American liquidambar, nyssa, taxodium and red oak. Nearby, the skyline of the garden's northern boundary is speared by the rocket shapes of giant and dawn redwoods, arranged in a horseshoe shape at the edge of a wide paddock in the company of golden conifers, big clumps of pampas grass, and specimens of the superb August-flowering, evergreen shrub *Eucryphia* × *nymansensis* 'Nymansay'. Raised by James Comber (its name being a corruption of 'Nymans A seedling'), it is one of around 40 plants named after the garden.

Meandering paths lead from this pinetum into a dappled plantation of large trees, rising from grass and shrubberies of camellia and rhododendron. Here there are fine specimens of *Styrax japonicus* 'Fargesii', *Nothofagus menziesii* from New Zealand, and the tree magnolias *M.* × *veitchii* and melon-scented *M. hypoleuca*. A young, seed-raised collection of the Chinese handkerchief tree, *Davidia involucrata* var. *vilmoriniana*, grows between box topiaries,

creatively shaped by Alistair Buchanan of the Messel family, and a new bamboo jungle bisected by a boardwalk. Many trees in the garden are from wild-sourced seed, with *Meliosma veitchiorum*, *Aesculus wilsonii* and *Thuja koraiensis* being among those collected by Ernest Wilson on his plant-hunting expeditions to China in the first decade of the twentieth century.

Magnolias are a Nymans speciality, and their pink and white waterlilies and goblets are major contributors to the long spring season in many parts of the garden, often accompanied by carpets of narcissi, fritillaries and other bulbs. Excellent hybrids, derived from the shrubby species, have been raised here, the best-known being

the lilac-pink *M.* × *loebneri* 'Leonard Messel', which grows beside its parents, *M. kobus* and *M. stellata* 'Rosea'. Tree magnolias were also planted with abandon. There are impressive plants of *M. campbellii*, its hybrid 'Charles Raffill', and *M. sargentiana* var. *robusta* in the nearby Wall Garden – all producing their blooms on bare branches in spring, often followed by impressive fruits – in addition to cultivars of *M.* × *soulangeana* and *M. liliiflora*, and the summer-flowering *M. sieboldii*. *Styrax hemsleyanus* and *S. obassia*, *Cornus kousa* (also striking when bearing its red fruit and crimson autumn leaves, as well as when covered in white bracts in June) and August-flowering eucryphias are also here as fine specimens.

On the night of 16 October 1987 drama came to Nymans, with winds of 160kph (100mph) ripping through the garden, taking down much of the shelter belt and more than 80 per cent of its specimen trees. That there is no sign of damage or absence of mature tree cover today is evidence of how over-stocked the garden was, and how quickly new plantings establish here – but the loss of so many heritage plants was a tragedy.

ABOVE The ruins of the house, destroyed by fire in 1947, seen across the cedar lawn, with drifts of anemones in the foreground.

Fortunately, there was much that could be salvaged. The detailed records held in the Trust's Woody Plant Catalogue – a continuously updated listing of the trees growing in the more important collections – gave the name and origin of the fallen species. Propagation material was taken from the rarest specimens and those with the most valuable genetic pedigrees and dispatched to nurseries. The resulting plants, together with those supplied by other tree collections and botanic gardens, and the spoils of more recent plant-collecting expeditions, formed the basis for a replanting programme, with the result that there is now a richer range of plants at Nymans than at any time in its history.

One notable collection that been expanding here recently centres around the plants associated with Harold Comber, James's son. Born in the old head gardener's cottage, and with his botanical education part-funded by the Messel family, Comber carried out two plant-hunting expeditions in Chile in the mid-1920s. Sheltered by the warm south-facing wall of the Wall Garden, a spectrum of Chilean plants is now displayed, ranging from shrubby *Luma apiculata*, *Cryptocarya alba*, *Desfontainia spinosa* and pungently scented *Escallonia illinita* to herbaceous *Lobelia tupa* and even species of spiky *Puya*.

Comber also collected in Tasmania, and a 'Tasmanian Walk' is going to be developed within the Wild Garden across the road – an area of some 3.2ha (8 acres), which also features collections of oaks and other woody species, notably *Quercus kelloggii*, *Pyrus pashia*, *Stewartia ovata* var. *grandiflora* and *Castonopsis sclerophylla*, arranged in loose groups among rough grass.

In the Top Garden, the trees and shrubs are spliced by double borders of predominantly June-flowering perennials, with loose drifts of daylilies, geraniums and other stalwarts interspersed with smaller clumps of contrasting shapes such as *Sanguisorba officinalis* 'Arnhem' and *Phlomis tuberosa* 'Amazone', as well as the Nymans form of *Philadelphus delavayi*, which has plum-coloured calyces around its highly scented white flowers. Elsewhere, new groupings of woodland perennials including varieties of *Disporum* and *Arisaema* have also been added.

Behind banks of fuchsias and salvias, you come to a formal garden of Shrub and Climbing roses, recently renovated and extended by the Trust to include longer-flowering English varieties. Roses were the enthusiasm of Maud Messel, who began collecting them in the 1920s during their lull in fashion; many were given to her by the rosarians Ellen Willmott and Edward Bunyard, others she found in France, and the collection became an important repository

of old varieties. Organic methods of pest and disease control are practised on them, with sprays of milk to control mildew and garlic solution against blackspot disease.

Down the main axis of the Wall Garden is the much-photographed pair of high-summer Edwardian borders, steeply tiered, kaleidoscopically coloured, and fuelled with a large proportion of annuals (watered sparingly so they become stocky and self-sufficient) to ensure a long and continuous performance.

They run either side of an Italian marble fountain, flanked by intricate yew topiaries, and in their structure and impact have changed little since they were installed by Ludwig Messel, taking advice on the design of this garden from the influential garden writer William Robinson.

The house looms over the wall to the east. It was built in 1928 in the style of a late-medieval manor house by Colonel and Mrs Leonard Messel as a replacement for his father's Victorian villa but, in the winter of 1947, it caught fire. The standpipes were frozen and before the flames could be brought under control the building was gutted, with the loss of almost all its contents, including a notable library of botanical books. So the 1987 storm was not Nymans' first disaster. The event was turned to advantage, however, for although its rear section was rebuilt, the remainder was left as a ruin, roofless, jagged-walled, and with its high mullioned windows glassless and gaping. Thus the garden gained a wonderfully romantic centrepiece. It stands, clothed in roses, honeysuckle, clematis, wisteria and (of course) evergreen magnolia, with some suitably quaint Old English accompaniments – fat topiary hens brooding on the gravel, a circular dovecote and a flock of white doves. Making use of the warm micro-climate beside them, bananas and other luxuriant foliage plants set an exotic mood, joined by flowers such as eucomis and ginger lilies, and a fine specimen of ferny-leaved *Lyonothamnus floribundus* subsp. *aspleniifolius*. The side gardens, featuring lavenders and pink 'Mevrouw Nathalie Nypels' roses, are a more restrained period piece.

There are further late nineteenth- and early twentieth-century touches on and beside the lawns that lead off to the south and east: a living basket, woven with winter jasmine and filled with red hydrangeas, and a sunken garden, where a Byzantine urn stands in a pattern of spring and summer bedding, backed by an Italian loggia. The shrubberies around the lawns have recently been refreshed with the clearance of old Hardy Hybrid rhododendrons and the planting of other shrubs, notably a collection of Ghent azaleas and hybrids of scented, June-flowering *Rhododendron viscosum*.

Although planting at Nymans continues to be adventurous and experimental, without historical constraints, the Trust is frequently guided in such work by the comprehensive plant survey compiled by Ludwig Messel's daughter Muriel in 1918, shortly before her untimely death in the flu pandemic.

The Kurume azaleas that Ernest Wilson selected in 1918 from a nursery on the southern Japanese island of Kyushu – Wilson's Fifty, as they are known – certainly used to be cultivated here, and those that are still available have been returned to a bank beside the Croquet Lawn. Other Japanese touches in this part of the garden include a long wisteria pergola and stone lanterns acquired from the Japan-British Exhibition of 1910.

Along the perimeter of the garden, colourful camellias, azaleas, rhododendrons and hydrangeas give way to landscaped ground of hillock and dell. The acid sand is well suited to heathers, and Ludwig Messel made a collection here – possibly the first heath garden in the country. The display includes many Sussex-bred varieties of our native *Calluna vulgaris*, such as 'Crowborough Beacon' and 'Scaynes Hill', and they grow in the company of low conifers, berberis, birches and some of the plant-hunters' dwarf rhododendrons such as *RR. anthopogon* subsp. *hypenanthum*, *calostrotum*, *saluenense* and *cerasinum*. Beyond, the ground falls and rises to give a fine view of the South Downs.

LEFT Nymans is known for its magnificent magnolias.

RIGHT The long herbaceous borders at Nymans are spectactular in late summer.

Ormesby Hall

ORMESBY, MIDDLESBROUGH

AREA 2ha (5 acres) within parkland • SOIL alkaline/heavy clay • ALTITUDE 47m (155ft)
AVERAGE RAINFALL 686mm (27in) • AVERAGE WINTER CLIMATE cold

The park and farm at Ormesby now form an island of greenery set in the suburbs and industrial development area of Middlesbrough, but the hall stands on a rise, surveying pasture and woodland belt. Designed in the fashionable Palladian style, it was built in the 1740s for James Pennyman, whose family had lived here since the sixteenth century. The garden is formal in design, with modest terraces of English roses and lavender, close-mown lawn and specimen trees. Beds of delphiniums, agapanthus and seasonal annuals add further colour, and the house walls are part-draped in Climbing roses and wisteria. Scarlet *Tropaeolum speciosum*, infiltrating the yew structures above the main lawn, is a memorable feature.

In contrast to this formality, a loop to the east of the croquet lawn takes you towards the church, where William Lawson, author of *A New Orchard & Garden* (1618), was vicar from 1583 to 1635. The ash, beech and oak copse is fringed in spring with snowdrops, aconites, daffodils and primroses, and later with cow parsley and aruncus; in the lower part of the west garden, you are led into a woodland walk and along a shady ribbon border of hydrangeas, azaleas and bergenias.

Much of the garden's character comes from its trees. Bolstered by Portuguese laurel, they shelter the exposed site, and within the garden give the rather thin composition some weight and substance. Limes, chestnuts, crab apples and walnut are among the company, and there is a fine 250-year-old copper beech by the old tennis lawn.

RIGHT Palladian Ormesby Hall, viewed across acanthus and other perennials.
FAR RIGHT Circular beds form part of the Pleasure Grounds at 18th-century Osterley Park.

Osterley Park

ISLEWORTH, MIDDLESEX

AREA 145ha (357 acres) • **SOIL** varied, gravel and clay • **ALTITUDE** 30m (100ft)
AVERAGE RAINFALL 610mm (24in) • **AVERAGE WINTER CLIMATE** moderate

'It is a pleasant drive between sweet little villages and villas to this park,' wrote one visitor in the autumn of 1786. How things have changed. Osterley has been engulfed in London's western conurbation, Heathrow is only 8km (5 miles) to the south-west, and the M4 has amputated the northern section of the park. But there are still 57ha (142 acres) of oasis remaining, and it is a surprise and relief suddenly to be able to exchange the roads, housing and light industry for a landscape of meadows, trees and lakes. The house itself, designed and refined by Robert Adam through the 1760s and '70s, is the park's principal ornament, standing in the centre of the flat parkland, and as you follow the circuit walk it provides a series of eye-catchers between the trees. From the east, there are views also of the stable block, the legacy of Sir Thomas Gresham, Chancellor of the Exchequer to Elizabeth I, who built the first great house here in the mid-sixteenth century.

The flowing landscape park, which is also quite likely to have been moulded by Adam, changed radically during the nineteenth century, in response to the taste for heavier and more varied scenery. By the 1980s the grounds were short-staffed and in serious decline, and it was then that a major project was initiated to restore its eighteenth-century character, which is now potently re-established.

On the west side of the house, you look out onto a large section of park, girdled once again with iron railings according to precedent. The Great Meadow within is grazed by impressive and benign Charolais cattle, and kissing gates allow you to wander across. It has never been ploughed or fertilised, and supports a wide range of wildflowers and insects. As well as the many isolated, scattered trees inside it, including black walnut and Turkey oak,

there are fenced-in plantations, comprising mixed trees such as horse and sweet chestnut, oak and hornbeam, but all underplanted with hazel or ringed with hawthorn, reminiscent of eighteenth-century clumps.

The trees in the adjacent pleasure ground gradually blend into a pinetum, with closely mown lawn lapping about them. The Temple of Pan, with its Rococo plasterwork, pre-dates Adam, but it was he who designed the handsomely decorated semi-circular Garden House, where the 45 tubs of orange and lemon trees listed in the comprehensive 1782 inventory (an invaluable resource in the garden's restoration) would have spent the winters. In front of it, Mrs Sarah Child had her flower garden, which has now been put back with gusto. The design is based on a pattern of myriad paisley beds in which the plants are arranged in theatrical tiers and flowering 'cones', some around wooden tripods. The flavour is lively and romantic, with billowing stands of verbascums and sweet peas, Canterbury bells and cornflowers, salvias and sweet rocket, and self-seeding poppies,

nigella and feverfew, following a wash of spring bulbs. It is
a delightful re-creation of a now rarely seen gardening style.

There are more flower displays inside the large Tudor walled
garden nearby, which includes annual and perennial cutting beds and
a Long Border as well as heirloom vegetables and beehives. There is
also colour in the American Garden. This was a popular feature in
eighteenth-century gardens, when plants from the New World were
coming into cultivation for the first time, and Mrs Child's collection
has been evoked here in the form of a broad border of trees, shrubs
and perennials she is known to have grown. The cast includes
liquidambar, calycanthus, chionanthus, echinacea, mertensia and
Shrub roses such as white *Rosa carolina* and pink *R. virginiana*.

Beyond the pinetum and meadow, the lazy wilderness walk
takes you through glades of Hungarian and other oaks, fringed with
foxgloves, campion and massed snowdrops, daffodils and bluebells,
to the lower lake and boathouse. Beginning as a narrow river, the

channel swells as it curves past the icehouse and the fine cork oak,
cedars and other specimen trees south of the house, to conclude in
a wide pool, elegantly rafted with waterlilies.

Beyond the drive, the second lake leads off to the north-east
corner of the park. The main eighteenth-century attraction here
was the menagerie of exotic birds on the east bank, reached by
a rope-drawn ferry. Now, it is the native species that provide the
entertainment, the park being large and peaceful enough for grebes,
jays, several species of owl and many other birds that have been
driven from the rest of London. There is even a small heronry on
the lake's island, a stone's throw from the rumbling motorway.

ABOVE Osterley provides a green oasis amid suburban West London.

RIGHT The mild climate at Overbeck's allows semi-exotic plants to thrive.

Overbeck's

SHARPITOR, SALCOMBE, DEVON

AREA 2.4ha (6 acres) • SOIL slightly alkaline • ALTITUDE 30m (100ft)
AVERAGE RAINFALL 1,016mm (40in) • AVERAGE WINTER CLIMATE mild

'It is so warm and beautiful here. I grow Bananas, Oranges, and Pomegranates in the open garden, and have 3,000 palm trees, planted out in my woods and garden.' So Otto Overbeck wrote in a letter to friends in 1933. Here on the balmy Devon Riviera, this subtropical mood is appropriate and achievable. The house, perched on a shelf of rock high above Salcombe estuary, looks down across a coastline spangled with white holiday villas and a broad channel of water bobbing with yachts. Summers are long and winters are usually very mild, and the hillside and hanging woods provide shelter from the wind.

The garden was already well established when Overbeck bought it in 1928. The grey stone walls that break the site into an irregular series of small enclosures, banks and terrace walks were set out by Edric Hopkins at the turn of the century, and the subsequent owners, Mr and Mrs George Medlicott Vereker, extended and embellished the plantings after 1913. Otto Overbeck followed their example, and the Trust, in its turn, continues to develop the garden actively.

In contrast to the more famous Devon gardens, the soil here is alkaline and fast-draining, so there is no springtime surge of camellias and rhododendrons. But below the formal statue garden is an unforgettable March sight: a hundred-year-old *Magnolia campbellii* holding its deep pink chalices against the sea. Soon afterwards, daffodils, anemones, primroses and the carmine-pink *Cyclamen repandum* appear in sheets on the rough grass banks. *C. hederifolium* follows in late summer. The slightly tender, evergreen climber *Holboellia latifolia* sends sugary scent over the flagpole wall,

and *Clematis armandii* wafts vanilla along the stairways. Other spring highlights include the long-racemed *Wisteria floribunda* 'Macrobotrys', camphor tree from the Far East, *Euphorbia mellifera* from Madeira and the startling young red foliage of *Euonymus lucidus* from the Himalayas.

In summer, the beds are packed with the rich colours and unfamiliar shapes of a vast array of tender and half-hardy border and bulbous perennials. By the house and its lawn, you come upon agapanthus, crocosmias, dahlias, crinums, cannas and, in early autumn, hedychiums, eucomis and amaryllis; *Lobelia tupa, Fuchsia splendens* and the curious shrubby *F. excorticata* grow in the rare damp and shady corners. By this time, the formal statue garden is a riot of osteospermums and argyranthemums, salvias, kniphofias, echiums, sunflowers and other chirpy annuals. Elsewhere, the colour is boosted by shrubs, including olearias and massed hydrangeas.

Structure and focal points are furnished as much by foliage as by the walls and castellated parapets and gate-posts. Phormiums, potted agaves and palm trees are ubiquitous, with additional

spiky notes coming from cordyline, yucca, astelia, fascicularia and beschorneria. The lush tropical flavour of canna and hedychium is echoed by the giant paddles of the hardiest banana, *Musa basjoo*, and by the great trumpets of daturas. Italian and golden Monterey cypresses make arresting pillars, and the various pittosporums unusually coloured domes and cushions. On the bank above the house lawn, the myrtle, *Luma apiculata*, creates a grove of cinnamon-suede trunks; like the Chusan palm, echium and *Cornus capitata*, this species self-sows freely.

This is merely a taste of what is here. The paths lead you to one treasure after another, each strikingly partnered for maximum impact. In another setting the variety might be excessive, but at Overbeck's there is always the tempering harmony of sweeping sea views. This is not a grand or historically important property; the only inspiring feature of the house – a plain, modestly sized Edwardian villa – is the conservatory, filled with the more tender pelargoniums and succulents. But the garden, with its citrus trees still growing in the open all year, is a treat.

LEFT Doorway into the Banana Garden at Overbeck's.

ABOVE Cannas, agapanthus and kniphofia are among the summer cast.

RIGHT One of the brightly coloured herbaceous borders at Oxburgh Hall.

Oxburgh Hall

OXBOROUGH, KING'S LYNN, NORFOLK

AREA 7.5ha (18½ acres) • **SOIL** alkaline-neutral/sandy, clay • **ALTITUDE** 30m (100ft)
AVERAGE RAINFALL 635mm (25in) • **AVERAGE WINTER CLIMATE** cold

'Beside the Gothic chapel, a path leads into the recently restored Victorian Wilderness'

This moated hall rises from flat ground into a broad Norfolk sky. Built and fortified for Sir Edmund Bedingfeld in about 1482, it was romanticised and remodelled for the 6th and 7th baronets in the mid-nineteenth century. The landscape has also been tamed, for the surrounding fields were marshland until drained and dyked in the late eighteenth century. Woods and belts of trees give some intimacy and shelter from the worst of the wind, and the warm red brickwork is cheery even on a grey day.

The garden's *pièce de résistance* lies beneath the hall's east front, an elaborately scrolled and patterned *parterre de compartiment* laid out by Sir Henry Paston Bedingfeld, 6th Baronet, and his wife Margaret, in about 1845. The design was taken from a garden they saw in Paris, and is very similar to one illustrated in *La Théorie et la pratique du jardinage*, published anonymously in 1709 by the French engraver and writer on the arts Antoine-Joseph Dezallier d'Argenville. Originally, the colour in such parterres was provided not by flowers but by gravels and other materials. Here, crushed chalk, black stone and painted cement were used, but in addition to massed annuals. It is remarkable that such a labour-intensive feature managed to survive for so many years, although it was in urgent need of attention by the time it came into the Trust's hands.

To reduce the amount of bedding required, blue rue and 'Hidcote' lavender have been added to some of the shapes, but each spring, the gardeners still plant out quantities of 'Paul Crampel' pelargonium, marigolds and ageratum – the violet-blue and yellow in the pattern being reversed each year to ring a subtle change in appearance. Crushed stone, tightly cropped grass, yew globes and

dwarf box edging complete the scheme, and the whole design is set off by lawn. Such a ground-hugging scheme preserves the sense of openness and isolation, for the hall stands alone in the smooth, empty plane of water, grass and gravel drives. The trees serve as a frame beyond the lawn, the tall oaks and beeches being joined by the favourite Victorian cedars and wellingtonias. Beside the Gothic chapel, a path leads into the recently restored Victorian Wilderness. The lime avenue here is sheeted with bluebells in late spring, and the meandering paths on either side are bordered with displays of snowdrops and daffodils.

Across the lawn from the parterre, a clipped yew hedge screens the long herbaceous border, where aconitum, lupins, delphiniums and irises rise behind a run of catmint, and the old wall is cloaked with clematis, roses and soft shrubs. The large Victorian kitchen garden behind, enclosed by castellated walls and turreted towers, is in the process of regeneration by the Trust, with produce such as pumpkins and asparagus, herbs and edible flowers now returned to the beds. The orchard has also been planted with traditional Norfolk apple and pear varieties, and the grass underneath them is managed as wildflower and bulb meadow. Sun-loving flowering and foliage shrubs bask against the potting-shed wall, on the site of the old peach and vinery houses. The scheme includes cistuses, romneya, potentilla, trumpet vine (*Campsis radicans*), woolly *Buddleja crispa*, ceanothus and the large-leaved vine *Vitis coignetiae*.

From the space and formal order of these areas, you can follow the stream beyond the border of spring bulbs and summer shrubs and walk across the wooden drawbridge that leads into My Lady's Wood. Now you are in the peaceful shadows of oak, beech and sycamore, among thickets of snowberry and carpets of snowdrops, winter aconites, violets and other wildflowers. The circular walk leads you to a thatched summer-house, recently rebuilt as part of the wood's restoration. A second circular walk has also been completed in woodland re-acquired by the Trust, south of the hall.

ABOVE The mid-Victorian parterre at Oxburgh was inspired by a Parisian garden, much enjoyed by Sir Henry Paston Bedingfield and his wife.

Packwood House

LAPWORTH, SOLIHULL, WARWICKSHIRE

AREA 3.2ha (8 acres) • SOIL alkaline/heavy soil • ALTITUDE 121m (396ft)
AVERAGE RAINFALL 686mm (27in) • AVERAGE WINTER CLIMATE cold

On rising ground to the south of this house is one of the great topiary gardens of Britain. Mystery surrounds its origins and theme, though by tradition it is a representation of the Sermon on the Mount, with The Master on the summit of the mound, the twelve Apostles and four Evangelists on the cross-walk below, and the lawn filled with the assembled Multitude. The 1723 plan may indicate some of these yews, but the Multitude does not appear to have been planted until the mid-nineteenth century. Whatever the true history, the topiaries are today an impressive sight. Leaning or bulging, cylindrical or conical, each is a character in the throng. Some now stand 15m (50ft) high, others are considerably less, either because they have a more taxing site or because they are replacements for earlier casualties (poor drainage and badgers being among the hazards). The cutting is done with the aid of a lorry-mounted hoist, and takes over three months to complete.

In the remainder of the garden, the flavour is more domestic, set by the house, bristling with gables and tall chimneys, and by the formal pattern of walls, gazebos, gateways and flights of steps that accompanies it. It is a handsome assembly of mellow orange brickwork, rich in design detail. The development of the garden's rectangular enclosures was probably begun after the Restoration by John Fetherston, whose father remodelled the existing timber-framed house. The raised terrace between the South Garden and the Yew Garden, affording a fine view of the lake and park, and the north-east gazebo, are attributed to him. They are both clearly depicted in a drawing of about 1756, as is the wall with its 30 recesses for bee skeps. The present appearance of this main South Garden, however,

reflects the sensitive hand of Graham Baron Ash, who devoted much of his early life to the rescue and embellishment of a neglected Packwood, bought for him by his father, a wealthy industrialist and racehorse owner, in 1905. It was he who rebuilt the missing gazebos, installed the Sunk Garden in the lawn and set out the double borders on the raised terrace.

Flowers are the third prominent element at Packwood, adding delicacy and complementary colours to the composition of greens and orange brick. They are arranged with a remarkable lightness of touch, capturing that romantic, mingled and deliciously carefree quality that you see in Victorian watercolours of cottage gardens. The style, adapted from that recommended by J.C. Loudon in his *Encyclopaedia of Gardening* of 1822, was perfected by E.D. Lindup, one of the Trust's first head gardeners, and has been developed by his successors. Perennials, climbing plants, and a host of spring and summer annuals and biennials contribute to the mix, with the structure, rhythm and harmony achieved by the continual repetition of the contents within each border. There are very few architectural plants, bold eye-catchers, or big clumps; everything here merges and intertwines.

Each border also has its colour scheme. Those in the East Court are in misty pinks and purples to give a heightened sense of depth in this smaller space, while over the wall in the main South Garden is the Yellow Border, its daisy-flowered heleniums and helianthus, golden hop and lemon potentilla tempered by a wash of catmint, nigella and corncockle. The new double borders, which flank the newly reinstated central axis path opposite the front door, are subtly liveried in plums, browns and silver-greys to echo the tints of the house – the cast including *Stipa gigantea* grasses, sanguisorba, cirsium, atriplex, artemisia, cardoons and *Yucca recurvifolia*. On the raised Terrace Walk, the daylilies, rudbeckias, red astrantias and the scarlet oriental poppy 'Beauty of Livermere' deliver hotter tones, complemented by the fresh, luxuriant foliage of *Euphorbia mellifera* and *Helianthus salicifolius* and the black of succulent aeoniums. The colour schemes are not always gentle. The rose beds, for example, which are set into bays of box and yew by the east wall, are shameless in their bands of brilliant red and yellow.

In 2007, the Sunk Garden, which had been flamboyantly bedded out in Baron Ash's time, was redeveloped as an exotic garden. The focus is now on more permanent planting, with the opportunity being taken to trial plants that are of borderline hardiness in the Midlands, for the beds are well-drained and sheltered. Succulent echeverias and Californian zauschnerias are among the company,

growing with other more reliable perennials with characterful appearance such as euphorbias, kniphofias, eryngiums and *Parahebe perfoliata*. Crushed red brick has been used as a top dressing to blend with the surrounding walls.

A series of fine wrought-iron gates offers glimpses into the park and connects the various courts. The two quietest courts are to the west and north of the house: Fountain Court is named after the strange plunge bath built in 1680, while the north court contains a well, shaded by a young collection of lime trees; there is a good show of snowdrops here in late winter.

Fruit and vegetable growing has also resumed in recent years. A new orchard has appeared between the Yew Garden and the lake, planted with pre-1920 trees associated with the region, such as 'Worcester Pearmain' apple, 'Warwickshire Drooper' plum and 'Black Worcester' pear. The ground beneath the trees is managed as wildflower meadow, with this theme also extending into the areas beyond – the diversity enriched by daffodils and experimental plantings of perennials such as blue *Iris sibirica* and orange *Hieracium aurantiacum*. Conversion to different mowing regimes has seen the return of numerous species, including orchids.

Across the road, the restoration of the walled kitchen garden is now under way, the vegetable and cut-flower beds set into a traditional quartered design around a circular dipping pond. Altogether, Packwood has been evolving into a very absorbing garden, rich in plantsmanship.

ABOVE Pink and white cosmos in the kitchen garden.

RIGHT Grasses and perennials in thwe double borders leading to Packwood's famous topiary garden.

Using semi-tender plants

Mick Evans, Head Gardener
PACKWOOD HOUSE, WARWICKSHIRE

With the more frequent occurrence of mild winters, it can be interesting to experiment with those plants whose hardiness lies on the boundaries of current winter temperatures; increasingly, plants such as osteospermum, penstemon, fuchsia and phygelius once considered too tender to make it through the British winter survive and flourish. Many semi-tender plants have strong architectural presence, providing important structure to a planting. Vivid flower colour and extended season of interest are also often attributes, with some flowering up to the first frosts and beyond. Generally speaking, a semi-tender plant is one that can withstand temperatures between 0°C (32°F) and 5°C (23°F), overwintering in the ground with little or no protection.

Various factors influence a semi-tender plant's chances of surviving the winter; temperature alone is not always decisive. Exposure to cold, drying winds or waterlogged soil can be as devastating as frost and a plant's age and period of establishment are important factors.

Exploiting micro-climates

Warm south- or west-facing walls, free-draining soil and established shrubs often create micro-climates that give a degree or two of extra protection throughout the winter months – for example, a warm south-facing wall with dry soil will enable the overwintering of plants such as the Australian bottlebrush (*Callistemon rigidus*). Other plants to try in favourable micro-climates include Mediterranean tree mallow (*Lavatera maritima*), which bears its lilac, hibiscus-like flowers until Christmas; the exotic hummingbird sage (*Salvia guaranitica*) from Brazil, which commonly produces its electric blue blooms through November and December; and silverbush (*Convolvulus cneorum*), with its attractive silvery-grey leaves. Other plants worth experimenting with in a sheltered spot include *Echium*, *Abutilon*, *Correa*, *Salvia* varieties and exotic geraniums.

Protecting semi-tender plants

In exposed positions, you will need to provide winter protection in the form of windbreaks, waterproof jackets, horticultural fleece, thick mulches or improved drainage. You can even overwinter the statuesque Japanese banana (*Musa basjoo*) by removing the leaves in November, wrapping the remaining stem with loft lagging and covering the whole with plastic compost sacks, leaving them in place until May. Tree ferns can be similarly treated.

Plants such as succulents stand a far greater chance of surviving the winter if their roots are kept dry. Grow them in pots, rooted in pure gravel for swift drainage, and cover them in November with fine nylon netting to protect them from icy winds.

Tips

- The larger the specimen you plant the greater the chance of its survival. As the plant matures it can withstand lower temperatures and minor changes in soil condition.
- Never prune semi-tender perennials in autumn or winter unless unavoidable, in which case protect the plant with either a thick mulch or fine nylon netting.
- Always experiment – it's the best way to learn.

Peckover House

WISBECH, CAMBRIDGESHIRE

AREA 0.8ha (2 acres) • SOIL neutral/rich alluvial loam • ALTITUDE 30m (100ft)
AVERAGE RAINFALL 381mm (15in) • AVERAGE WINTER CLIMATE cold

A thrilling example of the Victorian gardenesque style, this spacious town garden is one of the Trust's lesser-known jewels. The first impression is of Georgian elegance – a square, russet-brick house, standing in a handsome residential row on the north bank of the River Nene. Behind it, you might expect a sober composition of grass, evergreens and gravel walks, and these are indeed the ingredients of the garden's eastern section – but the lines of paths, croquet lawn and shrubberies surprise you by twisting and turning the moment they leave the house. The hollies, laurels, box and yew are joined by Victorian favourites such as spotted aucuba, golden privet and ferns; there is a wrought-iron seat with a fern design; and, as you walk onto the adjacent lawn, you suddenly come upon exotic specimens of monkey puzzle, California redwood and Chusan palm, a rustic summer-house, a circle cut in the grass for an ever-changing spring and summer bedding display, and a border where perennials, including thrift, saxifrages and purple sand cherry, play parts in a permanent bedding scheme.

In 1999, the Trust re-created Alexa's Rose Garden from archival photographs. Named after the Hon. Alexandrina Peckover, who gave the estate to the Trust in 1943, the rose arches now support old-fashioned highly scented roses that were popular in the Victorian and Edwardian eras, including 'Phyllis Bide', 'Aimée Vibert', 'Madame Grégoire Staechelin', 'Honorine de Brabant' and 'Céline Forrestier'.

The scenes now unfolding show both the best and 'worst' aspects of the gardenesque style, the term first proposed in 1832 by the author J.C. Loudon, to mean planting designed to display the character of each plant and the art of the gardener. There are crisp juxtapositions of shape, foliage and flowers – cypress next to bergenia and ivy; palm with variegated holly, yew and *Viburnum davidii* – and space is provided for each plant to grow and parade itself well. But there is also the frantic eclecticism that the style soon came to embody: a large and diverse plant collection, assembled in a startling variety and quantity of geometric and abstract beds, with no theme to unite them. Here, mercifully, walls and hedges do provide some visual barriers. However, it is all conducted with such panache, and tended with such minute attention to detail, that critical faculties are readily suspended.

Little is known of the garden's history, and the Trust has taken its cue for expanding this gardenesque theme from the layout, mature planting and garden buildings inherited from the Hon. Alexandrina Peckover, the last of the house's Quaker owners. It is a surprise to discover that the garden is not confined to a strip directly behind the house, but runs westwards along the backs of half a dozen other properties in the row. Behind the first dividing brick wall is a small enclosure, where a green and white pavilion overlooks an oval lawn and thyme-fringed waterlily pond. Beds of hydrangeas, peonies and lilies (excellent companions for a hearty soil), edged in sedum and liriope, complete the outer oval.

Through a gap in the hedge, a pair of double borders is revealed, segmented by short hedges and mixed in content. *Dianthus* 'Mrs Sinkins' runs either side of the gravel path, and iron supports holding Climbing roses and clematis punctuate the groups of shrubs and perennials, which include white 'Iceberg' roses, hydrangeas, guelder rose, asters, euphorbias, Japanese anemones and agapanthus.

The brick-based glasshouse in which the vista terminates is called the Orangery. Supported by other exotic pot plants, its centrepiece comprises three orange trees in glazed tubs; these are thought to be over 300 years old, and still bear heavy crops of fruit. The neighbouring glasshouse, adjoining cold frames and compost heaps (open to inspection), is used for propagation.

Vibrant beds of roses and tender perennials give you a thirst for the refreshing greens and shadows of the westernmost enclosure, where a quince and other fruit trees grow on the orchard lawn. Rambler roses hang from the hollies, and, silhouetted against a curving hedge of golden privet, a bed of fiery reds and purples is a final, potent sample of what Sir John Betjeman called Victorian 'ghastly good taste.'

LEFT Two topiary peacocks guard a gravel path bordered with pinks.

ABOVE The Orangery is used to display a wide range of flowering pot plants and three orange trees; in front is a metal arch for climbing roses.

Penrhyn Castle

BANGOR, GWYNEDD

AREA 19ha (48 acres) • SOIL neutral/sandy and stony • ALTITUDE 46m (150ft)
AVERAGE RAINFALL 1,092mm (43in) • AVERAGE WINTER CLIMATE mild

'Got up to look at the glorious view of the splendid range of hills lit up by the sun, which has not entirely risen … After breakfast I went out with Col. and Ly. L. Pennant, our children, & almost all the company & planted 2 trees in Albert's and my name … The view on the sea with Pen Man Mear [Penmaenmawr] rising above it is very beautiful,' wrote Queen Victoria in her journal in October 1859. The tree the Queen planted, a wellingtonia, is still standing and, with the many other exotic conifers and specimen trees added during the nineteenth century, continues to inject the sloping pleasure grounds with the flavour of that period. The views, south towards Snowdonia, east along the coastline and north across the Menai Strait to Anglesey and Puffin Island, remain spectacular. And, above and within the Walled Garden, there is the bonus of a treasure trove of rare plants.

The scene is, of course, dominated by the great mass of the castle built for G.H. Dawkins Pennant between 1822 and 1838, and considered the outstanding example of the short-lived Norman Revival. Its scale drops the jaw the moment it comes into view on the crest of the hill; picturesque Austrian pines and croaking jackdaws add to the ambiance. Dawkins Pennant accompanied his building with extensive tree planting, and the collection was steadily augmented over the years. From 1880, it was entrusted to the distinguished Scottish forester and botanist Angus Duncan Webster (son of Prince Albert's head forester at Balmoral), who, over a period of thirteen years, added many new and untried species.

The walks lead past this wealth of trees – redwoods, Douglas firs, bishop and Scots pines, evergreen and deciduous oaks, Caucasian and grand firs, sycamore, beeches, limes, ashes and self-sown strawberry trees (*Arbutus unedo*); tucked under the castle walls are some impressive Japanese maples. Quantities of bulbs and wildflowers accompany the trees on the slopes, and as you explore the glades you will come upon other features – the Gothic chapel to the former house, left as a romantic ruin; a heather slope; and a rhododendron walk – *R. arboreum, R. yunnanense, R. irroratum* and *R. decorum* are some of the highlights.

Descending this west side of the hill, through the plantations of evergreen broad-leaved shrubs, you sense you are moving into a warmer temperate zone. In the Walled Garden, you have arrived – for, with the benign influence of the Gulf Stream, the climate at Penrhyn is exceptionally mild and, given shelter from the wind, a very rarified vegetation can be staged.

Among the many surprises on the sunny walls are *Mutisia decurrens, Sophora japonica, Lomatia ferruginea, Lapageria, Decumaria, Camellia reticulata* and the pot jasmine (*Jasminum polyanthum*) – all shrubs and climbers from the world's softer climates. The very tender *Cordyline indivisa* is also here, together with *Pittosporum eugenioides* and huge-leaved *Magnolia tripetala*. But this is no lush subtropical scene; the exotics are displayed in

ordered fashion within a formal, period framework. Box-edged beds, lily ponds, fountains and loggia adorn the upper terrace, the whole composition remodelled from the original Victorian parterre by Lady Penrhyn in the 1930s. Formerly, the parterre would also have been a showpiece of complex exotic bedding, its planting supervised for many years by the noted head gardener, Walter Speed – one of the inaugural recipients of the Royal Horticultural Society's highest award, the Victoria Medal of Honour, in 1897; extensive fruit and vegetable gardens then complemented the flower garden, and Penrhyn had the reputation of being one of the best properties in the country for the training of young gardeners.

Below the upper terrace, the impressive collection of taller shrubs and trees is displayed on sloping lawns, divided into rectangles by the grid of gravel paths. Among the cast are *Drimys winteri*, *Davidia involucrata* (handkerchief tree), *Crinodendron hookerianum*, *Magnolia tripetala* and *Sciadopitys verticillata* (Japanese umbrella pine) along with a notable sequence of late summer eucryphias.

An ironwork pergola runs along the lowest terrace. This was reinstalled by the Trust and again plays host, according to precedent, to the dripping red flowers of *Fuchsia* 'Riccartonii' and the purple stars of *Clematis* 'Jackmanii Superba'. Accompanying it is one of the oldest specimens in Britain of *Metasequoia glyptostroboides* (dawn redwood), the Chinese conifer known only in fossilised form until rediscovered in the wild in 1941.

Dramatic contrast to this safe and steady formal layout is now revealed, for the garden drops abruptly into damp meadows and the scale changes. Rising from the grass are stupendous clumps of giant rhubarb, gunnera and tree ferns, New Zealand flax and bamboo, backed by holm oaks, eucalyptus and purple maples. The area was once a more intricate stream garden, again created by Lady Penrhyn in the 1930s, but the present scheme is perhaps more fitting – as a link with, and reminder of, the gigantic and slightly forbidding architectural spectacle on the hill above.

ABOVE A view of the ironwork pergola entwined with fuschia and clematis.

Petworth House

PETWORTH, WEST SUSSEX

AREA 12ha (30 acres) within parkland • SOIL acid/sandy loam and clay
ALTITUDE 33–130m (108–426ft) • AVERAGE RAINFALL 813mm (32in) • AVERAGE
WINTER CLIMATE moderate

By 1751, the reputation of Lancelot 'Capability' Brown was established, and for the next 35 years he would be the dominant force in English landscape gardening. The park at Petworth is arguably his finest remaining landscape, the scene surveyed by the magnificent, 98m (320ft) long, west façade of the house, created for the 6th 'Proud' Duke of Somerset in about 1690. The duke also created an important formal garden, almost certainly designed by the Royal Gardener George London. The park is a typical open and uncomplicated composition of grass, water and well-spaced specimens and clumps of trees, predominantly oak, beech and sycamore, concealing the bounds, outlining the contours and standing sentinel on the ridges. A large herd of fallow deer roams among them.

At the heart of the landscape is the serpentine lake, fashioned by Brown from an existing series of small fish ponds. Willow, birch and poplar fringe the water and cover the lake's islands, accompanied by some fine stands of swamp cypress; the Trust has recently replanted the clump of trees Brown planned at the head of the water. The boathouse was added by the 3rd Earl of Egremont, who is also responsible for the urns and sculptures that punctuate the park. J.M.W. Turner spent much time at Petworth during the time of the 3rd Earl, and his studio is often open for tours.

The Pleasure Grounds to the north of the house were devastated by the 1987 storm, and although the Trust has replaced the central original core of dense woodland as it was 180 years earlier, it will be many years before the new plantings restore the patterns of wood and glade. Yet there is much to see. Brown suggested the

Doric temple and Ionic rotunda as eye-catchers, and enclosed the whole with a ha-ha. He also enriched the planting, drawing on many ornamental species of tree and shrub introduced from America and southern Europe during the previous century. Further phases of adventurous planting took place in the late eighteenth, nineteenth and early twentieth centuries, and the tradition continues today under the care and guidance of the present Lady Egremont and the National Trust.

The greensand seams and the diversity of dry, damp, sunny and shady habitats allow a remarkable rate of tree growth, and a far wider range of plants than would grow in the exposed ground of the park. You walk from plantations of Shrub roses and crataegus, crabs, rowans and wild pear to banks of massed azaleas and rhododendrons, and marshy stands of willows and dogwoods.

Elsewhere, cornus, arbutus, aesculus, hydrangeas and Japanese maples provide highlights between laurel and aucuba, Hungarian and American oaks, tulip trees and the twisted trunks of Spanish chestnuts. In early spring, the Pleasure Ground is flooded with Lent lilies and primroses; later, there are bluebells, fritillaries and camassias, and an increasing population of common spotted and twayblade orchids: in short, colour and variety to complement the sublime expanses of landscape.

LEFT The Rotunda, built in 1766, with native daffodils, known as Lent lilies, in the grass.
ABOVE The West Front from the garden, showing the ha-ha.

Plas Newydd

LLANFAIRPWLL, ANGLESEY

AREA 16ha (40 acres) • SOIL varied • ALTITUDE 0–46m (0–150ft) • AVERAGE RAINFALL 1,118mm (44in) • AVERAGE WINTER CLIMATE mild

With yachts coursing the tidal water below its sloping lawns, the mountains of Snowdonia rising behind the Vaynol woods on the far shore, and, to the east, Robert Stephenson's Britannia railway bridge cutting across the curve of the Strait, Plas Newydd has as fine a setting as any coastal property in Britain. There is the further boon of a mild climate, announced immediately by the massive screens of the half-hardy New Zealand evergreen *Griselinia littoralis*, which flank your descent to the house. The summers here tend to be cool and sunny, the winters wet and windy and, given the sheltering woods, the site proves ideal for many woody plants from the warmer temperate regions of the world. The planting, however, is not in competition. The drifts of trees and shrubs are bold and harmonious, framing the views and providing expanses of green and islands of colour to echo the sinuous shapes of the landscape.

The bones of this layout were set out by the leading landscape designer of the late eighteenth century, Humphry Repton, engaged by Henry, Earl of Uxbridge, as work on the house was nearing completion. His proposals are contained in one of his famous Red Books, dated 1798–9. But much has happened since Repton's day. Lord Uxbridge's son, the 1st Marquess of Anglesey – the celebrated Waterloo commander – undertook a great deal of tree planting after 1815. Between the First and Second World Wars, the 6th Marquess added a range of conifers, specimen deciduous trees and ornamental shrubs, in particular rhododendrons and camellias, and the present Marquess continued to augment the collection through the 1950s and '60s. Since the transfer of ownership to the Trust, this momentum has been maintained, with several major new features

established. Within the historic framework, the garden thus reflects twentieth-century taste.

West of the house is the area known as the West Indies, a long and broad sweep of lawn fringed and broken by trees and shrubberies. In May, the shadows are lit with pastel-coloured azaleas and in summer with hydrangeas, whose blooms, indicating the increasing acidity, change from pink near the house to purple and intense sky blue and gentian as the garden flows deeper on to the greensand. *Magnolia* × *veitchii* 'Isca', *M. wilsonii* and *Prunus* 'Tai-Haku' add further early highlights, with eucryphias and hoherias giving showy white flowers in July and August. The hybrid *Hoheria* 'Glory of Amlwch' is a speciality and seems to perform better here than in any other Trust garden – appropriately, since it originated on Anglesey. Unfortunately, another noted feature, the hedges of *Viburnum plicatum* f. *tomentosum* 'Lanarth', have suffered from the spread of honey fungus in the grounds.

A small quarry dell, snaked with stone paths and stairways, adds to the adventure. Camellias, pink 'Donation' prominent among them, are massed here, with cherries, pieris and hedges of scented *Osmanthus delavayi* giving an April boost of colour. In the summer sunshine, the dell offers a cool and shady respite from the

ABOVE A Japanese maple in its autumn livery.
RIGHT Azaleas in the quarry dell in spring.

glare on sea and lawn. The garden's rarest tree, the tender Asian evergreen *Schima wallichii* var. *khasiana*, is found at this end of the garden; it produces its white flowers in autumn.

Following the line of the Long Walk, a double avenue of yew and *Chamaecyparis pisifera* 'Squarrosa' introduced as a windbreak in the 1930s, you arrive in the arboretum known as 'Australasia'. Planted in 1981 to replace the exhausted wartime orchard, this features a collection of eucalyptus and nothofagus grown among wildflowers and meadow grasses, with a fringe of Australasian shrubs. These are fast-growing trees and the Southern Hemisphere mood is well established.

The most recent improvements have centred on the formal terraces east of the house. On the upper level, a trellis garden house with bubbling tufa fountain has been erected, marking the site of the former Edwardian conservatory. On the levels below, the Italianate flavour set by the 6th Marquess has been reinforced with the introduction of pools and water features, additional hedging and clipped evergreens. In high summer, there is a fine show of agapanthus on the middle terrace, with hot borders opposite including crocosmias, heleniums, *Dahlia* 'Bishop of Llandaff' and marigolds.

Almost a mile's walk along the line of the Strait brings you to a quite different garden, a wild and exotic rhododendron wood. The 6th Marquess began introducing choice species and hybrids here in the 1930s, including *R. fortunei*, *R. thomsonii*, *R. praevernum*, *R.* 'Shilsonii', *R.* Nobleanum Group, *R.* 'Loderi King George' and *R. montroseanum*, which self-sows freely. The collection has been steadily augmented by the present Lord Anglesey, who received 'thinnings' from Bodnant as a wedding gift from the 2nd Lord Aberconway; for three seasons, beginning in 1948, lorry-loads of rhododendrons arrived, accompanied by two gardeners to plant them. Many of Bodnant's famous scarlet *R. griersonianum* hybrids were among them. Large-leaved species, such as *R. falconeri*, *R. maccabeanum* and *R. sinogrande*, perform particularly well here at Plas Newydd, and the climate is also mild enough for scented conservatory varieties such as 'Lady Alice Fitzwilliam', 'Princess Alice' and 'Fragrantissimum'. Open only until the end of May, this isolated corner of the Plas Newydd gardens is a bonus for springtime visitors and should not be missed.

LEFT Autumn colour in the garden at Plas Newydd.

Plas-yn-Rhiw

RHIW, PWLLHELI, GWYNEDD

AREA 0.4ha (1 acre) • **SOIL** acid/light loam • **ALTITUDE** 30m (100ft)
AVERAGE RAINFALL 1,016mm (40in) • **AVERAGE WINTER CLIMATE** frost-free, mild

Atlantic rollers may sweep into Porth Neigwl (Hell's Mouth Bay) below and the west wind may roar across the Llŷn Peninsula on which it sits, but Plas-yn-Rhiw seems to stay unruffled. Protected by hills and woods, the small granite house and its 0.4ha (1 acre) garden snuggle into the lower slope of Mynydd Rhiw, exposed only to the south and east. Thanks to the warming influences of the Gulf Stream, the climate is also mild, temperatures rarely dropping much below freezing.

It was their deep love for the Llŷn landscape, and a desire to protect it for future generations, which prompted the three Keating sisters, Honora, Lorna and Eileen, and their mother to buy Plas-yn-Rhiw and its 23ha (58 acres) in 1938; later they purchased more than 121ha (300 acres) with the express purpose of giving it to the National Trust. They planted in time-honoured cottage-garden fashion, pushing bulbs in here and slips of shrubs there, gradually building up a very large and varied plant collection, traditional favourites rubbing shoulders with exotics, and everywhere ferns and wildflowers. Things were getting a little out of hand by 1981, when Lorna, the last Miss Keating, died, and the Trust began a programme of gentle restoration.

To explore Plas-yn-Rhiw, you still have to squeeze between box hedges down narrow passageways and duck under arching pink rhododendrons and carmine camellias to follow the curving stone and cobbled paths. At each turn there is something to marvel at: great clumps of *Fuchsia magellanica*, its soft hazes of scarlet toning so well with the grey walls; an old pear tree and forsythia growing through the roof of the ruined dairy; or the superb *Magnolia*

campbellii subsp. *mollicomata*, planted by the Keatings in 1947, silhouetted against the bay below.

The garden is also full of scented plants and on warm days they can infuse the air. Viburnums, philadelphus, azaleas, daphnes, jasmines and clethra all contribute sweetness, and from the pillars of the Victorian verandah the fragrance of 'Zéphirine Drouhin' roses pervades the house. Forever drawing you away from the garden are the stupendous views, of the curve of Porth Neigwl, of the Gwynedd mountains and even, on a clear day, down the full length of Cardigan Bay to St David's Head in South Wales.

ABOVE Japanese anemones and a rambler rose are set off by a rough stone wall.

Polesden Lacey

GREAT BOOKHAM, DORKING, SURREY

AREA 12ha (30 acres) • SOIL alkaline/some clay and flint • ALTITUDE 91–143m (300–470ft)
AVERAGE RAINFALL 762mm (30in) • AVERAGE WINTER CLIMATE cold

From 1906, this was the home of the Hon. Mrs Ronald Greville, one of the most celebrated hostesses in the Marlborough House circle of Edward VII, and the mansion and gardens offer a delicious insight into the life of Edwardian high society. The present house, a yellow-washed and green-shuttered villa, was built in the 1820s, but enlarged and refurbished for the Grevilles in the French Neo-classical style by Mewès and Davis, the architects of the Ritz Hotel. Captain Greville died in 1908, and his plans for an equally grand scheme of parterres for the garden were never implemented. Instead, his wife enriched the planting within the inherited framework of avenues, formal walks, lawns and kitchen garden.

The setting is magnificent. The house stands just below the southernmost ridge of the North Downs, and the trees on the lower lawns frame sweeping views over the valley and across to the wooded crest of Ranmore Common. One of the garden's principal features is the panoramic Long Walk that stretches for 0.4km (¼ mile) eastward above the valley. This was begun in 1761, but considerably enlarged by the playwright Richard Brinsley Sheridan, who bought the property in 1797; it is the only remnant of his garden.

The chalk and sunny aspect make for a hot, dry hillside. Wildflowers do well among the hungry meadow grasses, and the open, mown lawns are stained purple by creeping thyme. But the site is well furnished with trees, and seams of richer, acid loam allow the chalk-tolerant beeches, oaks, maples and pines to be supplemented by sweet chestnut, wellingtonia, Douglas fir and other more fastidious species. The plantations were badly hit by the great storm of 1987, and to a lesser extent that of 1990, but new plantings are now maturing. Ornamental gardening is concentrated across the lawn to the west, except in the immediate vicinity of the house, which is hung with wisteria, yellow Banksian rose and other climbers and wall shrubs, and fringed with box-edged borders of spring and summer bedding.

Here, in the nineteenth-century walled kitchen garden, is Mrs Greville's rose garden. Set out in a simple cross pattern, with long, box-edged, wooden pergolas, adjoining seams of 'Dwarf Blue' lavenders, walls draped in clematis and a water tower festooned in an old Chinese wisteria, it is a mass of pink, white and crimson during the summer months. A little earlier in the year, the same colours occur in the first of the yew enclosures beyond, containing double borders of peonies. The other compartments present collections of lavenders – and of bearded iris, a selection of early hybrids, some of which have been invigorated through laboratory propagation of virus-free tissue.

As in the house, there is fine classical ornament at every turn. A Venetian well-head stands at the junction of the rose garden paths, a discus thrower disports in the lavender garden, and the theme is pursued elsewhere in the form of a Roman bath as well as further well-heads, urns and statues, all adding luxury to the compositions.

ABOVE An armillary sphere glimpsed through the Moon Window.
RIGHT Evening light in the Rose Garden, with a view towards the well-head.

To the west, the path leads past herbaceous borders to a winter garden, shaded by three large Persian ironwood trees. Beyond, a thatched bridge leads over the sunken estate road to the Edwardian kitchen garden, now mainly grassed over and patterned with limes and cherries, but with a large area given over to a series of annual food-production projects following on from the success of the pumpkin patch in 2015.

To the south run the main herbaceous borders, 137m (450ft) long and divided into four sections. The pastel colours rise into yellow climaxes of achilleas, daylilies and kniphofia, and spiky yuccas and blue-grey *Crambe maritima* contribute emphatic foliage to the corners. Agapanthus do particularly well in the hot, dry ground here, supreme among them a magnificent midnight blue form of the pendulous *A. inapertus*. Below, colour comes from the shrubs and trees on and adjacent to the bank of Westmorland limestone that plunges into the Upper Sunk Garden. Berberis, lilacs, hydrangeas and perovskia give a succession of flowers, beautifully complemented by pear trees with silver foliage (*Pyrus nivalis*), whitebeam, smoke bush, large-leaved *Viburnum rhytidophyllum*, a handkerchief tree and a massive Pfitzer juniper. The Lower Sunk Garden, sometimes referred to as Mrs Greville's Lost Woodland Walk, is now being opened up and filled with choice woodland plants.

Mrs Greville died in 1942 and lies buried outside the Walled Garden, in an enclosure presided over by eighteenth-century French statues of the Four Seasons.

PREVIOUS PAGE A kaleidoscope of annual poppies and cornflowers at Polesden Lacey.

LEFT *Clematis armandii* is the backdrop to a show of tulips.

RIGHT A view of the yew hedges that buttress the terraced gardens at Powis Castle. The garden was designed by Captain William Winde in the seventeenth century but the yew hedges have since swelled and subsided out of their original shape.

Powis Castle

WELSHPOOL, POWYS

AREA 10ha (25 acres) • SOIL acid woodland area, otherwise neutral to alkaline/clay
ALTITUDE 0–137m (0–450ft) • AVERAGE RAINFALL 813mm (32in) • AVERAGE WINTER
CLIMATE cold

It will annoy visitors following behind you, but I recommend slowing the car as you come to the ornamental wrought-iron gates between the park and the garden, on your way up the hill. Behind the railings, and from a platform of smooth grass, appointed with finely clipped topiaries, your eye is swept up over a canopy of mixed trees to a steep ridge in the middle distance. Mellow Baroque terraces, masked in shrubs and bordered by a gigantic hedge, ascend this in tiers towards the skyline. And here, seemingly among the clouds, is perched a massive fortress of red limestone – the medieval seat of Welsh princes and later the earls of Powis – crowned with battlements and lapped by domes of dark yew.

The appetite for exploration is whetted and there is no disappointment, for this is one of the Trust's richest flower gardens, with some of the most swashbuckling and sophisticated herbaceous planting to be seen anywhere in the country. The curving drive leads you on up the slopes, well wooded with oaks of such a size and quality that they were insisted upon by Admiral Rodney for his fighting ships during the American War of Independence. Groups of red and fallow deer can usually be glimpsed in the shadows.

You enter the garden just below the castle to be met by the reverse panorama: layers of herbaceous borders, topiaries, stairways and balustrades, descending to a 1ha (2½ acre) lawn; north of it, a large formal garden of fruit trees and rose beds; and opposite, another lower ridge, encased in oaks and yews, and backed by the patchwork of fields, villages and hills of the Welsh border countryside.

The grand terraces, incorporating an Orangery and Aviary, and an array of fine lead statuary from the workshop of the Flemish sculptor John van Nost, are a unique and remarkable legacy, having survived intact the destructive eighteenth-century taste for naturalistic landscaping. Legend has it (there is not shred of evidence) that Lancelot 'Capability' Brown visited and recommended that they be returned to the natural rock from which they were quarried, and that this was, therefore, a narrow escape.

Their exact history is something of a mystery. It seems most likely that they were designed by William Winde, the architect of the terrace at Cliveden, and that construction began in the early 1680s, when William Herbert, the 1st Marquess of Powis, was at the height of his political career. The Glorious Revolution of 1688 sent the Herberts into exile with King James II, and work is then thought to have come to a standstill until after 1703, when the family returned. In its entourage was now a Frenchman by the name of Adrian Duval and he, perhaps under the continuing supervision of Winde, completed the design. This included an impressive Dutch water garden on the site of the Great Lawn below, dismantled by 1809; a recent geophysical survey has revealed that its foundations correspond to the design shown in surviving drawings.

The cue for the lavish overlay of flowers comes from Violet, wife of the 4th Earl, who, in 1911, set about transforming a 'gradually deteriorating' garden into 'one of the most beautiful, if not the most beautiful, in England and Wales'. However, the garden

was once again in decline when it came to the Trust, and its present content – ever-changing and experimental in the spirit of Edwardian flower gardening – reflects the expertise of its head gardener and staff from the 1970s onwards.

The high, sheltering walls of the terraces, angled to the south-east, together with the comparatively mild climate, allow an adventurous range of shrubs and climbers. In late spring, deep blue ceanothus billow above the brick like thunderclouds, while against the Orangery, the buff-yellow roses *Rosa banksiae* 'Lutea' and 'Gloire de Dijon' pick up tones in the sandstone frontispiece, in the company of orange eccremocarpus and white abutilon. Later, there are curtains of flowering clematis, cream waterlilies from *Magnolia grandiflora*, a waterfall of pale green from honey-scented *Itea ilicifolia* and scarlet showers from wall-trained *Phygelius capensis*; less showy curiosities such as *Dregea sinensis*, *Rhodochiton atrosanguineus* and *Abutilon* 'Nabob' are to be discovered on every tier.

The display of tender perennials has been raised to the level of high art at Powis, where, with the backup of glasshouses, cuttings are grown on into bushy plants during the winter, brought into flower, hardened off and returned to the garden as early as April. Potfuls fill the pedimented niches in the upper terrace wall – the orange brick

fringed with the compact form of silver artemisia, brought here in 1972 and subsequently named 'Powis Castle' – and punctuate almost every balustrade and stairway. Fuchsias, an Edwardian favourite, are a speciality, with both the petticoated hybrids and scarlet-tubed *Fuchsia fulgens* and *F. boliviana* and dark-leaved *F.* 'Thalia' presented in old basketweave pots. Elsewhere, you come upon glorious salads made from the likes of glaucous-leaved melianthus, crimson-red cestrum, trailing yellow bidens, double red nasturtium, and the most sumptuous of all the pelargoniums, the damson, crimson-edged 'Lord Bute'.

Each terrace border has its theme. Drier conditions on the narrow Aviary Terrace have suggested plantings of sun-loving Mediterranean, Californian and Southern Hemisphere plants, including cistus, carpenteria, broom, lavender, iris and *Artemisia arborescens*. The Aviary itself, its roof studded with lead urns and draped in Japanese wisteria, contains troughs of half-hardy, scented rhododendrons in the company of the giant-fronded chain fern and webs of creeping fig.

On the third terrace, the deep, heavy soil allows lush herbaceous planting, and either side of the Orangery, pairs of long, boxed-edged borders recede into the distance. They are at their peak in late summer, and because of the milder light and temperatures here, the plants have a freshness and length of season rarely met in more southerly gardens. On one side of the Orangery, the tints are of violet, white and warm pink from perennials such as monkshood, cimicifugas, polygonums, asters and *Clematis* 'Jackmanii Superba', grown on balloon hoops; on the other side, the scene is of fire and brimstone, fuelled by orange crocosmias, yellow kniphofias, the vermilion hips of *Rosa moyesii* and *R. highdownensis*, and a plume of golden cypress.

The seasons of the lowest terrace's borders straddle this display, with one border focused on the euphorbias, galegas, verbascums and other perennials of early summer; the other on the chrysanthemums, sedums and Japanese anemones of early autumn – at which time the leaves of *Acer japonicum*, amelanchiers and euonymus on the adjacent grass slope are beginning to unite.

The yews are dramatic counterweights to this casual, ephemeral vegetation. The fourteen specimen 'tumps' that sit like jellies on the upper terrace, together with the stupendous, bulging hedge at the northern end, were probably planted in the 1720s, with darker Irish yews planted as companions a hundred years later. The boxwood is hardly less impressive, and on emerging through a gap in the yew

hedge, you meet a towering wall of it, running beside a sloping, serpentine walk. The smell is always intense.

This path leads down to the lower formal garden, made by the 4th Countess from the former kitchen garden. A long vine tunnel and lines of pyramidal apple trees are reminders of the earlier use – the latter including rare, old varieties like 'Mother' and 'Broad-Eyed Pippin', all set into silver and gold ground-cover plants, serving as permanent bedding. Beds of Floribunda and Hybrid Musk roses and other Edwardian favourites, including phlox, delphiniums, campanulas and hollyhocks, stretch away from the half-timbered gardener's bothy.

At the opposite end of the Orangery terrace, you are enticed out of the formal garden past an exposed face of rock, the path curving eastwards towards the opposite ridge. Paperbark maple, evergreen eucryphia, a tall maidenhair tree and shrimp-tinted *Acer pseudoplatanus* 'Brilliantissimum' are among the trees on this bank.

Remarkably, the ridge itself is formed of acid sandstone, in contrast to the limestone of the Castle ridge, allowing the 3rd Earl to indulge in the Victorian taste for rhododendrons.

The paths lead you to an icehouse and a Ladies' Bath, both probably dating from the nineteenth century, and here and there, you are given tree-framed prospects out to Long Mountain and the Breidden Hills and back across the daffodil and wildflower paddock and Great Lawn to the castle and its terraces. Few properties can offer such a variety of vantage points, or views of such breathtaking scale and detail. This is a garden that draws the visitor back again and again – several times a year, in my case.

LEFT The view from the terrace over the lower gardens and surrounding countryside.
ABOVE The red sandstone castle looms behind layers of trees, shrubs and topiaries.

Prior Park

BATH, SOMERSET

AREA 11ha (28 acres) • **SOIL** clay/loam • **ALTITUDE** 90m (295ft) • **AVERAGE RAINFALL** 762mm (30in) • **AVERAGE WINTER CLIMATE** sheltered, with frost pockets

An intimate Arcadian valley just 1.6km (1 mile) from the centre of Bath, Prior Park came to the Trust in 1993 in an advanced state of decay, but in its design remarkably little-changed since the death of its creator, Ralph Allen, in 1764. Thanks to generous bequests and donations from the public, and a large Heritage Lottery Fund grant in 2005, the major task of restoration has continued apace.

The 30 years of the park's development was a golden era in garden history, during which the new, 'natural' landscape style evolved from its early wooded, serpentine and allegorical phase to embrace the open, uncluttered panorama of lake and meadow. Allen responded, and his park both charts the changing fashion and preserves the work of some of the movement's most influential figures.

At the head of the combe stands the Palladian mansion built by John Wood from the honey-coloured stone that Allen, a self-made businessman, was quarrying in Combe Down for Georgian Bath; it has been a school since 1867. Below, the meadow sweeps down to a magnificent Palladian bridge and a chain of three ponds appearing as a curving lake, the whole prospect framed by woods. Beyond are the hills and skyline of Bath.

It is in the west woods that the oldest features of the garden are to be found. Here you come upon the Wilderness developed from the mid-1730s, where Allen was advised by his good friend Alexander Pope. Pope was one of the most persuasive advocates of the new style and of composing a garden as a sequence of varied, narrative and emotionally charged landscape pictures, influenced by the natural features and qualities of the site. He took a particularly close interest in this garden, even loaning his own gardener, John Serle.

Previously overcast by branches, dense with evergreen shrubbery, punctuated by black ponds, and with only remnants of its many architectural surprises visible, the Wilderness has now been opened up and renovated with an attendant loss of historic atmosphere. But in time, the new stonework will mellow and the plantings mature.

From the garden's entrance, the first feature you come upon is Mrs Allen's Grotto. Grottoes, with their origins deep in the ancient world, were very fashionable in the eighteenth-century garden, with Pope himself having one of the most celebrated examples in his villa garden in Twickenham. Prior Park's, partly disintegrated and currently under restoration, is also impressive, with its floor a starburst of stones, bones and ammonites, and its walls and roof formerly a wonderland of glinting shells and minerals.

Beyond, the river-like Serpentine Lake, newly restored, curls artfully along a level terrace between the steep wooded banks, terminating in a low Sham Bridge with arched openings and vermiculated pediments, and a view of the house above it – both reflecting elegantly in the water. Below the lake, the water crashes down a 'natural' rock Cascade, with a weir plate enabling an increased flow when Allen wanted to impress his guests, who would have been assembled in the circular gravel arena known as

the Cabinet at its base. Young oriental plane trees and decorative shrubberies of period plants – among them box, viburnum, phillyrea, ruscus, ferns, hydrangeas and magnolias – complete the scene.

This garden's main vista was refashioned several times. It began, in 1734, as a quite formal landscape, with a triangular lawn, circular basin of water and straight-edged woods. In the 1750s, it was greatly extended down into the combe, the woods were made to billow down the banks, the lower lakes were created by damming the stream and, in 1755, the Palladian bridge was built as its crowning ornament. After 1759, the naturalisation process was concluded, the circular basin with its accompanying cascade and plantations being removed to provide the present uninterrupted sweep of meadow. The leading landscape gardener was now Lancelot 'Capability' Brown, and it is possible that it was he who suggested the final alterations to Allen in the few years before his death.

The circuit of the park takes you around the meadow and down to the water by way of the eastern woods. In spring, there is a surge of wild garlic over the flank of the combe, and in among the trees there are many ferns and wildflowers. An oak-framed summer-house, moved here in 1912, surveys one of the glades, and at one point you can walk out onto the adjacent field for a broader panorama of the city.

As you descend, the lake is gradually revealed as three ponds standing at different levels, with another dam made under the bridge, so that the water gushed through the arches. The architect of the bridge, one of only three Palladian bridges to survive in Britain (the earlier examples being at Stowe and Wilton House), is unknown, but it was probably a copy of Wilton's built by Allen's clerk of works, Richard Jones; the stone was brought down via a new driveway to the north-west, with a Chinese gate at its entrance.

From the bridge, you have the equally impressive view back up the combe. Until 1921, this took in not only the mansion but also the Gothic Temple of 1753, perched on the edge of the Wilderness. A replica may replace it in due course: it is one of the final missing or broken pieces of the jigsaw that the National Trust has been gradually reassembling.

LEFT The Sham Bridge in the Wilderness, designed by Alexander Pope to appear as a bridge over a river although, in fact, it is on a pond with no watercourse running through it.

RIGHT Looking down over the lake with its Palladian bridge.

Quarry Bank Mill

STYAL, WILMSLOW, CHESHIRE

AREA 4.9ha (12 acres) • SOIL sandy loam/clay soil • ALTITUDE 96m (315ft) • AVERAGE RAINFALL 813mm (32in) • AVERAGE WINTER CLIMATE moderate

The Trust's acquisitions of Quarry Bank House in 2006 and the associated kitchen gardens in 2010, in addition to its existing ownership of the adjacent working cotton mill, Apprentice House and other buildings and land on the Styal estate, have contributed two more colourful parts to an already remarkably complete picture of a community living through the early years of the Industrial Revolution.

The Mill, built in 1784, is a vast expanse of russet-red brickwork, sitting in an unspoilt and well-wooded valley beside the River Bollin, which provided the necessary power to run the machines. Its owner was Samuel Greg, a wealthy young Manchester merchant, who together with his wife Hannah took an enlightened and paternalistic interest in the workforce – though, to modern eyes, they still endured a very harsh existence both domestically and in the heat and dust of the Mill. It is a sign of the Gregs' pride in their enterprise that in about 1800 they built their own house right beside the Mill, seeing it as an object of beauty and indifferent to the noise and smell which would later trouble the future Prime Minister William Gladstone, who visited in 1828.

A cream, bow-fronted villa of modest proportions, Quarry Bank House was intended as a country retreat, a periodic escape from the city, but eventually it became the family home. Its location, looking down a little river gorge, with red sandstone outcrops, high banks overhung with trees and even a small cave, perfectly suited the contemporary taste for romantic, layered, Picturesque landscape. The Mill itself was integral to it, its dominant architectural presence contributing much to the enjoyment of the views. As family and guests looked back towards the house, it provided that sublime uplifting drama of magnitude tinged with 'horror' which was so relished at the time, especially in mountain scenery.

Samuel and Hannah Greg clearly developed a fine garden here – 'truly picturesque and cultivated to the greatest possible extent', noted the visiting American naturalist John James Audubon in 1826 – and the framework of it still survives. Many plantings and garden features were subsequently added by their son, Robert Hyde Greg, and grandson, Edward Hyde Greg, so that the grounds attained a potent late Victorian overlay which the Trust – following a major programme of overgrown conifer and rhododendron clearance, painstaking path excavation and restoration, and garden renovation – is again fostering with the help of the 1872 Ordnance Survey map and old photographs.

On the valley floor below the Mill, Edward Hyde Greg created a Tennis Lawn out of the meadow parkland, and from here you look up at sloping banks thickly clad in tall beech woods; elsewhere Scots pines and other specimen trees, including a weeping ash and a young Brewer's spruce with pendulous swags of needles, add craggy and cascade-like silhouettes to enhance the site's natural romanticism. The crashing waters of the weir and the smaller manmade waterfalls are the accompaniment which in the past would have helped to lessen the noise of the Mill and today mitigate that from traffic.

ABOVE Autumn foliage and berries at Quarry Bank Mill.

RIGHT A view of the Mill showing its wooded setting.

Although only a mile from Manchester Airport, the garden is astonishingly tranquil and inhabited by a rich variety of wildlife. Dippers and kingfishers are often seen by the river, as are mink (which keep the rabbit population down), with northern divers and goosanders visiting in winter.

A rustic bridge crosses over the water into the pleasure grounds. Sloping lawns near the house harbour further trees, including a huge purple Japanese maple, but the path leads you away down a long river terrace, flanked by formal gardens and shrubberies. A principal highlight here, and indeed all up the steep banks and rich red sandstone undercliffs, are the azaleas and rhododendrons, which were an enthusiasm of Robert Hyde Greg and which he planted en masse between Quarry Bank House and his own house Norcliffe Hall, sited beyond the woods on this pathline. Spring therefore sees a terrific eruption of contrasting colours from thickets of yellow azalea, *Rhododendron luteum* (whose fruity scent fills the whole garden) to violet *R. augustinii*, blush-pink 'Loderi', and numerous carmine,

pink, deep purple and blood-red hybrids, some of which were raised by Greg, who was a keen rhododendron breeder.

They are interspersed with lush plantings of hostas, daylilies, ferns and hardy geraniums along the side of the river, and on the opposite side of the path is a small formal parterre, appointed with cast-iron urns and bedded out in spring with tulips and forget-me-nots, followed by summer bedding in the Victorian style. Above is the path to the Cave, with its steps hewn out of the rock, along which are more newly re-created linear borders of herbaceous plants, shrubs and bulbs.

The path then zigzags up the side of the gorge, past further trees and shrubs and a small lawn of sentinel yews, all the while giving attractive reverse views. Near the top, you are in the shadow of the overhanging oak and beech, where hydrangeas and ferns have been planted to join the carpet of bluebells sweeping under the yellow azaleas. Now 27m (90ft) above the river, you emerge into the upper parkland. There was a small Victorian orchard here with an apple walk, which is being restored, and in spring the meadow grass around is well studded with primroses. The adjacent paddock has some good trees, including a couple of enormous crab apples, *Malus hupehensis*, dating probably from the late 1940s, and in the corner is a massive and venerable beech tree, from which you are offered another fine prospect of the Mill and its landscape setting. In 2010, the Trust was also able to add another large section of this higher ground to its ownership, including the derelict, brick-walled kitchen garden, which still contains the shells of the 1830s glasshouses with their early examples of curvilinear glazing bars. As well as fruit and vegetables, the Upper Garden features new borders and a new row of mulberry trees, partnered with peonies and irises. The surviving pathways offer further dramatic clifftop views.

This pleasant mill owner's world is in sharp contrast to that presented by the Apprentice House. The apprentices were indentured child labourers who, from the age of nine or ten, were forced to work a twelve-hour day, six days a week, for a period of some seven years. The Apprentice House was home to these children who had been drawn from local workhouses, and later, from distant city slums. It housed up to 100 apprentices in a plain, whitewashed building, accompanied by a cluster of brick outhouses, a cobbled yard, and a productive garden, in which, under the supervision of the superintendents, the children grew food for themselves. Today, restored by the Quarry Bank Mill Trust, the site once again displays humble plots of fruit and vegetables, neatly divided by picket fences. With a few weeds between the cobbles and the grass a little shaggy, the rural nineteenth-century flavour has been recaptured.

One old apple and a few damson trees have survived; otherwise all the fruit and vegetable varieties now grown date from before the end of the nineteenth century, with many of local provenance. The garden is managed traditionally, using no chemicals. Among the apples are 'Irish Peach', 'Peasgood's Nonsuch', 'Lord Suffield' and the very rare, locally bred 'Withington Welter'; among the plums, 'Jefferson' and 'Imperial Gage' (syn. 'Denniston's Superb'); among the pears, 'Williams' Bon Chrétien' and 'Jargonelle'; and the damson is 'Cheshire Damson'.

The free-draining soil, well-laced with manure, supports an extensive selection of vegetables, many originally sourced from the heritage seed library at Garden Organic (formerly the Henry Doubleday Research Association) at Ryton-on-Dunsmore, near Coventry. These include the peas 'Champion of England' and 'Prince Albert'; the kale 'Ragged Jack'; the carrot 'Altrincham'; the turnip 'Manchester Market'; the onion 'Southport Red Globe'; and the

early maturing rhubarb 'Timperley Early'. The produce was stored in special tunnels.

There are also many herbs, which would have been used to make food more palatable, to treat minor ailments and, in the case of alkanet and woad, to act as dye plants. To add some cheer to the scene, there is a bed of cottage flowers, including stocks, pinks, columbines and dame's violet, which succeed the snowdrops, daffodils and cowslips that appear on the scythed grass bank in spring. This is a memorable place to visit.

LEFT Snowdrops on the grass bank, with the mill owner's house beyond.
ABOVE Ruby chard in the well-stocked vegetable plots.

Red House

BEXLEYHEATH, KENT

AREA 0.7ha (1¾ acres) • SOIL acid/clay and gravel • ALTITUDE 61m (200ft)
AVERAGE RAINFALL 635mm (25in) • AVERAGE WINTER CLIMATE moderate

In 1859, Bexleyheath was rural Kent, not London suburb, with hedgerows, apple orchards, and untamed heathland bisected by the Roman road of Watling Street, which had led Chaucer's pilgrims to Canterbury. These pastoral and romantic associations, together with a decent rail link to the capital, attracted William Morris, the artist, designer and inspiration behind the Arts and Crafts movement. In that year, newly married, he built his first home, Red House, designed by his friend, the architect Philip Webb.

The house dominates the garden. With its expanses of red brick and tile, and sparse array of windows in circular, Gothic-arched and arrow-slit shapes, the organic vernacular style suggests some learned ecclesiastical institution as much as a domestic house. Morris loved the simplicity, romance and colour of the Middle Ages, and the Red House garden was similarly set to a medieval tune, evoking the sort of enclosed 'pleasaunce' described by Chaucer and *Le Roman de la Rose*, the thirteenth-century allegorical poem about courtly love played out in a May-time garden. There were numerous formal compartments of varying design, with screens of wattle and rose-covered trellis (as featured in his celebrated 'Trellis' wallpaper), wildflower lawns, a bowling green and beds of old-fashioned flowers – many heavy with medieval symbolism, such as the white lily, signifying purity. Much of this was set around existing lines of orchard trees.

Today, some imagination is required from the visitor. The intricacies of its compartmented design have largely gone, together

LEFT A mass of red and white roses with Red House's rooftops in the background.

with most of the orchard trees. In Morris's time, for example, the entrance area comprised several formal enclosures, but is now a looser scheme of curving gravel drive, lawn and shrubbery, shaded by sizeable oaks, yews and pollarded limes, and sporting rhododendrons, camellias and Judas trees, *Cercis siliquastrum*. Recently, a nature trail has been created around the perimeter of the garden.

The Well House, on the east side of the house, is the garden's only architectural ornament, its conical roof echoing the steep roofline beyond, capped with fairytale turret and weather vane. Framed by the two wings of the house, it was always a working well and was originally intended as the centrepiece of an enclosed court, with the character of a medieval cloister. Morris planned to complete the court with buildings, in order to accommodate the Burne-Jones family, but although this was a gregarious household, his desire for a community of artists living and working together was never fulfilled. At present, the Well House stands in open lawn, broken by a couple of old apple and crab apple trees and a line of flower-beds, featuring a large strawberry tree (*Arbutus unedo*), and an assortment of roses, wildflowers, and cottage perennials, including teasel, iris, peony, aster and daylily. In his own borders, Morris eschewed fashionable Victorian exotics, garish bedding plants and even ferns, which he thought belonged to rock, waterfall and woodland. Double flowers were also to be avoided, he declared in a lecture of 1879, urging listeners to grow not the double sunflower but the single one, 'with its sharply chiselled yellow florets relieved by the quaintly patterned sad-coloured centre clogged with honey and beset with bees and butterflies'.

The two old pear trees on the west wall of the house, which once shared space with Climbing roses, jasmine and passionflower, face out across a brick pathway and a long, narrow border of lavenders and love-in-a-mist, *Nigella damascena*, in shades of blue and white. This, and the tunnel of Climbing roses behind, are the frame for the Bowling Green Lawn, one of the garden's original compartments where, according to Lady Burne-Jones, 'the men used to play when work was over'. But the section of orchard beyond, complete with old apple trees, was added to the property some years later, having previously been part of Aberleigh Lodge, where Morris and his wife stayed during the building of Red House. The kitchen garden in the south-west corner of the site was also extended at this time.

The originality of the garden fired the imaginations of those who saw it, its medieval detail an extension of the Pre-Raphaelite dream, and its sequence of formal compartments heralding the golden age of Arts and Crafts style.

Rievaulx Terrace and Temples

RIEVAULX, YORK, NORTH YORKSHIRE

AREA 25ha (62 acres) • **SOIL** alkaline/light soil • **ALTITUDE** 180m (591ft)
AVERAGE RAINFALL 686–813mm (27–32in) • **AVERAGE WINTER CLIMATE** cold

This serpentine grass walk, high on a wooded escarpment at the head of Ryedale, is one of the most beautiful products of the Picturesque phase of English landscape gardening. As at Fountains Abbey and Studley Royal, 48km (30 miles) away, the composition combines natural beauty with a suitably atmospheric eye-catcher – the majestic ruins of the great Cistercian abbey of Rievaulx, founded in 1131 (now an English Heritage property).

The terrace's story really begins across the combe at Duncombe Park, where, some time after 1713, Thomas Duncombe II broke from the French-inspired practice of designing wooded *allées* along straight axes, and commissioned instead a hillside ride that followed the natural contours of the terrain and curved in a crescent. Some 40 years later, Duncombe's son, Thomas Duncombe III, conceived this second terrace above the abbey. Superficially similar in shape to that at Duncombe, and also with Ionic and Doric temples at either end, the Rievaulx Terrace is, however, devoid of all its predecessor's residual formality. Undulating woods replace the hedges and linear plantations, and the walk meanders in a succession of curves, not enclosed by trees but revealing, through gaps in the woods, a series of superb views of the landscape – the abbey, the arched bridge over the river and the green patchwork of the Hambleton Hills and Rye Valley. Piles of dressed masonry found in the combe suggest that Thomas Duncombe III was planning a viaduct to connect the two terraces but, alas, it was never built.

Beech is the principal tree of the terrace's backdrop, supported by a range of other hardwoods including, unexpectedly, variegated sycamore. Further diversity is found on the woodland floor – the cast including martagon lilies, dog's mercury, columbines, lords and ladies and the parasitic pink toothwort – and on the rough grassy bank on the other side of the terrace, where there are rich communities of primroses, cowslips, oxlips, early purple orchids, bird's foot trefoil, hawkbits, clovers and many others, giving carpets of colour through spring and summer. Who says the eighteenth-century landscape garden lacks flowers?

ABOVE The eighteenth-century Ionic Temple, originally intended as a banqueting house.

Rowallane

SAINTFIELD, BALLYNAHINCH, CO. DOWN

AREA 21ha (52 acres) • **SOIL** acid/loam • **ALTITUDE** 61m (200ft) • **AVERAGE RAINFALL** 914mm (36in) • **AVERAGE WINTER CLIMATE** mild

The land at Rowallane, Hugh Armytage Moore was told, was 'not fit to graze a goat'. This is rough drumlin country. The fields are boxed small by dry-stone walls and sheltering hedgerows, and stands of gorse and massive outcrops of rock break from the grass. But the rainfall is moderately high, the summers cool and the winters comparatively mild. From 1903, Moore began planting, and his legacy is a large plantsman's garden of striking scenic beauty and distinctive character. In parts of the grounds, a foundation of trees and walls had already been set out by his uncle, the Rev. John Moore, who bought the property in 1860. The long entrance drive, now richly coloured by immense arboreal rhododendrons, already had its close fringes of deciduous trees and its sinuous grassy glades shaded by specimen conifers. The stone seats and arresting cairns of giant's marbles were also in place, complementing the exposed rock.

Behind the modest, apricot-painted farmhouse is the Rev. Moore's pleasure ground, a broad sweep of lawn and arboretum, featuring a pond and a circular stone dais, from which he is reputed to have delivered sermons. This looks less odd now that it is the base for the iron bandstand from Newcastle promenade, which was given to the Trust in a derelict state in 1985. Many trees have been added here over the past hundred years, but those planted by Rev. Moore still set the quiet mood. Monterey, Scots, bishop and umbrella pine, redwood, wellingtonia, cypresses, multi-stemmed western red cedar, Douglas fir, podocarpus, cunninghamia and *Fitzroya cupressoides* are among the many fine conifers framed by the beech trees. Recently, a new circuit path has been laid, with the accompanying extensive laurel removal now allowing views out into the fields.

The adjacent walled garden was also built by the Rev. Moore, but although it retains its formal kitchen garden pattern of gravel paths, its planting is now very different. In place of some of the vegetable beds, Hugh Armytage Moore introduced borders of choice perennials, shaded by ornamental trees, and this theme has been seized and developed in red-blooded fashion by the Trust. The moist climate allows wonderfully lush plantings. Drifts of Himalayan poppies – in particular, the scintillating turquoise-blue *Meconopsis* × *sheldonii* 'Slieve Donard' – course between lime-green hostas and bronze and tropical-leaved rodgersias. Species peonies are displayed in variety, followed by primulas, daylilies and astilbes. Phloxes and the Japanese *Kirengeshoma palmata* with its soft yellow shuttlecocks provide colour in late summer.

Low blocks of ornamental grasses, libertias and dwarf rhododendrons give contrasting flavours, while above and behind, ornamental trees, taller shrubs and climbers provide backdrops, evergreen structure and, in many parts, a dappled, woodland atmosphere - though, as is periodically required in mature gardens, much pruning has been taking place to create airier and healthier conditions. Cherries and spring- and summer-flowering magnolias are prominent, including forms of *M.* × *veitchii* introduced in the early part of the twentieth century by the Veitch nursery in Exeter, from which Hugh Armytage Moore obtained plants. *Rhododendron cinnabarinum* in many guises, *R. hanceanum* and the superb *R. shilsonii*, with blood-red flowers and cinnamon bark peeling to reveal purplish branches, are highlights among the shrubs, with *Hoheria lyallii* (which self-sows freely) and eucryphias giving later blossom.

A mature *Magnolia stellata* presides over box-edged beds of herbs and vegetables, while the compact form of *Viburnum plicatum*, raised from seed at Rostrevor but distributed from here and named 'Rowallane', grows in the centre of a small paved area, designed in the shape of a Celtic cross. The recently restored walls – unique in having projecting pierced tiles incorporated, through which supporting wires for climbing plants may be threaded, shelters *Acradenia frankliniae* from Tasmania and the conservatory rhododendron 'Lady Alice Fitzwilliam'.

The outer walled garden, formerly Hugh Armytage Moore's nursery area and currently being renovated by the Trust, springs further surprises, including *Helwingia japonica*, curious for producing its pale green flowers on the upper surface of the leaves. The unusual *Hydrangea aspera* subsp. *strigosa* is included in the large collection of hydrangeas, partnered with colchiums, and here also is the original plant of the popular garden japonica, *Chaenomeles* × *superba*

'Rowallane'. Crinums, watsonias, species dahlias, dieramas and a fat clump of *Lobelia tupa* add some exotic herbaceous interest.

In 1903, the rest of the ground now covered by the garden consisted of rock-strewn fields. Gradually, as his experience and enthusiasm grew, Hugh Armytage Moore annexed them. But he did no taming, levelling or ploughing. He kept the dry-stone walls, the gorse and the spongy turf, made a feature of the rock, and had his planting follow the undulating rhythm of the land. The result is an extraordinarily heady mix of the wild and exotic, and a succession of images that could belong to no other garden. Wildflower management here is outstanding.

The fields retain their age-old names. From the Haggard, or stackyard (a remarkable sight in July when the falling cotton seeds of *Populus maximowiczii* envelop it in a local blizzard), a gate leads first into the Spring Ground, long valued for its early-warming, southerly orientation. In spring, you are greeted by swathes of flowers. The foreground ridge is heavily planted with daffodils, including many old Irish cultivars; they are succeeded by colonies of devil's bit scabious and other wildflowers.

The view down the bank, framed by pine, beech and oak, is punctuated by eruptions of rhododendrons. Large hybrids, such as white 'Dr Stocker' and 'Loderi King George', give way to stands of sun-loving azaleas and pink and purplish *R. triflorum* species. Red Kirishima azalea, *Rhododendron × obtusum* and the scented *R. luteum* are prominent, the latter in its traditional garden partnership with wild bluebells. The white variety of *Magnolia campbellii* and summer-flowering *M. wilsonii* also grow here. Like many of the trees and shrubs in the garden, they have associations with the great plant-hunters of the early twentieth century. Moore corresponded with E.H. Wilson and George Forrest, and grew many of their introductions as they became available through both Irish and English nurseries.

More rhododendrons, this time in the company of specimen trees such as Dawyck beech, stewartias and deliciously fragrant *Malus toringo* subsp. *sargentii* entice you through the New Ground to the famous rock garden. Here, Moore exposed a gigantic outcrop of grey whinstone, smoothed and striated by glaciers, and imported cartloads of soil to make beds around it. The rock, gravel and grass paths curl and plunge past a huge range of ferns, bulbs and herbaceous plants, among which runs of silver-leaved celmisias are memorable incidents. Mats of mouse plant, *Arisarum proboscideum*, lie at the bottom.

In fact, there are rhododendrons everywhere. The rock fringes and streamsides are home to *Rhododendron orbiculare*, *R. baileyi*, the aromatic *R. glaucophyllum* and hybrids such as 'Yellow Hammer' and 'Blue Tit'. In sheltered corners grow the tender *R. virgatum* and lily-scented 'Countess of Haddington'. A fine pieris, from Forrest's seed, gives a spectacular show, as does the thicket of *Mahonia japonica* Bealei Group and the collection of streamside perennials, which includes Primula 'Rowallane Rose'.

Wooded enclosures lie ahead. Once planted as wind shelter for the grazing stock, this matrix of forest trees is equally important for the protection of the garden. A young shelter belt of beech is gradually replacing the felled larches on Trio Hill above the rock garden; among them are fine groups of embothrium, berberis and *Enkianthus campanulatus*, this last delivering sensational autumn tints. Recently rejuvenated plantings in Rock Garden Wood, composed with reference to Moore's diaries and correspondence, again feature rarified combinations such as *Boenninghausenia albiflora* with *Gentiana sino-ornata*, and meconopsis and primulas with *Arisaema griffithii*, as well as an assortment of tiny Himalayan rhododendrons overhanging the shady rocks.

Scots pine and beech form the mainstay of the plantations on the slopes running west towards the entrance drive. In these lower woods and glades, the contrast between the wild and the ornamental is at its most potent. For as you cross the bumpy terrain, past tree heathers, pieris and still more rhododendrons, between specimen maples, southern beeches, paulownia, davidia, sorbus, birch, chestnut and eucalyptus, you skirt the low boundary walls, over which you see land similarly contoured and compartmented, but empty. This is what Hugh Armytage Moore began with; behind you is what he made of it. Walks now opened up through the surrounding farmland, meadows and woods heighten the contrast further.

RIGHT A procession of Irish yews at Rowallane.

Rufford Old Hall

ORMSKIRK, LANCASHIRE

AREA 5.7ha (14 acres) • **SOIL** acid/sandy loam • **ALTITUDE** 8m (26ft)
AVERAGE RAINFALL 813mm (32in) • **AVERAGE WINTER CLIMATE** cold

A brick, red sandstone and black-and-white timbered Tudor house, framed by massed rhododendrons and azaleas in full bloom, is a heady sight. This is the moment, in late spring, to see early Victorian taste displayed at Rufford in glorious potency; at other times, the garden takes on a quieter, complementary role. The site is narrow and rectangular, wedged between canal and main road, but a tranquil, rural mood is struck the moment you enter the curving drive. Drifting into woodland to the north, Turkey oaks, sycamores, beeches, limes, sweet chestnut and silver willows shade the rough grass, in which appears a succession of bulbs and wildflowers through spring and early summer. There are good stands of osmunda fern and pampas grass and, near the house, a venerable weeping ash.

The first rhododendrons are here in island beds. Their variety and rich colour greatly appealed to Victorian gardeners, and the continual introduction of new species and home-bred hybrids kept appetites sharp. The acid, sandy soil at Rufford is well suited to them. On this west side of the garden, there are some gorgeous reds, including 'Britannia', 'Fusilier' and 'Bagshot Ruby', and the inclusion of yellow *Rhododendron wardii* and the scented azalea, *R. luteum*, in close proximity, satisfies the Victorian taste for contrast. Accompanying hydrangeas and berried hollies give continuity of bloom into the summer and autumn.

South of the house, some of the rhododendrons and azaleas are marshalled into a pair of long, open, formal borders, lapped by lawn and divided by a gravel path. Here, the yellows of azaleas associate with the pinks and purples of 'Mrs Davies Evans' and 'Praecox'. Other trees and shrubs – among them laburnum,

Rosa multiflora and *Magnolia kobus* – fuel the scheme and extend its season, with the help of bulbs, lilies and perennials such as geraniums, sedums, rudbeckias and daylilies, including the pale yellow variety 'Lady Fermor-Hesketh'. Bold clumps of blue and variegated hostas are a feature of the shadier parts of the garden's shrubberies. In the West Border, they partner weigela, philadelphus, viburnum, enkianthus, pieris and the summer-flowering chestnut *Aesculus parviflora*, and, with these, supply some lively autumn tints.

Set against this exotic woodland flora are ingredients more familiarly associated with such a domestic rural setting. White and mauve wisterias drape the high wall of the estate yard, beside beds of Floribunda and Bourbon roses and mounds of lavender. Quirky topiaries punctuate the lawns, most notable being the pair of squirrels at the head of the main vista, and in the south-west section of the garden is a small orchard, featuring old northern varieties of apple such as 'Keswick Codlin', 'Duke of Devonshire' and 'Lord Suffield'. Beyond and between the box-lined 'Lovers' Walk' is a small

paddock. Plans are afoot to develop a wildflower meadow in this area beyond the main garden, bordering the beech walk that leads to the village church. Beside the canal, *Rhododendron ponticum* thickets have been thinned to make a pleasant walk, between pine, yew and thorn, southwards to the meadow.

ABOVE A display of spring bluebells in the woodland.

St Michael's Mount

MARAZION, PENZANCE, CORNWALL

AREA 4ha (10 acres) • **SOIL** acid/loam • **ALTITUDE** 5–76m (15–250ft) • **AVERAGE RAINFALL** 889–1,016mm (35–40in) • **AVERAGE WINTER CLIMATE** frost-free/mild

This assembly of granite walls and towers perched on its rocky islet off the Cornish coast is one of the most heady architectural sights in Britain. Wind is the enemy here, and bold ridges of pines (*Pinus radiata* and *P. thunbergii*), sycamore and holm oak have been planted for protection, buttressed by salt-tolerant shrubs.

Aloes, aeoniums, echeverias and other tender succulents sprout from the Victorian stone walls of the East Terrace, the accompanying beds colourful with daisy-flowered osteospermums and gazanias. Dazzling blue *Scilla peruviana* is a feature in spring. The West Terrace, with its steep stone steps, is the warmest part of the garden and more exotic still, sporting magenta *Geranium maderense*, blue *Echium pininana*, *Leucodendron* and bird of paradise flower (*Strelitzia*), together with pelargoniums and kangaroo paws (*Anigozanthos*).

The three-tiered walled parterre garden has recently been redesigned. Inspired by the waves of the surrounding sea, the top terrace is now patterned in variegated *Tulbaghia violacea* 'Silver Lace', lilac *Parahebe catarractae* 'Porlock', white *Dietes grandiflora* and lavender *Pericallis lanata*. The middle terrace's pattern evokes water lapping the shore, and alternates panels of silver artemisia, convulvulus and helichrysum with the greens of kniphofia, echinacea, rudbeckia and pennisetum grass. On the narrow bottom terrace, domes of bay are set among gerberas, pelargoniums and cupheas.

The theme of the current renovation programme is to present a more co-ordinated overall landscape picture, while at the same time continuing to push the boundaries of what can be grown in these rarified micro-climates, framed by rock and sea.

RIGHT Cordylines and other tender plants on St Michael's Mount's steep terraces.

Saltram

PLYMPTON, PLYMOUTH, DEVON

AREA 9ha (23 acres) • SOIL acid/sandy loam • ALTITUDE 30m (100ft)
AVERAGE RAINFALL 1,016mm (40in) • AVERAGE WINTER CLIMATE mild

The sweeping views must have played a large part in persuading John and Lady Catherine Parker to move to Saltram from their estate at Boringdon, north of Plymouth, in the 1740s. Encompassing the estuary, the citadel, tiers of hills and the woods of Mount Edgcumbe, the panorama answered perfectly their fashionable aspiration for an elegant and undulating landscape in which to create a private rcadia.

Sadly, the outside world has since encroached upon the idyll. Housing estates and light industry now fringe the estate, and the park is bisected by the noisy Plympton bypass. Some of the open views, once carefully framed by trees, have had to be closed to make screens and shelter belts, but those to the south, accessible from the new Serpentine Walk, remain unspoilt and the grand classical façades of Lady Catherine's house, the stucco now washed a creamy-grey, continue to instil a civilised atmosphere through the grounds, the mood reinforced by smooth lawns, trim gravel walks and handsome garden buildings.

The pattern and content of the present enclosed garden derive from the following century, when formality returned to favour and a tradition of plantsmanship was established at Saltram in spite of the shallow stony soil and windy site. Shrub borders and spacious tree-studded lawns flow along the long, flat ridge west of the house, and the paths take you back and forth along parallel lines. The lowest walk is a long, vaulted avenue of sheltering limes, coloured with a succession of bulbs and wildflowers, from snowdrops and old varieties of daffodil to primroses, bluebells and cow parsley, before being mown in early July; in August, cushions of *Cyclamen hederifolium* appear between the boles.

On the adjacent lawn, impressive Monterey and stone pines, *Pinus radiata* and *P. pinea*, are indicative of the soft, maritime climate, while Chusan palm, *Trachycarpus fortunei*, strikes an exotic note. The balmy flavour intensifies as you walk back along the middle glade and pine-tree paths where numerous stands of half-hardy shrubs are revealed, including the cinnamon-trunked myrtle *Luma apiculata*, *Olearia macrodonta*, *Itea ilicifolia*, *Hoheria* 'Glory of Amlwch', *Acca sellowiana* syn. *Feijoa sellowiana*, *Drimys lanceolata* and loquat. Sober-leaved evergreens – in particular, large old rhododendrons and camellias – are the backbone of the shrubberies. Along the North Path, you find them in the company of ferns and other evergreen shrubs such as *Osmanthus delavayi*, *Drimys winteri*, *Umbellularia californica* and the rarified *Michelia doltsopa* and *Viburnum odoratissimum*. In spring, the warm coconut fragrance of double-flowered gorse infuses the air around the castle, the octagonal belvedere that is the conclusion of each walk running west, and the approach snakes through the plantings to give an attractive prospect of the river.

The northernmost path, the Melancholy Walk, leads between dark evergreens to another original vantage point, Fanny's Bower. Named after the diarist Fanny Burney, who visited Saltram in 1789 as part of the entourage of George III, this classical temple has now had its view up the valley carefully edited to remove the worst of the city sprawl. The Mediterranean flavour is strong in this north-east section of the garden. Large-leaved loquat, Chusan palm, yucca and Italian cypress surround the oval pond, and, in summer, pots of oranges and lemons are set out on the gravel. Traditionally, they were put out on Oak Apple Day (29 May) and taken in on Tavistock Goose Fair Day, the second Wednesday in October, but thanks to climate change the season has been extended. They spend the winter in the white Doric orangery that commands the vista across the West Lawn; partly destroyed by fire in 1932, this was restored by the Trust in 1961.

RIGHT The Managed Retreat Project on the River Plym, showing the river at high tide.

Scotney Castle

LAMBERHURST, TUNBRIDGE WELLS, KENT

AREA 12ha (30 acres) within parkland • SOIL neutral/sand, clay • ALTITUDE 76m (250ft)
AVERAGE RAINFALL 914mm (36in) • AVERAGE WINTER CLIMATE moderate to cold

'Bless'd too is he who, midst his tufted trees, Some ruin'd castle's lofty towers sees / Nodding o'er the stream that glides below.' In 1836, twelve years after the death of Richard Payne Knight, landscape gardener and the author of these lines, this same romantic vision began to take shape here. His friend Edward Hussey, the creator of Scotney, was determined to take advantage of the scenic potential of his site, and in that year he consulted W.S. Gilpin, the noted designer and nephew of the originator of the Picturesque style, William Gilpin. The 'picture' was to be fashioned in its entirety, with Anthony Salvin preparing plans for a new house, which was to command views across the ridge of hills to Goudhurst and down into the Bewl Valley.

The impulse for the composition lay below: a handsome 'medieval' castle, its surviving tower reflecting in a lake-like moat. Really a fortified manor, with sixteenth- and seventeenth-century additions, the castle was too cold and damp for habitation by the family, and Hussey had the walls selectively demolished to leave the present fairytale ruin. Gilpin's work centred on the terrace beside the new house, but Hussey's treatment of the entire valley landscape, with its planted quarry, sinuous sweeps of shrubbery and strikingly shaped trees dramatically sited, was clearly a red-blooded realisation of his and Knight's precepts.

Today, we see a post-1987 landscape, for the storm of that October ripped out many of the limes, beeches, oaks and yews that gave the slopes their curves, together with most of the cedar of Lebanon, Scots pines, incense cedars and Lawson cypresses that furnished the dashing horizontals and verticals between them. The long-term replacement trees, however, are now rising up, enabling fast-growing species such as Leyland cypress, installed as temporary accents, to be felled gradually and the landscape to recapture its old character.

From the bastion, you look out on a scene of great beauty, with the large numbers of deciduous trees and flowering shrubs ensuring a spectacular seasonal cycle. Bold and harmonious banks of shrubs, especially rhododendrons, were welcomed by the advocates of the Picturesque landscape. But for the array and succession of colour, much is owed to subsequent plantings by Christopher Hussey, the architectural historian, who, with his wife Betty, tended his grandfather's creation from 1952 until his death in 1970. Betty Hussey continued to have considerable influence at Scotney over the next 30 years.

Early in the year, waves of primroses and daffodils succeed the snowdrops, and large specimens of *Magnolia stellata* bloom in the quarry. This area, recently cleared and with its rock face exposed, has opened up many more dramatic planting opportunities. In late spring, it is the turn of rhododendrons and scented azaleas, in shades of yellow, cream and orange, accompanied by a mass of wildflowers. In June, the pink bells open on impressive mounds of *Kalmia latifolia*, to be succeeded in late summer by hydrangeas. And in autumn, the valley is filled with the mellow tints and flame highlights of leaves, furnished by Japanese maples, rhus, parrotia, liquidambar, nyssa and stands of royal fern.

The domestic garden is close to the new house and bastion, where Climbing, Shrub and Floribunda roses tumble about a Venetian font, and also in the forecourt of the castle, where Christopher Hussey set out a pattern of beds around the Venetian well-head installed by his aunt; its scheme of herbs was designed

by Lanning Roper, who was Mrs Hussey's garden adviser after her husband's death. Herbaceous and bedding plants fill the border, and roses, vines and wisteria explore the ruined walls.

The octagonal walled kitchen garden, 0.4ha (1 acre) in size, is also now being brought back into production, with the help of a local school, a regular team of volunteers, and members of Centrepoint, a charity for the homeless. Around by the lake, the invasive *Rhododendron ponticum* and its hybrids continue to be cut down and cleared to make way for more interesting plantings. Waterlilies and marsh plants accompany the serene reflections of trees

and castle, and a bronze figure, made and given by Henry Moore in tribute to Christopher Hussey, reclines on the isthmus. This is a powerfully atmospheric place.

LEFT The new house, designed by Anthony Salvin in 1835 in the Elizabethan style.

ABOVE The plantings of vivid colour were designed to fill the valley between the old castle and the new house in the Picturesque style.

Seaton Delaval Hall

WHITLEY BAY, NORTHUMBERLAND

AREA 5.2ha (13 acres) within parkland • SOIL slightly acidic sandy loam • ALTITUDE 30m (100ft) • AVERAGE RAINFALL 610mm (24in) • AVERAGE WINTER CLIMATE moderate

Remnants of a double lime avenue, over 1.6km (1 mile) in length and once accompanied by hefty gate piers, heightens the anticipation on your approach down the A190 (formerly the main estate road) and, turning the corner, you have the great house suddenly and theatrically upon you. A compact palace of now-blackened sandstone, bristling with architectural decoration, Seaton Delaval is one of the masterpieces of the English Baroque, and came to the Trust in 2009 following a major fund-raising campaign, with enthusiastic local support.

Constructed between 1719 and 1730, it was designed by Sir John Vanbrugh, the ebullient playwright and architect of Castle Howard, for Admiral George Delaval, whose Norman ancestor had been granted this estate in the eleventh century. For a more commanding presence and prospect over the sea, the coastal plain and the port of Blyth, Vanbrugh set the hall and its pleasure grounds on a raised platform, with a surrounding ha-ha and a three-quarter-circular bastion on each corner, a layout evocative of a Norman keep – as a former soldier, he frequently took inspiration for his designs from military fortifications. Each bastion sported a lead statuary group on a classical or Biblical theme from the workshop of John Cheere, some of which are now redistributed closer to the hall.

The earliest estate plan known to exist, from 1808 (the property's historical archive is far from complete), shows the hall standing in an asymmetric pattern of broad, formal grass corridors, framed by four large wilderness blocks of densely planted trees, and with a circuit walk above the ha-ha. Both Vanbrugh and Delaval died before the hall's completion, but the theatrical spirit in which it was conceived was savoured by those after them, for it was the setting for many parties and entertainments and the Delaval family were tireless and fun-loving hosts.

Today, as you stand under the rear, south-facing portico of the hall, remarkably little appears to have changed. In front of you, a sweep of grass, flanked by woody thickets containing old limes, beeches and sycamores, carries the eye to an obelisk 0.8km (½ mile) distant. You can still walk the perimeter from bastion to bastion, surveying the fields across the ha-ha, and, within one of the wilderness blocks, enter the little church that dates back to Norman times. The grounds are thus preserved as a rare and handsome survivor from the early transitional phase of English landscape gardening, when enclosed formality was giving way to an open parkland style.

Iron railings, however, now cut across the pleasure grounds close to the house. These were added later in the nineteenth century in Reptonian style to create an inner flower garden, safe from livestock. Its bones are visible in the Ordnance Survey plan of 1860, to which the present flower garden still adheres. The weeping ash, in the semi-circular lawn to the west of the portico, is presumed to date from this period, as do some of the box hedges in the adjacent parterre, which trace the footprint of a wing of the hall that was never built. The other wing to the East was destroyed in the fire

LEFT A view over the box hedging in the Rose Garden.
ABOVE The Baroque house seen from the laburnum walk.

of 1822, which also left the central portion of the hall the empty shell it remains to this day. For by then, the estate had transferred to the Astley/Hastings branch of the family, whose principal seat was in Norfolk.

After a long period of decline, culminating in the requisitioning of the hall for military use in the First World War and for prisoners of war in the Second, the flower garden was revitalised during the 1950s and '60s by the 22nd Lord and Lady Hastings with the help of the connoisseur plantsman James Russell of Sunningdale Nurseries, who, like Vanbrugh, has also left a legacy in the grounds of Castle Howard. The flower garden was revitalised again, after another lull, in the 1980s. A mixed border, featuring traditional favourites such

as delphiniums, hydrangeas, alchemilla, orange alstroemeria and sweet peas, now curves around the lawn, backed by scented yellow and apricot azaleas and stands of red, pink and white Hardy Hybrid rhododendrons.

This kaleidoscope of summer colour is echoed in the rose beds of the parterre, which feature *Rosa* 'Polar Star', *R.* 'Golden Wedding', *R.* 'Pink Peace' and other modern Bush roses in a maze-like pattern of box hedges and narrow gravel paths. Running behind it is a large border of irises, peonies, phlox and pink crinums, with shrubs and climbers such as lemon-scented verbena, jasmine and purple-blotched white *Cistus* × *cyprius* benefiting from the warm, protective south-facing wall. An imposing statue of Samson and a Philistine commands the scene. In quiet contrast beyond is Lady Hastings' Garden, an intimate hedged enclosure with summerhouse, lawn, lily pool and azalea border, accompanied by a small, orchard-like area of ornamental trees. An unexpected laburnum tunnel leads towrds the church, with a statue of the French Crown Prince Imperial by Bosio as its focus.

The principal set-piece scheme is the formal Sunken Garden. In alignment with the decorative wrought-iron gates and courtyard of the house's west wing, and with one of Vanbrugh's bastions forming one of its corners, this is also a ninteenth-century addition which was refurbished in the 1950s by James Russell. The central panel of lawn is flanked across broad gravel walks by side panels, patterned in box and infilled with silver santolina, white-variegated euonymus, hardy fuchsia and standard wisteria. These are backed by lines of grey-leaved whitebeams, clipped as mopheads, and the whole garden is contained within hedges of yew and beech. The central Haddonstone fountain was added in the 1990s.

Archaeological investigation continues across the estate, and there is much still awaiting repair, not least the abandoned walled kitchen garden, complete with its brick-lined pond and splendid stone Orangery. There is a good view across to it from Vanbrugh's north-east bastion.

LEFT A view past the statue of David slaying Goliath over the Rose Garden at Seaton Delaval Hall.

RIGHT Delphinium 'Blue Lagoon' in bloom.

Sheffield Park Garden and Estate

SHEFFIELD PARK, EAST SUSSEX

AREA 49ha (120 acres) within 107ha (265 acres) of parkland • SOIL acid/heavy clay
ALTITUDE 91m (300ft) • AVERAGE RAINFALL 889mm (35in) • AVERAGE WINTER CLIMATE
moderate

The reflections in the water of coloured leaves, soaring conifers, balustraded bridges, cascades and the towers and pinnacles of the gothick mansion give Sheffield Park an unmistakable sense of place. The axes of the garden are the four lakes, which are strung down the southerly slope below the house in an inverted 'T' formation. This is an ornamental landscape of dazzling scale and richness, planted above all for the drama of shape, trees, rhododendrons and autumn foliage, and encompassing nearly 162ha (400 acres) of meadow, marsh, woodland and glade.

The estate belonged to the Earls of Sheffield until it was purchased in 1909 by Arthur Soames, a Lincolnshire brewer, who had coveted the park since visiting it 20 years earlier. It was then that the rich overlay was applied. Scarlet oaks, Japanese maples, nyssas and amelanchiers were woven around the lakesides in the boldest drifts, complemented by new stands of giant conifers and seams of rhododendrons. But plant variety was always secondary to landscape impact, and Soames barely indulged in the new Chinese and South American introductions then being welcomed into other great woodland gardens.

These carefully conceived pictorial scenes were ravaged by the storm of October 1987. Shelter belts were devastated, ornamental trees brought down by the dozen, and much of the creative work of renewal and expansion carried out by the Trust over 30 years was undone. But the core of the garden survived largely intact, the native oaks were high-pruned and have regenerated splendidly and replanting has continued apace. Only those visitors acquainted with the previous landscape will now sense the loss.

The circuit of the park follows lazy figures of eight, and if all the tributary paths and glades are explored, and periodic pauses taken to savour the views, it lasts the best part of a day. No season is disappointing. In spring, the park wakes to camellias and a grass sward spangled with bulbs. You walk down banks sheeted with wild Lent lilies, *Narcissus pseudonarcissus*, and as the many old hybrid daffodils succeed them, there are the warm tints of amelanchiers and maples among the expanding greenery, and the scents of osmanthus on the air.

May brings the first great climax of colour, with pink and white dogwoods and the many thickets of rhododendrons and azaleas flowering in an ocean of bluebells. The palette is subtly graded, with the softer tones predominating through stands of tall, fragrant Loderi rhododendrons and other whites and pastels. Crimson, pink and purple Hardy Hybrids are grouped around the upper lake, and the more vibrant orange and gold Exbury azaleas (superb against copper beech), intense carmine and rose evergreen Kurume azaleas and electrifying violet-blue rhododendron hybrids (partnered with creams and lime-yellows) are gathered in their own glades. The zany group of 'Hinomayo' azaleas, clipped tight in late autumn and looking uncannily like a flock of brilliant pink sheep, is guaranteed especially to startle the eye.

By now, the purple beech and maples are reflecting sumptuously in the lakes, and the emerald leaves of the other deciduous trees have thrown the huge wellingtonias, redwoods, pines and cedars into deep relief. Every path has its quiet interludes, from sparkling glades of birch (the cream trunks looking well among the bluebells), to exotic and solemn groves of hardy Chusan palms, cypresses and hemlocks. Among these trees, the connoisseur will find rarities galore, including *Athrotaxis laxifolia* from Tasmania, *Pinus montezumae* from Mexico and *Fagus engleriana* from China.

One of the Trust's policies, as in many other woodland gardens, has been to enrich the summer display and, accordingly, an extensive collection of the late-flowering Ghent azaleas has been assembled (now the National Collection), together with hydrangeas – lacecaps in particular. There are no formal beds of herbaceous plants at Sheffield Park, but the lakes are edged in moisture-loving species and have their rafts of waterlilies. In 1979, the banks of the stream, west of the lowest lake, were also enriched.

The advent of the park's second climax is heralded by the red tints on spindle trees and *Prunus sargentii*. By mid-October, the landscape is alight with colour. At ground level, fiery hues break out among azaleas, fothergillas, enkianthus, blueberry and berberis, the

flames rising through amelanchier, parrotia, Japanese maples, *Acer circinatum* and *A. maximowiczianum* (syn. *nikoense*), to engulf the American oaks, the celebrated grove of tupelos (*Nyssa sylvatica*), and, a little later, the liquidambars. Simultaneously, the numerous birches have turned to butter yellow, the columns of deciduous conifers (*Taxodium* and *Metasequoia*) to orange-brown, and the native trees to copper and russet. Added to all this are plumes of white pampas grass, sky-blue streaks of autumn gentians (linear beds of *Gentiana sino-ornata* – another quirky touch), complementary domes and spires of evergreens, the lakes and James Wyatt's fantasy architecture.

In spite of its exotic content, the park is a tranquil place to stroll, the underlying mood set by the expanses of grass and water, the native trees and wildflowers. Beyond the third lake, the exotics melt away almost entirely as you follow the Trust's new walk that takes you, via rustic bridges of hornbeam, across a marsh. Native

sedges and bog plants grow here between thickets of alder and willow, and it is the haunt of kingfishers, grebe, marsh tits and several species of duck. The East Park, with its large population of spotted orchids, is tended as a wildflower reserve and is not at present open to the public, but the South Park, reattached to the estate in 2006 and spanning an additional 107ha (265 acres), is open and undergoing restoration. The park's cricket field, the scene of the first tour matches against the Australians between 1884 and 1896, has also recently been revived, with matches played throughout the summer months.

ABOVE An almost perfect reflection of autumn colour in the Middle Lake.

Sheringham Park

UPPER SHERINGHAM, NORFOLK

AREA 20ha (50 acres) within parkland • **SOIL** sandy, some clay • **ALTITUDE** 76m (250ft)
AVERAGE RAINFALL 508mm (20in) • **AVERAGE WINTER CLIMATE** mild

'After having passed nearly half a century in the study of Natural Scenery, and having been professionally consulted in the improvement of many hundred places in different parts of England, I can with truth pronounce that Sheringham possesses more natural beauty and local advantages than any place I have ever seen.' So declared the great landscape gardener Humphry Repton in his Red Book of proposals, watercolours and before-and-after overlays prepared for Sheringham's new owner, Abbot Upcher, in 1812.

Having lived in Norfolk on and off throughout his life (he is buried at nearby Aylsham), Repton had a special attachment to the county's landscape and knew this coastal estate well. When Sheringham came up for sale, it was his solicitor son William who handled its legal conveyance, and at the very moment Upcher came into William's office to sign the contract, Repton (by now wheelchair-bound following a carriage accident the previous year) was 'coincidentally' paying his son a visit. He secured the commission to design both the landscape and the hall, passing on the job of actually building the new house to another of his sons, the architect John Adey Repton.

Repton's skills were at their apogee, and this is considered one of the most complete and best-preserved of his commissions. Walking down the long entrance drive, you are taken over and around one of the wooded ridges and low hills that frame the hall and its pastoral coombe. The topography was well used by Repton to block and control the views and play with light and shadow, the upper ground being already well furnished with shelter belts, and the fields and slopes with old oaks, limes and beech which remain a feature of the estate.

As you descend, it is the sea that is first revealed, less than 1.6km (1 mile) away across the heathland, cliffs and shingle to the north, together with a windmill and coastguard cottages silhouetted against it. And then, as you veer east at a point known as The Turn, the hall comes handsomely into view, again with a flash of sea beyond. A large villa in the style of John Nash (its stone brought here by ship from Yorkshire), it looks inland across a ha-ha into meadow parkland, protected from the coastal winds by Oak Wood Hill. There is a small pond nearby and, enclosed in iron railings, a small pleasure garden (the hall is privately tenanted and, with the garden, is not open to the public). On the opposite flank of hill, the hall has its architectural eye-catcher in the form of a small domed Temple, designed by Repton but not in fact constructed until 1975. It is a fine scene.

Knowing the local weather conditions, Repton persuaded Upcher not to contemplate siting the house on the exposed side of the hill, so there is no sea view from the hall. But if you penetrate Oak Wood Hill you will find a remarkable gazebo in the form of a high wooden stairway and platform, offering a panorama of the locality. It was erected in 1975 on the site of a look-out post built during the Napoleonic Wars.

Repton liked his landscapes to offer diversion and variety, and this encompassed human and agricultural activity. From the outset he suggested that 'proper persons' be allowed to walk the estate one day in the week and admire its views. No doubt he would also have

enjoyed the white plumes, clatter and whistles of the steam trains of the North Norfolk Railway that run along the estate's coastline today. In front of the hall, he banished fences and cereal crops in favour of livestock roaming and grazing on a sweep of grass, which they continue to do. Nature also provides animation, the quiet habitats fostering a range of species from newts to nightjars (even, occasionally, golden orioles), with the orchids and wildflowers in the unimproved meadow grass attracting a diversity of butterflies, moths and other insects.

Sadly, Abbot Upcher died of fever in 1819 before the hall was completed, and it was not finally finished until 20 years later. But while Repton's vision for the broader landscape was adopted by successive members of the Upcher family, a major transformation took place in the woods flanking the main approach drive; from around 1850, and on through the twentieth century, the family indulged in the fashionable taste for rhododendrons.

The panoply of colour from some 20ha (50 acres) of hillside painted in purples, pinks, reds and assorted clashing tints is quite a spectacle, and there are two viewing towers that invite you to climb up among their cloud-like canopies. Many of the plants are so big and so densely packed that it is hard to appreciate them from below, until the flowers drop and create further carpets of colour on the ground. It seems puzzling that they would thrive so well in this dry climate, but the answer lies in the combination of overhead shade from the oaks, Scots pines, sycamores, sweet chestnuts and beech, their fine sponge-like root systems, and the high coastal humidity.

There is early action in the woods from groupings of shell-pink *Rhododendron* 'Christmas Cheer', together with thickets of camellias, but the climax comes in May and June when yellow and orange azaleas are scenting the air above the bluebells and red campion, and old hybrid rhododendrons such as blazing red 'Britannia', 'Pink Pearl', and purple-blotched, white 'Sappho' are in full eruption, all merrily arranged with little concern for colour scheming.

The paths lead under towering forms of *Rhododendron arboreum* and *R. ponticum*. Over the years, the latter – together with many hybrids, grown on *ponticum* rootstock, which have reverted to type – have spread extensively, and are gradually being extracted and replaced, though the job has to be done judiciously as they are valuable windbreaks.

Numerous other rhododendron species and selections add exciting ambushes as you walk down the drive and explore the side tracks. Blotched pink and white *R. calophytum*, slender-leaved *R. strigillosum*, white *R. niveum*, and large-flowered, scented pink and white forms of *R. decorum* and *R. fortunei* are among the company, with yellow-belled *R. cinnabarinum* subsp. *xanthocodon* notable not only for its beauty but for its resilience to the fatal mildew attack to which its tribe is peculiarly prone.

Importantly, many of these rhododendrons are from wild-collected seed, which Henry Morris Upcher obtained by subscribing to the Chinese expeditions of the plant hunter Ernest Wilson in the first decade of the twentieth century. Other Wilson plants here are *Magnolia sieboldii* subsp. *sinensis*, handkerchief tree (*Davidia involucrata*), the pink-berried rowan *Sorbus hupehensis*, and *Dipelta floribunda*, a large shrub with blush-white, funnel-shaped flowers in late spring, and a programme to propagate them to preserve their genetic heritage is in hand. In the 1950s, Henry's grandson Thomas Upcher continued to plant rhododendrons enthusiastically, holding champagne parties at peak flowering time.

All this creates a much more ornamental approach to the hall than Humphry Repton envisaged, but beyond the woods there is little intrusion upon his landscape, which remains calm and green and which he would still recognise as 'my most favourite work'.

LEFT A mysterious tunnel of old rhododendrons.

PREVIOUS PAGE *Rhododendron ponticum* in the wild garden in June.

Shugborough Estate

MILFORD, STAFFORD, STAFFORDSHIRE

AREA 9ha (22 acres) • SOIL acid/sandy loam • ALTITUDE 30m (100ft)
AVERAGE RAINFALL 686mm (27in) • AVERAGE WINTER CLIMATE cold

The capture of a Spanish treasure galleon in 1743 brought a fortune in prize money to Captain George Anson RN, later Admiral Lord Anson, and with this wealth, the fashionable improvements to the family estate at Shugborough, already being wrought by his older, bachelor brother Thomas, took on a new breadth and scale.

Entering the park through the belt of woodland beside the Stafford road (which is currently in the process of having its diseased and invasive understorey of *Rhododendron ponticum* eradicated), you get an immediate taste of the second phase of Thomas Anson's work. Down the drive, to left and right, three classical monuments appear in quick succession: on one side, the Lanthorn of Demosthenes, a cylindrical building with Corinthian columns, capped by a decorative tripod; on the other, mounted on a knoll, a Triumphal Arch, adorned with busts of Admiral and Lady Anson; and beyond, the Tower of the Winds, a slim octagon with windows and pedimented porches. The monuments are no longer part of a purely Picturesque landscape, for following a disastrous flood in 1795, which swept away many of Anson's other garden features, John Webb, a pupil of William Emes, was engaged to remodel the park, and with agriculture now the prime interest, its character altered. Trees, planted in great numbers in the 1820s and afterwards, have also changed the views. The setting is mellow and pastoral – flat, low-lying ground at the confluence of the rivers Sow and Trent (an attractive packhorse bridge crosses at the join), with the wild expanse of Cannock Chase rising behind.

The drive curves towards the east façade of the mansion, remodelled by Samuel Wyatt around the turn of the nineteenth century and rather ghostly in its milk-grey, ashlar-like cladding. But before you reach it, or explore the park, you are taken to the recently restored walled kitchen garden. Built in 1805, in its heyday this was one of the country's foremost productive gardens, with pioneering cultivation techniques, notably with pineapples. The gardening is now concentrated in the main 0.7ha (1¾ acre) enclosure, but this would have been part of a sequence of walled and hedged compartments. The design is traditional, with four beds set around a central oval dipping pond, and many old vegetable varieties are grown in them, including golden and striped beetroot and 'Scarlet Emperor' bean. Early nineteenth-century apples and pears are espaliered on the walls. To fuel the mood, gardeners work in period costume.

The old head gardener's house within the garden looks appealing, but it had a major drawback. Smoke from the flanking glasshouse heating systems used to be channelled into its upper storey during the day, to be released at night, so as not to disturb the serenity of Anson's landscape. The glasshouses are no longer here, but it is hoped they can be rebuilt in the future.

The walk down to the house leads past the model farm. There are some fine wisterias on the coach house, and in the midden yard you will find the celebrated edible blue-flowered pea *Lathyrus nervosus*, brought from Patagonia by Captain Anson's cook and known as Lord Anson's Blue Pea. But the gardens lie behind and to the sides of the house, and it is here that you encounter Thomas Anson's earlier, more eclectic structures, absorbed into a nineteenth-century layout of formal lawns and flower schemes, and gently meandering pleasure grounds, all strung along an arm of the River Sow, which flows directly below the house. To the south, on the site of Anson's shrubbery, is the loop of the Ladies' Walk, leading between oak, beech and lime trees (including a particularly fine weeping silver lime), past banks of ornamental shrubs and on to open lawn beside the water, where massed daffodils are followed by a riverside fringe of meadowsweet, lythrum, cow parsley and other wildflowers. The Blue Bridge invites you over the river to explore the arboretum and its collection of American and Asian oaks – an enthusiasm of the late Lord (Patrick) Lichfield.

Rhododendrons used to abound in the pleasure grounds, but are now gradually being replaced by period shrubs such as philadelphus, species roses and laurels. Brooms, snowberry, osmanthus and the late-flowering buckeye *Aesculus parviflora* are also among the cast along the Ladies' Walk. Around the lawns and glades to the north of the house, the colour is boosted by fiery plantings of Ghent azaleas and a lavish new herbaceous border, and here you will also come upon an impressive weeping holly and a common yew of gigantic proportions, noted in 1898 as being one of the most remarkable in the country, and shading 0.2ha (½ acre) of ground.

As you arrive in front of the house, the mood becomes strongly Victorian. A series of terraced lawns, set out by W.A. Nesfield in about 1855, replaces Anson's bowling green, and glowing cones of golden yew process down them towards the river, contrasting with the purple beech and plum woven into the backdrop of trees. This provocative yellow and purple contrast, much favoured at the time, has been intensified by beds of the canary-coloured Floribunda rose 'Bright Smile' and seams of 'Hidcote' lavender. Heliotropes, variegated helichrysums and blue lobelias are grown in the stone troughs and blue petunias in the urns. Close by, a rose garden in more delicate late nineteenth-century style has been reconstructed by the Trust. This takes the form of a pattern of small formal beds and ironwork arches arranged around a sundial, once more against the challenging backdrop of golden yew. But because of *Phytophthora* disease, the roses are now being replaced by clematis, accompanied by architectural blocks of herbaceous plants such as Japanese anemones, sedum and echinacea, in similar colours of pink, purple and white.

Beside the river, directly below the house, you pick up the first in the remaining series of garden buildings belonging to Anson's early phase of Rococo landscaping. Here stands the fragment of a ruin, with a rubble crag and the remains of a Coade-stone druid attached. At the turn of the river is the Chinese House, a white pavilion reflecting elegantly in the water; it was the first building Anson erected, in about 1747, and an early example of the new taste for chinoiserie. It is set off by a red iron bridge, and planting of an oriental flavour, including bamboo, stephanandra, berberis and Katsura tree (*Cercidiphyllum japonicum*). The scarlet lacquered stems of dogwood and some young dawn redwoods (*Metasequoia*) add to the atmosphere.

The Red Bridge leads you to an island between the two sections of the River Sow where, against a backdrop of yew, you meet the Cat's Monument – now widely believed to commemorate the ship's cat on Admiral Anson's circumnavigation of the globe in 1740–44. Returning to the main, curving gravel path, you encounter the Shepherd's Monument. A cryptic sequence of letters runs along its base, but the centrepiece is a marble tablet depicting a pastoral scene by Poussin and inscribed with a phrase that resonated in many an eighteenth-century landowner, '*Et in Arcadia ego*'.

LEFT The Chinese House was the first garden building erected by Lord Anson.

ABOVE Brilliant magenta and flame azaleas flourish here.

Sissinghurst Castle

SISSINGHURST, CRANBROOK, KENT

AREA 2.4ha (6 acres) • SOIL neutral/clay • ALTITUDE 61m (200ft) • AVERAGE RAINFALL 737mm (29in) • AVERAGE WINTER CLIMATE moderate

The sudden view of Sissinghurst's twin-turreted tower, rising from the open farmland, always brings a surge of anticipation. The garden's reputation, reinforced by talented head gardeners, sails before it, and anyone who has been here knows it is not exaggerated. The Trust, which must cope with the wear and congestion caused by the large numbers of visitors, discourages publicity and occasionally uses timed tickets, but people still return in their droves. Over 30 years, I have been one of them.

'To Vita Sackville-West, who made this garden,' reads the tablet under the Tower. Vita saw the castle for the first time in April 1930. 'I fell in love; love at first sight. I saw what might be made of it. It was Sleeping Beauty's Castle; but a castle running away into sordidness and squalor; a garden crying out for rescue.' An aerial photograph of July 1932 shows the site cleared and the gardens laid out in front of the South Cottage and Priest's House. By May 1938, when Sissinghurst opened to the public for the first time, all the bones of the garden were in place and the new plantings maturing.

Vita's husband, Harold Nicolson, was responsible for the pattern of the design. A diplomat, biographer, journalist and politician, he was also, according to Vita, an 'architect manqué', delighting in the pleasures of 'square-ruled paper … stakes and string'. They decided upon a formal, emphatic structure: 'Long, axial walks, running north and south, east and west, usually with terminal points such as a statue or an archway or a pair of sentinel poplars, and the more intimate surprise of small geometrical gardens opening off them, rather as the rooms of an enormous house would open off the arterial corridors,' wrote Vita. Comparisons with Hidcote

Manor are perhaps inevitable, though there is no evidence that Harold or Vita visited it before laying out their garden. The principal ingredient that distinguishes Sissinghurst from Hidcote, however, is the romance. At Sissinghurst are the ancient buildings, the moat and, above all, the fairytale tower, the garden's centrepiece, built shortly before Queen Elizabeth's visit in 1573; visible from most parts of the site, it lifts the eye from the enclosed spaces, and, from its roof, you have the opportunity of a bird's-eye view of the garden.

Then there is the all-pervading character of Vita herself. Her writing room in the Tower is much as she left it, with a cape primrose or other flowering pot plant on the table, for visitors intrigued by her intricate private life or admiring of her writing to come to inspect.

The tour begins in the courtyard, where Irish yews process from the entrance arch to the tower, between pads of tightly mown lawn. As at Hidcote, the mood of the beds and garden rooms is set by a clearly defined colour scheme. Here, there are plants echoing the salmon and copper tones of the brick: chaenomeles, evergreen magnolia with its suede-backed leaves, Climbing roses like 'Gloire

LEFT Agapanthus and anemone in the Rose Garden with the Tower in the distance
ABOVE Statue of Dionysus in the Nuttery in spring.

de Dijon' and apple-scented 'Paul Transon', and, in late summer, the burnished foliage and orange hips of *Rosa moyesii* 'Geranium'. But there are also contrasting notes: in spring, bushes of rosemary, injecting a rich shade of blue at the foot of the tower (the variety, 'Sissinghurst Blue', occurred here as a seedling); in summer, *Solanum crispum* 'Glasnevin', hanging a lilac veil over the east wall. Then there are the troughs and pots, the former simply filled with trailing blue *Euphorbia myrsinites* or white osteospermums, and the latter perhaps with the damson pelargonium 'Lord Bute'. In the main, plants at Sissinghurst are not blended into salads, but displayed as individuals, in generous groups, and with well-chosen partners that show off their shape and habit.

All this intensifies in the deep, south-facing border, where purple, violet-blue, mauve-pink and magenta perennials and climbers are assembled. The plant arrangement is masterly, with purple vine and clematis such as 'Perle d'Azur' and 'Ville de Lyon' cloaking the wall behind, and a well-matched succession of middle and foreground flowers, from tulips, wallflowers and dwarf irises to black-eyed *Geranium psilostemon*, platycodon (the campanula-like balloon flower), lythrum and asters.

At midsummer, the first path to take is to the Rose Garden, now awash with the petal-packed, scent-drenched flowers of the old-fashioned Shrub varieties that were Vita's passion. For her, they were infused with the romance of legend, poetry and the East – with the bazaars of Constantinople, where one afternoon, 'the rugs and carpets of Isfahan and Bokhara and Samarcand were unrolled in their dim but sumptuous colouring and richness of texture for our slow delight'. Irises, peonies, violas, pinks and alliums spread a Persian carpet beneath them, and on the curved wall at the west end of the garden there is that much-photographed curtain of *Clematis* 'Perle d'Azur'; this feat is achieved by regular training and tying-in of shoots through the spring and summer months. Plantings of Rugosa roses, single-flowered Hybrid Teas and Hybrid Musks extend the rose season beyond mid-July, and in autumn there is a second flush from many others. Japanese anemones, sedums, caterpillar-like pennisetum grasses, caryopteris, lavatera and felt-leaved *Hydrangea aspera* Villosa Group are then in full bloom.

Much of the late summer colour comes from tender perennials – plants that must be propagated annually by cuttings and over-wintered under glass. Vita would have known few of the many varieties now used here to take over from the biennial wallflowers, honesty and foxgloves. Their greatest concentration is in the adjacent Cottage Garden – from spring to autumn, a cauldron of oranges,

yellows and tropical reds. Wallflowers, tulips, irises, daylilies, euphorbias, helianthemums and coloured grasses fire up the garden earlier in the year, and then, from midsummer, it is the turn of Mexican salvias, argyranthemums, leonotis, cannas, dahlias and the sheets of the daisy-like arctotis hybrids, grown under the brick walls of the cottage. The contents of the verdigris laundry copper in the centre of the garden usually turn from the plum-splashed orange tulip 'Prinses Irene' to *Osteospermum* 'Orange Symphony'. Roses are ubiquitous partners. Together with figs and vines, Sissinghurst's old walls seemed to Vita to cry out for them: 'I planted them recklessly, and have never regretted it'. Here, the glowing red 'Parkdirektor Riggers' partners orange honeysuckle, and, from the cottage wall, 'Madame Alfred Carrière' gives soft white backlighting.

Below, a strip of lawn runs down to the moat, flanked on one side by a bank of deciduous azaleas – as fiery in their autumn leaf tints as they are in their flowers – and an old plantation of Kentish cobnuts, below which is an idealised woodland understorey of shuttlecock ferns and perennials such as geraniums, trilliums and uvularia. The richest spring surprise is sprung in the pleached lime walk, where primroses, anemones, muscari, species tulips, narcissi and a host of other bulbs are planted in mixed colours and assorted groups at the base of the trunks, to the accompaniment of alpine clematis spilling from Italian oil jars. This was Harold Nicolson's personal garden, and his diaries record the many happy hours spent planning and improving the display each year, aided by visits to the Royal Horticultural Society's spring shows at Vincent Square.

Herbs, with their historical and poetic associations, were assured a home at Sissinghurst. They are formally arranged in their own enclosure, around a camomile seat and a lion-guarded bowl, and with rugs of prostrate thymes laid at the entrance: patterned pink, white and crimson in summer, these are perhaps my favourite single feature, but, like so much of Sissinghurst's planting, do depend on a very high level of maintenance – intricate hand-weeding and frequent renewal of plants.

From here, you walk past the moat wall, hung with white wisteria and lapped, from August to October, with the lavender daisies of *Aster × frikartii* 'Mönch', and into the orchard. This area, bordered on two sides by water, is the garden's only open and expansive compartment, and provides a welcome interlude. In spring, gold, citron, cream and white daffodils, in separate but interlocking drifts, appear en masse under the apple and cherry trees. In summer, there are wildflowers in the grass and Rambler roses foaming lavishly in the branches.

Returning to the walls and hedges, there is still much to see. There is the Tower Lawn, with its 'Albertine' roses and a shady sunken garden; there is Delos, with its magnolias and ferns; and there is the most famous compartment of all. 'I am trying to make a grey, green and white garden,' wrote Vita in one of her weekly gardening articles for the *Observer* in January 1950. The idea transported her readers, and the garden itself prompted countless imitations. The images hardly need describing: *Lilium regale*, white delphiniums, irises, eremurus, galtonias and *Onopordum* thistles rising above cushions of artemisia and hosta; a weeping silver pear (the original fell in the great storm of October 1987; the present one is a replacement) sheltering the lead statue of a virgin; an ironwork bower covered in the white Rambler rose *R. mulliganii*, and the Priest's House in *R.* 'Madame Alfred Carrière' and *R.* 'Cooperi'. The colours span every tint and tone, with each plant sited for maximum impact of shape, height and leaf size.

'It may be a terrible failure,' added Vita with her customary modesty. 'All the same, I cannot help hoping that the great ghostly barn owl will sweep silently across the pale garden next summer in the twilight, that I am now planting under the first flakes of snow.' Whether or not it is twilight when you leave Sissinghurst, I recommend this enclosure as your departing image: a sorbet after the feast of colour.

Staffed separately from the main garden, and with the help of volunteers, Sissinghurst's new vegetable garden is now supplying large quantities of organic produce to the restaurant. A variety of crops is grown in large beds, edged in grass paths, including salads, leeks, potatoes, courgettes, brassicas and soft fruit such as gooseberries, raspberries, currants, rhubarb and strawberries. A new orchard has also been planted recently, adjacent to the car park, comprising apples, pears, cherries and plums.

ABOVE A carefully colour-schemed display of old roses and geraniums.

NEXT PAGE White cosmos, sweet peas and solanum in the White Garden.

Sizergh Castle

KENDAL, CUMBRIA

AREA 7.3ha (18 acres) • SOIL neutral/shallow loam overlying limestone • ALTITUDE 61m (200ft) • AVERAGE RAINFALL 1,270mm (50in) • AVERAGE WINTER CLIMATE mild to moderate

Just to the east of the castle's fourteenth-century tower is one of the most impressive rock gardens in the Trust's hands. Built in 1926 by the noted Ambleside firm of T.R. Hayes & Sons, it is an 0.1ha (½ acre) bowl of rough limestone terraces, contained within a dell and watered by streams, pools and falls fed from the natural pond above. Originally more open, the garden now has a fringe of sizeable conifers, including Bhutan, Arolla and mountain pines, maples and other ornamental trees, creating a quieter, leafier, more secret world within. On the lower banks, many of the dwarfer conifers, which punctuate the various meandering walks with numerous green and purple Japanese cut-leaved maples, have been allowed to mature into magnificent specimens.

The semi-prostrate Caucasian fir, golden Westfelton yew and weeping hemlock are among the most memorable, but every path takes you past curiosities in the form of miniature Norway spruce, noble fir, junipers and chamaecyparis, interspersed with taller gems such as the Japanese umbrella pine, *Sciadopitys verticillata*. A number of outsized conifers have been selectively felled to make room for them, to expose the contours of the bowl and to let in the sun. But as the high-altitude alpines have been shaded and elbowed out, the bowl has become filled with an alternative cast, appreciative of moisture and dappled light. The prime sources of flower colour are no longer the rock plants but the woodland geraniums and the bog and aquatic plants along the watercourses. Cool and moist, the dell has also become a paradise for ferns ranging from shield and sword ferns (*Polystichum*), bladder ferns (*Cystopteris*), delicate maidenhairs (*Adiantum*) to elegant forms of the royal fern, including the

miniature *Osmunda regalis* 'Gracilis'. Sizergh can now boast one of the finest plant collections in the country, including four National Collections.

Part of the success of the rock garden is that it is a locally inspired feature. This is limestone country and Sizergh's 607ha (1,500 acre) estate encompasses screes, cliffs and pavements, as well as panoramic views of the distant Lakeland fells (the walks also take in some fine tracts of ancient woodland). These habitats are rich in wildflowers, and there is a taste of this abundance on the bank east of the castle and in the meadow below the rock garden, where the wild Lent lily, *Narcissus pseudonarcissus*, is followed by a kaleidoscope of local species, including early purple, twayblade, fly and butterfly orchids, meadow geranium, ladies' smock, quaking grass, vetches and ox-eye daisies – the colours augmented by orange-tipped butterflies and much other insect life.

Elsewhere, natural themes are pursued with more decorative plants. The thin shady grass above the rock garden is lit in spring with crocus, scillas, dog's tooth violets and double white anemones,

ABOVE Looking over the yew topiary in the Dutch Garden towards the solar tower.
RIGHT The Rock Garden is a tapestry of conifers, ferns and Japanese maples.

to the accompaniment of the white Mount Fuji cherry, *Prunus* 'Shirotae'. Thousands of daffodils bloom under the orchard's fruit trees, which include many northern apple varieties such as 'Keswick Codlin' and 'White Melrose' as well as plums, damsons, quinces and medlars. The nearby kitchen garden was opened in 2003 and comprises beds of cut flowers, herbs, soft fruit and vegetables, structured by hedges of step-over apple trees. To the west of the house, you walk through a pyramid-shaped avenue of yews into an area of grassy glades, shaded by magnolias, handkerchief tree and more flowering cherries.

The castle itself, built originally as a defence against the marauding Scots and the home of the Strickland family for over 750 years, rises above the garden lake. Alternate pears and vines have recently been planted along the brick-faced hot wall beside the massive grey edifice, fronted by a narrow bed filled with bulbs for a long succession of colour. Thousands more bulbs accompany the cherry avenue on the second grass terrace below, formerly an elaborate Dutch parterre, which runs between a summer-house and flights of stone steps. The second stairway descends to a bastion over the garden lake, created from the former moat. Much of this is also the work of T.R. Hayes.

Everywhere, the walls, balustrades and paving are decorated with plants: fuchsias, honeysuckle, *Clematis montana* and big-leaved *Vitis coignetiae*. The mauve *Erinus alpinus* colonises the castle's own stairway, and the pink and white daisies of *Erigeron karvinskianus* has seeded high into the wall crevices. These details play against the grander scenery: the still sheet of water, in which the castle and fringe of manna ash, willow, sumach and weeping hornbeam are reflected; the rolling parkland, with its fine walnuts and field maples; and beyond, the looming Howgill hills.

ABOVE Plumes of aruncus in the herbaceous border in June.

Smallhythe Place

SMALLHYTHE, TENTERDEN, KENT

AREA 2ha (5 acres) • SOIL alkaline/loam, brown soil and gravel • ALTITUDE 5m (16ft)
AVERAGE WINTER CLIMATE mild

'There was something of wildness in her nature, something wilful and untamed, something almost fey, which assorts well with this brave old house, with these rich beams, these windows giving onto the green valley, this isolation among fields …' So wrote the critic E.V. Lucas, after visiting Ellen Terry here in her half-timbered farmhouse on the edge of Romney Marsh.

The most celebrated actress on the late nineteenth-century London stage, Ellen Terry discovered Smallhythe Place while on a drive with her theatrical partner Henry Irving in the 1890s. She asked a local shepherd to let her know if it should ever come up for sale, and in 1899 it was hers. She was then a widow in her fifties, and this was her escape from London, the house unpretentious with its leaning walls and geraniums on the windowsill, and the garden sleepy with roses and wildflowers.

Traffic on the adjacent road through the village now disturbs the idyll a little, at least on arrival, but there is still a sense of rural retreat as you look across the low-lying fields and pick up the croak of the frogs (a particularly vociferous Continental species, introduced in the 1930s) among the reeds and water iris of the pond. Hard as it is to believe of today's land-locked Smallhythe, this lung of water was once navigable from the sea, and part of a repair dock for ships.

A privet hedge, topped with mop-headed thorn trees and a run of pollarded limes, separates the garden from the road, and around the house the flower-beds are stuffed with cottage favourites such as marjoram, knapweed and love-in-a-mist. Terry loved roses. Red 'Étoile de Hollande', salmon-pink 'Albertine', flesh-pink 'Ophelia', and the continuous flowering, pinkish-yellow 'Phyllis Bide' climb up

the walls, and just beside the house, a grass path, edged in cottage pinks (*Dianthus*), leads you into a formal rose garden.

Renovated by the Trust, the rose garden is now a mixture of old-fashioned and repeat-flowering Shrub roses, such as lemon-white 'Kronprinzessin Viktoria von Preussen' and crimson 'De Rescht', together with late nineteenth- and early twentieth-century Floribundas and Hybrid Teas including white 'Yvonne Rabier' and the eponymous yellow 'Ellen Terry', introduced in 1925, the year she became a Dame. Violets, thyme, wild strawberry and poached egg plant contribute to the froth of herbaceous plants between them.

Elsewhere in the garden, there is a looser geometry of orchard, nuttery and tree-studded lawns, the few exotics – lilacs, magnolias and philadelphus for spring and summer, red oak and parrotia for autumn tints – blending with the native hedgerows and fruit trees. The old tennis court has a notable colony of snakeshead fritillaries, which turns the grass crimson-purple in late spring, and which, together with the daffodils and bluebells, adds to the display of wildflowers, including primrose, wood anemone, cuckoo flower and adder's tongue fern.

At the top of the garden looms the village church, as well as the cottage lived in by Terry's daughter Edy, complete with its topiary peacock. On her mother's death in 1928, Edy turned Smallhythe Place into a theatrical museum and converted the barn into a theatre, attracting an array of stars including Terry's great-nephew, John Gielgud. Performances are still staged here every year.

ABOVE The roses were laid out to Ellen Terry's design, such was her love of the flower.

Snowshill Manor

SNOWSHILL, BROADWAY, GLOUCESTERSHIRE

AREA 0.8ha (2 acres) • SOIL neutral to lime/light loam • ALTITUDE 229m (750ft)
AVERAGE RAINFALL 660mm (26in) • AVERAGE WINTER CLIMATE cold

From the mid-nineteenth century, the honey-coloured villages of the Cotswold hills – unspoilt, harmonious, rich in vernacular detail and an alluring antidote to the growing Victorian industrialisation – became an idyll and inspiration to a succession of painters, illustrators, craftsmen and other adherents to the Arts and Crafts creed. Charles Paget Wade, an architect, artist and woodworker, and a tireless collector of curios, saw a *Country Life* advertisement for the sale of Snowshill Manor in 1919. His legacy is one of the most extraordinary houses in the country, and the garden, anchored to the steeply sloping hillside below, is no less absorbing.

Here you will find a gold and green patchwork of intimate walled courts, narrow corridors, terraces, ponds and rustic outbuildings, idiosyncratically ornamented and sensitively planted. In spring and summer, a lively mix of cottage flowers, dispersed in repeated stands down the long outer path, injects a swathe of bright colour across the mellow composition: tulips, oriental poppies, lupins, foxgloves, veronica, lime-green alchemilla and purple sage are among the company. With white doves disporting on the roof of the medieval dovecote, the tops of clematis and roses visible beyond, and the fresh greens of the countryside all about, this is traditional England at its picture-postcard best.

All parts of the garden have their flower-filled moments. Here and there, you will come upon mixed beds of hellebores and Japanese anemones (an excellent, long-lasting partnership for partial shade), peonies, phloxes, lavender, acanthus, thalictrum and viola; steps fringed with red valerian; grass strewn with daffodils; and walls hung with roses. Wade found blue, mauve and purple toned best

with the stone, and these he allowed to predominate, with secondary use of salmons and creams, and sparing use of reds and yellows. Orange was banished.

This is emphatically an architect's garden. 'A garden is an extension of the house, a series of outdoor rooms,' Wade wrote, echoing contemporary philosophy. 'The plan is much more important than the flowers in it. Walls, steps and alleyways give a permanent setting, so that it is pleasant and orderly in both summer and winter.' Each room has its rustic details and crafted ornament: gate-piers, troughs and cisterns carrying the sound of water, a gilded armillary sundial crowning a stone column, a Venetian well-head, a bellcote with figures of St George and the Dragon, a shrine for a Madonna on the byre roof and a wall-mounted astrological dial. These last, like all the garden's wooden furniture, are painted in Wade's preferred shade of turquoise-flushed French blue, which, as with his favoured slice of the floral spectrum, he found the most satisfactory foil to stone and grass.

Beyond the walls and tiled roofs, there is the sweeping contrast of the Cotswold landscape. Though independent of it, the garden nestles into it as comfortably and organically as does the village, and any sense of claustrophobia engendered by the passages and small, introspective rooms is dispelled by the open views offered by others. Areas of rough grass, native trees, hedgerow shrubbery and wildflowers also create a bond. Common ivy, ferns, boxwood and ash are among the garden flora, and a dark tunnel of guelder rose, *Viburnum opulus* (a replacement for the aged elders planted by Wade), leads from the byre at the head of the Well Court; scillas, snakeshead fritillaries and primroses spangle the ground here in spring, followed by the pink and white Turk's caps of martagon lilies. This all adds to the rustic mood, and in sympathy, the National Trust maintains the garden entirely on organic principles. A small kitchen garden also provides organic produce to the restaurant.

LEFT The garden at Snowshill looking towards the dovecote, with poppies and Canterbury bells.

Speke Hall

SPEKE, LIVERPOOL

AREA 6.5ha (16 acres) • SOIL mainly acid/thin layer of loam over sand • ALTITUDE 30m (100ft) • AVERAGE RAINFALL 813mm (32in) • AVERAGE WINTER CLIMATE cold

In a landscape littered with industrial buildings, busy roads and airport runways, Speke offers seclusion and oxygen. Woods and fields provide an immediate welcome, and around the perimeter of the grounds, trees have been judiciously sited to block ugliness and frame desirable views of the Mersey estuary and the distant Welsh hills. To the south, a horseshoe-shaped soil mound muffles the noise of aircraft. Thus soothed, you can take in the wonder of the hall. A mesmerising expanse of black-and-white timberwork, sandwiched between mellow roof tiles and a base of red sandstone, it is one of the finest surviving Tudor manor houses in England.

A stone bridge leads across the moat – both sections of which were drained by the mid-nineteenth century – and into a warren of panelled rooms, filled with heavily decorated oak furniture and dimly lit through leaded and stained-glass windows. Contributing to the atmospheric gloom are the two yew trees in the cobbled courtyard, known as Adam and Eve. They were first referred to in the eighteenth century, but are reputedly as old as the present hall; surgery has recently been necessary to repair and rejuvenate them.

The present garden layout was established after 1855, when, after a long period of neglect, the hall was inherited by the 20-year-old Richard Watt and a programme of restoration and embellishment began. This was continued from 1867 by Frederick Leyland, who became the tenant after Watt's death, and from 1878 by Watt's daughter Adelaide. Since the Trust assumed control of Speke from Merseyside County Council in 1986, it has undertaken a further phase of major improvements in the late Victorian 'Old English' idiom, and a varied garden is once again emerging.

The most delicate planting is found in the small, low-walled enclosure outside the Great Parlour, where a pretty scheme of Floribunda and Shrub roses has been established, centred on the small-flowered varieties 'White Pet', rose-pink 'The Fairy' and yellow 'Amber Queen', grown as bushes and half-standards. The design was inspired by archive photographs and realised in 1985. The colouring echoes that of the moat border, where the marriage of white and warm pink roses, phlox, hydrangeas and Japanese anemones and damson-purple cotinus and berberis, with the sandstone and timberwork of the house, is a lesson in good planting; even the tones of the leaded windows are repeated in the white-flecked, grape-purple flowerheads of acanthus.

The sandy soil is well suited to rhododendrons, and these were planted in large numbers in the second half of the nineteenth century. Azaleas and pink and white Hardy Hybrids are the main feature of the North Lawn border, growing in the company of yucca, pampas grass, heather, pine, laburnum and crataegus. Rhododendrons are also prominent in the new wood and water dell, developed by the National Trust from 1987 out of derelict land. A stone tunnel leads into it, and ferns, primulas and other perennials flank the bubbling watercourse. With the fresh green foliage and autumn tints of azaleas, these provide light and colour to contrast with the blocks of sombre evergreen rhododendrons, yews and laurels that will, in time, re-create the shadowy, Gothic passages that delighted the Victorians.

ABOVE The Rose Garden, established outside the Great Parlour.
RIGHT The south front of the house and lawn at Speke Hall.

Springhill

MONEYMORE, MAGHERAFELT, CO. LONDONDERRY

AREA 18ha (45 acres) • **SOIL** acid/light soil • **ALTITUDE** 30m (100ft)
AVERAGE RAINFALL 889mm (35in) • **AVERAGE WINTER CLIMATE** cold to very cold

Touches of formality and grandeur are here heavily diluted by unpretentious domesticity and mellow landscape. Whitewashed walls, slate roofs and the matching pair of low, plain, roughly plastered staff houses counter the impact of the long, straight entrance drive and the late seventeenth-century elegance and symmetry of Springhill's façade, and in the garden, you are lured away from the mountain views into a sequence of service yards, small walled enclosures, shrubberies and copses.

Around the house, the stonework is only lightly ornamented with plants, but the white walls make a striking backdrop for the foliage of bay trees and the cinnamon trunks of the half-hardy myrtle *Luma apiculata*. East of the forecourt, flower colour comes into play. Roses and wisteria flower on the wall of the Costume Museum; the Bleach Green border has been given a crisp blue and yellow colour scheme, reflecting the livery of the Lenox-Conyngham family, who lived here for 300 years; and in the walled herb garden, marjoram, mint, rue and sage are among the plants grown in slate-edged squares around the camomile lawn, accompanied by wall-trained red- and whitecurrant bushes. Further fruiting plants grow on the high walls of the coach and stack yards, including grape- and kiwi vines and a magnificent 'Brown Turkey' fig, while the 2ha (5 acre) walled kitchen garden is now being used for allotments.

Generally, the plantings are relaxed, with mosses, *Erinus alpinus* and ferns colonising between the Climbing roses and clematis. Pulmonarias, martagon lilies, crocosmia, colchicums and willow gentian flower in succession in the Bleach Green border, while the walled flower garden will emerge from its restoration featuring rose beds and colour-schemed herbaceous borders, its design based on that depicted in an old photograph. Of Springhill's cast of roses, the most famous is the old specimen of the Macartney rose, *R. bracteata*. Lord Macartney brought this superb species home to Ireland from China, where he was Ambassador in about 1793, and is said to have planted the original one himself here against the barn wall.

'At Springhill are the finest trees in this county,' wrote G.V. Sampson in his 1802 *Statistical Survey of the County of Londonderry*. Subsequent phases of planting have ensured the estate remains well stocked with trees, and the sloping ground gives you varied vantage points from which to survey them. Mature oaks, horse chestnuts, beeches, sycamores, *Pinus radiata* and yews are among those prominent around the house and garden, while more recent additions include an avenue of red-fruited sycamores, *Acer pseudoplatanus* 'Erythrocarpum', and a collection of unusual birches. The beech walk to the rear of the house, established by Springhill's builder, William Conyngham, was replanted in 1984 after the original trees developed beech bark disease. But the yews in the woods are probably a vestige of the ancient forest of Glenconkeyne, which used to extend to Loch Neagh. Yellow azaleas, hybrid rhododendrons, snowdrops, daffodils and bluebells furnish contrasting swathes of colour in spring, and in summer there are hoherias and blue hydrangeas.

ABOVE The rear of the seventeenth-century 'Planter' house, taken from the Beech Walk, with the Sperrin Mountains beyond.

Stagshaw Garden

AMBLESIDE, CUMBRIA

AREA 2ha (5 acres) • SOIL acid/thin loam • ALTITUDE 75m (246ft)
AVERAGE RAINFALL 1,981mm (78in) • AVERAGE WINTER CLIMATE moderate

On a steep hillside above Lake Windermere, this garden combines plantsmanship, artistry and the natural beauty of the Lake District to produce what I consider sheer perfection in woodland gardening. Created on National Trust land from 1959 to 1979 by Cuthbert 'Cubby' Acland, the Trust's Area Agent for Cumbria, it has had a chequered history in recent years, but its future now seems secure.

As you enter the garden you immediately pick up the splash of the beck that bubbles down the length of the woodland on its eastern flank, over mossy boulders and small waterfalls. Red squirrels reside in the oaks and beeches, hollies and hazels, which were carefully thinned by Acland to make a series of planting spaces and grassy glades, and to expose the outcrops of rock. The framed view across Windermere to the Langdale Pikes is of epic quality.

Rhododendrons and azaleas in great variety supply much of the springtime spectacle. The discerning choice of species and hybrids, and the sensitive, painterly handling of colour reflect Acland's childhood at Killerton in Devon, his careful study of books and catalogues, and the fact that he took much advice from his friend Graham Stuart Thomas, the plantsman and artist. Near the house, the opening salvo is from yellow and salmon-orange azaleas, and as you explore the maze of paths snaking up and down the hillside a succession of painted pictures presents itself.

You turn one corner into an ambush of blood reds from the likes of *Rhododendron thomsonii*, *R. neriiflorum*, *R.* 'Romany Chai' and *R.* 'Grenadier'; turn another and you are among the oranges and apricot-pinks of *R.* 'Fabia', *R.* 'Margaret Dunn' and *R.* 'Champagne'. Here, a planting of pinkish-mauve, lavender and violet *R. yunnanense*, *R. oreotrephes* and *R. augustinii* is exchanged for the lemons and creams of *R. wardii* and *R.* 'Ightham Yellow'; there, the heavy purples of *R.* 'Old Port', *R.* 'Purple Splendour' and *R.* 'Moser's Maroon' for the cheery pastels of azaleas *R.* 'Daviesii' and *R.* 'Irene Koster'.

The topography of hillocks and dells prevents you from seeing too much at once and varies your vantage points. In one spot, a seat invites you to look up and contemplate the Palette, a sweep of largely pink, white and salmon Japanese azaleas and dwarf rhododendrons in the shape of a painter's palette, mounting the slope to a bluff of rock. In another, you find yourself looking down on a stand of large-leaved *R. falconeri* luxuriating on a moist sheltered bank beside the beck. The comparatively soft climate allows R. 'Lady Alice Fitzwilliam' to thrive and join its lily-like perfume to that of the great, pink-flushed white *R.* 'Loderi King George'. And it is good to be able to report the presence of healthy *R. cinnabarinum*, among the most beautifully coloured of the tribe, but also among the most vulnerable to rhododendron mildew.

Grass infiltrated with wildflowers, little outcrops of moss and heather and carpets of woodland perennials knit all these plantings together in a manner so natural as to belie the skilled planting and deft maintenance. Early crocuses are succeeded by erythroniums, wood anemones and numerous daffodil varieties. By early May, there is a flood of bluebells among the white stitchwort, and lily of the valley and Solomon's seal echo the white drifts of *Cornus canadensis* and *Maianthemum bifolium*. Gunnera, lysichiton and royal ferns expand giant leaves beside the beck. After a quiet summer, the woodland ignites again in autumn with the tinted leaves of maples, birches, nyssas, fothergillas, azaleas and other ericaceous shrubs.

ABOVE Pastel tints of azaleas in the oak and beech woodland.

Standden

EAST GRINSTEAD, WEST SUSSEX

AREA 4.9ha (12 acres) • SOIL acid/greensand • ALTITUDE 135m (443ft)
AVERAGE RAINFALL 965mm (38in) • AVERAGE WINTER CLIMATE moderate

This quirky assembly of tile-hung, weatherboard and warm brick and stone walls, high chimneys, gables and prospect tower is a product of the late 19th-century revival of unpretentious vernacular styles of architecture, built using local materials and traditional skills. Its architect, commissioned by London solicitor James Beale, was Philip Webb, one of the pioneers of the Arts and Crafts movement and a close associate of William Morris, whose wallpapers and textiles can be seen inside the house. The buildings are set into a wooded hillside, and in autumn when the trees turn copper, red and russet, the harmony is remarkable. The views are far-reaching, south and south-east across the Medway valley to the ridge of Ashdown Forest, the pastoral middle ground enhanced by the creation of Weir Wood Reservoir. Exposed faces of sandstone beside the winding entrance drive and in the quarry, from which stone for the house was excavated, add to the picturesque qualities.

In recent years the garden has been undergoing a comprehensive refurbishment in order to capture again the mood created by James's wife, Margaret Beale, who evolved the design features laid out by Webb and local landscape designer George Simpson in the 1890s, and gardened here enthusiastically until her death in 1936. She enjoyed experimenting with new plants, and recorded her successes and failures in garden diaries.

Standen was a working farm throughout the Beales' time and visitors arrived, as today, unpretentiously through the farmyard. The cottage overlooking the farmyard green is one of the three original farmhouses, and behind its picket fence its front garden sports a traditionally carefree mix of perennials, sweet peas and soft fruit in

contrast to the more sophisticated plantings around the main house. But in spite of its plantsmanship, Standen is throughout a relaxed family garden, its loosely compartmented design blending easily into its rural setting.

You reach the house's south front by way of a small enclosed lawn, presided over by a mulberry, and fringed in lavender, white roses, salmon alstroemerias and wisteria. From the terraces, the views to the landscape open up. 'Sander's White' and Banksian roses festoon the house walls, while the borders are a lively summer blend of perennials, grasses, exotic foliage plants, and annuals of mixed colours. *Tetrapanax papyrifer* and red *Lobelia tupa* are among the company. Tulips are a feature in spring, as they are in the courtyard behind the house, which is speared by Italian cypresses and enlivened by the continuous summer flowering of tender perennials, violet-blue Geranium 'Brookside', and the white daisies of *Erigeron annuus*.

On the slope above the house you are in the realm of trees and shrubs, with steps and paths leading through thickets of camellias and among maples and magnolias, eucryphias and scented yellow azaleas. The small steep-sided quarry here is wonderfully atmospheric, whether experienced from within or from the bridge above. Originally landscaped by James Backhouse, a well-known York nurseryman, and once considered one of the best natural rock gardens in the country (earning the approval of the great William Robinson of nearby Gravetye Manor), it has since become rather shady and overgrown. Work is now slowly under way to clean and restore it as a showcase for alpines and ferns.

Other parts of this higher section of the garden are broader and airier, with the tree and shrub plantings broken in one area by a wildflower meadow, spangled early in the year in cowslips and later in common spotted orchids, and in another area opening up into a long terrace walk, built by Cheals of Crawley in 1910, which concludes in a summerhouse and affords a superb panorama out towards Crowborough Beacon. The circular path here leads through pines, redwoods, birches and heathers to a new winter garden above the drive, which offers further long country views towards East Grinstead and Forest Row.

There is a parallel terrace and summerhouse, Grandfather's Walk, down by the main lawn. This is bordered by pollarded lime trees, *Tilia × euchlora*, while elsewhere fringing the lawn and the farm track below are good *Cercidiphyllum*, tulip and Japanese maple trees (some of them sent back to Standen from Japan during the Beales' world tour of 1906–7) as well as old-established plantings of hydrangeas and Loderi rhododendrons.

The family's croquet/tennis lawn and natural swimming pond are in the lower areas of the garden, accompanied by a small rhododendron dell and an orchard. The formal rose garden, with its curving pergola and beds of pink and white roses set around a sundial, is currently being re-established here.

The 1.2ha (3 acre) kitchen garden, with its original espalier apple trees still surviving, is also now being remade and brought back into full production, the beds filled with a range of heritage and modern vegetable varieties which supply the Barn Café. Herbs and cut flowers are included, as well as a coop of Sussex chickens. Plums, cherries and other fruit trees are also being planted. The poles and peasticks for the kitchen garden come from the surrounding estate, which offers a number of enjoyable walks through the woods of the High Weald.

BELOW Japanese maples provide autumn colour above the lower terrace at Standen.

Stoneywell

ULVERSCROFT, LEICESTERSHIRE

AREA 6.1ha (15 acres) of garden and woodland • SOIL acidic • ALTITUDE 183–201m (600–659ft) • AVERAGE RAINFALL 700mm (27½in) • AVERAGE WINTER CLIMATE moderate

Sitting within the wide expanse of Charnwood Forest, with its green hills, scattered woods and granite outcrops, Stoneywell feels remote even today. Fuelling the mood, the stone cottage is reached by foot along an old sheep track and comes into view between folds of trees and banks of heather and bilberry. Below it, the valley rolls down through a forest of purple foxgloves to a handsome conical-roofed pump house. It is a charming scene.

'When a cottage has been set on a rough hillside and the heather reaches to the door, a conscious garden scheme may be undesirable or even impossible,' wrote Gertrude Jekyll in *Gardens for Small Country Houses* after visiting Stoneywell, illustrating its pump house and admiring the rough simplicity of its accompanying circular pool – once used for bathing, and now home to two species of newt.

The cottage was built in 1898–9 for local industrialist Sydney Gimson, who had happy memories of exploring these lanes and woods as a young man, and had long wanted to make a home here as a summer retreat from Leicester. With the help of his eldest brother, Mentor, and his friend James Billson, a 4.04ha (10 acre) plot was purchased from the Ecclesiastical Commissioners and divided between them.

Sydney and Mentor invited their younger brother, Ernest, to design each of their cottages, as he also did later for their sister Margaret nearby. Influenced and guided by William Morris, whom he met when he was 19, Ernest Gimson was a prominent and accomplished architect, designer and furniture-maker in the Arts and Crafts movement. Stoneywell, constructed mostly of stone sourced

on site and curving organically into its hillside, is a fine display of his craft. It was lived in simply by the family, with drinking water drawn from the well by the lane and, until electricity was installed in 1938, was lit only by candles and paraffin lamps.

Ernest also made planting plans for the garden with an equally light touch on the landscape – native plants close to the cottage, elsewhere merged with fruit trees – but layers of more decorative plants have been added subsequently, especially around the garden's fringes. Nevertheless, Stoneywell remains an example of the quieter, less elaborate, and back-to-nature end of the Arts and Crafts gardening spectrum.

Entering the garden from the stableyard in spring, you are greeted by blankets of native daffodils, *Narcissus pseudonarcissus*, introduced by Sydney and since naturalised by self-seeding. In summer, the mown paths weave through flowering meadow grasses, with the wilder ground above and beyond thick with bracken. Among the rocks is a little stone fort, and here and there on the elevations you get long views into Bradgate Park (the birthplace of Lady Jane Grey, the Nine Day Queen) and its eighteenth-century folly, Old John, as well as a prospect of the city of Leicester, the resting place of King Richard III, 16km (10 miles) away.

In 1903, Sydney had the granite blasted from an area just above the cottage to create level ground for a grass tennis court, and later two small walled gardens were created for vegetables. The lower of these was converted to orchard in 1950, and as well as apples it sports a large white wisteria and a Judas tree. The upper garden, newly replanted by the Trust and with paths edged in alpine strawberries, supplies salad crops and soft fruit to the tea room.

Sydney's grandson, Donald, and his wife Anne inherited Stoneywell in 1953, bringing up their two children and living here full-time. They were both passionate gardeners, writing a diary and keeping plant records, and under their stewardship the richer planting layers you see across the grounds today evolved. 'Anne was Head Gardener and looked after herbaceous plants. I was Head Woodsman and looked after trees and shrubs. Most evenings we would walk around the garden and discuss what we had done and what needed to be done,' wrote Donald. One of their guiding principles was to give the impression that the garden had developed naturally, so they avoided straight lines and blurred the divisions between the wild and the cultivated.

Purple wisteria and scented trachelospermum now clothe the cottage walls, accompanied by heathers and potentillas, and on the north side is a scree bed containing an assortment of dwarf rhododendrons and enkianthus, underplanted with glossy-leaved *Galax urceolata*. The tightly pruned shrub of *Cornus mas* was installed next to the bird table so that feeding birds had a hiding place when a sparrowhawk appeared. The garden's flower beds have been undergoing restoration by the Trust since the property's acquisition in 2012, and as the brambles and couch grass are removed, sympathetic perennials such as geraniums, lysimachias, dicentras and euphorbias are being planted.

Rhododendrons are a principal feature of the garden. There are some 150 varieties here, fringing the drive and tennis court areas and extending into the wood, producing a succession of flower that begins early with plants such as pink 'Christmas Cheer' and rose-purple *R. dauricum* 'Midwinter' and extends into July with white 'Polar Bear'. In the 1970s, the Gimsons consulted Philip Brown, a rhododendron expert and gifted landscape gardener who was then employed at the University of Leicester Botanic Garden (he would later work wonders on the woodland garden at Portmeirion in Wales – where, as it happens, he gave me much of my own education in rhododendrons), so the choice and placing of the plants are unsurprisingly excellent.

The colours range from pastel 'Cowslip', 'Moonstone' and *R. lutescens* to bright pink 'Winsome', and potent scent is provided by yellow and white azaleas, *R. luteum* and 'Persil', and tender white 'Lady Alice Fitzwilliam', which finds sufficient protection under the trees. In the wood are striking large-leaved varieties including *R. sinogrande*, *macabeanum* and *rex* subsp. *fictolacteum*.

Magnolias, including pink *M.* × *loebneri* 'Leonard Messel', *M. liliiflora* 'Nigra' and white *M. denudata*, pieris and scarlet Chilean fire bush (*Embothrium coccineum*) add to the springtime picture, while the later company includes pendant white *M. sieboldii* and two Nymans eucryphia of impressive stature. Among the many fine trees – splendid beech, oak and sweet chestnut – there is a nice pin oak, *Quercus palustris*, standing by the gulley below the house and an elegant Bhutan pine, *Pinus wallichiana*, along the entrance walk. A handkerchief tree (*Davidia involucrata*) displays its white bracts in early summer, and in autumn *Stewartia pseudocamellia* and *Cornus kousa*, both with patterned trunks, join the Japanese maples and rowans as highlights in the panorama of copper and russet tints.

The 4.45ha (11 acres) of ancient woodland below the house were bought by Sydney in 1922 at the Grey family's big sale of Bradgate. Composed mainly of sessile and pedunculate oak, with silver birch on the higher ground and moisture-loving trees lower down, they are carpeted with bluebells in spring and woven through with stitchwort, rushes and acid grassland species. There is a circuit path by which to explore them. Woodpeckers and woodcock are found here; other parts of the grounds are home to bats and a good population of slow worms.

LEFT A view of the house across banks of bilberry and heather.

ABOVE Native daffodils (*Narcissus pseudonarcissus*) blanket the approach to the stableyard.

Stourhead

STOURTON, WARMINSTER, WILTSHIRE

AREA 38ha (93 acres) • SOIL acid/greensand • ALTITUDE 213m (700ft)
AVERAGE RAINFALL 1,016–1,118mm (40–44in) • AVERAGE WINTER CLIMATE moderate

'The most bewitching and beautiful of this country's landscape gardens'

Here we have probably the most bewitching and beautiful of this country's landscape gardens, an eighteenth-century Arcadia of hills and hanging beechwoods, water and classical architecture, but dashingly overlaid with a later collection of exotic broad-leaved trees, conifers and richly coloured rhododendrons. A few purists balk at the combination, but they are in the minority. The balance, however, is fine, and the Trust has been working to recapture more of the flavour of the earlier phase by reopening vistas and reordering the planting, eliminating disjointed patches of colour and strong contrasts in favour of gentle harmonies and smooth transitions.

The valley landscape is the work of various members of the Hoare family, beginning in the early 1740s, with Henry Hoare II, son of the founder of Hoare's Bank. Motivated by the new-born idea of garden-making not as an exercise in geometry but as a branch of landscape painting, and freshly returned from a three-year tour of Italy, he set about creating a poetic landscape inspired by the Roman Campagna – scenes from the much-admired era of peace and artistic accomplishment under Augustus, alluding allegorically in part to the epic journey of Aeneas. Hoare's architectural advisor was Henry Flitcroft, an associate of William Kent, the new landscape movement's leading designer, and the scenes are very much in his style. It was his grandson, Richard Colt Hoare, who, responding to the current influx of new plants from America and Asia Minor, introduced *Rhododendron ponticum*, cherry laurel and the tulip tree into the landscape, and the exotic planting continued in the late nineteenth and early twentieth centuries, under the direction of Sir Henry Hoare.

The valley is tucked between folds of chalk downland and divorced from the grand Palladian villa, which stands back on the ridge to the north. One way of entering is to bypass the house by walking immediately downhill from the car park and arriving at the lakeside through the little estate village of Stourton, with its inn, church and row of cottages. The most dramatic approach, however, is to descend the wooded hillside across the lawn from the house, and have the first surprises sprung from above.

A line of ancient sweet chestnuts, a vestige of an earlier avenue to Stourton Castle, flanks part of the curving driveway to the mansion, and to the left are the old stable yard and walled kitchen gardens, currently being renovated by the Trust with the active involvement of students, community groups and volunteers, and planted with a wide variety of fruit, vegetables and ornamental plants. A Foster and Pearson glasshouse, dating from 1902, stands in the lower walled garden and houses a fine collection of pelargoniums. Ahead looms the house, designed by Colen Campbell for Henry Hoare I, but with a later portico and flanking pavilions; the backdrop is of tree belts and open countryside carrying the eye across the edge of Salisbury Plain.

Opposite the south front, across a lawn lined with rows of beech trees, Edwardian-style shrubberies of purple, red and white rhododendrons – hybrids such as 'Britannia', 'Mrs Charles E. Pearson' and 'Loder's White' – colour the way, and there is a particularly good icehouse concealed down a laurel passage. Specimens of Persian ironwood (*Parrotia persica*), *Philadelphus* 'Belle Etoile' and *Ligustrum compactum* (syn. *L. chenaultii*) feature among the trees and in the eighteenth-century shrubbery on the lawn edges.

Magnificent tulip trees mark the beginning of the valley landscape. First, there is a view down to the village church, past sweet chestnuts and Himalayan whitebeam, and then you enter the wood, the path winding downhill between the beech and the rough carpets of ferns, grasses and wildflowers – the browns and greens seasonally washed with snowdrops, bluebells and the native Lent lily, *Narcissus pseudonarcissus*. An obelisk, surmounted by a gilded solar disc, is the focal point for Richard Colt Hoare's broad, straight Fir Walk, now regenerated with young western hemlocks. Cherry laurel, kept low by annual pruning, gives a glossy evergreen understorey to the woods, with the more interesting rhododendrons appearing in loose drifts: Ghent azaleas and large-leaved Himalayan species; cool-coloured Hardy Hybrids like 'Blue Peter', 'Cynthia' and 'Nobleanum Venustum'; *R. barbatum*; and fragrant yellow *Rhododendron luteum* continuing into high summer with *R. auriculatum* and 'Polar Bear'.

Between the trees, two of the garden buildings suddenly appear – first, the Temple of Apollo, a pale cylinder with domed roof and Corinthian columns, perched on its hill across the valley, and then, on the far bank of the lake, the portico and rotunda of the Pantheon. No sooner glimpsed than lost; enveloped by the wood, you continue down to the valley floor, where a more ornamental cast of trees again takes over from the beech and oak – handsome flowering species such as snowdrop tree, handkerchief tree, Italian maple (*Acer opalus*) and tree magnolias, including a champion *M. campbellii* subsp. *mollicomata* and *M. denudata* (syn. *M. heptapeta*); conifers such as Macedonian pine, cryptomeria, dawn redwood and noble fir.

This assortment of exotics, backed by the hanging woods, extends around the lakeside. There are the evergreen rockets of wellingtonias and thujas (an immense broad-skirted specimen awaits across the water); the elegant uprights of tulip trees, punctuating the banks and rising from the central island; a number of purple beech trees; blasts of springtime rhododendron colour; and an exciting autumn panorama of red Japanese maples, American oaks and russet cypresses. Inside this rich canvas, you follow the circuit walk from one poetic building to the next, passing from sunlight to shadow. The reflections in the water add greatly to the composition, not only of the main lake but of the flanking pools – to the west, a lily lake, with a view beyond, up Six Wells Valley, where the River Stour rises; to the east, Turner's Paddock Lake, fed by a cascade and married with trees and a newly restored water wheel.

The path leads through a tunnel of yew, under a rustic stone arch, and into one of the most impressive of English grottoes, dank and gloomy but alive to the sound of water splashing from the natural springs; a nymph sleeps above the cascade, and from the opening in the lakeside wall there is a view across the water to the village church and arched bridge, framed in limes and sugar maples. A river god in the adjacent cave points in the direction of the Pantheon, and you leave by way of a rustic stairway, edged in hart's tongue fern. Now you come to the old Watch Cottage, Gothicised by Richard Colt Hoare in 1806 and with a good Japanese maple, *Acer palmatum* 'Osakazuki', beside it. From here, an array of features is visible – the Temple of Apollo on its mount, the slim and skeletal sculpture of the Bristol High Cross in the village and, on the opposite bank, the pediment and Doric columns of the elegant Temple of Flora.

A statue of Hercules and other classical figures stand inside the rotunda of the Pantheon, and thence it is around the edge of the lake, and on to the temples of Apollo and Flora, from where you obtain the equally glorious reverse views of the lake, trees and architectural ornament. These vistas are as close to perfection as any artist gardener can compose, and, thanks to their exotic plant content, they pass through a breathtaking sequence of colours. This is a landscape to visit at every season.

ABOVE Autumnal bronze foliage in the trees by the water.

NEXT PAGE The Palladian bridge and Pantheon at Stourhead, lit by an October sunset.

Pruning trees

Alan Power, Garden and Estate Manager
STOURHEAD, WILTSHIRE

It is inevitable that trees will need pruning at some stage during their life as part of the garden, but how this is carried out will depend upon the reason for doing it.

To promote a healthy tree

When dealing with a specimen tree in a garden, prune any dead and diseased branches back to a healthy growing point. Regular inspections of young trees will highlight the need to remove branches that will potentially form tight and therefore weak forks, or any crossing, rubbing branches. If these tasks are carried out when the tree is young you may prevent the need for major surgery in later years.

To extend the life of a tree

The pruning already described helps to extend the life of a tree, but with certain trees, when they achieve great size and status in the garden, structural weaknesses can become apparent. In some instances you will need to reduce the weight on an individual limb by thinning out the branch network. It may even be necessary to carry out an overall crown reduction; this will reduce the weight on each limb and also the wind sail capacity of the tree (the amount of pressure the wind places on the tree) and take some pressure off the main stems.

For aesthetic or safety reasons

A visual inspection of a young tree will highlight any imbalances within the crown, and when they are caught at an early age it is easier to remove small branches that may lead to a lopsided tree, unwanted double leaders, low-growing branches and inward-growing branches.

It is sometimes necessary also to remove branches that may obscure attractive views. It is always worth aiming to prune a tree at as young an age as possible in order to eliminate the need to leave a large pruning wound on a mature tree. Finally, if a limb has become potentially dangerous its removal is essential, whether the season is ideal or not.

When to prune

Spring Early in spring is a good time to pollard or prune back willows, conifers and broad-leaved evergreens, but avoid leaving the pruning too late in the season, when the sap will be rising.

Summer When you are busy in the garden keeping up with routine maintenance it is easy to forget the needs of the trees, but conifers can be pruned during the summer along with broad-leaved evergreen trees.

Autumn and winter Deciduous specimen trees are best pruned late in the autumn or in winter. Specimen ornamental evergreen trees can be pruned in autumn in the milder areas of the country, but avoid pruning them in winter unless they are unsafe.

Tips

- Make sure pruning tools are sharp and clean.
- Remove suckers at ground level on ornamental trees.
- Avoid heavy pruning in summer.
- Remove pruning debris as soon as possible as this can play host to pests and diseases.
- If in doubt about when or how to prune always seek advice from an expert, such as your local tree surgeon.

- Pruning a tree forms part of your overall tree-care regime. You should also ensure the base of a young tree is free of weeds in order to reduce competition for nutrients. Inspect any supports on the tree, making sure that stakes are firm and ties are not loose or too tight. Feeding a young tree with natural well-rotted leaf mulch helps it to establish, reduces competition at root level and keeps moisture in the soil.

Stowe Landscape Gardens

BUCKINGHAM, BUCKINGHAMSHIRE

AREA 101ha (250 acres) • **SOIL** alkaline/clay and gravel • **ALTITUDE** 120m (394ft)
AVERAGE RAINFALL 660mm (26in) **AVERAGE WINTER CLIMATE** cold

'The visitor should prepare to be impressed,' wrote John Martin Robinson in a past Stowe guidebook. This is one of England's foremost landscape gardens. At the Buckingham entrance, the scale is immediately heroic – 2.4km (1½ miles) of beech and chestnut avenue splicing across the undulating, wooded ridges of the countryside and carrying you to a triumphal Corinthian arch, the landscape's crowning monument. The New Inn to the side of it, built to accommodate Stowe's eighteenth-century visitors, has been restored and reopened, enabling visitors to follow in the footsteps of eighteenth-century tourists and enter the grounds through Bell Gate. This provides one of the most celebrated views, across the Octagon Lake to the Palladian mansion, now Stowe School, which is the centrepiece of the 101.1ha (250 acre) garden. The house is periodically open to the public for guided tours by the Stowe House Preservation Trust.

This stupendous composition is the work of the socially and politically ambitious Temple-Grenville family, beginning with General Sir Richard Temple, later Viscount Cobham, who, funded by his marriage in 1715 to a wealthy heiress, Anne Halsey, set about transforming his father's small terraced garden in splendid style. This was a momentous period in landscape design, with the pendulum about to swing towards more natural and less formal composition. Stowe would not only reflect but pioneer the change in taste, with many of the leading architects, designers and sculptors employed here including 'Capability' Brown.

The early phase was executed by the royal gardener, Charles Bridgeman, and adorned with buildings designed by Sir John Vanbrugh, the architect of Blenheim Palace and Castle Howard. Very little of this layout remains today, for it was gradually dismantled in the 1740s, and then, in the 1750s, finally converted by Cobham's nephew, Earl Temple, into the more confidently sweeping style of the time, in harmony with the later parts of the landscape.

The main garden axis, below the majestic south façade of the house, is now broad and open. Where once the eye would have been channelled over an elaborate parterre, between an avenue of poplars and across an octagonal pond, there is empty lawn, informal flanks of forest trees, and a seemingly natural pool of water, strewn with the native white waterlily. Beyond, Earl Temple widened the axis between Vanbrugh's pavilions, giving the present grand vista into the park, terminated by his masterstroke, the Corinthian Arch. To the west of the house, Vanbrugh's domed rotunda, once the centre of radiating gravel walks, was set into a more informal wooded glade.

Bridgeman's principal legacy is the ha-ha. This French device of a sunken ditch, giving gardens protection from grazing animals yet allowing them to merge uninterrupted with the countryside, had a decisive impact on the development of the landscape garden. Stowe was the first English property in which it was used extensively. The runs were constructed like military fortifications and punctuated by projecting bastions, and on the south-west and south-east corners, these are adorned with monuments, a Palladian Temple of Venus and a Tuscan Temple of Friendship added by Earl Temple and now a ruin, following a fire in the nineteenth century.

The second phase of the garden's development under Lord Cobham took place from 1734 and is centred in a narrow dell, a little to the east – once occupied by Stowe village and its public road, of which only the fourteenth-century church remains. Garden design was now being compared to landscape painting, with landowners beginning to yearn for the sort of pastoral landscapes depicted by the likes of Claude Lorrain and Salvator Rosa. The pioneer of this Picturesque style was William Kent, who was engaged by Lord Cobham to create these Elysian Fields (the Romans' mythological paradise) here at Stowe.

It is the most intimate portion of the garden. Access, as in the myth, is across the serpentine River Styx, spouting from a newly restored grotto and created by damming the existing stream (the upper dam being the Shell Bridge). You enter into bright glades, fringed by trees and filled with monuments, but presided over, on the west bank, by the Temple of Ancient Virtue, an Ionic rotunda erected in 1736, and on the east, by the Temple of British Worthies, a curved screen in which the busts of distinguished men of action

and of contemplation are displayed in niches (along with that of one woman, Queen Elizabeth I). The cast ranges from King Alfred and Walter Raleigh to William Shakespeare and Isaac Newton, and includes Cobham's friend Alexander Pope, the poet and influential landscape theorist – all Whig heroes. This was one of the first monuments intended to be 'read' by visitors, who would have noticed the pointed omission of Catholic priests. Exploring the Arcadian landscape was intended to be as much an exercise for the mind as for the feet. Here at Stowe, there are not only classical and literary references to pick up but also the family's strongly held beliefs and prejudices, often conveyed with satire.

At the base of the Elysian Fields, you are enticed further east, across Hawkwell Field, which rolls down to another naturalistic stretch of water, spanned by one of the garden's best-known monuments, the Palladian Bridge by James Gibbs. Lord Cobham

began developing this area in the late 1730s as ornamental pasture, combining classical decoration with agricultural use; it was an early example of *la ferme ornée*, and is still grazed today. Presiding over the scene, on a ridge far to the north, stands the Queen's Temple, a Corinthian temple built as a summer-house for Lady Cobham, and on the same axis, halfway to the water and flanked by young and old cedar trees, the Gothic Temple, a monument to the 'Liberty of our Ancestors'.

The last part of the garden to be completed was the Grecian Valley, north-east of the house. A carefully contoured sweep of hay meadow – full of wildflowers, including massed cowslips – and framed by broad and muscular banks of deciduous trees, cedars

ABOVE View across the Octagon Lake towards the Lake Pavilions and Corinthian Arch.

and pines, this marks the arrival of a more open and bold style of naturalistic landscaping. It was begun in 1746, by which time Lord Cobham's head gardener was none other than the young Lancelot, later 'Capability', Brown.

The Grecian Valley contains one of the most impressive of Stowe's monuments – the Ionic Temple, completed by Earl Temple with the addition of a magnificent carved pediment, showing Britannia receiving the tribute of the world; it was transferred here from the Palladian Bridge, structures being moved about the garden like chess pieces. Named the Temple of Concord and Victory in line with Earl Temple's development of the garden on still grander lines, it embraces not only national but imperial achievements.

Stowe is the most complex of English gardens, but no deep understanding is needed in order to appreciate its beauty – the open meadows, the lofty plantations of beech, lime, oak and chestnut with their yew, holly, cherry laurel and box understorey, the waterside fringes of alder and ash, and the golden architecture. It presents a succession of magnificent landscape pictures, changing in response to every phase of light and season.

Only after the Second World War, when the study of garden history grew, did Stowe School begin to realise the landscape's true significance and the scale of the rescue work demanded. Repairs were tentatively begun, gathering momentum in the 1960s. But the scale of the declining landscape and the sheer quantity of crumbling buildings was alarming. In 1990, following offers of support from a benefactor, English Heritage and the National Heritage Memorial Fund, Stowe School conveyed the gardens to the National Trust, and a major appeal was launched. Numerous individuals and public and private bodies have contributed subsequently, a comprehensive historical survey has been commissioned, and lake by lake, plantation by plantation, and temple by temple, the work has proceeded, involving archaeology, lake dredging, skilled stonemasonry and the planting of thousands of trees. It continues to be one of the most ambitious garden restoration projects ever undertaken.

PREVIOUS PAGE The Oxford Bridge on a frosty day at Stowe Landscape Gardens.

ABOVE The Palladian Bridge, built in 1738, with the Gothic Temple designed by Gibbs on the skyline.

Sunnycroft

WELLINGTON, SHROPSHIRE

AREA 2ha (5 acres) • **SOIL** sandy and silty lawn • **ALTITUDE** 113m (371ft)
AVERAGE RAINFALL 533mm (21in) • **AVERAGE WINTER CLIMATE** moderate

It is a nice conceit that the entrance avenue at Sunnycroft is formed of wellingtonias, *Sequoiadendron giganteum*. Introduced into Britain in the 1850s, and named after the Iron Duke, they were widely planted in the late nineteenth century and today, with their soaring silhouettes and fibrous bark that glows orange in the sun, they set an immediate period mood. Here, interplanted with pollarded limes for contrast, they lead from the lodge to a red-brick Victorian villa, built in 1880 and extended in 1899, complete with Gothic tower and airy verandah.

This is not a grand house. Rather, it gives an insight into the life and aspirations of the well-to-do local business class of that time, who created in the suburbs their own scaled-down version of a country estate, with a small household of staff. It passed in ownership from John Wackrill, who ran the Shropshire Brewery, to Mary Jane Slaney, a wine and spirits merchant, and then in 1912 to her brother-in-law J.V.T. Lander, a Wellington solicitor, whose family lived here for three generations.

On her death in 1997, his granddaughter Joan – a spinster, former radiographer and accomplished embroiderer – presented the Trust with a house and grounds so little altered (although somewhat frayed, as upkeep was by now a severe financial strain) that even the medicine cabinet contained little evidence of the modern era. Surrounded as it is now by dense residential development, this sense of stumbling upon a time capsule is pronounced.

The front of the house looks onto a spacious lawn, the setting for croquet and afternoon tea (promptly served at 4pm). A further assortment of large conifers fringe its boundaries, including cedar, yew and various forms of Lawson cypress, with white and pink-flowering May trees (*Crataegus*) in the grass to lend some summer shade. Beside the house a lively, even garish, display of pot and bedding plants is staged, the wallflowers, tulips and pansies of spring followed by pelargoniums, petunias, purple heliotrope and scarlet salvias in summer.

Planting at Sunnycroft is not sophisticated. In the absence of many photographs or other records, the National Trust has set out simply to conjure up the typical charm and tastes of a provincial villa garden in its Edwardian heyday. The garden compartments, although formally delineated, are overlaid with fairly relaxed planting schemes – the most prim, and modern, being the small rose garden by the house's west wall, which contains pink and apricot Hybrid Tea and Floribunda varieties from the 1950s.

This sits in front of a very fine conservatory, with stained-glass panes and lantern roof, by R. Halliday & Co. of Middleton, near Manchester, who also built glasshouses for Lord Rothschild at Waddesdon Manor in the 1880s. Joan Lander's speciality was her pots of white arum lilies (*Zantedeschia*) which, after being dried out during the summer on their sides, were brought into the heat in early October to bloom in time for the Easter services at St Eata's church in Atcham – a tradition the Trust continues. A collection of scented-leaved pelargoniums provides the year-round supporting cast.

The double herbaceous borders, like much of the garden, have required thorough restoration, having become overcast with outsized laurels and conifers. They are now restocked with a mixed succession of cottage garden stalwarts from aquilegias, oriental poppies, geraniums and daylilies to phlox, crocosmia, and Michaelmas daisies. Further period walks, tile-edged and punctuated by rustic wooden arches, are flanked by flowering shrubs such as viburnum, mahonia, philadelphus, spiraea and flowering currant.

The straight path lines are broken at one point by a circular bed of hostas and bergenias, presided over by a central clump of pampas grass, a Victorian favourite (the new plumes particularly striking when accompanied by the golden autumn tints of the hosta leaves), and you emerge from the shrubberies to find a cut-flower border, bright with dahlias, cornflowers, clarkias and Shasta daisies. The small, shady flower garden on the other side of the lawn – planted in the cool green and white colours of snowdrops, narcissi, geraniums, dicentra, ferns and euphorbia – is bordered by a culverted stream, flowing down into the garden from the Ercall woods and crossed by a rustic bridge. Here, you also come to a pleasant garden of soft fruit.

Sunnycroft under the Lander family was largely self-sufficient, with surplus produce sold at market. In the Edwardian era, there was a widespread yearning for the good life – a bountiful, rural idyll amid increasing industrialisation and urban expansion – and J.V.T. Lander, who was brought up on a large farm, was able to achieve it here on his miniature estate, which was a hive of fruit-bottling, jam-making, and much else besides.

Behind the conservatory are a tomato house and a little vinery and peach house, recently restored, while beyond the drive is the vegetable garden, which Joan Lander ensured was kept productive until she died. The plots are now run as allotments. The family kept pigs, as well as a milk cow which grazed the paddock separating the garden from the main road. Livestock may well return to this field, but meanwhile chickens are still to be found scratching about in their coop among the apples, pears, greengages and Shropshire damsons of the adjoining orchard.

ABOVE A fine avenue of Wellingtonias at Sunnycroft.

RIGHT Old-fashioned borders of delphiniums, campanulas, penstemons and ligularia line the path on the east side of this gentleman's suburban villa.

Tatton Park

KNUTSFORD, CHESHIRE

AREA 24ha (60 acres) • SOIL acid/sand • ALTITUDE 60m (197ft) • AVERAGE RAINFALL 28in (711mm) • AVERAGE WINTER CLIMATE cold

'A grand domain of great verdure, and with a noble lake; these are the charms: the *per contra*, no inequality of ground; the timber of neither stature nor girth,' wrote the diarist Lord Torrington in 1790. The terrain is certainly flat. The estate lies at the northern end of the Cheshire plain, amid pastureland and meres. The trees, however, have become one of the chief assets. Before, and in the decades after Lord Torrington's visit, a considerable number were planted as clumps and woods, and these, with their replacements, now bring shape and texture to the setting; an extensive arboretum has also grown up beside the house. Herds of red and fallow deer graze the meadows, together with sheep, and there is further animation from the boats coursing the lake – sailing being one of many recreational activities for which the park is available to the public.

A varied landscape thus presents itself, much in the style of Humphry Repton, who paid a visit here in 1791 and prepared one of his Red Books of proposals the following year, though, in fact, it owes more to one John Webb, a pupil of William Emes, who worked here in the second decade of the nineteenth century, and to planting by the 1st and 2nd Lords Egerton in the 1870s and 1880s.

Surveying the scene is an imposing Neo-classical mansion of pinkish-grey sandstone, built by Samuel Wyatt and his nephew Lewis Wyatt, between 1790 and 1812. And to accompany it are gardens: the full panoply of parterre and croquet lawn, herbaceous borders and topiary, glasshouses and aviaries, kitchen gardens, shrubberies, water gardens and pinetum, which would provide a string of diversions for the leisured Victorian and Edwardian family and their guests.

Below the portico, terraced lawns flow down to the Italian Garden, constructed in the 1880s and restored by the National Trust a hundred years later, using archive photographs. Grass, gravel, box and bedding (polyanthus and forget-me-nots, followed by armeria, ageratum and the single, mauve-pink 'Princess Marie José' dahlia, in adherence to precedent) provide the pattern, sculpted around marble vases and a Neptune fountain. The upper parterre has also recently been restored, with the bedding set among ribbons of armeria and the original top-dressings of white marble and local red shale.

The decorative glasshouses stand to the west. The Conservatory, built by Lewis Wyatt in 1818, is stocked with oranges and lemons. Formerly, these would have stood outside on the terrace for summer, but now they are permanent inhabitants accompanied by clivias, passion flowers and mimosa. Many other gardens have a conservatory on this scale, but none has as impressive a fernery. Dating from the 1850s, its architect was probably Joseph Paxton, the designer of the Crystal Palace and the conservatory at Chatsworth. The speciality is the Australian tree ferns collected on his travels by Captain Charles Randle Egerton RN, the brother of the 1st Lord Egerton. The path curves under their crowns – mesmerising traceries of emerald, as you look through them towards the roof glass – passing a dry-stone wall studded with maidenhairs and cyrtomiums, while the enormous fronds of the chain fern, *Woodwardia radicans*, brush against your legs. The connecting conservatory, also rebuilt, is now a traditional riot of colour.

Beyond are further flower gardens: a long L-shaped border, colour-coded within buttresses of yew, and backed by walls densely clothed in climbers and shrubs (including the rare *Magnolia acuminata* var. *subcordata*, which gives a good show of yellow flowers in summer); a garden partially restored in the sinuous and curious gardenesque style of the early nineteenth century, where specimen plants are shown off as individuals in small beds; and a walled enclosure of roses and scented plants set beside a pool. Topiary yews, a fountain, a shady pergola and trellis arbour, and a castellated sheep-watcher's tower, dating from before 1750, add further incident.

The walled kitchen and orchard gardens, each 1ha (2½ acres) in size, have been the subject of a major restoration programme and are now very impressive. In the kitchen garden, heritage and unusual vegetables, such as salsify and scorzonera, are grown on a rotation system in four equal-sized beds. A central cross of apple tunnels, fig houses with twelve varieties of fig, including the very early 'White Marseilles', and forcing pots, used for sea kale as well as rhubarb – of which there are some 40 varieties – add to the scene, all presided over by the Tea House of the adjacent Japanese Garden (open only on certain days).

The orchard garden now boasts restored glasshouses for vines, tomatoes, peaches and even pineapples, whose three-year fruiting cycle is once again being mastered. There are also glasshouses for begonias and orchids, the latter comprising four temperature-controlled sections, restocked with the help of the North of England Orchid Society. Outdoors, the hardy fruits, including the wonderfully named 'Bloody Ploughman' apple are all varieties grown in Cheshire before 1900. The soft fruits are set around the central pergola and twin herbaceous borders, and the tree fruits grown in an array of goblet, fan and espalier shapes. These demonstrate old pruning and training skills now rarely encountered in Britain.

By now, the rich variety of trees and shrubs in the garden will have impressed themselves on you. The view from the house towards the distant hills beyond Congleton encompasses fine evergreen and Turkey oaks and cedar of Lebanon, and, in the dell below, high conifers, beeches and sweet chestnuts (the twisted, deeply fissured trunks are a memorable motif). Around the lawns of the flower gardens, you will have come upon handkerchief tree, *Malus hupehensis, Magnolia obovata* syn. *M. hypoleuca*, large-leaved *Emmenopterys henryi*, blue-podded *Descaisnea fargesii* and choice conifers such as Brewer's weeping spruce and the red-coned Chinese spruce, *Picea likiangensis*.

These are a taste of what awaits in the arboretum's many hectares of grassy and pool-side glades. The cast is arranged fairly erratically, and often very closely packed, but it is an interesting catalogue of what will thrive in a cold northern climate, and there are also some magnificent specimens, not least among the conifer collection, which is being continually augmented.

The pinetum was well established by 1795, though the oldest of the present plants date mostly from the late nineteenth and early twentieth centuries. In addition to the extensive range of tall American and Far Eastern species, such as *Pinus jeffreyi, P. wallichiana, Abies recurvata* var. *ernesti* and *Picea purpurea* syn. *P. likiangensis* var. *purpurea*, there are contrasting plumes from Sawara cypresses (*Chamaecyparis pisifera*) and cryptomeria, dawn redwoods grouped in a glade, and swamp cypresses (*Taxodium distichum*) beside a stretch of water. Among deciduous trees, there are cherries and parrotia, styrax and halesia, a very tall bay willow (*Salix pentandra*) and a prickly curiosity in the form of *Kalopanax septemlobus* syn. *K. pictus*, whose maple-like leaves are among the last to drop in autumn.

In summer, the glades are predominantly green, but in spring, there are blasts of colour from massed rhododendrons. The collection was built up by the last Lord Egerton in the 1940s, during his enforced confinement in Britain away from his beloved estate in Kenya. The walls of the Tenants' Hall are covered with the heads of game that crossed his path, and at one point in the garden tour you come upon a heather-thatched African hut.

En route, you encounter two surprising vestiges of an earlier layout. One, tucked into shrubbery, is a small beech maze, a rare feature that was established here before 1795 and said to be the same plan as at Hampton Court. The other, splicing the arboretum into two parts, is an avenue predominantly of beech. Known as the Broad Walk, it dates from the 1730s, and in the 1820s the family installed a grand monument at its head, inspired by that to Lysicrates, the chorus or storyteller, in ancient Athens. This marks the boundary of the garden, from where you can look out over the park.

I have left the jewel in Tatton's crown until last. The opening of Japan to foreigners in the late nineteenth century brought a fascination with all things Japanese, culminating in the Japan-British Exhibition of 1910. Almost immediately, the 3rd Lord Egerton embarked on a Japanese garden in one of the dells at Tatton. It is probably the finest in the country. A fusion of the various styles of classical garden, it has a still, dark pool as its centre, fed by four streams that flow over cascades, under flat bridges, past stone lanterns and key rocks (including a mound of white stones representing Mount Fuji), and between a carefully placed cast of plants, including maples, bamboo, water iris, cherry, pine and particularly fine specimens of *Picea pungens* Glauca Group. Cranes and other mythically charged animals are met on the way, and the centrepiece, standing on the Master's island, is a thatched Tea House. Beyond the arched bridge a Shinto shrine, brought from Japan, adorns the island on the adjacent lake – made for Lady Charlotte Egerton, wife of the 1st Baron, out of disused clay pits. These Japanese features are heavy with a symbolism that passes most of us by, but the craftsmanship and tranquillity of the setting are there for all to savour. A Japanese gardener may well have supervised or advised on the original work, and recently, under Japanese guidance, the garden has been comprehensively restored.

So there are large and varied gardens at Tatton, full of interest and reflecting the enthusiasms of many generations of the Egerton family, who lived here from 1598 for more than 350 years.

PREVIOUS PAGE The Japanese Garden at Tatton Park with the 'flying goose' bridge and the ornamental tea house in the background.

ABOVE The restored kitchen garden is on a very large scale.

Tintinhull Garden

TINTINHULL, YEOVIL, SOMERSET

AREA 0.8ha (2 acres) • SOIL neutral/loam over marl clay • ALTITUDE 30m (100ft)
AVERAGE RAINFALL 762mm (30in) • AVERAGE WINTER CLIMATE moderate

'Nothing is out of place, and the result is a garden that is the embodiment of peace'

The west front of Tintinhull House, part-hidden by a high wall at the edge of the village, is as dreamy a façade as you are likely to come upon. Compact, symmetrical, built of a warm and welcoming honey-coloured stone (quarried at nearby Ham Hill), and adorned with pediment and pilasters, mullioned windows and carved scrolls, it is the picture of early eighteenth-century elegance. The lines and proportions of the manor have been extended to create an equally exceptional garden: an open and varied sequence of rooms, or courts, formally set out over the more or less flat terrain, and decorated with a varied but discerningly chosen range of plants. 'Nothing is out of place, and the result is a garden that is the embodiment of peace,' wrote the cottage gardener Margery Fish.

From the sitting-room door, a long, straight path, flanked by low domes of clipped box, invites you west through three enclosures. The first, Eagle Court (named after the pair of birds mounted on its gate-piers), is the oldest part of the garden, dating from the eighteenth century, with the stone paving added, and the further enclosures formally connected and shaped, some time after 1905, probably by Dr S.J.M. Price, a churchman of private means who was then the tenant.

But the planting, the design of the larger courts and the character of the present garden is the inspiration of Phyllis Reiss, who, with her husband, Captain F.E. Reiss, came to live here in 1933, having already made a garden near Cheltenham – not far from Hidcote, to which Tintinhull owes more than a passing acknowledgement. She had an ordered and distinctive approach. 'Her special gift,' wrote the garden designer Lanning Roper, was

'for selecting and placing plants to create an effect … If a plant is distinguished in form and texture it is used boldly and often repeated, this making a unity of design.'

Within the parameters of colour and mood set by Mrs Reiss, the Trust's former tenants, the distinguished garden writer Penelope Hobhouse and her husband the late Professor John Malins, continued to experiment and rejuvenate. As at Hidcote, there is an exciting tension between the plants and their trim and emphatic framework. The design is very firm, with the new courts running parallel with the old, and bound together with strong east-west and north-south axes in the form of stone paths, terraces and channelled views leading to a seat or other ornament.

Thus, from the central old court, you gain a prospect down the length of a rectangular waterlily pond to a stone loggia; this garden was made from the old tennis court in 1947, and the loggia erected by Mrs Reiss in memory of her nephew who was killed in the Second World War. From the Fountain Garden beyond, the eye is led between rivers of catmint down the centre of the Kitchen Garden, to a farm gate and then out into a woodland walk, edged in bulbs. The Kitchen Garden itself is full of unusual crops, many from the Heritage Seed Library of Garden Organic (formerly the Henry Doubleday Research Association); 'Rat's Tail' radish, 'Tiger Tom' tomato and the chilli pepper 'Long Green Buddha' are among the selection of curiosities.

Often, the symmetry of Tintinhull's design is reinforced in the planting. Lavender is repeated either side of the Eagle Court's terrace steps, for example, and beds of the Apothecary's rose, *Rosa*

gallica var. *officinalis*, either side of the southern entrance to the Kitchen Garden. A clump of variegated flag iris stands in each corner of the waterlily pool; and a pair of white-tiered *Cornus controversa* 'Variegata' (introduced by the Trust, and perhaps a touch too flashy for Tintinhull) preside over the extension to the Fountain Garden, teamed with foliage plants.

But everywhere, there is the contrasting exuberance: hellebores filtering between evergreen *Itea ilicifolia* and *Mahonia × media* 'Winter Sun', oak-leaved hydrangea and mock orange, in a north-facing bed; *Iris sibirica* 'Flight of Butterflies' interplanted with *Allium christophii*. As at Hidcote, colour is the medium that orders the mixed cast of plants. The beds around the circular pool in the Fountain Garden have a crisp white theme, founded on the flowers of tulips, roses, penstemons, argyranthemums and cosmos, and set off by silvery foliage and a dark backdrop of yew hedges.

The large north-eastern court has a border of smouldering crimson and bronze-red leaves, provided by various berberis and the young growth of Bush roses, partnered with the magenta-red flowers of *Rosa* 'Zéphirine Drouhin' and 'Rosemary Rose', alliums and penstemons; a more subdued, old-world mood than the red borders at Hidcote, with their brilliant scarlets and oranges. Flanking the rectangular waterlily pool is a contrasting pair of schemes, one with the soft, feminine tones of pink and lavender phlox, veronica and aster, and the other with the more potent, advancing shades of blood-red 'Frensham' roses, dahlias and yellow achilleas, but harmonised by the presence of white and silver in the form of stachys, crambe, sweet rocket and *Clematis recta*.

Because most of the garden is seen from the upstairs windows of the house, Mrs Reiss planned the borders for an all-year display, and wherever possible, bulbs, annuals and biennials are used to give each piece of ground a second season of colour. Thus, snowdrops, winter aconites, anemones, chionodoxas and scillas are ubiquitous (the blues particularly striking beneath plants whose young leaves are in shades of red); tulips and daffodils appear in advance of roses; pink and white cyclamen follow the spring magnolias. There is an additional boost from pots, notably around the waterlily pool, where tulips perform ahead of pink verbena and *Anisodontea*, white *Argyranthemum* and grey-leaved marguerites. In the cool shade of the loggia stand pots of hostas and ferns.

In every enclosure, large and small, there is a sense of space and tranquillity, an impression fostered by the central uncluttered expanses of lawn or water. The terraces are generous, appointed with steps wide and shallow to 'emphasise the change of level on what is a

relatively flat site', as Lanning Roper observed. The trees are also of an unexpected scale: there are just a handful to lift the eye and draw in the sky, including yew, cedar, and holm oak, *Quercus ilex* – all evergreen and nicely in period with the house.

All this, together with the various sub-divisions and wealth of detail, makes it very hard to believe that the entire composition encompasses only about 0.8ha (2 acres), as many writers have commented. The ideas and lessons here for all owners of small gardens are legion.

PREVIOUS PAGE Evening light streams across catmint and lime-green smyrnium in the Kitchen Garden.

ABOVE The Pool Garden at Tintinhull, viewed from the Summer House.

Townend

TROUTBECK, WINDERMERE, CUMBRIA

AREA 0.1ha (¼ acre) • **SOIL** acid/loam • **ALTITUDE** 165m (541ft)
AVERAGE RAINFALL 2,006mm (79in) • **AVERAGE WINTER CLIMATE** moderate

From the Ambleside road, the lane leading to Townend climbs
and winds into the Troutbeck Valley, with fine views down to Lake
Windermere and up into the fells. This small, lime-washed yeoman's
farmhouse, home to the Browne family from the mid-sixteenth
century, is tucked into a sheltering bank of old yew trees, presiding
over outbuildings, barns and an unpretentious little yard.

The last George Browne – the tenth generation to carry that
name – was an antiquary, woodcarver and keen gardener. With the
benefit of his notebooks, the Trust maintains the garden much as
it was before his death in 1914. The small, formal flower garden is
entered from the lane through a rustic gate and arch, covered in the
blush-white Victorian Climbing rose 'Madame d'Arblay'. Bounded
by low, grey stone walls and gravel paths, it is an attractive period
piece, featuring Hybrid Musk and other roses amid a host of cottage
perennials, including alchemilla, bellflowers, geraniums, comfrey,
daylilies and the blue spires of Browne's favourite delphiniums. A lilac
tree and a row of white burnet roses frame a cutting bed of dahlias,
chrysanthemums and old-fashioned sweet peas, including rose and
white 'Painted Lady', blue 'Lord Nelson' and orange 'Henry Eckford'.
In the yard beyond, more roses and perennials bring the wash of
summer colour right up to the house, *Geranium macrorrhizum*
'Album' handsomely topping one low garden wall in white icing.

Above the garden, separated by a bank of rowan, lilac and
laburnum, is an orchard of damsons and old apple varieties, such as
'Lady Henniker', 'Court of Wick' and 'Keswick Codlin', accompanied
in spring with a flush of wild daffodils.

RIGHT The gate at Townend framed by an arch formed by a Victorian climbing rose.

Treasurer's House

MINSTER YARD, YORK, NORTH YORKSHIRE

AREA 0.1ha (½ acre) • SOIL silty loam with clay pockets • ALTITUDE 11m (36ft)
AVERAGE RAINFALL 559mm (22in) • AVERAGE WINTER CLIMATE cold

'Eighteenth-century French statues of gods and goddesses evoke the city's Roman past'

The medieval bulk of York Minster casts long shadows across this garden, which stands behind the Chapter House within the cobbled lanes of the Close. The Minster's treasurers lived on this site until the Reformation, but the present Treasurer's House, with its pale limestone façade and Dutch gables, dates from the mid-sixteenth and early seventeenth centuries, when it was owned by Thomas Young, Queen Elizabeth I's powerful Archbishop of York and Lord President of the Council of the North, and his descendants.

After a long period of decline in the nineteenth century, when it was subdivided into at least five separate dwellings, Treasurer's House found its champion in Frank Green. Thanks to the Wakefield engineering business begun by his grandfather, Green could enjoy the rich lifestyle of a bachelor connoisseur, and indulge himself fully in the contemporary taste for exploring and reviving the romance of the past. In 1897 he began buying and piecing together the front sections of this historic house – the rear section, owned by the Gray family, remaining separate – and, with the help of his architect Temple Moore, stripping away Victorian alterations to reveal the earlier bones. By 1900 the evocative period refurbishment was to a standard that was fit for the Prince and Princess of Wales, who came to stay that June.

Over much the same period, the walled garden in front of the house was also reunited from separate plots and redesigned in its present form by Moore. Green wanted a simple setting to complement rather than compete with the house, and the resulting formal green court comprises a narrow terrace walk around a sunken lawn. A robinia and a large ash shade one side of the garden, together with an avenue of pollarded London planes, presented in panels of cobbles either side of the York stone pathway. They are balanced on the opposite side by a younger ash and quince tree planted by the Trust, which has owned Treasurer's House since 1930.

In Green's time, the principal detailing was in the architectural decoration. Eighteenth-century French statues of gods and goddesses evoke the city's Roman past – Neptune and Venus flanking the front door, and Vulcan, the god of fire, at the head of the lawn – together with Mercury (a replacement for the original lead statue of him, which was stolen) on top of the circular fountain. An assortment of architectural fragments is also incorporated into niches in the garden walls to handsome effect.

It is the National Trust which has added an overlay of flowering plants to the scene, to make the garden a more interesting place for visitors to stroll around and sit in. In the recent replanting, the colour scheme has been confined to whites and blues to meet Green's desire for simplicity, and to foster the sense of cathedral calm (to which end, routine mowing and pruning is carried out with silent hand tools).

A mass of white 'Thalia' narcissi and 'White Triumphator' tulips illuminate the beds in spring, and these are followed by a succession of perennials including bearded irises, peonies, geraniums, agapanthus and Japanese anemones. The dry, limy soil, tree roots and shade make this a challenging site. Accompanying shrubs, including a pair of evergreen *Viburnum × globosum* 'Jermyns Globe' by the wrought-iron entrance gate and *Magnolia grandiflora*, pyracantha and blue Japanese wisteria on the house walls, give the beds some year-round structures.

Quirkily, there is an additional pocket of garden to the rear of the property, within the curtilage of Gray's Court. Formerly a small orchard, this was first turned into a herb garden by the Trust but is now being redesigned to incorporate espaliered fruits and cut flowers for the house. Very attractive modern ironwork gates, featuring hart's tongue ferns, lead into it, and there is a beehive at the back. Like the front garden, this area is also towered over by medieval architecture, in this case a section of York's castellated city wall.

RIGHT A lead statue of the Roman god Mercury, which is also a fountain, at the western end of the garden.

Tredegar House

NEWPORT, MONMOUTHSHIRE

AREA 46ha (113 acres) • SOIL deep reddish, fine and loamy • ALTITUDE 43m (141ft)
AVERAGE RAINFALL 841mm (33in)

Mystery surrounds the origins and early layout of these gardens, and indeed surrounds the great house itself, for exactly when it was built and who the architect was are unclear. The house is arranged in a square and, of its four sides, one range is Tudor, dating from the 1540s, while the grand, red-brick front and side ranges date from 1670. What is not in doubt is its magnificence – the luxury of its interiors and the elegance of its warm brick façades, dressed in carved limestone – which proclaims the taste and social standing of the Morgan family, descendents of the Welsh princes who had owned this land since the Middle Ages. It was probably William Morgan who commissioned it, following his marriage to his cousin Blanche, a wealthy heiress, in 1661. It replaced his existing Tudor house, and it was set in a pattern of formal courts and radiating tree avenues in the Baroque manner.

The principal approach was from the north, and here the oak avenue still stands, crossing the park in slightly skew alignment with the front door, which is screened from the outer stable courtyard by a superbly ornate and gilded ironwork *clairvoyée* made by the Edney Brothers of Bristol in about 1715. Two of the avenue's original oaks survive, the other trees being of assorted ages.

The gardens run past the house's south-west front as a series, or *enfilade*, of three walled compartments (together with an outer rectangular strip, the Slips, which is of much later date and likely to have been purely utilitarian). The first record of them is in an estate plan of 1770, but they are likely to have been built in the second or third decade of the eighteenth century, incorporating earlier walls

and gardens. Formal gardens of this age are extremely rare, and today they still impress with their scale – well over 1.6 ha (4 acres) – and with the beauty of their high brick walls, gates and gate piers, capped with urns. The long axis paths would once have connected to stately tree avenues beyond.

Restoration by the Trust, which acquired Tredegar on a 50-year lease from Newport Borough Council only in 2012, is at a very early stage, so much of the present content of the walled gardens has been inherited. The largest compartment, the Orchard Garden, appears to have combined large productive areas with display elements at least by the nineteenth century – an era when the walled gardens would surely have been lavish, though again there is surprisingly little historical documentation or illustration. There were further extensive walled kitchen gardens, which no longer exist.

The Orchard Garden is now managed by the charity Growing Space, whose mixed planting, from herb beds to tropical bedding, gives it a lively atmosphere. On the lawns are older fruit trees and conifers, including Monterey and stone pines (*Pinus pinea*), and in one corner are remnants of a series of Victorian glasshouses, together with a bothy, a potting shed, and the footings of a vanished vinery. Here Evan Morgan, 2nd Viscount Tredegar, who died in 1949 and was the last member of the family to live at Tredegar, kept part of his idiosyncratic menagerie of animals and birds, which included a kangaroo, honey bear and baboon.

The central compartment, adjacent to the house and divided into panels of lawn, is known as the Cedar Garden. There may have been six cedars of Lebanon here in the past, but only one remains, dating from the early nineteenth century and now accompanied by several other trees including magnolias. The garden is fringed by some very attractive herbaceous borders, and as its centrepiece has an obelisk monument commemorating Sir Briggs, the horse that carried Captain Godfrey Morgan, 1st Viscount, in the Charge of the Light Brigade in 1854 and died here twenty years later, aged 28.

The third and smallest compartment is the Orangery Garden. The large brick Orangery – probably built at the same time as the gardens – is, like the adjoining Stables, a grand and handsome statement. The pots of orange and lemon trees housed over winter would once have been kept warm by concealed hot-air ducts in the floor and rear wall. Today, they share their indoor accommodation with the Cefn Mably shovelboard, which at 12.8m (42ft) is the longest single-plank oak table in the world, and outdoors sojourn with topiary bay trees in a parterre patterned with coloured sands, shells, and brick and coal dust, devised by the Council following an archeological excavation in 1990. On the walls are espaliered apples, pears, plums and cherries, with the Orangery itself sporting figs and an evergreen magnolia.

Tredegar's park once spanned 404ha (1,000 acres). Most of this land has now been swallowed up by industrial, motorway and housing development, which on the east side comes very close to the house, almost overshadowing the small green Italianate sunken garden here. To the north, though, there is still a green lung of 36ha (90 acres) inviting exploration.

Responding to the swing in gardening taste towards more naturalistic landscape, John Morgan engaged Adam Mickle – who had worked for 'Capability' Brown – to remodel this North Park, and his plan of 1788 survives. A principal alteration was the new entrance drive, now edged in deodar cedars, curving in through the park, while retaining the oak avenue (it appears that Mickle's ideas for dismantling elements of the formal gardens were often vetoed).

Beyond the drive he introduced the handsome serpentine lake, which is fed by the Ebbw River. Spanning 4ha (10 acres) and containing several islands, now silted up, its shores bristle with pines, cedars and wellingtonias, which are one of the planting motifs of the Park's pleasure grounds, together with self-seeded alders. Striking clumps of wellingtonias also stand sentinel close to the stable courtyard.

The walk around the lake – with views across rafts of native white waterlilies sheltering large carp and, in summer, offering the sight of whirling house martins and perhaps also the flash of a kingfisher – takes you past a timber boathouse and cascade, and into a belt of mixed woodland and laurel jungle. In spring, a colourful shrubbery of hardy hybrid rhododendrons enlivens the return journey from the gate lodges.

BELOW The Orangery Garden parterre at Tredegar House.

Trelissick Garden

FEOCK, TRURO, CORNWALL

AREA 10ha (25 acres) • SOIL acid/loam • ALTITUDE 30m (100ft) • AVERAGE RAINFALL 1,016mm (40in) • AVERAGE WINTER CLIMATE frost-free, mild

Cornish gardens spring many surprises, but the apparitions at Trelissick take some beating. Detached from the Neo-classical mansion, the grounds are on an intimate scale, a tranquil composition of plunging lawns, specimen trees, shady paths and stream-fed dell framed by woods and the expected masses of rhododendrons and camellias. There are occasional glimpses of the River Fal below, a ribbon of light between the tree-clad banks. But as you emerge from the shrub walks to the north, the jaw drops – for the water near the river mouth is deep, and at anchor on the garden's boundary is likely to be a substantial cargo ship. Like the land approaches to the Suez Canal, where great tankers suddenly appear, gliding between folds of empty desert, not only their size but their very presence is a shock.

It would be more appropriate if the ships were galleons, for this is a country of creeks and secret coves, of smugglers' legend and historical romance. The house commands an excellent view of Carrick Roads and beyond to Falmouth Bay, while the road that bisects the garden drops to the King Harry Ferry, connecting Truro with the isolated Roseland Peninsula. The garden acquired its present richness after 1937, when the estate became the home of Mr and Mrs Ronald Copeland. Since 1955, the Trust has developed the grounds considerably in response to various losses from drought, frost and storm by extending the shrubberies and tree collection into Carcadden, the land across the Ferry road, as well as boosting the post-spring displays.

Entering the garden beside the walls of the old kitchen garden, you plunge immediately into flowers. In spring, Chinese and Japanese wisterias, with violet abutilon, accompany clove-scented *Viburnum × juddii*, while in summer, hot-coloured cannas, dahlias, hedychiums and heliotrope are backed by scented evergreen *Trachelospermum jasminoides* and *Magnolia grandiflora* 'Galissonière'. There is also a collection of figs further on, near the shop.

The climate, though not quite as benevolent as at Glendurgan or Trengwainton, is mild and moist, and the shrub display that draws you into the woodland walks begins early. Brazen stands of 'Cornish Red' rhododendrons and the blood-red form of *R. arboreum* give way to groves of *Camellia japonica* and *C. × williamsii* in their many red, pink and white cultivars. There are splashes from blush-pink *Rhododendron sutchuenense* and red *R. thomsonii*, the pink *R. williamsianum* cultivars and other Cornish hybrids such as 'Penjerrick' and 'Beauty of Tremough'. And so the succession continues, with appearances from evergreen azaleas, violet-blue *R. augustinii* hybrids, scented white 'Avalanche', scented deciduous azaleas, numerous Hardy Hybrids and a large collection of blood-scarlet rhododendrons from early 'Little Bert' and 'Earl of Athlone' to 'May Day' and 'Romany Chai', and the Trelissick speciality 'Gwilt-King'. The more tender varieties, such as *R. magnificum*, grow on the sides of the dell, on the far side of the main lawn. The huge Australian tree ferns inevitably steal the show here, but the collection of white, lily-scented *maddenii* rhododendrons is

bewitching. The shelter and moisture is also enjoyed by large-leaved species, such as the rose-tinted form of *R. rex* subsp. *arizelum* and by the beautiful sulphur-yellow hybrid 'Mary Swaythling'.

The wet ground below is at its most brilliant in early summer, when awash with variously coloured candelabra primulas, but earlier it is lit by the yellow flares of skunk cabbage in spring, and, later in the summer by lemon-scented *Primula florindae* and astilbes. The accompanying fern and hosta leaves are as large and lush as you will see anywhere.

Hydrangeas, extensively planted by the Copelands, have been still further exploited by the Trust, so that now the banks of spring shrub colour have their match in summer and autumn. A walk of blue and white hydrangeas, overhung with cherries and the snowdrop tree, *Halesia carolina*, skirts the dell, and more white varieties, grown near eucryphias and orange kniphofias, illuminate the view over the river to the gothick mansion of Tregothnan. Hydrangeas are also massed in Carcadden. This young arboretum, reached by a new bridge – the original of which was part of the system of carriage rides set out in the early nineteenth century – is a former orchard and nursery, and was brought into the garden in the 1960s. Magnolias

and viburnums, as well as rhododendrons, camellias and cherries, now feature here, together with a range of unusual trees and larger shrubs, including two fine plants of the frost-tender Chilean hazel, *Gevuina avellana*.

Much of the garden's attraction comes from the vistas, across from one side of the plant-filled valley to the other, along the undulating lawns and meandering paths, and, of course, down over the River Fal and the estuary. Daffodils, anemones and wildflowers carpet these views in spring and summer, and the mixed deciduous and evergreen trees provide an ever-changing frame; the highlights include *Acer platanoides* 'Cucullatum' in Carcadden and, most memorably, C.D. Gilbert's Japanese cedar, *Cryptomeria japonica*, stretching its many limbs in the centre of the main lawn, surrounded by deep exotic borders of cannas, ginger lilies and bananas.

LEFT Wisteria in flower on the Entrance Walk, with the Water Tower beyond.
ABOVE The new entrance and landscaping at Trelissick Garden in May.

Trengwainton Garden

MADRON, PENZANCE, CORNWALL

AREA 10ha (25 acres) • SOIL acid/loam over granite • ALTITUDE 75–120m (246–394ft)
AVERAGE RAINFALL 1,220mm (48in) • AVERAGE WINTER CLIMATE mild to moderate

The south-west corner of the Cornish peninsula enjoys one of the mildest climates in Britain, and in some of the dappled glades and old walled enclosures at Trengwainton you feel you could be in some lush subtropical garden. The long growing seasons, high rainfall and moist sea air promote fast growth, mosses and lichens, and the soft winters allow trees, shrubs and climbers from some of the world's temperate regions to flourish. The exotic flavour is appropriate, for it was wealth from his family's Jamaican sugar plantation that enabled Sir Rose Price to lay the foundations of the garden in the early nineteenth century.

It was he who built, in about 1820, the series of small walled compartments close to the entrance lodge, of great interest to garden historians for their sizeable raised brick vegetable beds, specially angled to take advantage of the winter sun; though known to have existed elsewhere, these are thought to be the only survivors. The southernmost compartments are now mysterious and jungly plantsman's plots, with wild ferns running through the grey granite walls, primroses and anemones spreading around the skirts of shrubs, and old, spring-flowering tree magnolias, *M. × veitchii* and forms of *M. campbellii*, shading a mossy carpet patterned with scented plants and areas of wildflower meadow.

The micro-climates here suit a mouth-watering range of tender trees and shrubs. *Eucryphia moorei* and *Panax laetus* syn. *Pseudopanax laetus* from Australia, *Magnolia doltsopa* syn. *Michelia doltsopa* from China and the Himalayas, and the South American

Fuchsia excorticata have all grown into fine specimens, as have hardier Asian species such as *Enkianthus campanulatus* and *Stewartia sinensis*, appreciative of the additional warmth, shelter and moisture.

Tender rhododendrons abound, among them the Formosan azalea *R. oldhamii*, and white-flowered, lily-scented species and hybrids of the *maddenii* series. The soaring biennial *Echium pininana*, from the Canary Islands, is a luxurious sight, as is *Geranium palmatum* from Madeira. The abundance of broad-leaved evergreens and scarcity of conifers contributes much to the balmy flavour of the gardens, but a few Southern Hemisphere coniferous species add exotic notes, among them *Podocarpus salignus* from Chile and *Athrotaxis selaginoides* from Tasmania.

Trengwainton began sampling such treasures after 1925, when Lt Col Edward Bolitho (who gave this garden to the Trust in 1961) inherited. The foundation for his collection of rhododendron species was Frank Kingdon-Ward's 1927–8 plant-hunting expedition to north-east Assam and the Mishmi Hills in Upper Burma, in which he was offered a share of the spoils by G.H. Johnstone of Trewithen. A number of species, including *Rhododendron maccabeanum*, *R. elliottii* and *R. cinnabarinum* subsp. *xanthocodon* Concatenans Group, flowered here for the first time in the British Isles. Over a long spring season, their flower trusses colour the woodland fringes

LEFT Colourful azaleas and rhododendrons grow in colourful thickets.
ABOVE Tree ferns surround the pond at Trengwainton.

and grassy glades through which the curving drive and its parallel long walk climb towards the house, following the old carriage drive.

At the height of the display, strong patches of magenta and pink Kirishima and Kurume azaleas draw the eye through the softer rose tones of *R. vaseyi*, the violets of 'Penheale Blue' and 'Saint Breward', and a great many other handsome selections, some bred here and most growing in the company of daffodils or wildflowers. The scents are rich and heavy, from deciduous azaleas and tender rhododendrons such as *Rhododendron johnstoneanum* and *R.* 'Lady Alice Fitzwilliam', and in the shadows and moist troughs, you come upon the elephantine foliage of *R. grande*, *R. magnificum*, *R. falconeri* (layers from the original specimen dating from the 1880s), and, of course, *R. macabeanum*.

Camellias are also here in quantity, massed into *allées* and scattered in drifts; and, later in summer, the drive and woodland walks are flushed blue and white with hydrangeas. Shortly after beginning the walk up the hill, you hear the sound of water.

The hills are laced with underground springs, and the stream beside the drive is fringed with lysichitons, candelabra primulas, astilbes, polygonums, arum lilies, hydrangeas and crocosmias. This contrasts with the jungle mood recaptured in the shady, sheltered pockets between the trees and rhododendron thickets, where wooden bridges cross the water and the mossy streamside banks support self-sporing colonies of Australian tree ferns; the open zones of bamboos, grasses and phormiums give a special theme to the Jubilee Garden.

In front of the Victorian house, the trees give way to falling lawns and, from the terrace, a stunning view of St Michael's Mount rising from the sea. The garden's chief threat – the wind – may also become apparent. The westerlies can be savage, and without extensive tree planting to protect the slope, little ornamental gardening could have been attempted. The shelter belts need continual management, and much restoration has been necessary following the severe gales of January 1990. Unusual plants continue to be sampled at Trengwainton, ensuring that the collection retains its pioneering flavour and can always spring exotic surprises.

ABOVE Candelabra primulas flower in the Stream Garden in June.

Trerice

KESTLE MILL, NEWQUAY, CORNWALL

AREA 2.4ha (6 acres) • **SOIL** neutral to alkaline/sandy loam • **ALTITUDE** 30m (100ft)
AVERAGE RAINFALL 940mm (37in) • **AVERAGE WINTER CLIMATE** moderate

This is bald, windswept, coastal countryside. High hedges flank the winding lanes that lead here, and the house is tucked into the hillside, sheltered by belts of pale-trunked sycamore, beech and other tenacious trees. The garden is a far cry from the exotic woodlands of the south coast. It is small and intimate, comprising a series of formal terraces and grass banks, enclosed by walls and hedges.

In fact, it is a rare survivor from the sixteenth century. The house was probably completed in 1573, and recent archeological surveys have also started to reveal more of the garden's ancient bones. This is likely to inspire considerable change and restoration, and already there have been period additions including, near the Great Barn and the productive vegetable garden, the installation of an Elizabethan grass labyrinth.

Above the house is the bowling terrace, known as the Kayling Lawn after the traditional Cornish game of skittles. This is now considered to be one of a suite of gardens that would have surrounded the house in Tudor times, and it would have been a prestigious and scenic addition, as it is today, offering views over the countryside to Newquay.

The Long Walk below is currently planted for a long flower display, with prostrate rosemary, euphorbia and tulips for spring, geraniums and lavender for early summer, and the hardy fuchsia 'Chillerton Beauty' blooming into autumn, alongside asters and penstemons. There is more rich colour in the form of gold and purple foliage, clematis and mock orange in the borders of the Front Court. This is a handsome walled enclosure presided over by a pair of early eighteenth-century lions made for the Cornish branch of the Arundell family, who owned Trerice for nearly 500 years. It was the house's original entrance court, and in Tudor times would have had a different geometric layout, possibly including a pond.

A vast double herbaceous border of blue and white, again with a long flowering season, divides the Front Court from the orchard and the recently planted knot garden in the new Ladies' Garden. The knot garden is the result of recent archaeological research, which revealed evidence of a sunken area and raised walks, and the patterns of its design, inspired by the magnificent plasterwork of the interiors, can be savoured from the windows of the Great Chamber. This formality contrasts with the soft meadow planting surrounding it. Native Tenby daffodils carpet the orchard in spring, followed by a succession of later daffodils and English irises.

ABOVE The east front of Trerice House viewed over the garden wall.

Tyntesfield

WRAXALL, BRISTOL, SOMERSET

AREA 18ha (45 acres) • SOIL neutral/loam over limestone • ALTITUDE 40–78m (131–256ft)
AVERAGE RAINFALL 1,054mm (41½ in) • AVERAGE WINTER CLIMATE mild

In April 2002, this High Victorian timepiece – a complete estate and ensemble, just 11.3km (7 miles) from the centre of Bristol – came blinking into the limelight, secured for the National Trust by a grant from the National Heritage Memorial Fund and a fundraising campaign to which 70,000 donors contributed. It had been a well-kept secret even in its locality, with Richard Gibbs, 2nd Lord Wraxall, guarding his privacy.

Although Lord Wraxall kept the walled kitchen garden in continuous production and the pleasure grounds mown and clipped, the decorative buildings, glasshouses, boating lake, tennis court and flower gardens were allowed to deteriorate. So the grounds required major restoration, and, in a departure from traditional practice, the Trust has been sharing this complex and fascinating task with trainees, volunteers, schoolchildren, and other members of the public wherever possible.

Walking onto the terrace, you are met by the wide, tranquil landscape of the Yeo valley, seen over layers of shapes and silhouettes – Irish yews against deciduous trees and trees against distant hills – while behind bristles the Gothic fantasy of the house, with golden towers, turrets and chimneys. The house was rebuilt in the 1860s for William Gibbs, whose virtual monopoly of the Peruvian guano trade (the bird dung used as an agricultural fertiliser) made him the richest commoner in England. His principal architect, John Norton, may also have designed the terrace, which wraps around two sides of the house, bounded by a balustrade.

Before 1917, the terrace culminated in a great conservatory, with a domed roof modelled on St Mark's in Venice, and its footprint is still visible below camellias, magnolias and Chusan palms (*Trachycarpus fortunei*). A mature lemon verbena, growing near wisteria and yellow Banksian roses elsewhere on the terrace, indicates the mildness of the climate here.

As you would expect, the High Victorian taste for artful, 'unnatural' gardening finds expression in bedding schemes, formality and coloured foliage. The central feature of each of the ten patterned terrace beds is a circle of green or golden hollies, topped by a stone urn; these are accompanied by rich, ever-changing displays of spring and summer bulbs, annuals, biennials and hothouse exotics, which, it is hoped, will be increasingly innovative and experimental over time. The formality then extends down a double stairway into a grand avenue of Irish yews (formerly interplanted with yuccas), and between topiary spheres of Portuguese laurel. Off to the west, a procession of hollies, pruned into mushroom mounds, leads you past an ornamental wooden aviary and into the pleasure grounds. The other decorative elements in the surrounding woods and farmland are part of an extensive designed landscape, while the pleasure grounds' tree collection is the nucleus of a vast planting scheme. Its sloping lawns are dotted with favourite Victorian curiosities, from blue cedar, monkey puzzle and variegated cypress (*Thujopsis dolabrata* 'Variegata') to gingko, oriental plane, and cut-leaved lime. There are also trees of champion size, including *Acer triflorum*, *Cercis siliquastrum* and *Zelkova serrata*. New plantings are being influenced by the discovery of some 400 zinc and terracotta tree labels, though curiosities such as Wollemi pine are also being added.

A High Church man (with his own resident chaplain), William Gibbs funded the building of the chapel at Keble College, Oxford,

and this is commemorated in the planting of a hybrid Algerian oak, *Quercus canariensis × robur*. The cedars of Lebanon were grown from seed brought from the Holy Land by the family in 1858. Frequently, the lawn dissolves into wilder areas, with colonies of daffodils, cowslips and other wildflowers, or thickets of bamboo and pampas grass. Indeed the lawns, which are presumed never to have been treated with fertiliser or weedkiller, are themselves rich wildflower habitats and home to orchids – twayblade, bee, green-winged, early purple and hundreds of autumn ladies' tresses. They are also rich in fungi, notably waxcaps.

Stone seats invite you to pause and survey the scene, one flanked by a pair of slim columnar cypresses, *Chamaecyparis lawsoniana* 'Wisselii'. Below the terrace, you meet rhododendron clumps and a little maze of yellow azalea. Another surprise among the trees is a large terraced rose garden, patterned in box hedges

and ironwork tunnels, and with a pair of Minton-tiled gazebos as architectural eye-catchers. Deer make rose-growing difficult here, so bedding and other plants make up today's palette. Lavenders and pink peonies, disliked by deer, present a good display, while to the side is a fernery and a rock bank, which will be developed as an intricate alpine garden. A sloping theatre lawn, backed by a hedge, rises behind the rose garden.

The walled kitchen garden is downhill from the house, the curving drive taking you past rhododendrons and specimen trees, including yellow buckeye, *Aesculus flava*. After 1896, when it was redesigned by architect Walter Cave, the kitchen garden was on show to guests as part of the garden tour and suitably ornamented

LEFT Lady Wraxall's Garden, with exotic planting around the edges of the red brick walls.
ABOVE Agapanthus flowers on the terrace with formal beds beyond.

with wrought-iron gates, a small flowery entrance garden, and an Italianate loggia in brick and sandstone – a classical contrast to the Gothic of the house, which would have been filled with seasonal pot plants, such as carnations and pelargoniums. The accompanying Lady Wraxall's Garden is warm and sheltered and contains tree ferns, hedychium and lemon verbenas.

Beyond is the range of glasshouses, already restocked with peaches, vines, tomatoes and cucumbers, and gardeners' sheds (including a packing room, where produce would have been prepared for the kitchen and for dispatch to London in boxes embossed with the family coronet). The Cut Flower or Jubilee Garden is lively with dahlias, sweet peas and other cutting flowers, and there is an extremely decorative classical orangery, recently restored. This would probably have been used as much for entertaining as for growing plants.

The main walled garden has a central dipping pool, and glasshouses on its southern side for figs, peaches and other tender fruits. With a full range of vegetables being returned to its beds, and hardy fruits newly trained on its walls (which were inset with vine-eye supports as they were built), this is once again reaching full production. Outside, the derelict orchard house and other outbuildings are projects for the future.

ABOVE A display of dahlias in the Cut Flower Garden.

Uppark

SOUTH HARTING, PETERSFIELD, WEST SUSSEX

AREA 22ha (54 acres) • SOIL alkaline/brown earth, chalk • ALTITUDE 150m (492ft)
AVERAGE RAINFALL 940mm (37in) • AVERAGE WINTER CLIMATE cold

Uppark suffered more than its fair share of calamity at the end of the twentieth century. In October 1987, and again in January 1990, its garden, park and woods were devastated by gales. In August 1989, when the restoration of the house was nearing completion and while the roof was being leaded, the building caught fire and was severely damaged. But the house has been painstakingly reconstructed, plaster wall by ceiling, door hinge by bracket, and looks uncannily unchanged; the scars suffered by the garden from the building works are gone and trees are growing up to re-create the former lushly wooded setting.

Its position, high on the South Downs with a view between flanking hills to a distant band of sea, is the chief delight. The house stands proud in this landscape, an elegant Dutch-style building with steeply pitched roof, pediment and red-brick walls, dressed in pale stone. It was built in about 1690 for Lord Grey of Warke, later 1st Earl of Tankerville, and in the mid-eighteenth century was given its supporting pair of large brick outbuildings, a stable block and kitchen-laundry range (later becoming the Orangery), each with a clock tower. Your first sight is of its rear, north façade and portico, at the head of a short drive, informally bordered by grass glades, groups of free-growing yew and other evergreens, and a young avenue of Norway maple.

Clearly, this is not a 1690s setting. The early, grander formal gardens, which seem to have had terrace walks, courts, orchards and a bowling green, had mostly disappeared by about 1730 in favour of parkland sweeping up to the house walls. The present rear garden of sinuous lawns, meandering gravel paths and shrubberies evolved

afterwards. It may well be that they were worked on by Lancelot 'Capability' Brown, for there is a plan dating from about 1750 attributable to him. But the principal protagonist behind today's garden is Humphry Repton, who advised Sir Harry Fetherstonhaugh from 1793, and produced one of his celebrated Red Books of proposals and sketches in 1810. He redesigned the north approach drive and portico, and most likely designed the game larder, the pathway to which is gruesomely inset with deer vertebrae. He probably also designed the iron gratings in the light wells over the intriguing underground service passages in the rear forecourt, which link the house to the kitchen, laundry and stables. The upstairs-downstairs world here was experienced at close hand by the young H.G. Wells, whose mother was housekeeper for twelve years until being dismissed for incompetence in 1892.

In the flower gardens and shrubberies either side of the drive, the Trust has embarked on a programme to capture more of the

flavour of Repton's Picturesque style. To the east, broad grass walks and glades curve around belts and island beds of loose, serpentine planting, the ingredients arranged in defined groups of gently contrasting form and habit, and graded in height for theatrical effect and plays of light and shade. To the west, there is a small scented garden. Repton commented on the 'atmosphere of sweets': 'I may truly say that in no place have I ever seen such accurate attention given to olfactory joy as at Uppark – every window has its Orange Tree or Tube roses – and admits perfume from the surrounding beds of Mignionette and Heliotrope.' Everywhere, the emphasis is on

shrubs and perennials of Repton's period, such as Shrub roses, lilacs, philadelphus and strawberry tree. There is a good show of bulbs, and also of chalkland wildflowers which thrive in the unimproved grass of the lawns and meadows and, with the trees, connect the garden to its breathtaking setting.

PREVIOUS PAGE A distant glimpse of Uppark, a late seventeenth-century house set high on the South Downs.

ABOVE Red valerian edges one of the island beds, planted in the Picturesque style.

Upton House

BANBURY, WARWICKSHIRE

AREA 15ha (37 acres) • SOIL neutral/iron-sandstone • ALTITUDE 211mm (693ft)
AVERAGE RAINFALL 686mm (27in) • AVERAGE WINTER CLIMATE cold

Upton stages one of the great *coups de théâtre* of English gardening. The opening scene is sober, even austere. The house, a wide, plain and symmetrical building, constructed of the local honey-brown Hornton sandstone, stands at the head of a straight drive, enclosed by tall beech and Scots pine, holly and yew. Its core was built by Sir Rushout Cullen, the son of a London merchant, in 1695; its additions date from the late 1920s, when the estate was bought by the 2nd Viscount Bearsted, a noted art collector and philanthropist.

The garden front is cheerier. There is clematis, wisteria and pink 'Albertine' rose on the walls; a succession of bedding plants, including wallflowers, tulips, Canterbury bells and seed-grown dahlias, fringing and spilling over the flagged terrace; and a stand of the hybrid Scots briar rose *Rosa × harisonii* 'Williams Double Yellow' complementing the stone. Opposite, a broad platform of lawn, framed on one side by yews and on the other by eighteenth-century cedars of Lebanon, sweeps to a ha-ha, beyond which the land climbs up a hillside, dotted with sheep and clumps of trees. It is a gentle and pleasing scene. Some visitors may look out upon it and turn back. On my first visit, I nearly did, but luckily decided to continue to the lawn edge.

As you peer over, the contents spring up at you like a jack-in-the-box. A valley is revealed, the nearside bank tamed by terraces of flowering shrubs and perennials, double herbaceous borders running down to a copper beech tree, a garden of roses, sloping yew hedges, a grand Italianate stairway, a large fruit and vegetable garden and, at the bottom, a rectangular lake. A complete garden landscape is hidden here. The walls are contemporary with

the older part of the house, and it seems that for three centuries the slope has been providing fruit and vegetables for the household. Angled to the south, the plots absorb all the available warmth, and they are still managed intensively, with greenhouses used to raise seedlings and cloches to protect young plants. The gamut of vegetables, grown on a four-year rotation, runs from French beans and Brussels sprouts to kohlrabi and onions. Falling rows of salad crops, asparagus beds, apple trees and blocks of soft fruit, including worcesterberry and jostaberry, complete the scene.

But while this productive section remains as the centrepiece, and a reminder of the priorities in the late seventeenth- and early eighteenth-century garden, the remainder of the slope has been developed for purely ornamental purposes. This was undertaken for Lord and Lady Bearsted by their architect, Percy Morley Horder, and the plantswoman and garden designer Kitty Lloyd-Jones, whose practical skills and artistry were employed by clients on both sides of the English Channel. In the present five-year refurbishment of the garden, the Trust is intending to reflect more of this 1930s flavour in its plantings – notably Kitty Lloyd-Jones's colour drifts in the Gertrude Jekyll style, and use of bulbs, annuals and tender perennials to extend the season. Family photographs and other archive material are helping in this.

With the construction of the stone stairway, the Baroque grandeur of the house was extended into the composition. The flights descend elegantly either side of a crown of wisteria, and at the base, where once the greenhouses stood, you come to the formal rose garden with beds of China and Hybrid Musk roses around a statue of Pan; Lady Bearsted's paved garden with pink and white perennials, shrubs and bedding plants; and a garden of blue flowers, woven

around *Hibiscus syriacus* 'Oiseau Bleu' (syn. 'Blue Bird'), and framed again by double yellow hybrid Scots briar roses.

Soft and carefully focused associations of colour distinguish the planting here on the terraces, with blue and yellow, alone or in partnership, as a principal motif. There are many memorable passages: Dutch lavender, running beside the upper grass walk, accompanied by ceanothus, romneya, laburnum, salvia and agapanthus; a wave of creamy, iris-like *Sisyrinchium striatum*, beneath outcrops of phlomis, santolina, cistus and purple aubrieta; and fine displays from the apricot Tea rose 'Climbing Lady Hillingdon', the buff Noisette rose 'Rêve d'Or', *Lonicera etrusca*, and, in autumn, from the leaves and fruits of stag's horn sumach and numerous berberis, including *B. wilsoniae*.

The Mediterranean and Californian flavour of these upper borders is in response to the sunny, dry conditions, but where the light and soil changes, you meet a different cast. On the cool, shady side of the vegetable garden's brick wall, for example, a National Collection of asters has been assembled: not the mildew-prone *novi-belgii* hybrids, the true Michaelmas daisies, but the various cultivars of the taller, smaller-flowered *A. ericoides* and *A. cordifolius*, which include so many desirable garden plants, interspersed with varieties of short, starry *A. amellus*. They are at their peak in early October. As you reach the lake, water sets a new theme – for this is one of a chain of six former stewponds, formalised by Sir Rushout Cullen, but dating back to medieval times, when the land was held by the Church. The water, fed from a spring on top of Edgehill, collects first in the Monk's Well, south-west of the house, passes through the stewponds and flows eventually into the Thames. The lake you see from the lawn above is part of this, and was given its irregular shape and temple in 1775, when the property was owned by the banker Robert Child. The sunken lawn off to the west is now explained, for as you arrive through the nuttery (another essential in the productive garden), you realise that it too, together with the other water-filled depression now revealed – bordered by rushes and trees, including an impressive hornbeam – is part of the sequence.

Upton's second big surprise is now sprung. For beyond this pond, yet another garden of distinctive character opens up – a water garden of meandering grass paths and sinuous pools, presided over by a Dutch-style banqueting house, now looming between the trees. The building, like the formal framework of the gardens, dates back to the late seventeenth century, but the area was re-landscaped and planted in the 1930s, by which time the stewponds here had become an overgrown marsh. Lush marginal plantings of hostas, rodgersias,

ligularias and rheums contrast with the more elegant foliage of ferns, astilbes and the multi-stemmed Katsura trees (*Cercidiphyllum japonicum*), and there are strong flashes of colour from lysichiton, primulas, and irises. Yew terraces, dating from the seventeenth century, lead back up to the main lawn.

This is by no means a complete catalogue of the garden's horticultural attractions. There is Lady Bearsted's limestone rock garden beside the swimming pool on the main lawn; the secret scented garden with its Shrub roses, stocks and sweet peas; the south lake border with its lush foliage; the spectacular delphinium, lupin and peony border; the orchard with its damsons, medlars and greengages; and the Wilderness, where Queen Anne's lace and campion follow the daffodils and bluebells. All contribute to a mood of luscious 1930s country house life.

PREVIOUS PAGE Lady Bearsted's garden, planted in pinks, whites and mauves, at Upton House.

ABOVE Cedars of Lebanon mark the boundary of the lawn and lower gardens.

RIGHT Garden steps leading from the top terrace down into the gardens, with the Mirror Pond beyond.

The maintenance of mixed borders

Heather Aston, Head Gardener
UPTON HOUSE, WARWICKSHIRE

The mixed border is the main backbone of any garden and is part of what makes gardening so exciting. After planting, it is very important to follow a good routine and annual programme of maintenance to get maximum benefit from the border.

Establishing a routine

Your routine for general maintenance will include weeding, feeding, hoeing, putting support systems in place, planting bulbs, sowing annual seeds, planting tender perennials after the last frosts and removing and protecting them before the first, checking for pests and diseases and introducing natural predators to control them. Some of these tasks will need to be done weekly, while others just need your attention once or twice a year. But the more you work and the more time you spend in the border, the more you will see and appreciate the plants around you.

To maintain a healthy stock, shrubs and plants will need to be propagated throughout the year at the optimum times. For example, most shrubs, such as buddleja and rock rose (*Cistus*), can be propagated in early autumn by taking softwood cuttings; other shrubs, such as dogwood (*Cornus*) and willow (*Salix*), can be propagated by hardwood cuttings. Many herbaceous plants, such as asters and achillea, can either be divided in the spring or propagated by soft cuttings taken as growth starts to appear, while some are better propagated by root cuttings. For instance, anemone root cuttings need to be taken in the autumn and overwintered indoors before replanting out in the spring as healthy new plants. This will ensure a clean and healthy border throughout the year.

Annual maintenance is paramount, as it sets the standards for the border for the following year and will also help with soil structure and moisture retention. It is usually done in the winter, but some of your plants might well be winter flowering and some spring bulbs might be early, so when you choose to do it will very much depend on your location and the plants in your border.

Plant maintenance

This is easily divided into the various types of plant you have in your borders:

- Herbaceous perennials: removal of dead foliage and support systems, dividing and replanting.
- Bulbs: splitting up and replanting.
- Shrubs: removal, replanting, pruning to maintain shape and size, removal of diseased, damaged and diverting branches.
- Trees: removal of lower laterals and overcrowded, diseased, damaged and diverting branches.
- Wall shrubs and climbing plants: prune and train branches to maintain shape and structure.

When the plants have all been pruned into shape the border will then need to be lightly forked over to relieve any soil compaction before applying a generous helping of organic matter spread evenly over the border to a depth of 7.5cm (3in). Homemade compost is ideal, but any organic matter will do. This is very important in maintaining an open and fibrous soil structure and also maintaining a level of moisture retention for the plants.

Tips

- Establish a good routine of plant husbandry – in other words, do not leave it for several years and then do it all at once!
- Research your plants and get to know what they like before planting. Do they prefer dry or wet conditions, heavy or light soil?
- Keep a diary of maintenance routines, noting dates of planting, feeding, propagating, composting and so forth.
- Constantly stand back and view the border analytically. There is always room for change and improvement, trying out new planting combinations, such as planting different varieties of clematis around wooden pillars to add height and colour. Pruning shrubs slightly differently can also add a fresh focal point to the border.

The Vyne

SHERBORNE ST JOHN, BASINGSTOKE, HAMPSHIRE

AREA 5ha (13 acres) • SOIL neutral/clay • ALTITUDE 61m (200ft)
AVERAGE RAINFALL 762mm (30in) • AVERAGE WINTER CLIMATE moderate

This composition of spacious pleasure grounds and crisp, clear colours fills a quiet hollow just a few miles from Basingstoke. The house was built for William Sandys, later Lord Chamberlain to Henry VIII, in the early part of the sixteenth century, and modified by Chaloner Chute, Speaker of the House of Commons, after 1653. It is a wide and welcoming building of rose-red brickwork, dressed in stone and decorated with purple header-bricks in diamond pattern (diapering), and when you approach the north façade of the house, it springs the surprise of a white Palladian portico – the earliest known example to adorn an English country house.

The low-lying position makes for a lush, green setting. Towering limes, together with an old horse chestnut and ancient oak, shade the south lawns (flooded with daffodils in spring), and on the north side, a vast expanse of close-mown grass rolls gently down to a lake, flanked by cedars, walnuts, Scots pines and other trees. You can see carp basking in the water and there is much other wildlife besides, including kingfishers, which often dart over the lower lake beyond the weir. A circular walk takes you across two bridges at either end of the lake (the brick piers of which are the remains of a fine Victorian bridge that replaced a Chinese-Gothic structure put up by John Chute in the eighteenth century) and passes through Morgaston Wood, full of bluebells in spring.

The other, more ornamental wilderness area was developed by Sir Charles Chute in about 1907, following the woodland and meadow gardening ideas of the writer William Robinson. Here, snowdrops, daffodils, anemones and snakeshead fritillaries are naturalised in the grass, accompanied by clumps of geraniums,

Gunnera manicata and the summer-flowering scented *Philadelphus* 'Beauclerk'. These areas are in contrast to the architectural and more formal touches that John Chute incorporated, or which were reinstated or added in the Victorian and Edwardian eras, when the grounds were reshaped and replanted; they include the gravel walk in front of the house, the narrow avenue of red-twigged limes dating from 1884, and, at its head, the splendid domed brick pavilion, in the shape of a Greek cross, dating from the 1630s. Standing next to it is one of the oldest oak trees in Hampshire. Nearby, beside the Chapel, you also come upon two evergreen *Phillyrea latifolia*, with ancient twisted trunks.

In summer, the most colourful area of the garden is the small enclosure beside the west front of the house. Here, backed by a yew hedge, is a colourful herbaceous border planted in the 1960s, where violet-blue, purples, pinks, carmines and whites (catmint, *Campanula lactiflora*, acanthus, phlox, sedum, Japanese anemone and others) melt into a scheme of yellows, apricots, creams and scarlets (ligularia, daylilies, macleaya, crocosmia) – all finely associated for height and foliage contrast. I caught this border, designed by the late Graham Stuart Thomas, at its peak in July and it has lodged in my memory as one of the best formal herbaceous schemes I have come across in National Trust gardens. Opposite, the two beds of the fragrant pink Bush rose *Rosa* 'Madame Knorr' (syn. *R*. 'Comte de Chambord') are flanked by a pair of purple vines grown on frames. These are a reference to the house, thought to have been named after *Vin Domus*, or House of Wine, in Roman times.

In recent years the eighteenth-century walled garden has been brought back into production, with large areas of soft fruit, vegetables, and fruit trees, including many historic varieties of apple. You meander through the beds to the soft sound of clucking chickens. The new glasshouse, built on the site of its Victorian predecessor, displays plants such as citrus trees and pelargoniums, which were once grown in the house's Stone Gallery.

RIGHT Swans on the main lake at The Vyne, with the porticoed north front of the house in the background.

Waddesdon Manor

WADDESDON, AYLESBURY, BUCKINGHAMSHIRE

AREA 67ha (165 acres) • SOIL alkaline/clay, sand • ALTITUDE 76m (250ft)
AVERAGE RAINFALL 864mm (34in) • AVERAGE WINTER CLIMATE cold

Baron Ferdinand de Rothschild rejected the initial design for his country house, intended as a weekend retreat for himself and his guests, as being rather too ambitious. His French architect, Gabriel-Hippolyte Destailleur, told him he would regret his decision, commenting that 'one always builds too small'. 'He prophesied truly,' said the Baron. 'After I had lived in the house for a while I was compelled to add one wing and then another . . .'

The manor, revealed at the end of a double avenue of trees (recently replanted with young English oak), is a fantastic sight: a broad expanse of Loire château perched on a cold, windy Buckinghamshire hill, bristling with conical towers, high-pitched pavilions, spires and ornament. Accompanying it is sweeping parkland with swirling belts of beech, lime, horse chestnut and other trees – many of which were planted in a semi-mature state, brought to their sites by teams of Percheron draft horses, specially imported from Normandy.

The tree collection was considerably enriched by his sister Miss Alice de Rothschild after Baron Ferdinand's death in 1898, and is characterised now by its sumptuous stands of specimen exotics, arranged, species by species, for landscape impact. Unfortunately, there were comparatively few subsequent introductions in the years after her death, with the result that a major programme of replacement planting for the future has been required of the Rothschild Foundation, the Rothschild family charity that manages the property on behalf of the National Trust. Horse chestnut, silver lime and Austrian pine are among those you pass as you ascend the curving drive from the village, and at the head of the oak avenue

weeping limes drench the air with summer scent around the grand fountain of Triton and Nereids riding on sea monsters.

Coloured-leaved trees, much favoured in the late Victorian garden, are prominent here on the approach, as elsewhere, with blue Atlas cedar, purple beech and Norway maple (*Acer platanoides* 'Schwedleri') used as highlights among the tapestry of greens. Golden yew and the golden Lawson cypress 'Stewartii' supply the yellow through the grounds. But the trees are just one element in this composition, which was planned as a series of varied and impressive entertainments for the family and their weekend guests.

The changes in terrain provide some drama, not just the contrast of the levelled areas and the falling hillside, but also the more picturesque additions, in particular the eruptions of rock to the west of the oak avenue. These seem natural, but in fact were made up of stone removed during the creation of the plateau on which the house is built, and are layered with artificial stone, brick and concrete. They were built by the noted rockwork specialists Pulham & Sons and, until the smell became too offensive, were used as shelter by Baron Ferdinand's flock of mountain sheep. Further down the hill, you come upon a deep gulley (excavated for part of the tramway installed to transport materials for building the house) spanned by a bridge and with its steep sides planted with ferns and bamboo. The grass here is full of bluebells, primroses and daffodils, an echo of the great sloping wildflower and daffodil meadow, planted by Mr and Mrs James de Rothschild as a memorial to Miss Alice, further to the south.

The contrasts of artful gardening and natural landscape, man-made eye-catchers and plant forms play throughout the grounds. Beyond Pulham's rustic rockwork is the most splendid structure of all: a magnificent Rococo ironwork aviary, each compartment housing an assortment of exotic birds. The raucous calls, including those of the dashing white Rothschild's Mynah from Bali, can be heard deep into the park, and on my first visit here, years ago, there was the astonishing sight of macaws flying free over the trees. This policy had to be discontinued because of the damage they inflicted on plants.

The grandest piece of formal gardening, however, is to be found to the south of the house. Here, below the terrace, is the great parterre, designed by the Baron and the arena where he could demonstrate to his guests his gardeners' mastery over plants. With an ornate fountain displaying Pluto and Proserpine as their centrepiece,

LEFT View of the house from the west garden.

and a stone balustrade and clipped hedges of green and golden yew as their frame, the beds heave with many thousands of seasonal bulbs, annuals and tropical dot plants. Elsewhere in the gardens are modern recreations of a 19th-century phenomenom pioneered by the Rothschilds – three-dimensional carpet bedding, in which bedding plants are set into sculptural frames, in this case in the form of giant birds (a reference to the bird and floral basket created by Miss Alice). Across the parterre, there is a panoramic view, past the pink- and white-candled chestnuts, down into the Vale of Aylesbury and towards the Rothschild pavilion at Eythrope, near Upper Winchendon – formerly Alice de Rothschild's house, to which her brother Baron Ferdinand would conduct his guests in a procession of landaus on a Sunday afternoon. In the morning, they would have toured Waddesdon's series of show glasshouses and rose, fruit and cutting flower gardens, all formerly attached to the 2.8ha (7 acre) kitchen garden, which is outside the Trust's boundary and of which nothing much remains. The ornamental Dairy and Water Garden, which were also on the tour, have by contrast been restored and can be visited by appointment.

It was a sumptuous world, and present-day Waddesdon has re-created the spectacular flamboyance of the past with innovation and showmanship – not least in the manor's interiors, which are one of the treasure chests of Europe. The gardens are also now home to several pieces of contemporary sculpture alongside the historic collection, with the exhibitions programme inviting contemporary artists to create responses to the gardens and landscape.

RIGHT An impressive spring display of tulips and wallflowers in the great parterre.

Summer bedding

Paul Farnell, Head Gardener
WADDESDON MANOR, BUCKINGHAMSHIRE

Summer bedding can be the crowning glory of any garden – the intensity of the colours, the longevity of the flowers and the sheer diversity of the plant range mean there is always something new to try. As with all things, there are good practices and bad practices when picking a bedding scheme, but there are only a few simple rules to follow.

Choosing bedding plants

When looking for a bedding plant there are several things to be taken into account. Colour is important, together with the ultimate height and spread of the plant, the longevity of its flowering season, its ability to cope with hotter, drier summers and, perhaps the most important and often overlooked, a good healthy plant to start with.

Putting your schemes together

People often talk about shape and form when they are looking at plants, but bedding is less about shape, form and permanence than colour, lashings of it, put together in a way that is pleasing on the eye. For this I find an artist's colour wheel invaluable, of which plenty of examples can be found on the Internet.

There are four ways of describing colour schemes:

- Monochromatic: using a single colour in its various hues and tints.
- Analogous (related): colours are used that are neighbours on the colour wheel, such as red and orange.
- Contrasting: colours directly opposite each other on the colour wheel are used, such as yellow and violet.
- Polychromatic (rainbow): colours from all parts of the wheel are used in Victorian style.

Discounting the polychromatic scheme, which generally turns out to be too much of a good thing, there are three ways of putting colours together in a harmonious way, the most subtle of which is to use tints and shades of a single colour. The most restful way is to match analogous colours that lie next to each other on the colour wheel, while the boldest is to use contrasting colours. However, it is important to remember that you are not dealing with a block of colour as you would when painting a wall, for example, as you always have the various shades of green that make up the background of the plant showing through and the flowers often have a different colour eye, perhaps starting off with a very intense colour that then fades as they age. All these factors need to be considered when designing a bedding display.

The care of bedding plants

Bedding plants are usually quite robust, but it is important to have a good, healthy plant to start with. Soil is the next consideration. Soil science has come a long way over the past few years, confirming what our forefathers knew – that adding well-rotted organic material to the soil improves the quality of the plant. We now know that it is due in part to micro-organisms within the compost that are beneficial to the plant, so good soil preparation is essential.

Most bedding plants are annuals and their sole purpose is to flower and set seed to continue their species. Regular deadheading of the plants will prolong the flowering of your bedding, and while doing this you are close up to the plant so you can tell if there are any problems with pests or diseases that may be present.

Feeding

Some bedding plants can be quite heavy feeders; applying an organic seaweed-based fertiliser at the start of the season and giving a supplementary feed with an organic liquid fertiliser every two weeks or so during August will keep them in good heart. If you are using liquid feed, dilute it to half the recommended strength – your plants will flower just as well and will be tougher and more disease-resistant.

Gardening in a changing climate

While debate about climate changes rages in the media, gardeners are faced with real, tangible changes in weather patterns that affect their plants significantly. For several years the UK has had periods of intense summer heat without precipitation, then violent pulses of rain and winters without prolonged periods of frost, and although bitter winters are not a thing of the past the trend is towards a warming world.

The most basic step towards coping with dry summers is to acquire a water butt – your acid-loving plants will in any case prefer rain water to that from the tap. While you can buy ornamental tanks, a simple, inexpensive plastic butt with a tap at the base will do the job perfectly well. You will also need a diverter kit, so that once the butt is full the excess water will run down into your drain or into another butt. Place the water butt on a flat surface, raising it on to a platform if necessary so that you can get a watering can beneath the tap with ease.

Once you have to carry water to and fro rather than just turning on a hose you will feel less inclined to water so often, and your plants will actually benefit from this. Experiments have shown that a low-watered plant is a tougher one, less reliant on human intervention – and while your bedding plants may be more compact you may find you have a lesser incidence of aphids, perhaps because there is less soft, sappy growth for them to feed on.

Finally, accepting the now-popular principle of gardening with nature rather than against it will make your gardening life easier and the plants in your borders healthier. If you live in one of the more arid parts of the country, such as Essex, research the plants that will live happily in the conditions that you provide for them – you will find you can still have a garden rich in colour, form, texture and fragrance no matter where you live.

Tips
- Regular deadheading will prolong the flowering season of your plants.
- Check regularly for pests and diseases.
- Pinch out foliage bedding plants regularly to encourage more foliage.

Wakehurst Place

ARDINGLY, HAYWARDS HEATH, WEST SUSSEX

AREA 73ha (180 acres) • SOIL acid to neutral/sandy, clay • ALTITUDE 61–152m (200–500ft)
AVERAGE RAINFALL 889mm (35in) • AVERAGE WINTER CLIMATE moderate

The setting for this mind-boggling collection of trees and shrubs is the unspoilt countryside of the Sussex Weald, with its rolling hills and tracts of ancient woodland. The gardens spill down grassy and rocky slopes below a high plateau, on which stands the Elizabethan mansion, built for Sir Edward Culpeper and restored by the Edwardian architect Sir Aston Webb.

The tall redwoods, formal lawns and small garden lake and rockery that accompany it are part of the nineteenth-century legacy, but it was in 1903 that the exotic planting began in earnest. The estate was bought by Gerald Loder, later Lord Wakehurst, who, following his father and his brother Sir Edmund at nearby Leonardslee and his nephew Giles at The High Beeches, began tapping into the stream of new trees and shrubs becoming available from the Americas, the Far East and Australasia. In 1965, the garden came, by way of a 99-year lease from the National Trust, to the Royal Botanic Garden, Kew, whose influence now shows in the stricter rationalising policy of grouping plants by geographic region and habitat, so that one has a sense of walking through the world's temperate woodlands, among relatively natural associations of leaf and flower.

The great storm of 1987, which tore through Wakehurst with the loss of around 20,000 trees, accelerated this shift in display in various parts of the grounds, including near the house, where sheltered and shady woodland beds were converted overnight into a sunny, exposed hilltop. Replanted with dwarf rhododendrons, junipers, potentillas, and *Daphne bholua*, ground-cover perennials including roscoeas and carpets of *Bergenia ciliata*, and a copse of birch, rowan and maples behind, this now gives a taste of the sub-alpine heathland and scrub of Taiwan, Korea, Japan and the Sino-Himalayas – a region which was of special interest to Tony Schilling, the plant-hunter and former curator.

Such innovations interplay with older and more ornamental features. Around the lawns, white-tiered *Cornus alternifolia* 'Argentea' and golden cypresses share ground with botanical rarities such as *Aesculus wilsonii* and aromatic *Zanthoxylum ailanthoides*. There are displays of autumn colour, and on the other side of the mansion an area has been planted for winter, presenting witch hazels and other flowering shrubs in a scheme of heathers, conifers and white-trunked birches. Nearby are the formal walled gardens, one with an inner enclosure of yew hedges and bedding schemes, and the other with a cottage-garden mood, set by silver-leaved and pastel-flowered shrubs, perennials and roses; the walls shelter many interesting climbers, including a noted specimen of the Chilean coral plant, *Berberidopsis corallina*.

Outside one of the walls, the botanical and geographical themes are picked up again with a pair of borders devoted to bulbs and other monocotyledons, divided according to their Northern or Southern Hemisphere origins. The cast includes some ravishing ginger lilies (*Hedychium*), many of which are hardier than is often supposed. Reputedly tender plants also spring surprises in the Southern Hemisphere Garden by the croquet lawn, where *Banksia integrifolia* subsp. *monticola*, *Hakea*, *Pseudopanax*, *Leptospermum*, and *Telopea* appear among the more familiar genera.

As you walk south, away from the house and the mansion pond, the ground suddenly drops away, and from the semi-circular balustrade of the viewing bastion, you find yourself looking down into a steep glen, known as the Slips, the entrance to one of the two planted valleys that ring the house like a horseshoe. A stream flows down, falling over ledges and feeding into pools of various sizes, bordered by a rich array of moisture-loving perennials, including blue poppies, osmunda fern, arisaemas, and, in well-manured ground, a spectacular colony of the giant Himalayan lily, *Cardiocrinum giganteum*. Magnolias and nyssas thrive on the grassy banks, joined by a range of other garden-worthy trees such as *Stewartia pseudocamellia*, *Trochodendron aralioides* and *Maytenus boaria*. Curving paths, short flights of steps and small bridges over the water beckon this way and that, at one point leading you into the Iris Dell, ringed by a steep bank of Japanese maples and Kurume azaleas. In late June and early July, the numerous forms of *Iris ensata* turn it into a bowl of colour, which you cross by a boardwalk.

The glades and depressions are framed by native oaks and beeches and soaring North American conifers – the western hemlocks and Douglas firs in particular have reached a notable size. There is a concentration of unusual conifers, such as *Picea farreri* and *Keteleeria davidiana*, in the Pinetum. Rhododendrons and azaleas are also a major presence at the head of Westwood Valley, and among the moister pockets and shadier banks, you wander among extensive plantings of the larger-leaved kinds, such as *Rhododendron fulvum*, *R. rex* and the Loderi Group.

To the west, a massive outcrop of weathered grey sandstone is the centrepiece for a wilder and more rugged Himalayan scene, with viewing points down the valley. Here, some of the thickets of *Berberis wilsoniae* have been cleared to expose more of the rock, which is an important habitat for rare mosses, liverworts and lichens, and the native filmy fern, *Hymenophyllum tunbrigense*. In line with Kew's involvement with plant conservation worldwide, much effort is directed towards wildflower and habitat management at Wakehurst, ranging from different mowing and maintenance regimes of the garden's lawn and grass areas to helping in the heathland restoration of Ashdown Forest – visitors are encouraged to inspect the extensive recycling operation on the eastern edge of the garden, where bracken from the Forest is composted.

An extensive sweep of meadows, woods and wetlands in the Loder Valley is also managed as a nature reserve. The public is admitted only by permit, but you get an idea of its content to the south of the garden's lower lake, where an area of swamp, surrounded by woods, has been made accessible by means of a raised wooden walkway, enabling you to pass through reed beds and over watermint and other aquatics, looking down at fish, tadpoles and dragonflies; grebe are usually present, and occasionally you catch a glimpse of a kingfisher. It is a complete change in mood.

Beside Westwood Lake, rhododendrons and other Asian exotics again reappear, and in autumn there is another bonfire of coloured leaves from American species such as *Cotinus obovatus*, *Acer rubrum*, *Oxydendrum arboreum* and liquidambar. The walk back up the western valley takes you through further American forest types, including atmospheric groves of Douglas fir and wellingtonia; a belt of high Arctic species; slopes of Mediterranean pines, oaks and arbutus; a Southern Hemisphere wood of *Nothofagus* (a National Collection) and eucalyptus; and plantings made up of the world's birches (another National Collection). Bluebells, Lent lilies and numerous other wildflowers carpet

the banks in spring and summer. This is one of the Trust's largest gardens, and a full day is never long enough.

Opened in 2000, the Millennium Seed Bank is a further addition to the garden. With its laboratories and storage rooms on display through glass panels in a specially designed building, the Bank already conserves 10 per cent of the world's flora, and some 97 per cent of British flora, as an insurance policy against the dangers of extinction in the wild, and to help in the research and restoration of natural ecosystems.

ABOVE Wakehurst Place seen from across the lake.

Wallington

CAMBO, MORPETH, NORTHUMBERLAND

AREA 26ha (65 acres) • SOIL neutral to acid/medium loam • ALTITUDE 152m (500ft)
AVERAGE RAINFALL 838mm (33in) • AVERAGE WINTER CLIMATE moderate to cold

The moorland road from Hexham to Rothbury and Cragside runs through the heart of the Wallington estate, crossing the River Wansbeck over the stone-balustraded bridge designed by James Paine in 1755, and then climbing the wooded hill to skirt the eastern front of the Palladian mansion. Four dragons' heads, embedded in the lawn, grin at you as you pass. Sir Walter Calverley Blackett embarked on the creation of his Georgian idyll some time in the mid-1730s, helped principally by a 'Mr Joyce', and possibly later in the 1760s by the assiduous Lancelot 'Capability' Brown, whose childhood home was only a mile away.

So, you arrive at Wallington to a taste of the eighteenth century. Either side of the house are the remnants of Sir Walter's elaborately designed plantations: dark walks, straight and serpentine, leading between the beeches, oaks, limes and sycamores, and their laurel and yew understorey, to open pools colonised by waterlily, iris, great water dock and many other native species. Red squirrels still live in these woods, and there is a rich birdlife, including nuthatch, wood warbler and pied flycatcher.

From the house, there is the contrast of sweeping views across the ha-ha, down into the parkland and up over the rolling Northumbrian hills towards Hadrian's Wall and the distant Shaftoe Crags. Urns draw the eye east and west across open lawn, the west view taking you down an avenue of laurel hedges. But there are also more colourful touches, added in Victorian and more recent times: mixed shrubberies of golden yew, golden lonicera, red-purple plum and bronze-purple sloe (*Prunus spinosa* 'Purpurea'); the Bourbon rose 'Madame Isaac Pereire' successfully trained as a climber up the south front of the house, in the company of other roses, sage, rosemary and fuchsia; and, where the entrance drive curves into the clock-tower courtyard, an unexpectedly pretty midsummer partnership of deep violet *Campanula lactiflora*, rich red valerian, moonlight-yellow tree lupin and white philadelphus backed by purple sloe.

All this is an appetiser for what awaits in the Walled Garden, 0.8km (½mile) to the east. The route takes you through the wood, past prospects of Sir Walter's triumphal archway (he had it repositioned here in an upper field, as a folly, after it proved too narrow for coaches to pass through); alongside his handsome, recently restored Portico House, built into the north wall of the original kitchen garden; and then, at the head of the easternmost wilderness pond, to a modest oak gate.

The surprise is sprung. Ahead are stone terraces and curving stairways, lawns and hedges, ponds and rockeries, conservatory and pavilion, ornamental trees and border after border of flowering shrubs, herbaceous plants, roses and bulbs, all backed by views of parkland and woods. The walls and central erect pavilion (the Owl House, now, as formerly, the head gardener's office) were built by Sir Walter to enclose his new kitchen garden, but the internal design is largely the work of Sir George Otto Trevelyan, who inherited in 1886 and gardened here enthusiastically until his death in 1928, at the age of 90. The planting, on the other hand, is almost entirely the work of the Trust, which took over a garden weedy, overgrown and in structural disrepair.

There is a wealth of detail to investigate. The brick, fern-flecked wall of the eighteenth-century upper terrace faces inwards, unlike those at Powis Castle (*qv*), onto a summer border of pastel-tinted Hybrid Musk roses and the almost single-flowered,

richly scented 'Souvenir de St Anne's' (a sport of the popular Bourbon rose 'Souvenir de la Malmaison'), accompanied by alliums, eryngiums and a froth of white valerian. *Rosa glauca* (well teamed with black-eyed, magenta *Geranium psilostemon*) terminates the view in a haze of purplish grey. Since 2008, vegetables, soft fruit and herbs have been cultivated in the nuttery within the Walled Garden, as a reminder of the garden's earlier role.

The colour schemes of the Walled Garden are loose, but there is an underlying theme to most of the borders. In front of the conservatory, purple smoke bushes billow over hot plantings of yellow, orange and scarlet. Metal arches of honeysuckle and blue clematis (an echo of the fruit tunnels of the original garden) span beds of blue irises and nepeta, yellow loosestrife, inula and marjoram. White martagon lilies partner golden yews; salmon alstroemerias are teamed with violet campanulas. The wide lower north-facing border is graded from soft to strong colours.

Elsewhere, the planting is dictated more by the nature of the habitat. Dwarf conifers, brooms, potentillas and hebes are grouped along the rocky beds beside the paths and stream, while the damp western fringe of the garden supports large and lush colonies of hostas, water irises and ligularias, accompanied by a comprehensive range of elders.

When bad weather threatens, there is Sir George's conservatory for shelter. The very highest standards of cultivation underpin this splendid Edwardian scene, where pink and red flowers are arrayed against white-painted timberwork and furniture, marble busts and stone-slabbed floor. Pelargoniums and begonias, interspersed with palms, ferns and trailing ivy, fill the display bench with colour. Scent is provided by *Heliotropium arborescens* and a huge lemon verbena, said to pre-date the house.

LEFT The Pump House, partly covered by trees and undergrowth, can just be seen behind the China Pond.

ABOVE View of the Owl House, conservatory and hot border at Wallington.

Washington Old Hall

WASHINGTON VILLAGE, TYNE AND WEAR

AREA 0.6ha (1½ acres) • SOIL neutral to slightly acidic/clay • ALTITUDE 50m (164ft)
AVERAGE RAINFALL 546mm (21½ in) • AVERAGE WINTER CLIMATE cold

A pair of American eagles on the garden steps and, on occasion, the Stars and Stripes flying from the terrace flagpole announces the place of this old manor house in the history of the United States. In fact, the branch of the Washington family that produced the first President moved to Lancashire in 1292, over 300 years before the present hall was built, and then to Northamptonshire, from where, in 1656, George Washington's great-grandfather departed for the New World. But the family took their name from this village, and lived in an earlier house on this site from around 1180.

Parts of that medieval house are still visible within the sober, sandstone structure of the hall, which was rebuilt for the James family in the early seventeenth century. It stands behind an impressive gateway near the heart of the village, which is preserved as a pocket of leafy old England within the New Town conurbation. But the hall's history is far from romantic, it having become slum tenements by late Victorian times, and then been threatened with demolition. It was saved through the enthusiasm of local people, and restored with donations from both sides of the Atlantic.

The garden's restoration draws together typical Jacobean features. Nothing is known of the original layout; probably it was far more utilitarian and less polished. A well-executed knot garden of woven box, surmounted by narrow terrace beds of lavender and Shrub roses, now welcomes you into the otherwise rather bleak entrance court and is the appetiser for the splendid patterned flower and herb parterre installed below the hall's main façade.

Here, two large diagonal crosses of box hedging formalise the open ground either side of a sundial, while buttresses of yew punctuate the high retaining wall below the terrace lawn. Against these are set the favourite scented culinary, medicinal and strewing plants of the seventeenth century. Petal-packed Shrub roses, including pink Moss and *Rosa* 'Complicata', bloom above feverfew, comfrey and germander; sweet violet and golden marjoram alternate with sweet woodruff and *Dianthus* 'Sops-in-wine'; grapevines and old pear varieties ripen their fruits behind Madonna lilies, teazel and summer irises. In spring, the beds are lively with tulips.

Although Jacobean gardens were formally designed as a series of enclosures in alignment with the house, they often included some sort of organised wilderness to bring a change of mood. Here, the romantic source of inspiration has been the 'flowery mead', or flower-rich lawn, of medieval times, and to the east of the house you find a little lawn in which daffodils and snakeshead fritillaries are succeeded by ox-eye daisies, poppies and corncockles. A double form of wild cherry stands in the grass, and foxgloves, celandines and herb robert grow in the shady shrubbery fringe, in front of holly and hawthorn.

The wildflower riches are much greater beyond the lower parterre, where the nuttery gives way to open, sunny meadow and large populations of bees, butterflies and dragonflies. The resident redwood tree here strikes an anachronistic but not incongruous note, given the American connection, and as you look back to the hall, you see the cloak of Virginia creeper, blazing scarlet in autumn – a tangible connection with the state in which the Washingtons settled 350 years ago.

LEFT The seventeenth-century manor house from the lower garden.
ABOVE The beautifully patterned knot garden.

The Weir

SWAINSHILL, HEREFORD, HEREFORDSHIRE

AREA 4ha (10 acres) • **SOIL** alkaline/sand • **ALTITUDE** 61m (200ft)
AVERAGE RAINFALL 762mm (30in) • **AVERAGE WINTER CLIMATE** moderate

A picturesque curve of the River Wye, and an accompanying patchwork of fields and woods stretching away towards the Black Mountains, provide the setting for this individual garden of trees and wildflowers. It extends over 4ha (10 acres) of high, steep riverbank – with its plain whitewashed villa, now a retirement home, perched above – and you cover them by a network of meandering and plunging paths, stairways and adventurous bridges. The sense of exploration is heightened by the pockets of more formal gardening that reveal themselves between the trees: clipped tumps of yew, box and laurel hedges bordering the river, and a rock garden of Cheddar limestone, spangled with pools and shaded by Japanese maples. In summer, when the tracts of rough grass and flowers around them are high, the whole place takes on an abandoned air, while the bulbs and wildflowers are given time to seed and die back naturally.

The paths and early plantings are largely the work of R.C. Parr, a Manchester banker who bought the property as a fishing lodge in 1922 – assisted, from 1942, by his companion, Victor Morris. Parr's most colourful legacy is the surge of bulbs. Sheets of snowdrops, chionodoxas, scillas, daffodils and bluebells appear in bold succession under the trees, to be followed by patches of snakeshead fritillaries, blue camassias, martagon lilies, and, in late summer, cyclamen and colchicums. This is a display that continues to be augmented by the Trust's gardeners, who install a range of bulbs each autumn with the aid of a long-handled, step-on planter.

However, it is the range of wildflowers that is most remarkable. The poor, alkaline soil enables a wide variety of species to compete with the grasses, and as well as dry, sunny slopes and shady woodland, there is damp ground and waterside. This is, therefore, a rich and diverse preserve, all the more precious for being set inside a wide, 'improved', arable landscape. Primroses and thick carpets of violets appear with the bulbs early in the year, and as the summer advances, the sunny banks are stained and scented with crosswort, thyme, marjoram, vetches, yarrow, wild carrot, scabious and ox-eye daisies. Purple loosestrife, figwort, eupatorium and Himalayan balsam colonise the river's edge, and in the more heavily shaded woodland the bluebells and wild garlic are followed by swathes of pink campion.

At every turn, something catches your eye, whether it be drifts of twayblade orchid and quaking grass, or eruptions of parasitic toothwort, blooming in late spring along the surface-feeding roots of the poplars. At the end of July, when the growth is becoming rank, the garden is cut by rotary mower, and it then enters a period of green calm until the first autumn leaf tints appear in late September.

Nearly completed is the restoration of the eighteenth-century walled garden, now open to visitors, which includes a splendid Foster & Pearson vinery glasshouse, which Parr installed in around 1923.

ABOVE Wild daffodils and blue chionodoxa are among the bulbs carpeting the riverbank.

Westbury Court Garden

WESTBURY-ON-SEVERN, GLOUCESTERSHIRE

AREA 2ha (5 acres) • SOIL alkaline/alluvial silt, clay • ALTITUDE 6m (20ft)
AVERAGE RAINFALL 686mm (27in) • AVERAGE WINTER CLIMATE moderate

The Tall Pavilion offers an elevated vantage point of this handsomely appointed walled garden. The view is of tranquil canals, mown lawns, neat hedges and topiaries, white-painted benches, flashes of flower colour and fruits espaliered against mellow brick. Little seems to have ruffled the scene for 300 years. In fact, when Westbury Court came to the Trust in 1967, it was in an advanced state of dereliction.

Enthusiasm for the major restoration project sprang from the garden's rarity. Very few formal gardens in Britain survived the long era of naturalistic landscaping of the eighteenth century, and among them, Westbury Court was the only example to show a Dutch-style layout from the reign of William of Orange. The low-lying meadows bordering the River Severn make an ideal site for a water garden, but it may also have been the influence of his Dutch neighbour, Catherine Boevey of Flaxley Abbey, that prompted Maynard Colchester to embark on its construction. He began in 1696, with the excavation of the Long Canal, and work continued apace until his death in 1715. The garden was then embellished and altered by his nephew, Maynard Colchester II.

Within the walls, the parallel lines of yew hedges create a series of rectangular framed vistas down the waterways and lawns, with the flowering plants, topiaries and pot plants conveying the Dutch absorption and expertise in the art and craft of horticulture. Some of the hedges themselves sprout yew cones and spheres of holly, while balls and cones of box feature in the flower-filled 'cut parterre' beyond the T-shaped canal. A quincunx of standard trees and clipped evergreens surrounds it, including domes of *Phillyrea angustifolia*, umbrellas of Portuguese laurel, and thorns sporting nests of mistletoe

(established by pressing the ripe berries into the cracks of branches in late winter).

The espaliered fruit trees, reminders of the garden's important productive role, contribute to the formal patterns. Evocatively named varieties, all in cultivation before 1700, include the apples 'Calville Blanc d'Hiver', 'Catshead' and 'Court Pendu Plat'; the pears 'Beurré Brown', 'Forelle' and 'Bellissime d'Hiver'; and the plums 'Red Magnum Bonum' and 'Catalonia'. Peaches, apricots and Morello cherries are also here. In spring, bulbs make a patchwork of colour between them. The mid-seventeenth century saw the height of 'tulipmania' in Holland, when freakish tulips exchanged hands for vast sums, and although those famous varieties no longer exist, the selection of species and cultivars here evokes that period. Drifts of daffodils, anemones, muscari, ranunculus and crown imperials accompany them.

In the small walled enclosure beside the gazebo is a collection of the border perennials grown at the time. Campanulas, astrantia,

ABOVE Honeysuckle arch in the walled garden.

hellebores, veratrums and meadow sages are among the cast filling the pine-edged beds, and at midsummer they are showered with the scented blooms of old Shrub and Climbing roses. A small collection of dianthus is grown outside the walls, in beds specially raised and gritted. Vegetable plots, as shown in Kip's engraving of about 1707, have been replanted, and recently the original path layout around the Long Canal, and between the fountain and summerhouse, have been re-established.

The garden is essentially intimate and introspective, but framed views of the countryside are given by the two ironwork grilles, or *clairvoyées*, in the north wall – one surmounted by stone pineapples made in 1704, and the other capped by vases made after 1715. There are some fine trees in the neighbouring fields, including, to the south, a line of rare native black poplars. An avenue of 'Barland' pears, willow and alder shade the glades beyond the canalised stream, which forms the garden's eastern boundary, while within the formal garden itself stands a superb tulip tree and a stupendous evergreen oak, presumed to pre-date the Dutch layout and thought to be one of the largest and oldest specimens in Britain. Recently, a small rabbit warren has also been re-created – the original warren was seven times larger and would have kept the kitchen well supplied with meat.

ABOVE Bed of globe artichokes in June at Westbury Court Garden.

RIGHT The Tall Pavilion seen from the parterre.

West Green House Garden

WEST GREEN, HARTLEY WINTNEY, HAMPSHIRE

AREA 2.8ha (7 acres) • SOIL heavy clay • ALTITUDE 69m (225ft) • AVERAGE RAINFALL 762mm
(30in) • AVERAGE WINTER CLIMATE moderate

General Henry Hawley is remembered chiefly as 'Hangman
Hawley' for his brutality to the defeated Scots Highlanders after the
Battle of Culloden – but he shows a different side to his character
at West Green, where a tombstone in the garden remembers his
dog Monkey, 'The best black spaniell that ere wag'd a taile'. The
house that he remodelled in 1750 is a perfect piece of Georgian
symmetry, built of warm brick, modest in size, and grandly crowned
with pedimented dormers and stone vases. And it sets the tone for
the garden around it, which is revealed as a sequence of immaculate
walled and hedged enclosures, with crisp lawns, gravel paths and
patterns of box. Quite how it evolved is something of a mystery, but
by 1773, fourteen years after Hawley's death, there was a complete
landscape here, in a formal style that was by then distinctly
old-fashioned even then.

The surviving framework was relished and expanded in the
Arts and Crafts style – a *Country Life* article of November 1936
describes 'an idyll of roses, herbaceous borders, vegetables and fruit,
croquet on the lawn and tea on the terrace'. Unusually, after coming
to the Trust in 1957, the garden has been allowed to respond to the
enthusiasms of the house's tenants, who pay for its maintenance, and
it has been developed with great gusto, first by Lord McAlpine and,
since 1993, by the Australian gardener Marylyn Abbott.

From the approaching country lane, your appetiser is a
Memorial Column, one of a number of handsome theatrical follies
commissioned by Lord McAlpine from the architect Quinlan Terry.
It stands at the head of a young lime avenue. The entrance drive then
brings you round past the magnolia-clad south front where, through
railings, you look into a polite little parterre of fruit trees, ringed in
doughnuts of box.

The main walled garden, however, keeps its secrets until
you step through the door. Suddenly, you are in one of the most
sumptuous English potagers, a triumphant restoration of Lord
McAlpine's architectural design by Marylyn Abbott, overlaid with
her own swashbuckling approach to planting. Centred on a fine
wrought-iron well-head, narrow box-edged flower borders run
alongside the lawns and gravel paths, punctuated by fruit trees
and pyramids of clematis. They are packed with annuals as well as
perennials and roses, the content constantly changing but always
co-ordinated by colour – some areas palely ethereal in lavenders,
whites and pinks, others in unusual biscuits, apricots and browns,
and still others brooding in burgundy, purple and battleship grey.
Quantities of spires and umbels, as from foxgloves, eremurus,
verbascums, alliums and pink cow parsley add a dreamy wildness
to the mix. A pair of ornamental fruit cages presides over patterns
of clipped rosemary, lavender and silver santolina and a spectacular
array of hardy and exotic vegetables, which are arranged to a different
extravagant theme every year. A new plant house and a red and white
Alice in Wonderland garden add to the variety.

In the rear wall of the main walled garden, added before 1936,
you are led through a moon gate to the *trompe-l'oeil* Nymphaeum,
also by Quinlan Terry and modelled on a fountain in the Via
Garibaldi in Rome. Restored, fronted by patterned paving, and with
its flanking cascading rills splashing down the slope in the company

of a new box and yew parterre, this makes a lively change of mood. A sister water garden, a modern interpretation of a paradise garden, has been completed beyond the hedge.

In the adjacent Lake Garden, the formality is exchanged for a miniature Arcadian landscape of water, trees and architectural follies, from Doric gazebo to Chinese bridge, and with a pineapple-topped aviary on the lake's island. An ever-expanding carpet of naturalised bulbs in the grass, from crocuses to massed daffodils and snakeshead fritillaries, accompanies them. Allegorical references to Heaven and Hell were intended, and the cave-like Smoke House, from which visitors were meant to emerge spluttering, symbolised

Purgatory. Afterwards, you ascend the Olympian mount to the song of blackbirds, the scent of balsam poplars, and the sway of weeping willows over water.

Equally serene, but formally so, is the Green Theatre to the north of the house, to which the green tiers of lawn descend below an eighteenth-century Orangery adorned with cartouches of painted garden implements. Opera is staged here every summer.

LEFT A view of the lake at West Green House. The still water is surrounded by trees and covered in algae.

ABOVE The parterre of fruit trees, ringed in box.

West Wycombe Park

WEST WYCOMBE, BUCKINGHAMSHIRE

AREA 19ha (46 acres) • **SOIL** alkaline • **ALTITUDE** 76m (250ft) • **AVERAGE RAINFALL** 762mm (30in) • **AVERAGE WINTER CLIMATE** cold

The red-blooded passion for life and art held by Sir Francis Dashwood, politician, antiquarian, connoisseur, practical joker, party-giver and founder member of the Society of Dilettanti and of the notorious Hellfire Club, is behind the creation of this Elysian landscape. The mansion, sitting on rising ground and commanding northerly views down its own wooded Chiltern coombe and up to Church Hill opposite, was remodelled by Dashwood over a period of 45 years, from 1735 – by which time he had spent the best part of eleven years on successive cultural tours through Europe and Asia Minor – until his death in 1781. The coombe was landscaped over the same long period.

By 1752, the first phase had produced a semi-formal composition, combining straight-edged plantations and avenues with serpentine walks and an irregularly shaped lake, made by damming the River Wye. From 1770, there was a fresh impetus, as Dashwood responded to the current taste for a parkland of more sweeping views and flowing contours. Although this phase – probably directed throughout by Thomas Cook, a pupil of 'Capability' Brown – did much to soften the earlier formality, many of the Baroque and Rococo elements were retained and absorbed, leaving the evolution of the garden clearly exposed.

Little has disturbed the scene since, although a programme of restoration and replanting was much needed by the middle of the last century and was conducted by the Trust and the late 11th Baronet, with assistance from the Historic Buildings Council. The circuit of the park unfolds a succession of composed views and architectural surprises. From the north front of the house, you look down the greensward to the lake, where, on the largest of three islands, a colonnaded music temple by Nicholas Revett shines against the trees. On the hill to the west, above the plantation screening West Wycombe village, stands St Lawrence's church, topped with its gilded sphere or Golden Ball.

Past the Palladian east portico, the double colonnades of the south front, the great stone and flintwork arch of the Temple of Apollo, the blue cedars and banks of shrubs, you walk up the slope to find the Round Temple suddenly revealed, a circular dovecote designed by Revett in about 1775. From here, the dog-leg ha-ha draws you between open pastureland above and dark straight-edged

plantations of deciduous trees below to the Temple of the Winds, a flint and stuccoed wonder, built in about 1759 and one of the earliest reproductions of an ancient classical monument in the country. The old entrance drive now takes you down to the lakeside and cascade. The early garden's impressive rock arch and accompanying River God were replaced by 1781 with the present simplified structure of piers and reclining nymphs, but the water still gushes over the knobbled steps into the stream. Across the lake, the view is more tranquil, the eye channelled between the islands and down the Broad Walk opposite, the only survivor of the two great avenues shown on the 1752 survey.

Daphne's Temple and Kitty's Lodge mark the original entrance to the park, and from here you skirt the top end of the lake and enter the woods where, by means of little bridges crossing sinuous streams, you pass the eighteenth-century Temple of Venus, cross the Broad Walk, and return to the mansion. But *en route*, the mind must be allowed to wander, conjuring up visions of the Bacchanalian feasts, musical spectacles and other lavish entertainments the park has borne witness to.

ABOVE The Temple of Music creates a reflection in the lake on this hazy day.

Wightwick Manor

WOLVERHAMPTON, WEST MIDLANDS

AREA 6.9ha (17 acres) • SOIL acid/varied, clay-sandstone outcrops • ALTITUDE 76m (250ft)
AVERAGE RAINFALL 686mm (27in) • AVERAGE WINTER CLIMATE cold

Nostalgia for a more romantic past was a natural accompaniment to the nineteenth century's relentless industrialisation and urban sprawl. Beside the old manor and malt-house at Wightwick, the paint and varnish manufacturer Theodore Mander commissioned Edward Ould to build a neo-Tudor mansion, with feudal great hall, spiral brick chimneys and elaborately patterned black-and-white timbered walls. For the garden, Mander called upon Alfred Parsons, who, as well as being an accomplished landscape painter and illustrator, was a practised designer of gardens in the 'old-fashioned' style.

The formal compartments, clipped yew hedges, cottage-garden flowers, topiary peacocks and roses arrived at Wightwick between 1887 and 1906, in which year the famous Thomas Mawson of Windermere strengthened and embellished the patterns with beds, hedges and topiaries, and bonded house and garden by means of a broad, stone-flagged terrace, steps and oak balustrade. Parsons' and Mawson's yews have now swelled into massive cylinders and high screens, and they are an imposing presence both in the rose garden, where they complement rose beds and herbaceous borders, and on the lawn below the terrace, where they process to the southern boundary. Here, the fringes of colour include two shrub borders, and four small mixed borders dedicated to the memory of the National Trust's garden advisor, Bill Malecki, who died tragically young.

In late spring, the two large ponds, recently cleaned by the Trust and restocked with trout and carp, reflect the rich colours of massed rhododendrons; wildflowers bloom on the banks, while the air is stirred with the scents of bluebells and yellow azaleas. Mixed deciduous trees provide the backdrop, and their varied autumn tints follow the summer greens; maidenhair tree and red oak are among the highlights. Such tranquil pockets make the garden a haven for kingfishers, jays, woodpeckers and other wildlife. The adjacent paddocks add to the country flavour, and on the other side of the house there are further productive areas including a hazel coppice, a second orchard and, in front of the Peach House, a new kitchen garden based on the original Mawson design. Over the road, spanned by a copy of the 'Mathematical' bridge at Queen's College, Cambridge, is the former fruit garden, now cleared and replanted with early spring bulbs. With limes, beeches and other great trees all about, it is easy to forget you are in the Wolverhampton suburbs.

ABOVE The meadow at Wightwick Manor.

RIGHT Great drums of yew occupy the lawn below the half-timbered façade.

Wimpole Hall

ARRINGTON, ROYSTON, CAMBRIDGESHIRE

AREA 24ha (60 acres) • SOIL alkaline/clay • ALTITUDE 30m (100ft)
AVERAGE RAINFALL 584mm (23in) • AVERAGE WINTER CLIMATE moderate

A ridge of chalk meets the Cambridgeshire plain to the north and west of Wimpole Hall, giving sudden views of rising woods and grassland, the scene picturesquely animated by flocks of rare antelope-like sheep and herds of hefty (but docile) huge-horned cattle. The approach, however, is across level ground, from which the red-brick Georgian façade ascends imposingly. This is the county's grandest country house, and it is fitting that its park should have been moulded by some of the most famous names in landscape gardening.

A 3.2km (2 mile) long double avenue, conceived by Charles Bridgeman in the 1720s, slices across the flat farmland opposite the south front. Sadly, the original elm trees here, and in the older west avenue, fell victim to Dutch elm disease in the 1970s, but in a major, phased planting project the Trust replaced them with limes, some propagated from ancient trees in the park. Flanked by laid hedges, they are now a fine sight.

From the mid-eighteenth century, the landscaping at Wimpole was essentially directed along more 'natural' lines. The first phase was conducted for the 1st Earl of Hardwicke by Robert Greening, advised by the garden architect Sanderson Miller. It was Miller who produced the design for the Gothic Tower that serves as the distant eye-catcher from the north front of the hall, though it was not built until 1774, and then in a modified form. The broad sweeps of hilly pasture and the clumps and tiers of trees that frame this folly have also been moulded by later designers. For ten years from the mid-1760s, the park was in the hands of 'Capability' Brown and, from 1790, his contemporary William Emes. As you walk across the park towards the tower, you will come upon the lakes Brown created from the former fish ponds and enhanced with islands and a Chinese bridge.

The last great name in this extraordinary roll call of designers is Humphry Repton, who came here in 1801. He planned a new approach to the hall from the Cambridge road, filled out Brown's tree clumps, and set out the present formal pattern of neat lawns and paths, exclaiming that: 'It is called natural, but to me it has ever seemed unnatural that a palace shall rise immediately out of sheep pasture.' The parterre is planted with contrasting displays of tulips for spring and some 12,000 pelargoniums and salvias for summer, while in the adjacent Dutch Garden fuchsias follow a mass of blue and white anemones.

Trees are one of Wimpole's chief glories, and while the native oaks, beeches, limes and ashes give the artful backdrop, ornamental varieties, planted over the past two centuries, enhance the foreground. Oriental plane, copper beeches and Indian bean trees are highlights in the formal areas, and in the pleasure grounds, the meandering path to the walled garden takes you past cherries, crab apples and a range of American species, including good specimens of redwood, Cornelian dogwood and a National Collection of walnuts. There was much replanting here in the wake of the 1987 storm, and the cast now includes a generous percentage of conifers, which have proved surprisingly tolerant of the heavy alkaline soil. Western red cedar, Spanish fir, incense cedar and Serbian spruce are among the species added.

Scented shrubs such as mock orange and winter-flowering honeysuckle accompany the trees, and there is a great show of daffodils. These were the passion of Elsie Bambridge, daughter of Rudyard Kipling, who, with her husband, Captain George Bambridge, took on the property in 1936 and made a start on the formidable task of restoring the house and grounds after a long decline. The collection includes many varieties that have long disappeared from the nursery lists – among them 'Bath's Flame', 'John Evelyn' and 'Mrs Barclay'. Species tulips and orchids also flourish in the grass here.

The recent restoration of the walled garden has added a further panoply of attractions to the garden tour. The outer walls date from the 1840s, and contain orchard plots of old and local apple and pear varieties, wall-trained apricots, and a soft fruit cage. A group of double-flowered white cherry, *Prunus avium* 'Plena', boosts the display of blossom in spring, and a long, superbly composed herbaceous border, with contemporary themes of grasses, alliums,

verbena and textured foliage, sustains colour and drama through the summer.

The 0.8ha (2 acre) inner walled garden, dating from the 1790s, also has its decorative features, with tremendous displays of dahlias, fuchsias, peonies and Korean chrysanthemums, as well as box-edged, double herbaceous borders of epic length. Within a traditional quartered design, centred on a circular dipping pond, a wide range of vegetables is cultivated, including sweet corn, gherkins, chicory, kohlrabi, pak choi and variegated horseradish. A Squash Extravaganza is held at the end of September, and a Tomato Day

in August – an astonishing 60 varieties of tomato being grown here, including the particularly delicious black forms. However, the garden's principal feature is its splendid glasshouse, re-created from the original eighteenth-century design by Sir John Soane.

ABOVE The north front of Wimpole Hall seen across the parterre.

Winkworth Arboretum

HASCOMBE ROAD, GODALMING, SURREY

AREA 45ha (110 acres) • SOIL acid to neutral/sandy • ALTITUDE 61–107m (200–350ft)
AVERAGE RAINFALL 762mm (30in) • AVERAGE WINTER CLIMATE cold

Autumn colour is Winkworth's chief glory, and as the surrounding countryside assumes its mellow wash of russet, copper and gold, its steep hillside takes on the more potent livery of Chinese mountains and New England forests. Wilfrid Fox, a skin specialist and amateur arborist, began clearing the brambles and bracken in 1938, working mainly alone but with the help of friends and neighbours at weekends.

The oak and bluebell wood beside the former lower lake (now wetland), he left largely undisturbed, but for a flash of Japanese maples. The ground is colonised by tussock grass and native marsh plants, and the banks are part-fringed by tangled stands of elder and alder. The hillside, too, remains rough and unmanicured, the exotics having been planted among native trees in a natural carpet of grasses, ferns, bracken, primroses, stitchwort, wild garlic and other flowers. So there is still a sense of wilderness, and often the only sounds are from birds – among them, the hammering of woodpeckers and the piercing cries of water rail. The stream goes on to fill the lake at Bramley House, where the influential Edwardian gardener Gertrude Jekyll spent her childhood.

Elsewhere, you find yourself in a plantsman's domain. Near the hill-top entrance is a glade planted for winter, with cherry, camellias, early rhododendrons, scented witch hazels and *Symplocos paniculata*, with ultramarine-blue berries. Further on, you are drawn by the exposed trunks of birches, snakebark and paperbark maples; the stands of Scots pine, blue cedar, Serbian spruce and other conifers rising from the orange bracken; and the traceries of branches against the silver lake and the sheep-grazed hillside opposite.

Spring sees the tints of expanding leaves and blossom on cherries, dogwoods and magnolias, the last massed in the shelter of a plantation of coppiced hazel. Dr Fox fringed the flight of over a hundred steps leading down to the old boathouse with evergreen Japanese azaleas to make a May cascade of carmine, pink and white. Elsewhere, there are white handkerchiefs on *Davidia involucrata*, musk-scented vases on *Magnolia tripetala* and clouds of young white leaves on the collection of whitebeams. Thickets of the yellow deciduous azalea *Rhododendron luteum* fill the bluebell glades with honeysuckle fragrance. A little later, snowbells hang from styrax and melon-scented waterlilies open on *Magnolia obovata*. Hydrangeas then give a blue and white flush to the shadows, and in August the massive evergreen columns of *Eucryphia × nymansensis* 'Nymansay', planted by the Trust to guard the memorial to Dr Fox above the escarpment, open their white saucers.

Mountain ashes were among Dr Fox's favourite trees, and a large collection grows on the slope above the lake. The berries ripen in succession from August onwards. The orange and scarlet fruits on species such as *Sorbus commixta*, *S. pohuashanensis* and *S. esserteauana* and on *S. aucuparia* 'Rossica Major' from Kiev, standing beside the water, are vulnerable to birds, of course, though Dr Fox noted that berries on foreign species tend not to be consumed as voraciously as on forms of the native rowan. Trees with amber-yellow berries, such as *S.* 'Joseph Rock', and with pink or white berries, such as *S. vilmorinii*, *S. hupehensis* and *S. cashmiriana*, also often persist well into winter.

LEFT A panoply of Japanese maples and other autumn tints at Winkworth Arboretum.

The peak period for autumn leaf colour is mid- to late-October, but some trees, notably *Prunus sargentii* and its fiery clone 'Rancho', begin much earlier, while others, such as liquidambar, *Acer carpinifolium* and the shrubby *Photinia villosa* can delay until November. Japanese and other maples, amelanchier, sumachs, and *Enkianthus perulatus* turn orange-scarlet; fothergilla and deciduous azaleas a deeper crimson. Rich reds come from the fastigiate red maple *Acer rubrum* 'Columnare', *Oxydendrum arboreum*, *Viburnum cassinoides* and the compact ash *Fraxinus angustifolia* subsp. *oxycarpa* 'Raywood'; bright yellows from *Acer cappadocicum*, *A. platanoides* and the cherry birch *Betula lenta*; and orange-browns from the many kinds of oak found here at Winkworth.

There are arresting views from all angles. In one spot on the upper path, you look down at a bank of red maple, *Acer rubrum*, dashingly partnered with the flame and yellow of *A. rufinerve* and *A. pensylvanicum* and the blue of cedar and Bhutan pine, the whole scheme silhouetted against the lake. From the lakeside you look up at slopes of parrotias and Japanese maples, and walk past stands of *Nyssa sylvatica* and *Cercidiphyllum japonicum*, the latter – on the right day – infusing the air with caramel scent from falling pink and parchment-coloured leaves.

ABOVE Foxgloves are among the many wildflowers here.

RIGHT Sunlight filters through the canopy of a Japanese maple.

Woolbeding Gardens

MIDHURST, WEST SUSSEX

AREA 11ha (26 acres) • **SOIL** neutral/sandy loam and some clay in parts • **ALTITUDE** 30m (100ft) • **AVERAGE RAINFALL** 813mm (32in) • **AVERAGE WINTER CLIMATE** moderate

The road through Woolbeding village has for a long time tantalised passers-by with a glimpse over the gate of well-composed double borders running up to the porticoed façade of a substantial house. Until 2011, this was a very private world. The property came to the Trust as far back as 1958 but without the accompanying funding, and from 1973 onwards it was leased to the philanthropist and grocery magnate Simon Sainsbury and his partner Stewart Grimshaw, a trained botanist, as a weekend home.

The garden owes its present exceptional standard of presentation and rich content, and the house and outbuildings their quality restoration and finish, to the attentions and tastes of these tenants – and when Simon Sainsbury died in 2006 he provided a healthy endowment for the maintenance of the garden that he and Stewart Grimshaw had created, eventually enabling it to be opened up for visitors. It is a fresh and contemporary composition, not engaging in new trends in planting or design but reflecting the late twentieth century's more mainstream preoccupations – a renewed fascination with colour-schemed formality, an awakened delight in garden history, and the manipulation of a sophisticated palette of plants – with some of the leading contemporary designers and craftsmen commissioned to help develop it.

The setting is the intimate pastoral and wooded valley of the River Rother, which curves through the grounds between willows and alders close to the house, its surrounding meadows grazed by Belted Galloway cattle and Jacob, Herdwick and Welsh Black sheep. The house was remodelled in the eighteenth century in fairly plain classical style, and is closely accompanied by a small lodge and a

mellow cluster of sandstone, brick and tile farm buildings, with an arched gateway leading into the entrance courtyard.

On this west side of the garden the mood is more formal, set by the long eighteenth-century oak and beech avenue, which carries the vista across the village road and up a ridge into the woods. A series of hedged and walled garden rooms have sprung up here, packed with horticultural interest. Lanning Roper, the talented American designer of post-war English country house gardens, helped with the layout and planting through the 1970s, visiting initially three days a year. The garden certainly reflects his mingled and overflowing style, but so much was also initiated by Simon Sainsbury and Stewart Grimshaw themselves, and so much enthusiastic development has taken place over subsequent decades, that Roper's work has now been largely subsumed.

The long double borders, flanking the principal vista's gravel walk and side panels of lawn, are on a blue, violet and white theme, illuminated by cracks of soft yellow. Clematis 'Perle d'Azur' and a big Chinese wisteria cloak the walls, with gypsophila, tree poppy (*Romneya*), agapanthus, phlox, alchemilla and scabious among the foreground company, arranged with an eye to leaf contrast. The informal addition of bedding plants such as tulips, wallflowers and violas in spring and salvias, roses, echiums and white *Ammi majus* in summer ensures a long season of interest.

The openings into the adjoining enclosures are marked by yew topiaries. To the north, you pass under a brick pergola, covered in scented *Trachelospermum* and other climbers, and enter a gravel courtyard. The space is dominated by a large and fairly new conservatory, comfortably appointed for sitting in on chilly days, and maintained with enough heat and humidity to support begonias, Dutchman's pipe vine (*Aristolochia*), palms, *Cymbidium* orchids, and tender jasmines and ferns. The hardy Japanese banana *Musa basjoo* and a pollarded foxglove tree (*Paulownia*) extend the exotic foliage theme outside, with pots of pelargoniums, fuchsias, cannas and shrubby mimulus placed around an Italian well-head – all presented in a haze of self-seeding verbascum and purple *Verbena bonariensis*.

South of the double borders you are in a network of rooms. The herb garden, designed by Roper, is placed on a platform of brick and stone paths and structured by box hedges and spiral topiaries, with the herbs arranged in four beds according to colour – white, red, blue and yellow – and with figs and cordon apples on the walls. Beyond is the swimming-pool garden, enclosed in hornbeam hedges, with a brick dining gazebo and orangery/pool house designed in the 1970s by the architect Philip Jebb. Lawns and yew topiaries then provide a green interlude.

LEFT The domed temple was built to commemorate a tulip tree lost in the 1987 storm
ABOVE Topiary cones lead to yew-enclosed garden compartments.

The small vegetable garden, accompanied by a fruit cage, takes the form of a decorative potager, with a pattern of lettuces, beets, chard and sorrel, path edgings of chives, pyramids of sweet peas and French beans, and cordon apples underplanted with grape hyacinths, love-in-a-mist and corncockle, all set around a topiary dove.

The Fountain Garden takes its name from its central ornament, featuring Neptune and dolphins. This is a replica of the Renaissance original, now in the Victoria & Albert Museum, which was acquired from nearby Cowdray Park by Lord Robert Spencer, son of the second Duke of Marlborough, who lived here between 1791 and 1831. The surrounding flower planting is intricately woven through the subtlest of apricot, brown, plum, pink and lilac colour tints, using a rarified cast of shrubs and perennials including Rosa 'Hot Chocolate', *Colutea × media* 'Copper Beauty', and Digitalis 'Spice Island'. Daphnes, favourite shrubs of Stewart Grimshaw, add their scents, as they do to many parts of the garden.

The balancing Well Garden, with box-edged beds around an Italian well-head, sports green-flowered plants including echinacea, zinnia and nicotiana, complemented by green foliage such as miscanthus grass and a narrow-leaved form of hart's tongue fern; they are set off by the creamy-yellow flowers of plants such as *Schizophragma hydrangeoides* 'Moonlight' and scented *Trachelospermum asiaticum* growing on the walls.

You emerge from this botanical reverie beside the Saxon church, which stands just across the lawn from the house, its churchyard wall partly obscured by a pre-1973 shrubbery of rhododendrons, azaleas and camellias. The garden now opens up informally into the landscape, and across the open lawns towards the river are some large and venerable eighteenth-century trees, including cedars of Lebanon and two magnificent oriental planes which have layered themselves over a vast area. A towering tulip tree which collapsed in the great storm of October 1987 has had a domed Temple erected in its honour, while the demise of a large cedar has recently prompted the commissioning of a polished steel water sculpture by William Pye; by extraordinary coincidence, Pye had sat under this very same cedar tree while visiting Woolbeding as a child.

Turning north along the riverbank, the path curves through a rustic nineteenth-century hornbeam tunnel, guarded by lions, and on past the weir and brick pump house. The rough, shady ground hereabouts is coloured by crocuses, daffodils, primroses and bluebells in spring, followed by violet and white *Campanula latifolia* in summer; occasionally a kingfisher flashes over the water. Climbing back up towards the house, you pass through an open terraced garden, inspired by holidays in the Mediterranean, featuring straight rows of plants such as figs, irises and lavender between bands of retaining wall.

Turn south across the house lawn and you are led over the ha-ha and through a kissing gate into the paddock, alongside the old cricket field, and downhill into a wooded and watery dell. The garden here was designed in 2000 by Julian and Isabel Bannerman, and in its architectural flourishes and rich layers of historical allusion is a typically colourful example of their work. Simon Sainsbury and Stewart Grimshaw had already landscaped the area, introduced water, and commissioned structures including an octagonal gothick summer-house from Philip Jebb, but felt the potential had not been fully exploited.

So, the Bannermans enlarged the lakes, resculpted the surroundings, and added a succession of romantic buildings and other evocative features to enliven the circuit walk. You first encounter the 'ancient' ruins of a chapel and then, further down the slope, a rustic hermit's hut, its thatched roof held up by burr elm supports on paddle stones. A wildflower meadow, punctuated by taxodium and liquidambar trees, rolls down to the water, which you cross by a Chinese bridge.

The path then meanders past waterside plantings devised by Stewart Grimshaw, featuring gunnera, rushes, ferns and candelabra primulas, until you come to a statue of the River God, sitting in a ferny grotto and pouring water from his urn. Nearby, a cascade gushes from a cliff under the summer-house, while up in a glade among the trees, presided over by statues of the Four Seasons, is the quiet 'source' of the water, bubbling from a mossy fountain, or spugna, into flint-edged rills.

Nearer the house, a second garden designed by the Bannermans is a welcoming entrance for visitors. A formal water garden, with the water moving and reflecting in a series of stone-edged tanks, is reminiscent of giant farmyard troughs, which descend in height from eye to ground level. The informal perennial planting enlivens the surrounding gravel, together with pots and troughs filled with bulbs and sophisticated bedding plants.

Overall, Woolbeding provides a glimpse into contemporary country life of a very luscious and rarified kind. It has produced a very fine garden.

LEFT A view towards the house from the herb and sundial garden at Woolbeding House.

Wordsworth House and Garden

COCKERMOUTH, CUMBRIA

AREA 0.2ha (½ acre) • SOIL rich alluvial • ALTITUDE 50m (164ft) • AVERAGE RAINFALL 254mm (10in) • AVERAGE WINTER CLIMATE cold

William Wordsworth was born in this house in 1770, and had fond memories of it as a happy childhood home where he played with his three brothers and his sister Dorothy, who would be his companion and muse throughout his life. The idyll ended with the death of his mother in 1778, after which he was sent to boarding school, but he continued to spend his school holidays here until the age of thirteen when, on the death of his father, he went to live with his mother's family.

The house stands in the heart of the town, soberly elegant with its terracotta-washed façade, portico and sash windows, and separated from the street by high walls and gate pillars. Through the gate, you are met by a small entrance courtyard, paved in red sandstone and decorated with a symmetrical pair of circular beds, each planted with the pale pink old Shrub rose 'Great Maiden's Blush' within rings of purple aquilegia, lavender and clipped box.

There are few records of how Wordsworth House's gardens looked in the late eighteenth century, but drawing on general research into town gardening of that period, coupled with geophysical investigations on site, the National Trust has undertaken the most plausible Georgian restoration possible – and it gives a rare insight into a type of garden of which we have very few surviving examples. Overall, the design is formal and symmetrical, but since this was a family home rather than a showcase (and the family employed only a jobbing gardener), the finish is neat but not overly polished, with cottage-garden plants, fruits and vegetables setting a relaxed mood. Most of the plants are varieties known to have been grown in the north before 1770.

The restoration had been largely completed when, in November 2009, the town was devastated by floodwater from the River Cocker, 2.4m (8ft deep) and racing down Main Street at 40mph (25mph). At the end of the garden, the River Derwent also burst its banks. Garden walls collapsed, the rear garden was strewn with the floating contents of local shops, and part of the Terrace was washed away. Many plants were also lost, including the Terrace's large 150-year-old trees, which had to be felled. But thanks to a large team of volunteers, a remarkable amount of the contents was also saved, including fruit trees and stretches of box hedging, and today the garden is in an advanced state of recovery and repair.

There is a good view of the walled back garden from the landing window of the house, a vantage point that also reveals the geometry of the plot to be somewhat askew. A gravel pathway runs around the edge of the garden, with espaliered apples and pears and a young fan-trained plum and greengage on the walls. They are accompanied, inside their box-edged borders, with evergreen *Viburnum tinus* and simple kinds of perennials such as geraniums, daylilies, solidago, lychnis and cottage peonies.

Since the growing of food was probably very important for a family with five children, the Trust has put a strong emphasis on fruit and vegetables in the garden. The central plot is divided into a number of productive beds. Three are run on a rotation system, the many heritage crops including asparagus pea, 'Painted Lady' runner bean, and black Spanish radish, which the gardeners say tastes horrid. Crops are supported with traditional ash poles, hemp twine and 'brashings' (twiggy branches). Herbs such as sage and winter savory are mixed among them, together with pot marigolds, borage and other plants with edible flowers – it is quite likely they would have been used here in the old English dish *salmagundi*.

Gooseberries, currants and permanent vegetables such as horseradish, sorrel and Welsh onions are grown in other beds, and along both the side paths are six 'Greenup's Pippin' apple trees, an eighteenth-century Cumbrian variety which was eaten as both a dessert and cooking apple. Clipped into goblet shapes, they are underplanted with herbs that were used medicinally at the time, such as tansy, feverfew, bistort and hyssop. At either end of the garden are flower-beds, one for perennial cut flowers such as globe thistle, yellow asphodel and soapwort, and the other filled with old Moss and Gallica roses accompanied by catmint. The garden is well endowed with scent.

In spring, Wordsworth's 'host of golden daffodils' appears throughout the beds – though not the 'ten thousand' he saw on his walk around Ullswater with Dorothy in April 1802, which inspired his most famous poem. The daffodil he encountered would have been our native Lent lily, *Narcissus pseudonarcissus*. It grows here with other long-grown varieties of daffodil, and also tulips, such as *Tulipa clusiana* and colour forms of 'Duc van Tol', which prove reliably perennial in the garden's drier areas of silty soil.

There is a smaller walled garden at the river end of the neighbouring property which has always belonged to Wordsworth House. Here, accompanying more cut-flower and herb beds, is a little grass orchard plot with 'Keswick Codlin' and 'Lady's Finger' cider apples, and a Georgian hen house behind a split oak palisade.

The raised gravel Terrace Walk beside the River Derwent was a favourite spot for William Wordsworth. In his time, 'a thick hedge of privet and roses provided impervious shelter to birds who built their nests there', and the loss of the big trees in the 2009 flood has enabled the Trust to reinstate it. The scene beyond is now less pastoral, but there is still a good sweep of the meadows (where the family also grazed their cow), the woods and the water that were his playground. He reminisced in *The Prelude Book 1* (1805–6)

> *When having left his Mountains, to the Towers*
> *Of Cockermouth that beauteous River came*
> *Behind my Father's House he pass'd, close by*
> *Along the margins of our Terrace Walk,*
> *He was a Playmate whom we dearly lov'd.'*
> *Oh! Many a time have I, a five years' Child,*
> *A naked Boy, in one delightful Rill,*
> *A little Mill-race sever'd from his stream,*
> *Made one long bathing of a summer's day,*
> *Bask'd in the sun, and plunged, and bask'd again*
> *Alternate all a summer's day, or cours'd*
> *Over the sandy fields, leaping through groves*
> *Of yellow grunsel, or when crag and hill,*
> *The woods, and distant Skiddaw's lofty height,*
> *Were bronz'd with a deep radiance, stood alone*
> *Beneath the sky, as if I had been born*
> *On Indian Plains, and from my Mother's hut*
> *Had run abroad in wantonness, to sport,*
> *A naked Savage, in the thunder shower.'*

RIGHT Foxgloves and alliums in the garden.

NEXT PAGE A border of shrub roses and lavender in the walled garden.

Other Gardens

Not all these gardens are open to visit on a regular basis. Some are cared for by tenants, or are infrequently open by appointment, or by booked tours only. Please check the current National Trust Handbook or visit www.nationaltrust.org.uk before visiting.

Ashdown House
Lambourn, Newbury
Berkshire RG17 8RE

Avebury Manor
nr Marlborough
Wiltshire SN8 1RF

Bradenham Manor
High Wycombe
Buckinghamshire HP14 4HF

Carlyle's House
24 Cheyne Row
London SW3 5HL

Castle Coole
Enniskillen
Co. Fermanagh BT74 6JY

Cherryburn
Station Bank
Mickley, nr Stocksfield
Northumberland NE43 7DD

Claydon House
Middle Claydon
nr Buckingham
Buckinghamshire MK18 2EY

Coleridge Cottage
35 Lime Street,
Nether Stowey
Bridgwater
Somerset TA5 1NQ

Derrymore House
Bessbrook, Newry
Co. Armagh BT35 7EF

Dinefwr Park
Llandeilo
Carmarthenshire SA19 6RT

Dorneywood
Dorneywood, Burnham
Buckinghamshire SL1 8PY

Downhill Castle
Castlerock,
Co. Londonderry BT51 4TW

Eastbury Manor House
Eastbury Square, Barking
London IG11 9SN

Elizabethan House Museum
4 South Quay
Great Yarmouth
Norfolk NR20 2QH

Fell Foot Park
Newby Bridge, Ulverston
Cumbria LA12 8NN

Grantham House
Castlegate, Grantham
Lincolnshire NG31 6SS

The Greyfriars
Friar Street, Worcester
Worcestershire WR1 2LZ

Ilam Park
Ilam, Ashbourne
Derbyshire DE6 2AZ

Leith Hill
nr Coldharbour Village, Dorking
Surrey RH5 6LY

Lindsey House
99–100 Cheyne Walk
London SW10 0DQ

Little Clarendon
Dinton, Salisbury
Wiltshire SP3 5DZ

Morden Hall Park
Morden Hall Road, Morden
London SM4 5JD

Morville Hall
nr Bridgnorth
Shropshire WV16 5NB

Mount Grace Priory
Staddle Bridge, Northallerton
North Yorkshire DL6 3JG

Mr Straw's House
7 Blyth Grove, Worksop
Nottinghamshire S81 0JG

Newark Park
Ozleworth
Wotton-under-Edge
Gloucestershire GL12 7PZ

Oakhurst Cottage
Hambledon, nr Godalming
Surrey GU8 4HF

The Old Manor
Norbury, Ashbourne
Derbyshire DE6 2ED

Owletts
The Street, Cobham, Gravesend
Kent DA12 3AP

Paycocke's
West Street, Coggeshall
Colchester
Essex CO6 1NS

Philipps House
Dinton, Salisbury
Wiltshire SP3 5HH

Quebec House
Quebec Square, Westerham
Kent TN16 1TD

St John's Jerusalem
Sutton-at-Hone, Dartford
Kent DA4 9HQ

Sandham Memorial Chapel
Harts Lane, Burghclere
near Newbury
Hampshire RG20 9JT

Shaw's Corner
Ayot St Lawrence
nr Welwyn
Hertfordshire AL6 9BX

Sprivers Garden
Horsmonden
Kent TN12 8DR

Stoneacre
Otham, Maidstone
Kent ME15 8RS

Sudbury Hall
Sudbury, Ashbourne
Derbyshire DE6 5HT

Tintagel Old Post Office
Fore Street, Tintagel
Cornwall PL34 0DB

Tudor Merchant's House
Quay Hill, Tenby
Pembrokeshire SA70 7BX

Westwood Manor
Bradford-on-Avon
Wiltshire BA15 2AF

Whipsnade Tree Cathedral
Whipsnade, Dunstable
Bedfordshire LU6 2LL

Woodchester Park
Ebworth Estate
The Camp, Stroud
Gloucestershire GL6 7ES

The Workhouse
Southwell
Nottinghamshire NG25 0PT

Acknowledgements

Katherine Lambert undertook the task of collating research in the National Trust's archives, while I waltzed around the gardens. I am deeply indebted to her. My job was made much easier by the efficient frontline management of the project by Kristy Richardson and Lucy Smith of Pavilion and Amy Feldman at the National Trust. Mike Calnan, Head of Gardens, has been generous with his help, sharing the resources of his team, and commenting on the text, Lin Ewart has kindly fact-checked and been at the thick of communications between Gardens Advisors and gardens, and Rhonda West Pollard has given Katherine valuable assistance in her research. Further sensitive editing was undertaken by Diana Vowles. My literary agent, Anthony Goff, has been a much valued sounding board and advocate. And not least I must thank the Head Gardeners and Gardeners in Charge, whose guided tours have been one of this project's principal pleasures.

National Trust Garden Collection

The National Trust has been caring for special gardens for over 110 years and now looks after over 200 gardens and parks including 32 Plant Heritage National Plant Collections and over 70,000 plant species. We employ over 450 professional gardeners, ably aided by 1,500 volunteers.

Many gardeners have been inspired by spending time in beautiful National Trust gardens and parks. The National Trust has teamed up with carefully selected British companies to develop and design an eclectic mix of National Trust inspired products, with greenhouses, sheds, gates, furniture, paving, garden tools and much more in the range. Each product is carefully designed and produced using traditional crafts and techniques to bring you the kind of quality you would expect from the National Trust. Moreover, each sale helps us continue our work in conservation and restoration of the places and spaces in the Trust's care including that of gardens: for ever, for everyone.

To find out more or purchase online, please visit our website www.nationaltrustgardencollection.co.uk.

Bibliography

The National Trust's detailed guides to individual properties and gardens have been the prime source of reference. In addition, I have had access to a vast store of information on file, including Gardens Advisers' reports and observations, management plans, park and garden surveys by Katie Fretwell, John Phibbs, Keystone Consultants and others, entries in the Woody Plant Catalogue compiled by Michael Lear, and articles from journals and magazines past and present, most especially from *Country Life* by John Cornforth, Arthur Hellyer, Christopher Hussey, Gervase Jackson-Stops, John Sales and others. All has been grist to the mill.

A great many books have helped me understand better the evolution of British gardens, and of certain gardens in particular. The following were principal references:

Anscombe, Isabelle, *Arts & Crafts Style* (Phaidon, 1991)

Brown, Jane, *The English Garden in Our Time* (Antique Collectors' Club, 1986)

Brown, Jane, *Sissinghurst, Portrait of a Garden* (NT/Weidenfeld & Nicolson, 1990)

Brown, Jane, *Vita's Other World* (Viking, 1985)

Calnan, Mike et al., *Rooted in History: Studies in Garden Conservation* (National Trust, 2001)

Clarke, Ethne, *Hidcote, the Making of a Garden* (Michael Joseph, 1989)

David, Penny, *Hidden Gardens* (Cassell, 2002)

Elliott, Brent, *Victorian Gardens* (Batsford, 1986)

Festing, Sally, *Gertrude Jekyll* (Viking, 1991)

Gordon, Catherine, *The Coventrys of Croome* (National Trust/Phillimore, 2000)

Greeves, Lydia and Michael Trinick, *The National Trust Guide* (National Trust, 1989)

Hayden, Peter, *Biddulph Grange: a Victorian Garden Rediscovered* (National Trust/George Philip)

Hayward, Allyson, Norah Lindsay (Frances Lincoln, 2007)

Jacques, David, *Georgian Gardens, the Reign of Nature* (Batsford, 1983)

Jellicoe, Geoffrey and Susan, *The Landscape of Man* (Thames & Hudson, 1975)

Jellicoe, Sir Geoffrey, Susan Jellicoe, Patrick Goode and Michael Lancaster, *The Oxford Companion to Gardens* (Oxford University Press, 1986)

McLean, Teresa, *Medieval English Gardens* (Barrie & Jenkins, 1989)

National Trust Head Gardeners, Gardening Secrets (National Trust, 2008)

Nicholson, Shirley, *Nymans, the Story of a Sussex Garden* (National Trust/Alan Sutton, 1992)

Ottewill, David, *The Edwardian Garden* (Yale University Press, 1989)

Pearson, Graham S., *Lawrence Johnston* (Hidcote Books, 2010)

Plumptre, George, *British Gardens* (Collins, 1985)

Richardson, Tim, *The Arcadian Friends* (Bantam Press, 2007)

Robinson, John Martin, *Temples of Delight, Stowe Landscape Gardens* (National Trust/George Philip, 1990)

Scott-James, Anne, *Sissinghurst, the Making of a Garden* (Michael Joseph, 1975)

Strong, Roy, *The Renaissance Garden in England* (Thames & Hudson, 1998)

Stroud, Dorothy, *Capability Brown* (Faber & Faber, 1975)

Stroud, Dorothy, *Humphry Repton* (Country Life, 1962)

Stuart, David, *Georgian Gardens* (Robert Hale, 1979)

Stuart, David, *The Garden Triumphant, a Victorian Legacy* (Viking, 1988)

Thomas, Graham Stuart, *Gardens of the National Trust* (National Trust/Weidenfeld & Nicolson, 1979)

Plant Index

cedar of Lebanon *21*, 26, 172, 188, 244, 298, 348, 356, 365, 369, *370*
Cedrus brevifolia 186
Cyprus cedar 186, 188
deodar cedar 50, 188, 357
golden cedar 24
incense cedar 195, 298, 398
Japanese cedar 359
weeping cedar 24
western red cedar 289, 398
celandine 387
Celastrus orbiculatus 78, 114
Centaurea cyanus 210
Ceratostigma 202
Cercidiphyllum 111, 135, 328
  C. japonicum 122, 311, 370, 402
Cercis siliquastrum 12, 60, 144, 154, 202, 228, 287, 330, 364
Cestrum 278
  C. elegans 214
Chaenomeles x superba 'Rowallane' 289–90
Chamaecyparis
  C. lawsoniana 'Erecta' 188
  C. l. 'Kilmacurragh' 188
  C. l. 'Wisselii' 188, 365
  C. pisifera 348
  C. p. 'Squarrosa' 270
chard, ruby 211
cherry *see Prunus*
chestnut 28, 32, 55, 73, 82, 94, 108, *111*, 205, 290, 292, 342
  Spanish chestnut 267
  sweet chestnut 22, 52, 105, 129, 144, 251, 272
  variegated sweet chestnut 24
Chilean coral plant 382
Chilean fire bush 57, 143, 331
chilli peppers, 'Long Green Buddha' 350
Chimonanthus 16, 108, 111
Chionanthus 252
Chionodoxa 17, 111, 115, 204, 352, 388, *388*
  C. luciliae 43
  C. tommasinianus 17
chives *158*
Choisya 16, 188, 214
Chrysanthemum 278, 399
Cimicifugas 164, 278
Cineraria 30, 186, 214
Cirsium 257
Cistus 197, 199, 256, 278, 370, 372
  C. x cyprius 302
Clarkia 343
Claytonia 22
Clematis 12, 30, 39, 47, 67, 76, 78, 96, 104, 121, 164, 186, 228, *228*, 238, 248, *264–5*, 373
  C. armandii 100, 222, 253, *276*
  C. cirrhosa var. *balearica* 222
  C. x durandii 239
  C. x d. 'Juuli' 239
  C. x d. 'Prince Charles' 239
  C. flammula 210, 230
  C. 'Jackmanii' 126, 210

C. 'Jackmanii Superba' 265, 278
C. x jouiniana 43
C. montana 32, 98, 168, 210, 320
C. 'Perle d'Azur' 222, 314, 404
C. recta 352
C. tibetana 43
C. 'Ville de Lyon' 314
C. vitalba 186
C. viticella 230
C. v. subsp. *campaniflora* 43
Clerodendrum 201
  C. bungei 112
Clethra 201, 271
Clianthus puniceus 238
Clivia 347
clover 288
Cobaea 23
cobnut 190, 314
Colchicum 230, 289, 326, 388
  C. tenorei 128
Coleus 25, 222
Colletia
  C. cruciata 144
  C. paradoxa 144
columbine 143, 166, 222, 285, 288
Colutea x media 'Copper Beauty' 407
comfrey 44, *105*, 244, 353, 387
companion planting 132–3
conifers 56, 71, 141, 200, 348, 382, 383
Convolvulus 294
  C. altheoides 183
  C. cneorum 261
Cordyline 71, 116, 174, 254, *294–5*
  C. indivisa 264
corncockle 257, 387
cornflower 251, *274–5*
Cornus (dogwood) 16, 52, 53, 71, 79, 81, 95, 111, 118, 134, 152, 233, 267, 311, 372
  C. alba 'Spaethii' 101
  C. alternifolia 'Argentea' 382
  C. canadensis 168, 327
  C. capitata 95, 144, 155, 254
  C. controversa 'Variegata' 352
  C. kousa 143, 154, 195, 247, 331
  C. k. var. *chinensis* 57
  C. mas 230, 331, 398
Corokia 241
Correa 261
Corylus avellana 'Contorta' 16
Cosmea 224
Cosmos 30, 89, *114*, 128, *258*, *316–17*, 352
Cotinus (smoke bush) 29, 81, 102, 145, 164, 181, 216, 276
  C. coggygria 105, 181
  C. obovatus 383
Cotoneaster 16, 181
  C. microphyllus 47
cow parsley 180, 311
cowslips 137, 152, 216, 218, 285, 288, 328, 339
crab apples 44, 100, 111, 216,

232, 285
'Ballerina' 156
Crambe 30, 89, 196, 228, 352
  C. cordifolia 15, *129*
  C. maritima 276
cranesbill 10, 202
Crataegus 267, 324, 343
  C. persimilis 'Prunifolia' 102
Crinodendron 92, 118
  C. hookerianum 56, 155, 265
  C. patagua 45
Crinum 29, 30, 67, 69, 84, 101, 224, 238, 290
Crocosmia (montbretia) 29, 46, 52, 89, 92, 94, 164, 200, 204, 270, 278, 326, 362, 374
  C. paniculata 134
Crocus 17, 52, 97, 111, 318, 327
  C. nudiflorus 43
  C. pulchellus 43
  C. speciosus 43
  C. tommasinianus 43
  C. vernus 43, 202
crossword 388
crown imperials 12, *125*, 208
Cryptocarya alba 248
Cryptomeria 50, 114, 155, 333, 348
  C. japonica 195, 359
  C. j. 'Lobbii' 195
cuckoo flower 321
cucumber tree 81, 115
cucumbers 213
Cunninghamia 289
  C. konishii 144
  C. lanceolata 144
Cuphea 94, 294
Cupressus see cypress
currants 75, 117
Cyathea 144
Cyclamen 34, 46, 97, 105, 111, 196, 201, 220, 230, 388
  C. coum 195
  C. hederifolium 17, 195, 253, 296
  C. repandum 155, 195, 201, 253
Cymbidium 405
cypress (*Cupressus*) 22, 56, 188, 239, 289, 333
  columnar cypress 365
  Cupressus sempervirens 'Stricta' 188
  golden cypress 278, 382
  Italian cypress 162, 296, 328
  Lawson cypress 29, 298, 343, 377
  Leyland cypress 238, 242, 298
  Monterey cypress 195, 254
  Nootka cypress 104
  Sawara cypress 348
  swamp cypress 112, 202, 267, 348
  variegated cypress 364
Cyrtomium 347
Cystopteris 318
Cytisus 'Moyclare Pink' 21

Dacrydium 154
daffodil *see Narcissus*
Dahlia 28, 30, 47, 52, 89, 104,

112, *112*, 114, *114*, 116, 117, 118, 128, 154, 164, 172, *174*, 175, 183, 195, 216, 217, 224, 227, 290, 314, *366*
  D. 'Bishop of Llandaff' 270
  D. 'Ella Britton' 13
  D. imperialis 201
  D. 'Madame Simone Stappers' 13
  D. 'Princess Marie José' 347
daisy 328
  Michaelmas 370
  ox-eye 318, 387, 388
  Shasta 12, *22*, 27, 118, 166, *212*, 343
damsons 44, 89, 201, 320, 370
  'Cheshire Damson' 285
  'Shropshire Damson' 218
Daphne 108, 111, 174, 199, 271, 407
  D. acutiloba 94
  D. bholua 52, 57, 94, 382
  D. x burkwoodii 29
  D. laureola 142
  D. odora 22
  D. pontica 142
Darmera 24, 134
  D. peltata 99, 211
Dasylirion 128
Datura 224, 254
Davidia 290
  D. involucrata 57, 59, 79, 114, 143, 154, 246, 265, 276, 303, 309, 331, 333, 348, 401
  D. i. var. *vilmoriniana* 122, 246
daylily (*Hemerocallis*) 19, 30, 46, 52, 53, 69, 85, 89, 97, 108, 112, 117, 121, 134, 231, 248, 257, 276, 284, 314, 353, 374
  Hemerocallis citrina 101
  H. dumortieri 29
  'Lady Fermor-Hesketh 292
Decumaria 264
Delphinium 12, 13, 24, 27, 47, 51, 68, 89, 112, 210, 222, 224, 239, 256, 279, 315, *344–5*, 353
  D. 'Blue Lagoon' *303*
Dendromecon rigida 238
Descaisnea fargesii 348
Desfontainia spinosa 248
Deutzia 38, 113, 172
devil's bit scabious 290
devil's walking stick 44, 59
Dianthus (pink) 44, 116, 118, 128, 161, 172, 199, 321, 390
  D. 'Mrs Sinkins' 263
  D. plumarius 12
  D. 'Sops-in-wine' 387
Diascia 142
Dicentra 331, 343
Dichroa febrifuga 92
Dicksonia 144
Dierama 21, 56, 101
Dietes grandiflora 294
Digitalis *7*, 74, 84, 85, 98, 104, *147*, 166, 178, *183*, *223*,

225, 244, 314, 323, 330, *402*, *409*
  D. 'Spice Island' 407
  D. Excelsior 200
Diorama 290
Dipelta floribunda 86, 309
Disporum 248
dog's mercury 288
dogwood *see Cornus*
Dregea sinensis 278
Drimys 129
  D. winteri 143, 265, 296
Dryopteris
  D. affinis 239
  D. pseudomas 239
dyer's greenweed 208

Eccremocarpus 278
Echeveria 116, 257, 294
Echinacea 86, 252, 311
Echium 241, 253, 254, 261
  E. candicans 238
  E. pininana 294, 361
Eglantine 231
Ehretia dicksonii 195
Elaeagnus (oleaster) 16, 111
  E. umbellata 95
elder 77, 121, 197, 401
Elecampane 208
elm 60, 119, 163, 225, 398
  Chinese elm 115
  English elm 67
  weeping elm 68
Embothrium 92, 95, 99, 143, 239, 241, 290
  E. coccineum 71, 79, 331
  E. c. var. *lanceolatum* 'Norquinco' 57
Emmenopterys henryi 348
Enkianthus 99, 292, 304
  E. campanulatus 290, 361
  E. perulatus 122, 402
Epimedium 43, 50, 111
Eranthis 17
Eremurus 315, 392
Erica arborea var. *alpina* 98
Erigeron
  E. annuus 328
  E. karvinkianus 109, 320
Erinus alpinus 320, 326
Eryngium 24, 258, 385
Erysimum (wallflower) 30, 62, *105*, 186, 224, 314, *378–9*
  E. 'Jacob's Jacket' 101
  E. 'Persian Carpet' *63*
Erythronium (dog's tooth violet) 17, 108, 202, 318, 327
Escallonia 21, 113, 145, 181, 242
  E. illinita 248
Eucalyptus 97, 155, 239, 270, 290, 383
  E. globulus 238, 241
Eucomis 67, 113, 204, 249
  E. bicolor 97
Eucryphia 18, 68, 92, 95, 99, 114, 118, 134, 144, 154, 247, 268, 279, 289, 331, 359
  E. cordifolia 239
  E. glutinosa 56, 79, 122, 178
  E. lucida 56

E. moorei 361
E. 'Nyman's' 168
E. x nymansensis 'Nymansay' 246, 401
E. 'Rostrevor' 207
Euonymus 242, 278, 303
  E. 'Emerald Gaiety' 16
  E. lucidus 253
Eupatorium 15, 388
Euphorbia 94, 128, 164, 174, 181, 183, 200, 227, 263, 278, 331
  E. mellifera 253, 257
  E. myrsinites 314
Exochirda 145

Fagus see beech
Fascicularia 94, 207, 238, 254
  F. bicolor 71
Feijoa selloviana (*Acca sellowiana*) 71, 92, 114, 233
fennel *204*
ferns 22, 50, 52, 62, 68, 91, 117, 166, 188, 196, 201, 202, *319*
  adder's tongue fern 321
  Australian tree fern 347, 362
  bladder fern 318
  filmy fern 383
  lady ferns 99
  maidenhair fern 201
  Osmunda fern 50, 196, 292, 382
  polypody fern 150
  Polystichum 200
  royal fern 318
  shuttlecock fern 114, 314
  sword fern 318
  tree fern 84, 144, 154, 261
  Woodwardia 129, 154, 347
feverfew 133, 224, 252, 387
  golden feverfew 132
Ficus (fig) 12, 30, 38, 45, *46*, 104, 128, 160, 187, 202, 222, 278
  F. 'Brown Turkey' 326
  F. 'White Marseilles' 347
figwort 388
Filipendula 23
fir (*Abies*) 22, 26, 56, 71, 99, 186
  Abies. grandis 26, 264
  A. recurvata var. *ernesti* 348
  Caucasian fir 104, 264, 318
  Douglas fir 104, 199, 264, 272, 289, 383
  noble fir 104, 333
  silver fir 143
  Spanish fir 398
Fitzroya cupressoides 201, 289
forget-me-not 85, 116, *148*, 205
  Chatham Island forget-me-not 238
Fothergilla 304, 327, 402
foxglove tree 84, 155, 156, 405
foxgloves *7*, 74, 84, 85, 98, 104, *147*, 166, 178, *183*, *223*, *225*, 244, 314, 323, 330, *402*, *409*
  Excelsior 200
Fraxinus (ash) 22, 45, 97, 105,

General Index

Picture credits